CLINICAL MANAGEMENT *of* CARDIAC ARRHYTHMIAS

G. Neal Kay, MD
Director, Cardiac Electrophysiological Catheterization Laboratory
Associate Professor of Medicine
Arrhythmia Service, Division of Cardiovascular Disease
Department of Medicine
University of Alabama at Birmingham

Rosemary S. Bubien, MSN, RN
Cardiovascular Research Associate
Arrhythmia Service, Division of Cardiovascular Disease
Department of Medicine
University of Alabama at Birmingham

AN ASPEN PUBLICATION®
Aspen Publishers, Inc.
Gaithersburg, Maryland
1992

Library of Congress Cataloging-in-Publication Data

Kay, G. Neal.
Clinical management of cardiac arrhythmias /
G. Neal Kay, Rosemary S. Bubien.
p. cm.
Includes bibliographical references and index.
ISBN: 0-8342-0281-6
1. Arrhythmia. 2. Arrhythmia—Nursing. I. Bubien, Rosemary S. II. Title.
[DNLM: 1. Arrhythmia. 2. Arrhythmia—therapy. WG 330 K23c]
RC685.A65K39   1991
616.1'28—dc20
DNLM/DLC
for Library of Congress
91-25952
CIP

The authors have made every effort to ensure the accuracy of the information herein, particularly
with regard to drug selection and dose. However, appropriate information sources should be
consulted, especially for new or unfamiliar drugs or procedures. It is the responsibility of every
practitioner to evaluate the appropriateness of a particular opinion in the context of actual clinical
situations and with due consideration to new developments. Authors, editors, and the publisher
cannot be held responsible for any typographical or other errors found in this book.

Editorial Services: Barbara Priest

Library of Congress Catalog Card Number: 91-25952
ISBN: 0-8342-0281-6

Printed in the United States of America

1 2 3 4 5

Aspen Series in Cardiovascular Nursing
Donna R. Packa, RN, DSN, Series Editor
Professor of Nursing
The University of Mississippi Medical Center
Jackson, Mississippi

Sudden Cardiac Death: Theory and Practice
Patricia Owen

Essentials of Cardiovascular Nursing
Linda S. Baas

To Linda and Jim
for their encouragement
and understanding

Table of Contents

Preface

From the outset, our goal in writing this book has been to place into clinical perspective the major advances that have occurred in basic and clinical research and antiarrhythmia device technology. Innovations in these areas have been rapidly applied to the practical management of arrhythmias culmunating in important improvements in patient care. Our intent is to provide the reader with current, concise, and practical guidelines for the management of cardiac arrhythmias. Each of the topics is discussed in a manner that we hope will enable the reader to understand the rationale for our approach and what to expect as a consequence. The trends in arrhythmia management that we discuss have been rapidly evolving. In this light, we have attempted to emphasize both those diagnostic and therapeutic approaches that we believe are most likely to show promise as effective clinical management strategies in the near future.

Acknowledgments

The authors wish to thank their colleagues, Andrew E. Epstein, M.D., George H. Crossley, M.D., Sharon M. Dailey, M.D., and Vance J. Plumb, M.D., for their contribution and review of the manuscript. The authors also thank electrophysiology technicians Mr. Craig Porter and Mr. Judson Brown and electrophysiology research nurse Ms. Sylvia McLaughlin for their assistance. The authors wish to acknowledge the secretarial assistance provided in the preparation of this manuscript by Ms. Michele Bryan, Ms. Margaret Burchfield, and Ms. Natasha Hubbert. For their technical assistance with the photography, the authors thank Mr. David Fisher, Ms. Margaret Lasakow, Mr. Craig Porter, and Mr. Michael Strawn. The authors also wish to express their appreciation to the editor, Ms. Barbara Marsh, for her invaluable assistance.

Chapter 1

The Anatomic Basis for Conduction of the Cardiac Impulse

THE SINUS NODE

The normal cardiac impulse arises within the sinus node, a specialized region of the right atrium with intrinsic pacemaker activity. The sinus node is located in the high lateral right atrium in the sulcus terminalis, a groove extending between the vena cavae (Figure 1-1). The sinus node is normally located at the junction of the superior vena cava and the base of the right atrial appendage. Shaped as an ellipse, the sinus node is 10 to 20 mm in length with a maximum thickness of approximately 3 mm. In a small proportion of individuals the sinus node is a horseshoe-shaped structure extending anteriorly around the superior vena cava as it joins the right atrium. The ultrastructure of the sinus node consists of several specialized cells, including P-cells from which the normal automaticity of the node arises. P-cells are small, pale-staining, ovoid cells with a decreased quantity of contractile myofibrils. The sinus node also contains transitional cells, with characteristics that are intermediate between P-cells and normal atrial myocardial cells, and occasional Purkinje fibers that surround the node. The P-cells are dependent on calcium rather than sodium currents, a feature that distinguishes the functional properties of the sinus node from those of Purkinje fibers or ordinary atrial myocytes.

The sinus node is richly innervated with both sympathetic and parasympathetic fibers, leading to the marked responsiveness of this structure to autonomic influences. The parasympathetic fibers that innervate the sinus node are carried by the vagus nerve. These vagal fibers slow the rate of impulse generation in the sinus node. Sympathetic fibers influencing the sinus node are postganglionic fibers arising in the right and left stellate ganglia. The right stellate ganglion has predominant influence over sinus node function, leading to an increase in the rate of impulse generation when the right stellate is stimulated. The net effect of the antagonistic sympathetic and parasympathetic nervous influences differs from rest to exercise. At rest, the parasympathetic influence on the sinus node predominates, with a slowing of the sinus rate. With exercise, parasympathetic tone is withdrawn and sympathetic tone is enhanced, resulting in the expected increase in heart rate. Total blockade of the autonomic nervous system with atropine and propranolol normally results in an increase in resting sinus rate to 90 to 110 beats per minute. The intrinsic sinus rate is dependent on the age of the individual, with a gradual decrease in sinus rates with age. An elevated resting heart rate is observed in denervated patients, such as those who have undergone heart transplantation or who have disorders of the autonomic nervous system (e.g., diabetic neuropathy).

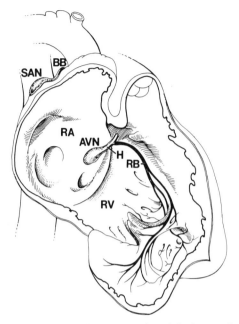

Figure 1-1 Schematic representation of the intracardiac conduction system. The sinus node (SAN) is located in the high lateral portion of the right atrium (RA) at the junction of the right atrial appendage and the superior vena cava. The sinus node may be a horseshoe-shaped structure in some individuals that encircles the superior portion of the right atrium. A thick band of muscle ascending from the right atrium to the left atrium, known as Bachman's bundle (BB), is illustrated. The AV conduction system is a continuous structure. The AV node (AVN) lies in the interatrial septum. The bundle of His (H) emerges from the distal extent of the AV node as it enters the interventricular septum. The His bundle branches into the right bundle branch (RB) and left bundle branch in the interventricular septum where the bundle branches form a network of Purkinje fibers. The RB lies in close proximity to the right ventricular (RV) endocardial surface.

The arterial blood supply to the sinus node is provided by the sinus node artery, a branch from the right coronary artery in approximately 55% of individuals. The sinus node artery may normally arise from the left circumflex coronary artery in approximately 45% of patients. Richly perfused, the sinus node also responds quickly to circulating catecholamines, as evidenced by the increase in heart rate that occurs in denervated heart transplant recipients with exercise. The sinus node also contains a fibrous stroma that increases with the age of the individual. Because of the progressive increase in the proportion of fibrous tissue in the sinus node over the lifetime

of the normal individual, an age-related decrease in the maximum sinus rate that can be achieved with exercise is observed. This gradual replacement of the sinus node by fibrous elements is the probable explanation for the high frequency of sinus node dysfunction that is observed in elderly patients.

INTERNODAL CONDUCTION

Although internodal tracts connecting the sinus node to the atrioventricular (AV) node have been proposed, the existence of these connections has not been universally accepted. Recent studies utilizing serial histologic sections through the atria have failed to confirm the presence of discrete internodal conducting fibers. Thus specialized structures joining the sinus and AV nodes cannot be identified. Despite this, propagation of electrical impulses through the atrial myocardium has not been demonstrated to be uniform. For example, depolarizing wavefronts of activation spread rapidly when propagation is along the axis of myofiber orientation but slowly when the direction of propagation is transverse to this axis. This phenomenon relating to the effect of fiber orientation on conduction velocity is termed anisotropy. Although specialized internodal tracts are unlikely to exist, the apparent preferential conduction observed within the atria is likely to be related to the longitudinal orientation of atrial fibers from the high to the low right atrium. Conduction of the atrial impulse from the right to the left atrium is accomplished by a longitudinal bundle of fibers known as Bachmann's bundle. These longitudinal fibers allow the left atrium to be depolarized before the activation wavefront traverses the AV node. Anisotropic conduction may also be an important determinant of the mechanism of clinical arrhythmias such as atrial flutter.

THE ATRIOVENTRICULAR NODE
AND BUNDLE OF HIS

The AV node is located within the lower interatrial septum. The location of the AV node can be identified from the right atrium within Koch's triangle, an important surgical landmark. Koch's triangle is bounded by the septal leaflet of the tricuspid valve, the ostium of the coronary sinus, and the tendon of Todaro, a fibrous ridge that extends from the inferior vena cava to the central fibrous body of the heart. The AV node is an elliptical structure with the proximal portion oriented caudally and the distal portion oriented anteriorly and cephalad. The AV node is composed of cells that are specialized for AV conduction. Unlike the normal working atrial myocardium, the specialized AV nodal cells are characterized by slow conduction of electrical impulses, produced predominantly by the inward calcium current (to be discussed in Chapter 2). The AV node is surrounded by transitional cells with characteristics that are intermediate between those of atrial myocytes and the specialized AV nodal cells. These perinodal cells may be the substrate for a reentrant arrhythmia involving the AV node, AV nodal reentrant tachycardia.

The bundle of His arises from the distal extent of the AV node and penetrates the tough, fibrous skeleton of the heart, the central fibrous body. The bundle of His lies within the thin, membranous interventricular septum and descends into the thick, muscular interventricular septum, where the right and left bundle branches arise. The bundle of His is thus located in the center of the heart, in close proximity to the annulus of the aortic valve, the right atrium, the crest of the left ventricle, and the superior extent of the tricuspid valve. Because of its location, the bundle of His is vulnerable to injury from disorders affecting any of these structures. The AV node is in close proximity to the mitral valve annulus. Because of these anatomic relationships, it is not surprising that the bundle of His may be injured at the time of aortic valve replacement, whereas the AV node may be damaged during mitral valve replacement. In addition, aortic stenosis related to calcification of the aortic valve is frequently associated with AV block due to impingement of the calcific process on the His bundle. Mitral annular calcification, a common disorder in elderly patients, is often accompanied by evidence of AV nodal dysfunction.

The AV node is richly innervated by inhibitory parasympathetic fibers carried by the vagus nerve and excitatory postganglionic sympathetic fibers arising in the right and left stellate ganglia. Because of its innervation and dependence on the inward calcium current, the AV node is highly responsive to autonomic influences. Thus enhanced vagal tone related to drug effects or autonomic reflexes (e.g., nausea, vomiting) may produce a conduction block within the AV node. In addition, the augmented vagal tone in trained athletes or in normal children and young adults is often manifested by AV block occurring in the AV node during sleep. Wenckebach block may be seen in otherwise normal individuals during times of enhanced vagal tone, such as during sleep. Exercise and emotional excitement improve AV nodal conduction by withdrawal of vagal tone and enhancement of sympathetic stimulation. In contrast to the AV node, the bundle of His is sparsely innervated and only minimally influenced by the autonomic nervous system. This difference in the effect of the autonomic nervous system on the AV node and the bundle of His can be helpful in the clinical evaluation of AV block. In general, AV block that improves with exercise or atropine is usually localized to the AV node. AV block that worsens with exercise or with atropine is usually related to disease in the bundle of His or infrahisian conduction fibers.

The arterial blood supply to the AV node is provided by the AV node artery. In over 90% of individuals the AV node artery arises from the distal right coronary artery. In approximately 10% of patients the left circumflex coronary artery supplies the AV node artery. The bundle of His is perfused by septal perforating branches from the left anterior descending coronary artery. Thus inferior myocardial infarctions (usually related to right coronary artery thrombosis) are frequently complicated by transient dysfunction of the AV node. Anterior myocardial infarctions, which are related to occlusion of the left anterior descending coronary artery, may be complicated by AV block or bundle branch block related to permanent destruction of the His bundle or bundle branches.

The AV node has several unusual functional properties. The most important property of the AV node is the normal delay in conduction that it imposes on the electrical connection between activation of the atria and the ventricles. The AV node delays propagation of the electrical wavefront of depolarization, allowing time for transport of blood across the tricuspid and mitral valves. The normal PR interval is largely determined by the conduction time through the AV node. Thus the AV node serves to synchronize electrical and mechanical events, optimizing the hemodynamic transport function of the atria and cardiac output. The normal AV node also demonstrates decremental conduction properties, that is, progressive slowing of conduction at faster atrial pacing rates. Consequently if the atria are paced at progressively increasing rates, the PR interval progressively prolongs until physiologic AV Wenckebach block in the AV node is produced. In contrast to the atria, ventricles, or His bundle, which demonstrate increased conduction velocity at increasing heart rates, conduction through the AV node worsens with artificially induced increases in heart rate in response to rapid atrial pacing. However, normal increases in the rate of sinus node firing related to emotion or exercise (withdrawal of parasympathetic tone and enhanced sympathetic stimulation) result in improved AV nodal conduction. Thus pathologic atrial tachyarrhythmias are often associated with a longer PR interval during the tachycardia than during sinus rhythm. In contrast, during physiologic sinus tachycardia, the PR interval is usually shorter than during normal sinus rhythm at slower heart rates. This observation regarding the PR interval has clinical relevance and can be useful to differentiate pathologic atrial tachycardias from sinus tachycardia.

BUNDLE BRANCHES AND THE PURKINJE SYSTEM

As the His bundle courses through the membranous interventricular septum and into the muscular interventricular septum, it gives rise to the right and left bundle branches (Figure 1-2). The right bundle branch arises from the distal His bundle near the left side of the muscular interventricular septum and follows an intramyocardial course to the right, coming to lie just under the right ventricular endocardium. The

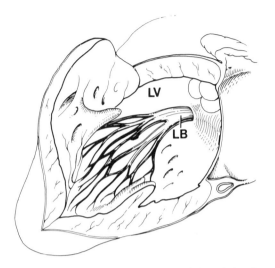

Figure 1-2 Schematic representation of the left bundle branch (LB) as seen from the left ventricle (LV). In this diagram the left bundle branch is seen to emerge below the aortic valve. The left bundle branches into a network of fibers that traverse the left side of the interventricular septum. Because of its proximity to the aortic valve, the His bundle and left bundle branch are susceptible to injury by disorders affecting the aortic valve.

right bundle branch is a thin structure measuring only 1 to 2 mm in thickness. Because of its small size and close proximity to the right ventricular endocardial surface, it is vulnerable to injury during catheterization. The left bundle branch demonstrates widely variable anatomy. In many individuals it is a wide, fan-shaped structure coursing near the left side of the interventricular septum. In others, it may arise with a narrow proximal portion, only widening after several millimeters. Although the electrocardiographic terms left anterior and left posterior hemiblock suggest two discrete fascicles bifurcating from the left bundle branch, the actual anatomy is much more complex, with most pathologic specimens demonstrating an interlocking syncytium of fibers. Despite the anatomic reality that the left bundle branch is a widely branching structure, the electrocardiographic concepts of hemiblock have practical clinical value.

As the right and left bundle branches spread distally, they form an interlocking network of cells specialized for rapid conduction, the Purkinje fibers. The Purkinje fibers are broader and shorter than ordinary working myocardial cells.

An important function of the Purkinje network is the relatively homogeneous depolarization and repolarization that this system normally provides for both the right and left ventricles. Since the Purkinje cells are located subendocardially, the endocardium is depolarized prior to the epicardium. In addition, the apex of the heart is activated before the base. The rapid spread of conduction in the Purkinje fibers produces a well-synchronized activation pattern and a normal, narrow QRS complex. The normal process of repolarization occurs in a direction that is opposite that of depolarization. Thus repolarization proceeds from epicardium to endocardium and from the base of the heart to the apex. Because of the opposite direction of depolarization and repolarization, the base of the ventricles is depolarized last but repolarized first. The reversed sequence of ventricular depolarization and repolarization allows both ventricles to be repolarized relatively homogeneously, decreasing the risk of arrhythmias that may be induced by the situation of having some areas refractory and other areas fully recovered. This situation, termed dispersion of refractoriness, is avoided by the normally functioning Purkinje network.

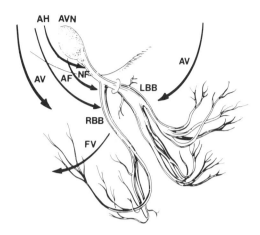

Figure 1-3 Schematic representation of accessory pathways of the conduction system. The AV node (AVN) lies in the interatrial septum and gives rise to the His bundle, which penetrates the central fibrous body and muscular interventricular septum. A Kent bundle (AV) is an accessory connection joining the atrium to the ventricle that bypasses the AV ring. In this way the atrium and ventricle are in electrical continuity. Mahaim fibers may be of the nodofascicular (NF) or the fasciculoventricular (FV) type. The nodofascicular fiber joins the AV node to the right bundle branch (RBB). In addition, fibers that join the atrium to the right bundle branch (atriofascicular) fibers have also been reported. An atriohisian fiber (AH) joins the right atrium or interatrial septum to the His bundle directly. LBB indicates left bundle branch.

ANATOMIC SUBSTRATES FOR PREEXCITATION

The normal AV conduction system provides a single electrical connection between the atria and ventricles, the AV node and His bundle. Other than these specialized structures, there is no electrical connection between the atria and ventricles, as these chambers are separated by the tough fibrous skeleton of the heart provided by the tricuspid and mitral valve rings. However, in patients with reentrant supraventricular arrhythmias, there is often an additional pathway of electrical conduction that provides the substrate for reentry (Figure 1-3). This additional (or accessory) pathway of conduction is usually a small strip of myocardium that crosses the AV valve ring to join the atrium to the ventricle. Preexcitation is the term given to the functional state that occurs when the ventricles are activated earlier than would occur if conduction had been solely over the AV node and His bundle.

The Wolff-Parkinson-White syndrome is the clinical constellation of (1) a short PR interval; (2) a distorted, slurred onset of the QRS complex; and (3) supraventricular arrhythmias. This syndrome results from antegrade conduction of electrical wavefronts from the atria to the ventricles by accessory AV connections. These accessory AV connections are composed of ordinary working atrial myocardial cells that bridge the fibrous AV rings and are actually a form of congenital heart disease. Accessory AV connections (previously referred to as Kent bundles) may be located at any point around the tricuspid valve ring and around the posterior and lateral mitral valve ring from the crux of the heart to the left atrial appendage. Since the anterior portion of the mitral annulus is joined to the aortic annulus, accessory AV connections cannot be located in this area. Accessory AV connections crossing the mitral valve ring are usually located in the epicardial fat pad that protects the coronary sinus and left circumflex coronary artery. Right-sided accessory pathways may also traverse the tricuspid valve annulus subepicardially. However, pathologic specimens of right-sided accessory pathways have shown that they may also penetrate the tricuspid annulus in a subendocardial position.

In addition to these free wall locations, accessory pathways may be located in the anterior or posterior septum. In the posteroseptal location, the accessory pathway joins the right or left atrium to the posterior-superior process of the left ventricle in the posterior pyramidal space. This is a trihedral space bounded on the left by the mitral annulus, on the right by the tricuspid annulus, and superiorly by the interatrial septum at the junction of the right and left atria. The apex of this space is formed by the central fibrous body, and the base of the triangle is formed by the crux of the heart and the coronary sinus. Accessory pathways can be located anywhere in this posterior space, sometimes in close proximity to the AV node and bundle of His. The complex anatomy of this area and the proximity to the normal AV conduction system present an increased risk of AV block during surgery to divide these accessory pathways.

The short PR interval observed on the ECG with the Wolff-Parkinson-White syndrome is explained by rapid conduction over an accessory AV connection that bypasses the normal delay imposed by the AV node. The delta wave is produced by eccentric activation of the ventricles, with slow conduction through the ventricular myocardium and without the synchronizing action of the Purkinje network. In addition to these typical electrocardiographic features of Wolff-Parkinson-White syndrome, accessory AV connections may conduct only in the retrograde direction, from the ventricle to the atrium. Patients with these pathways capable of retrograde but not antegrade conduction have neither a short PR interval nor a delta wave but are nevertheless predisposed to reentrant supraventricular arrhythmias utilizing the AV node–His bundle as the antegrade limb of a reentrant circuit and the accessory pathway as the retrograde limb. These AV connections are referred to as "concealed" accessory pathways because of the absence of antegrade preexcitation.

Preexcitation may also occur with abnormal connections from the AV node to the right bundle branch (nodofascicular fibers) or from the right bundle branch to the ventricular myocardium (fasciculoventricular fibers). These abnormal connections are together referred to as Mahaim fibers. Newer evidence suggests that some fibers may actually arise from the arteromedial right atrium rather than from the AV node and insert into or very near the right bundle branch. These fibers are capable of antegrade conduction with the absence of retrograde conduction (or very slow retrograde conduction). Since preexcitation with Mahaim fibers involves early activation of the right ventricle or right bundle branch, the QRS is typically a left bundle branch block variety. Nodofascicular fibers are frequently involved in a reentrant tachycardia with antegrade conduction over the nodofascicular fibers and retrograde conduction over the His bundle and AV node. Fasciculoventricular fibers are not associated with reentrant arrhythmias. Both varieties of Mahaim fibers may coexist with accessory AV connections of the usual WPW variety.

Atriohisian (Brechenmacher) fibers are rare pathways connecting the medial right atrium to the His bundle. Since the His bundle rather than the ventricles is preexcited by these pathways, the PR interval is short but the QRS is normal. Atriohisian fibers may participate in reentrant tachycardias with antegrade conduction over the AV node and retrograde conduction over the accessory connection from the His bundle to the atrium. These pathways have also been found in patients with coexisting fasciculoventricular fibers.

BIBLIOGRAPHY

Anderson RH, Becker AE. Accessory atrioventricular connections. *J Thorac Cardiovasc Surg.* 1979;78:310–312.

Anderson RH, Becker AE. Stanley Kent and accessory atrioventricular connections. *J Thorac Cardiovasc Surg.* 1981;81:649–658.

Becker AE. Anatomic substrates. In: Zipes DP, Rowlands DJ, eds. *Progress in Cardiology.* Philadelphia, Pa: Lea & Febiger; 1988;2–1:519–537.

Becker AE. Pathologic substrates of arrhythmias. In: Brogada P, Wellens HJJ, eds. *Cardiac Arrhythmias: Where to Go from Here?* Mt Kisco, NY: Futura Publishing Co; 1987:3–26.

Becker AE, Anderson RH. Morphology of the human atrio-ventricular junctional area. In: Wellens HJJ, Lie KI, Janse MJ, eds. *The Conduction System of the Heart: Structure Function and Clinical Implications*. Leiden: Stenfert Kroese BV; 1976:263–286.

Guyton C. *Textbook of Medical Physiology*. 7th ed. Philadelphia, Pa: WB Saunders Co; 1986.

James TN. The sinus node. *Am J Cardiol*. 1977;40: 965–986.

Kirklin JW, Barratt-Boyes BG. *Cardiac Surgery*. New York, NY: John Wiley & Sons; 1986.

Chapter 2

Basic Electrophysiology and Mechanisms of Arrhythmias

RESTING MEMBRANE POTENTIAL

The fundamental property of excitable tissue (nerves and muscle) is the existence of an unequal number of positive and negative charges on the inside compared to the outside of the cell membrane. For the various types of cardiac cells, the inside of the cell is electrically negative compared to the outside, with a membrane potential (the electrical potential energy) of -60 to -90 mV. This separation of charges across the membrane is the result of an excess of sodium ions on the outside of the cell. The voltage created by the separation of charges across the cell membrane is a measure of the electrical force required to separate the positive and negative charges. It is also the force that would allow charged ions to flow across the membrane if ion movement were not restricted. However, charged sodium ions cannot flow into the resting cardiac cell because of the normally high resistance to ion movement that is an inherent property of the cell membrane.

CARDIAC CELL MEMBRANES AND CHANNEL PROTEINS

The cardiac cell membrane is composed of two layers of phospholipids, molecules that have a charged end and a neutral end. The phos-pholipids in the two layers of the membrane are oriented such that the neutral, lipid-soluble ends point toward the center of the membrane and the charged, hydrophilic ends are pointed toward the periphery. Because of its structure, the cell membrane allows interaction of water-soluble solutions on both the inside and outside of the cell. The lipid-soluble center of the membrane serves as an effective insulator against the flow of electrically charged particles and offers the resistance necessary to separate positive and negative charges across the cell membrane.

In order for electrical charges to pass through the cell membrane at appropriate times during the cardiac cycle, specialized proteins that form the channels that regulate ion movement are present in the membrane. These proteins are suspended within the lipid bilayer and present a hydrophilic pore that is relatively specific for the different ions carrying charges into and out of the cell—sodium, potassium, and calcium. Thus different channels are present that have selectivity for sodium, potassium, and calcium ions. Membrane channels regulate the movement of charged ions by a gating mechanism in which the channel proteins change conformation in response to changes in transmembrane potential, to chemical activators such as acetylcholine or catecholamines, and to the opening and closing of other channels. Channels may open for less than 1 millisecond (characteristic of the sodium

9

channel) or hundreds of milliseconds (typical of the potassium channel). It is estimated that opening a single sodium channel allows approximately 10,000 sodium ions to enter the cell. The number of sodium channels in cardiac cell membranes is estimated to be on the order of 5 to 10 channels per square micron of the cell membrane. Currently available experimental techniques allow the opening and closing of individual sodium channels to be recorded. The sodium channel has recently been shown to be composed of two polypeptides (molecular weight 39,000 and 37,000 daltons) that are associated with a large glycoprotein with a molecular weight of 270,000 daltons. The protein has regions of positively charged amino acids and clusters of negatively charged amino acids. The negatively charged region may function as the pore through which sodium ions may pass, while the positively charged region may function as the "gate" that opens in response to changes in the transmembrane voltage.

THE SODIUM-POTASSIUM EXCHANGE PUMP

The cardiac cell membrane is not a perfect insulator. Because there is a passive leak of positively charged sodium ions into the cardiac cell, an active pump to remove this ion from the cell must be involved to maintain the resting membrane potential. The sodium-potassium adenosine triphosphatase (ATPase) pump is a membrane-bound transport mechanism that moves sodium out of the cell and potassium into the cell and is an important regulator of ion homeostasis within the cardiac cell. The ratio of sodium ions extruded from the cell to potassium ions transported into the cell is 3:2. Thus this transport mechanism generates a net negative electrical charge within the cell. Because ions are moved "uphill" against an electrical gradient, this transport system requires energy in the form of adenosine triphosphate (ATP) to regulate the movement of sodium and potassium ions. The function of the sodium-potassium ATPase pump is sensitive to disruptions of cell metabolism that generate ATP by oxidative metabolism. It is also influenced by several factors, including (1) the concentration of sodium ions inside the cell; (2) the concentration of potassium ions outside the cell; (3) the high-energy molecules ATP and adenosine diphosphate (ADP), and inorganic phosphate; (4) cardiac glycosides such as digoxin, which inhibit the pump; (5) catecholamines, which increase pump activity; (6) thyroid hormone, which stimulates pump activity; and (7) insulin, which stimulates the sodium-potassium ATPase pump.

THE SODIUM-CALCIUM EXCHANGE PUMP

In addition to the sodium-potassium pump, cardiac cells also regulate the concentration of sodium and calcium inside the cell by an active pump that exchanges sodium inside the cell for calcium outside the cell. Since intracellular calcium concentration is an important intracellular second messenger for regulation of cardiac contraction and the effects of catecholamines and hormones, the ratio of sodium to calcium must be strictly controlled for normal cardiac function. The interaction of sodium and calcium currents during the cardiac action potential will be described in subsequent sections of this chapter. The sodium-calcium pump is also active during diastole and results in a net movement of positive charges out of the cardiac cell by moving three sodium ions out of the cell in exchange for one calcium ion that moves into the cell. Thus this pump also contributes to the maintenance of the normal resting membrane potential.

INTRACELLULAR IONS

In addition to the function of the cell membrane to separate positive and negative charges, charged ions are also sequestered within specialized structures in the interior of cardiac cells. Since the calcium ion is an important activator of contractile proteins in cardiac muscle, the concentration of this ion is strictly regulated within the cell cytoplasm. Calcium ions are regulated by and concentrated within the endoplasmic reticulum, an internal network of tubules and vesicles within the cell. The mitochondria are also able to sequester calcium ions in higher concentration than within the cytoplasm. The ability to actively concentrate calcium ions is provided by the ATP-dependent calcium pump. In contrast to the positively charged cations that move across the cell membrane through specialized channels, negatively charged anions within the cell are relatively nondiffusible and therefore fixed. Much less is known regarding the intracellular regulation of anions such as chloride, phosphate, and bicarbonate.

TRANSMEMBRANE POTENTIAL IN DIFFERENT VARIETIES OF CARDIAC CELLS

Several distinct types of cells are found within the heart, including (1) sinus node cells (P-cells), (2) AV nodal cells, (3) His-Purkinje cells, (4) atrial myocytes, and (5) ventricular myocytes. The P-cells in the sinus node are specialized for pacemaker activity, that is, for generating spontaneous action potentials. In order for pacemaker cells to generate a spontaneous action potential, the cell must spontaneously depolarize. Thus in these cells the resting membrane potential is not constant. Rather, there is a gradual depolarizing drift in the membrane potential (decreasing negativity) until the threshold for generation of an action potential is reached. It is this gradual drift in the resting membrane potential that is referred to as the pacemaker potential or spontaneous diastolic depolarization. Since the rate of the depolarizing drift in the pacemaker potential is usually most rapid in the sinus node, it is this structure that normally controls the cardiac rhythm. His-Purkinje cells also have the capability for pacemaker activity, though usually at a slower rate than that of the sinus node. Under abnormal conditions, ordinary atrial or ventricular myocytes may be relatively depolarized and thus achieve threshold, generating abnormal pacemaker activity. Factors leading to a fall in the transmembrane potential (making it less negative or closer to 0 mV) increase the likelihood of abnormal pacemaker activity. Factors that may result in abnormal pacemaker activity in atrial or ventricular muscle include hypokalemia, cate-

cholamine stimulation, ischemia, or mechanical stretch.

THE CARDIAC ACTION POTENTIAL

Nerves and muscle have the capacity to respond to an electrical stimulus with a response that is out of proportion to the intensity of that stimulus. This response to electrical stimuli is an active membrane process rather than simple passive conductance along the cell membrane. This property of an exaggerated response to stimulation is referred to as excitability. If a small depolarizing current is applied to the cell, a small shift in transmembrane potential from the resting state toward neutral voltage results. However, if the transmembrane potential is further depolarized to a critical level (threshold potential), an action potential is generated. The action potential is thus triggered by depolarization to the threshold potential.

There are five phases of the action potential (Figure 2-1). The action potential of Purkinje fibers is characterized by an initial steep, rapid rise in voltage (upstroke, or phase 0) so that the inside of the cell becomes positive with respect to the outside. The rapid depolarization phase is related to a transient increase in the permeability of the membrane sodium channels, allowing sodium ions to rapidly move across the membrane. For a very brief period after the rapid depolarization phase, the inside of the cell becomes positively charged (phase 1). This overshoot voltage is quickly dissipated (early rapid repolarization) by a net flow of potassium ions out of the cell and is followed by a plateau phase (phase 2) during which the transmembrane voltage approximates 0 mV. Phase 2 of the action potential is related to a combination of cellular currents including an outward potassium current and an inward calcium current. During phase 2, the cell is depolarized and cannot respond to another extrastimulus. The plateau phase, which is unique to cardiac cells, lasts several hundred milliseconds and is followed by a phase of rapid repolarization as the cell regenerates its negative resting potential (phase 3). Near the end of phase 3 the cell regains the capability of responding to another

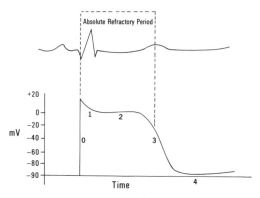

Figure 2-1 Phases of the cardiac action potential. The resting membrane potential of the normal ventricular myocyte is approximately −90 mV, with the inside of the cell being negatively charged as compared with the outside of the cell. The onset of ventricular depolarization occurs synchronously with the onset of the QRS on the surface ECG, shown above. The upstroke of the action potential (phase 0) is largely related to the influx of sodium ions from outside the cell through specialized sodium channels in the membrane. This results in an abrupt change in the membrane potential from approximately −90 mV to approximately +20 mV. This is followed by a rapid repolarization phase (phase 1), at the conclusion of which the membrane potential approaches 0 mV, signifying that phase 2 has been reached. During phase 2 the cell is refractory to further stimulation. Phase 2 is followed by a phase of repolarization (phase 3) during which the cell is made progressively more negatively charged as compared with the outside. During this phase, electrical stimuli of varying strengths may be able to elicit another action potential if delivered following repolarization of the cell. The cell undergoes a gradual loss of membrane polarization (phase 4) during diastole, prior to the next action potential.

extrastimulus with an action potential. Following repolarization the resting membrane potential is generated, which may gradually drift toward threshold potential at a rate that is specific for each type of cardiac cell. This upward drift (known as the pacemaker potential) represents phase 4 of the action potential.

REFRACTORINESS

As described in the preceding section, the cardiac cell cannot respond to an extrastimulus that is delivered during the plateau phase of the action potential. During this period, the cell is refractory to stimulation. However, as the cell repolarizes in phase 3, the capability for

responding to a stimulus with another action potential is regained. The period from the onset of the action potential to the return of responsiveness is termed the refractory period. The duration of the refractory period is determined by the action potential duration, with a longer duration occurring at slower heart rates and a shorter duration occurring at faster heart rates. The duration of the refractory period is also dependent on the intensity of the electrical stimulus applied to the cell, with more intense stimuli being capable of evoking propagated responses somewhat earlier in the cardiac cycle than stimuli of less intensity.

THE INWARD SODIUM CURRENT

As mentioned previously, the concentration of sodium outside the resting cardiac cell greatly exceeds the concentration of sodium inside the cell. The current responsible for the upstroke of the action potential (phase 0) is carried by sodium ions flowing through specialized membrane protein channels into the cell. The conductance of sodium through the membrane-bound sodium channels occurs as a voltage-dependent process and is induced to occur at threshold voltage. The inward sodium current lasts only several milliseconds and reaches maximum at a transmembrane potential of −10 to −20 mV. The rapid depolarization phase is followed by abrupt inactivation of the inward sodium current. The threshold potential for activation of the inward sodium current has been shown to be approximately −60 mV.

Regulation of the sodium current is theorized to be due to the interaction of two gates in the sodium channel. When membrane voltage reaches threshold potential, an activation gate (m gate) in the sodium channel is opened, allowing sodium ions to flow through the channel into the cell. Following opening of the m gate, a second, inactivation gate (h gate) rapidly closes the channel and interrupts the flow of sodium current. Two inactivation states are likely to be present in the sodium channel, one acting rapidly, the other slowly.

The velocity of the rapid depolarization phase is dependent on the resting membrane potential, with a more rapid upstroke occurring at more negative resting potentials. Thus relatively depolarized cells (as occurs with hyperkalemia, hypoxemia, or ischemia) may have a slow upstroke of the action potential and impaired conduction. The inward sodium current is selectively blocked by tetrodotoxin. Class I antiarrhythmic drugs are also effective inhibitors of the inward sodium current.

THE INWARD CALCIUM CURRENT

In addition to the sodium current, a second inward depolarizing current that is carried by calcium ions has been found in all cardiac cells. The inward calcium current has been demonstrated to be the predominant inward current in the sinus and AV nodes. The calcium current has far slower kinetics than the sodium current and is often referred to as the ''slow'' current. The inward calcium current is associated with a much slower upstroke velocity than the sodium current demonstrates. The calcium current is carried by a different membrane channel than the sodium current, one that is selective for divalent cations (calcium, strontium, barium). Inward calcium flow occurs during the depolarized plateau phase of the action potential (phase 2) and persists far longer than the sodium current. In contrast to the sodium current, the calcium current is enhanced by β-adrenergic stimulation and cyclic adenosine monophosphate (AMP). The calcium current is blocked by drugs such as verapamil and adenosine and by high intracellular or low extracellular calcium concentrations.

THE OUTWARD POTASSIUM CURRENT

Repolarization of the cardiac action potential is primarily the result of outward currents that move positively charged ions out of the cell. The major outward current is carried by potassium. The outward potassium current is inactivated at both low membrane potentials (near 0 mV) and when the cell is repolarized to its high, resting potential. However, at membrane potentials between the plateau (depolarized) and resting (repolarized) phases of the action potential, the

outward potassium conductance is maximal. Thus maximal potassium conductance occurs during phases 1 and 3 of the action potential. This self-limiting property of the potassium current at both high and low membrane potentials is referred to as rectification. The potassium current is also activated by the high intracellular calcium concentration that develops following activation of the calcium current. A second repolarizing current may be related to the inward flow of chloride ions. Thus repolarization during phase 3 of the action potential is accomplished by the combination of inactivation of the inward calcium current and activation of the outward potassium current and possibly an inward chloride current. The electrogenic sodium-potassium pump also contributes to repolarization. The outward potassium current is stimulated by epinephrine, hypoxia, and high extracellular concentrations of calcium. Since repolarization occurs faster during these conditions, the action potential shortens. The outward potassium current is decreased by drugs such as quinidine, resulting in delayed repolarization and prolonged action potential duration.

SUMMARY OF EVENTS OF THE NORMAL CARDIAC ACTION POTENTIAL

In summary, the normal cardiac action potential is generated by the action of membrane-bound protein channels that allow the movement of sodium, calcium, potassium, and chloride ions across the cell membrane. The rapid upstroke of the action potential is produced by the flow of sodium ions into the cell and is followed by a slower-developing inward calcium current. The outward potassium current and possibly an inward chloride current regenerate the transmembrane potential, allowing the cell to respond to another electrical stimulus.

PROPAGATION OF THE ACTION POTENTIAL

The propagation of the action potential through the intact heart is equally important for normal cardiac electrophysiology. Normal conduction of action potentials depends on both active and passive membrane properties. Rather than an action potential being conducted passively along the cell membrane from its site of initiation, as down an electrical cable (passive propagation), the action potential is repeatedly regenerated along the membrane. Propagation is dependent on the action potential of one area of the membrane (the electrical "source") causing depolarization of neighboring areas (the electrical "sink") sufficient to reach threshold voltage and open sodium channels. Thus the interaction of the source (the action potential, due to active membrane properties) and the sink (due to passive cable properties) determines whether the action potential will be normally propagated.

The propagation of an action potential through intact myocardium is not uniform in all directions. The spread of activation is not simply in a radial manner but is related to the orientation of muscle fibers. For example, conduction has been demonstrated to be much more rapid along the longitudinal axis of fibers than along the transverse axis (Figure 2-2). This property of nonuniform propagation based on fiber orientation (anisotropy) is an important factor in both normal and abnormal cardiac rhythms.

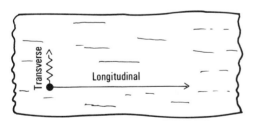

Figure 2-2 Anisotropy in a strip of atrial myocardium is illustrated diagrammatically. Cardiac muscle is arranged in sheets of fibers with longitudinal and transverse fiber orientation. When an electrical stimulus is applied at a point along the muscle sheet (black dot), the wavefront spreads rapidly along the longitudinal axis of fiber orientation and very slowly in the transverse axis. Anisotropy leads to preferential conduction of cardiac activation along the axis of fiber orientation. This feature of cardiac conduction can have a profound influence on the pathways of conduction seen with arrhythmias.

MECHANISMS OF ARRHYTHMIAS

Automaticity

Automaticity is the repetitive, spontaneous generation of action potentials. No stimuli are required for automatic cells to produce action potentials, though the process may be accelerated or suppressed by such factors as catecholamines, drugs, and hormonal transmitters. Automaticity is a normal property of several types of cardiac cells, most notably the sinus node. Other cells such as the AV junction and Purkinje fibers also have the capability for automaticity, which provides escape rhythms in the event of sinus node dysfunction. There is experimental evidence that there are also cells with latent pacemaker activity in the atria. The common property of all automatic cells is spontaneous diastolic depolarization during phase 4 (the pacemaker potential). The slope of the pacemaker potential determines the rate of cell discharge, with a more steep slope resulting in a faster rate. Whether the pacemaker potential is due to increased inward calcium current or decreased outward potassium current is not certain.

Alterations in Normal Automaticity

Alterations in normal automaticity may result in clinically relevant arrhythmias. For example, acceleration of the discharge rate of automatic atrial cells may result in incessant ectopic atrial tachycardias, which are more common in children and young adults. Automatic atrial cells may be involved in the genesis of the wandering atrial pacemaker syndrome. These arrhythmias share the normal properties of the sinus node, including suppression by overdrive pacing (pacing at a rate faster than the spontaneous rate, commonly referred to as overdrive suppression) and acceleration by increased catecholamine concentrations. Automatic arrhythmias also tend to demonstrate a gradually increasing rate ("warm-up") following overdrive suppression and a wide variability in the fluctuation of their spontaneous rate. Accelerated junctional rhythms following cardiac surgery, inferior

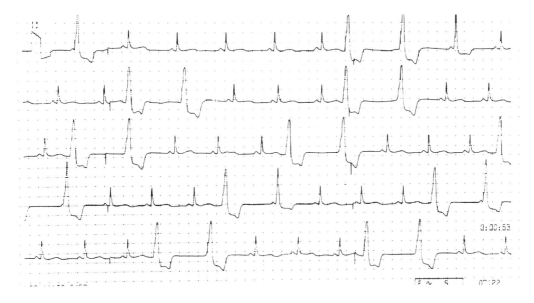

Figure 2-3 Ventricular parasystole. Notice that there is a wide QRS morphology that seems to march through the underlying sinus rhythm. Also note that the coupling intervals between the preceding sinus beat and the ventricular complexes are variable. This represents a protected focus in the ventricle and is typical of parasystole. The parasystolic focus allows exit of the electrical discharge from a focus that is protected from entrance by the underlying ventricular rhythm.

myocardial infarction, or digoxin therapy are also likely to be related to enhanced automaticity. Some forms of ventricular arrhythmias, including parasystole (Figure 2-3), accelerated idioventricular rhythm, and exercise-induced ventricular tachycardia, are likely to be due to automaticity. The electrocardiographic phenomenon of parasystole, spontaneous discharge of a focus with dissociation from the underlying cardiac rhythm, is likely to be related to automaticity in an area of myocardium with ''entrance block'' into the focus. In this circumstance, the automatic focus is protected and not influenced by the prevailing cardiac rhythm because of conduction block into the site of automatic discharge. The rate of discharge of a parasystolic focus tends to be slow, in keeping with the expected rate of subsidiary pacemakers.

Abnormal Automaticity

In addition to alterations in the discharge rate of cells with the capability for normal automaticity, under some conditions atrial or ventricular

myocytes may develop abnormal automaticity. Ischemia may result in partially depolarized cells that do not achieve the normal resting membrane potential. Under conditions of partial diastolic depolarization, threshold potential may be reached by passive sodium or calcium leak into the cell, with generation of a spontaneous action potential. Atrial or ventricular tachycardias occurring in the presence of ischemia, hypokalemia, or mechanical injury may be the result of abnormal automaticity. Clinical arrhythmias related to automaticity cannot be terminated by cardioversion or pacing techniques.

Because abnormal automaticity is likely to develop in infarcted or ischemic cardiac tissue, conduction block to neighboring areas of myocardium may not occur. However, if sufficient passive transfer of depolarizing current occurs across areas of conduction block, triggering of action potentials in contiguous abnormal myocardium may develop. In such situations, complex interactions of ectopic pacemakers may result in clinical arrhythmias. This passive interaction of ectopic foci has been termed ''modulated parasystole.'' In such situations, evidence of a precise mathematical relationship between foci may be observed. Examples of modulated parasystole have been reported in patients with premature ventricular depolarizations.

Afterdepolarizations and Triggered Activity

Afterdepolarizations are cellular phenomena related to abnormal depolarization of the membrane following the upstroke of the action potential. Afterdepolarizations that occur during the repolarization phase of the action potential (phase 3) are termed early afterdepolarizations. Afterdepolarizations that develop after the cell has repolarized (in phase 4) are referred to as delayed afterdepolarizations (Figure 2-4). If afterdepolarizations are of sufficient amplitude to result in threshold, an action potential is "triggered." Thus triggered action potentials require the presence of a preceding action potential. This requirement for a previous action potential distinguishes triggered activity from automaticity. Experiments in a variety of species have demonstrated that triggered activity may develop with high extracellular concentrations of calcium, epinephrine, or digitalis.

Delayed afterdepolarizations occur during conditions of cellular calcium overload, when there is a high concentration of calcium within the cytoplasm. The classic model of delayed afterdepolarizations and triggered activity has been digitalis toxicity. Digitalis results in an increased intracellular calcium concentration via poisoning of the sodium-potassium exchange pump. Since this results in increased intracellular sodium, the sodium-calcium pump is stimulated, which leads to increased calcium entry into the cell. Toxic concentrations of cardiac glycosides result in oscillations in the cell membrane potential in phase 4. In general, the higher the concentration of these drugs, the higher the amplitude of the delayed afterdepolarizations. It has also been shown that the amplitude of delayed afterdepolarizations and the likelihood of triggered activity developing is increased at faster heart rates. Delayed afterdepolarizations are also exaggerated by hypokalemia and hypercalcemia, conditions long

Figure 2-4 Cardiac action potentials demonstrating afterdepolarizations. In the left portion of the figure, a normal cardiac action potential is demonstrated. Notice that the action potential has minimal change in membrane potential during diastole. In the center panel of the figure, an action potential followed by a delayed afterdepolarization (DAD) is demonstrated. Notice that the action potential duration is somewhat shorter than normal, and there is a small hump following repolarization. These spontaneous afterdepolarizations can reach threshold and trigger another action potential. Delayed afterdepolarizations are generally found during conditions of excess intracellular calcium and have been strongly associated with digitalis intoxication. On the right side of the figure an action potential with an early afterdepolarization (EAD) is demonstrated. Notice that the action potential duration is quite prolonged, and there is a hump in the beginning of phase 3 that occurs prior to repolarization of the cell. Early afterdepolarizations arise during abnormalities of repolarization with a prolonged action potential duration. Early afterdepolarizations are associated with conditions that prolong the QT interval, such as class IA antiarrhythmic drug therapy, hypokalemia, or hypomagnesemia. *Source:* Adapted with permission from BP Damiano and MR Rosen, Effects of pacing on triggered activity induced by early afterdepolarizations, in *Circulation* (1984;65[5]:1013–1025), Copyright © 1984, American Heart Association.

known to worsen clinical arrhythmias during digitalis toxicity. Factors suggesting that the mechanism of an arrhythmia may be triggered activity related to delayed afterdepolarizations include (1) a clinical setting of increased catecholamine concentrations, digitalis toxicity, hypokalemia, or hypercalcemia; (2) worsening of the arrhythmia during rapid heart rates; (3) a more rapid rate of the arrhythmia during faster spontaneous heart rates; and (4) shortening of the interval between the last spontaneous beat and the first beat of the arrhythmia at faster spontaneous heart rates.

Clinical arrhythmias related to delayed afterdepolarizations and triggered activity may include the atrial tachycardia with AV block seen in digitalis toxicity, the junctional tachycardia seen in inferior myocardial infarction or digitalis toxicity, multifocal atrial tachycardia, and exercise-induced ventricular tachycardia in the setting of a structurally normal heart. Because of the requirement for calcium overload for the genesis of delayed afterdepolarizations, drugs such as β-blockers or verapamil may be especially useful for the therapy of arrhythmias based on triggered activity. Drugs such as β-agonists or theophylline should be avoided.

Early afterdepolarizations are depolarizing shifts in membrane potential that develop before the cell repolarizes. If early afterdepolarizations reach sufficient amplitude, action potentials may be triggered. Early afterdepolarizations may be produced during experimental conditions by aconitine, quinidine, procainamide, or cesium and are usually associated with a prolonged action potential duration. In contrast to delayed afterdepolarizations, early afterdepolarizations are more likely to develop during bradycardia than during tachycardia. These observations suggest that abnormalities of the repolarizing currents result in the conditions for early after-depolarization development. Cesium, which inhibits the outward potassium current, has been demonstrated to result in bradycardia, prolonged action potential duration, early afterdepolarizations, and ventricular tachycardia with features typical of torsades de pointes.

The clinical arrhythmia most likely to be related to early afterdepolarizations is torsades de pointes, a form of ventricular tachycardia related to abnormal prolongation of the QT interval (see Chapter 7, "Congenital and Acquired Long QT Syndromes"). Features suggesting torsades de pointes include (1) a prolonged QT interval (the sine qua non); (2) bradycardia; (3) a long coupling interval between the last normal QRS and the first beat of the tachycardia; (4) a long-short initiating sequence in which a pause precedes a normal QRS and the first beat of the tachycardia; (5) a twisting, polymorphic QRS during tachycardia; and (6) an appropriate clinical setting (i.e., quinidine, procainamide, complete AV block, phenothiazines, hypokalemia, hypomagnesemia). Since prolongation of the action potential appears to play a critical role in the development of early afterdepolarizations, therapeutic maneuvers that shorten the QT interval (rapid pacing, intravenous magnesium) are effective treatments for drug-induced torsades de pointes.

Reentry

The concept of reentry is based on the observation that a single wavefront of depolarization may propagate through a complete circuit of myocardium and continue to propagate around the circuit without the need for further pacemaker discharge. Reentry is the best-understood mechanism of clinical arrhythmias and probably the most frequent. Reentry has been conclusively demonstrated to be the underlying mechanism of tachycardias related to the Wolff-Parkinson-White syndrome. This clinical condition also serves as the prototype for understanding the mechanism of reentry underlying a variety of other clinical arrhythmias.

In order for a wavefront of activation to complete a circuit and continue to propagate, the myocardium at each point in the reentrant loop must have had time to recover the capability to respond to a depolarizing wave. Thus the conduction properties of at least a portion of the loop must be slow enough, or the reentrant circuit must be long enough, for recovery of excitability at every point. The fundamental requirements for reentry (Figure 2-5) were postulated by Mines in 1914: (1) an area of unidirectional block; (2) traverse movement of the depolarizing wave through the entire circuit, to arrive back at the site of origin; and (3) slow conduction of the impulse around the circuit, allowing time for the recovery of excitability. In the Wolff-Parkinson-White syndrome, for example, the area of unidirectional block is usually the accessory AV pathway. Thus a premature atrial depolarization will conduct through the atria to the AV node and the accessory pathway. If the premature beat conducts antegrade down the AV node but blocks in the accessory pathway, the wavefront enters the ventricles over the normal His-Purkinje system. The wavefront may then spread through the ventricle to enter the accessory pathway in the retrograde direction and reactivate the atria. If the AV node has had sufficient time to recover excitability, the wavefront may then again conduct to the ventricles and cause a sustained reentrant tachycardia (orthodromic reciprocating tachycardia). Thus in Wolff-Parkinson-White syndrome, the accessory pathway is often the site of unidirec-

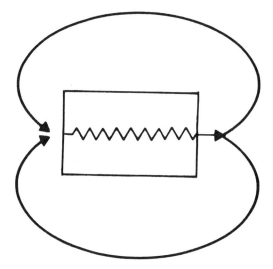

Figure 2-5 Anatomic model of reentry. The rectangular area in the middle of the figure demonstrates a region of slow conduction in cardiac tissue. A wavefront of depolarization enters the proximal portion of this region of slow conduction and slowly traverses it to arrive at the distal portion. Following this, the wavefront of activation spreads in two directions through more normal myocardium to arrive back at the proximal end of the region of slow conduction, to complete the reentrant circuit. Because of the time required for traversing the region of slow conduction, there is a gap of excitability in the circuit during which portions of the reentrant circuits are not refractory to stimulation.

tional block. Slow conduction in this arrhythmia is provided by the normally functioning AV node. Failure of conduction at any point along the circuit (atria, AV node, ventricle, or accessory pathway) will result in termination of the reentrant rhythm. Other clinical arrhythmias that are likely based on the anatomic obstacle form of reentry include ventricular tachycardia following myocardial infarction, AV nodal reentrant tachycardia, and classic atrial flutter.

In addition to the clinical model of reentry provided by Wolff-Parkinson-White syndrome, which is due to a discrete anatomic circuit, a second form of reentry without an anatomic obstacle has been demonstrated. Allessie demonstrated that an activation wavefront may continuously circle around a fulcrum in isolated pieces of normal rabbit atrium. The length of the circuit is determined by the refractory period of the involved myocardium. In this form of reentry, the leading edge of the advancing wavefront

follows the receding trail of refractory tissue. This form of reentry is known as the leading-circle model (Figure 2-6) and is determined by the electrophysiologic properties of the myocardium involved. Therefore interventions that shorten the refractory period of the tissue will tend to speed the rate of the reentrant arrhythmia by making the circuit functionally smaller. Drugs that lengthen the refractory period of the tissue will slow the reentrant tachycardia by prolonging the time required for a wavefront to circulate. Atrial fibrillation, ventricular fibrillation, and rapid atrial flutter are likely based on the leading-circle form of reentry.

In addition to the anatomic obstacle and leading-circle models of reentry, clinical reentrant arrhythmias may combine the features of both forms in their mechanism. Since myocardium demonstrates nonuniform conduction properties (anisotropy), the anatomic orientation of muscle

Figure 2-6 A micro–reentrant circuit without an excitable gap is illustrated diagrammatically. During this form of reentry the electrophysiologic properties of the myocardium determine the size and conduction velocity of the reentrant circuit. An advancing wave of depolarization (large black arrow) pursues a receding trail of refractoriness. There is no excitable gap during this reentrant circuit. In the middle of the circuit the myocardium is kept constantly refractory by continuous activation of the revolving wave of depolarization. *Source:* Adapted with permission from MA Allessie, FIM Bonke, and FJG Schopman, The "Leading Circle" concept: a new model of circus movement in cardiac tissue without the involvement of an anatomic obstacle, in *Circulation Research* (1977;41[1]:9–18), Copyright © 1977, American Heart Association.

fibers is certain to play a role in the circuit of either reentrant model.

From the preceding discussion it may be obvious that reentrant arrhythmias may be terminated by factors that interrupt the circulating wavefront. Both the anatomic obstacle and leading-circle forms of reentry may be terminated by cardioverting shocks that depolarize the entire circuit simultaneously. The anatomic obstacle form of reentry can also be terminated by rapid pacing, which results in conduction block at any point in the circuit.

Reflection

Experimental preparations of Purkinje fibers bathed in solutions with low electrolyte concentrations to suppress conduction of action potentials have demonstrated a phenomenon in which the action potential in one area of myocardium can ''jump'' a gap of nonexcitable myocardium to induce an action potential in a nearby region without actual propagation. This is possible because depolarization on one side of the gap leads to depolarization on the other side by means of passive, static electricity. If the passive (electrotonic) positive shift in the membrane potential is enough to reach threshold, an action potential will result. The newly generated action potential may then be ''reflected'' back across the nonexcitable gap by the same electrotonic depolarizing mechanism, resulting in reactivation of the original site of action potential generation. In order for an action potential to be reflected back across the gap, the myocardium must have had time to recover its excitability. Thus an inherent requirement for reflection is a time delay for transmission of electrotonic charge across an inexcitable gap. Under certain experimental conditions, repetitive runs of tachycardia can be generated by the mechanism of reflection. Whether or not reflection results in clinical arrhythmias is not certain.

BIBLIOGRAPHY

Allessie MA, Bonke FIM, Schopman FJG. The ''leading circle'' concept: a new model of circus movement in cardiac tissue without the involvement of an anatomic obstacle. *Circ Res.* 1977;41:9–18.

Allessie MA, Wim JEP, Lammers PL, et al. Determinants of re-entry in cardiac muscle. In: Zipes DP, Rowlands DJ, eds. *Progress in Cardiology.* Philadelphia, Pa: Lea & Febiger; 1988;1–2:3–18.

Antzelevitch C. Reflection as a mechanism of reentrant cardiac arrhythmias. Mechanisms. In: Zipes DP, Rowlands DJ, eds. *Progress in Cardiology.* Philadelphia, Pa: Lea & Febiger; 1988;1–1:3–16.

Antzelevitch C, Jalife J, Moe GK. Characteristics of reflection as a mechanism of reentrant arrhythmias and its relationship to parasystole. *Circulation.* 1980;61:182–191.

Arnsdorf MF. Basic understanding of the electrophysiologic actions of antiarrhythmic drugs: sources, sinks, and matrices of information. In: Zipes DP, ed. Cardiac Arrhythmias II. *The Medical Clinics of North America.* Philadelphia, Pa: W B Saunders Co; 1984;68: 1247–1280.

Baumgarten CM, Fozzard HA. The resting and pacemaker potentials. In: Fozzard HA, Haber E, Jennings RB, et al, eds. *The Heart and Cardiovascular System Scientific Foundations.* New York, NY: Raven Press; 1986:601–62.

Berne RM, Levy MN. Electrical activity of the heart. In: *Physiology.* St Louis, Mo: CV Mosby Co; 1983.

Brachmann J, Scherlag BJ, Rosenshtraukh LV, et al. Bradycardia-dependent triggered activity: relevance to drug-induced multiform ventricular tachycardia. *Circulation.* 1983;68:846–856.

Brown AM, Yatani A. Ca and Na channels in the heart. In: Fozzard HA, Haber E, Jennings RB, et al, eds. *The Heart and Cardiovascular System Scientific Foundations.* New York, NY: Raven Press; 1986:627–636.

Chung EKY. Parasystole. *Prog Cardiovasc Dis.* 1968; 2:64–81.

Cranefield PF. Action potentials, afterpotentials and arrhythmias. *Circ Res.* 1977;41:415–423.

Damiano BP, Rosen MR. Effects of pacing on triggered activity induced by early afterdepolarizations. *Circulation.* 1984;65:1013–1025.

Davidenko JM, Naw GJ. Parasystole. In: Zipes DP, Rowlands DJ, eds. *Progress in Cardiology.* Philadelphia, Pa: Lea & Febiger; 1988:171–186.

Fozzard HA, Arnsdorf MF. Cardiac electrophysiology. In: Fozzard HA, Haber E, Jennings RB, et al, eds. *The Heart and Cardiovascular System Scientific Foundations.* New York, NY: Raven Press; 1986:1–30.

Gilmore RF, Zipes DP. Abnormal automaticity and related phenomena. In: Fozzard HA, Haber E, Jennings RB, et al, eds. *The Heart and Cardiovascular System Scientific Foundations.* New York, NY: Raven Press; 1986:1239–1258.

Guyton AC. *Textbook of Medical Physiology.* 7th ed. Philadelphia, Pa: WB Saunders Co; 1986.

Hoffman BF, Cranefield PF. *Electrophysiology of the Heart.* New York, NY: McGraw-Hill Book Co; 1960.

Jalife J, Michaels DC. Modulated parasystolic rhythms as mechanisms of coupled extrasystoles and ventricular tachycardias. In: Zipes DP, Rowlands DJ, eds. *Progress in Cardiology*. Philadelphia, Pa: Lea & Febiger; 1988; 1–1:47–64.

Jalife J, Moe GK. A biological model of parasystole. *Am J Cardiol*. 1976;43:761.

Janse MJ. Reentry rhythms. In: Fozzard HA, Haber E, Jennings RB, et al, eds. *The Heart and Cardiovascular System Scientific Foundations*. New York, NY: Raven Press; 1986:1203–1238.

Janse MJ, van Capelle FJL, Morsink H, et al. Flow of "injury" current and pattern of excitation during early ventricular arrhythmias in acute regional myocardial ischemia in isolated procine and canine hearts: evidence for two different arrhythmogenic mechanisms. *Circ Res*. 1980;47:151–165.

Langendorf R, Pick A. Parasystole with fixed coupling. *Circulation*. 1967;35:304–315.

Nau GJ, Acunzo RS, Aldariz AE, et al. Electrocardiographic observations on the mechanisms of ventricular premature beats. *Clin Prog Electrophysiol*. 1986;4:141.

Nau GJ, Aldariz AE, Acunzo RS. Concealed ventricular parasystole uncovered in the form of ventricular escapes of variable coupling. *Circulation*. 1981;64:199–207.

Rosen MR, Hoffman BF. Electrophysiology determinants of normal cardiac rhythms and arrhythmias. In: Rosen MR, Hoffman BF, eds. *Cardiac Therapy*. Boston, Mass: Martinus Nijhoff; 1983:1–19.

Rosen MR, Wit AL. Triggered activity. In: Zipes DP, Rowlands DJ, eds. *Progress in Cardiology*. Philadelphia, Pa: Lea & Febiger; 1988;1–1:39–46.

Schechter E, Freeman CI, Lazzara R. Afterdepolarizations as a mechanism for the long QT syndrome: electrophysiological studies of a case. *J Am Coll Cardiol*. 1984;3:1556–1561.

Scherlag BJ, El-Sherji N, Hope RR, et al. Characterization and localization of ventricular arrhythmias resulting from myocardial ischemia and infarction. *Circ Res*. 1974; 35:372–383.

Vassalle M. The relationship among cardiac pacemakers: overdrive suppression. *Circ Res*. 1977;41:269–277.

Verrier RL. Autonomic substrates for arrhythmias. In: Zipes DP, Rowlands DJ, eds. *Progress in Cardiology*. Philadelphia, Pa: Lea & Febiger; 1988;1–1:65–86.

Wit AL, Rosen MR. Afterdepolarizations and triggered activity. In: Fozzard HA, Haber E, Jennings RB, et al, eds. *The Heart and Cardiovascular System Scientific Foundations*. New York: Raven Press; 1986:1449–1490.

Wit AL, Rosen MR. Cellular electrophysiology of cardiac arrhythmias. In: Josephson ME, Wellens HJJ, eds. *Tachycardias: Mechanisms, Diagnosis, Treatment*. Philadelphia, Pa: Lea & Febiger; 1984:1–27.

Chapter 3

Noninvasive Evaluation of Cardiac Arrhythmias

INTRODUCTION

Effective management of the patient with cardiac arrhythmias is dependent upon establishing an accurate rhythm diagnosis. The most important test for diagnosing clinical arrhythmias remains the 12-lead ECG. Based on careful analysis of the surface ECG, arrhythmias can be correctly categorized as either supraventricular or ventricular in origin in the vast majority of cases. In addition, by correlation of the ECG with the patient's symptoms, most arrhythmias can be satisfactorily treated. Although the surface ECG is an extremely valuable clinical tool, there are important limitations of this technique relating to the transient and random occurrence of paroxysmal arrhythmias and the limited ability of surface recordings to differentiate intracardiac events. In order to address these limitations of the surface ECG, the noninvasive techniques of ambulatory electrocardiographic (Holter) monitoring, exercise stress testing, signal-averaged electrocardiography, and transtelephonic event recording and the semi-invasive tools of esophageal and epicardial recordings have been incorporated into clinical use for the diagnosis and management of cardiac arrhythmias. Lastly, observations associated with physical diagnosis, response to carotid sinus massage, and intracardiac pressure tracings can facilitate the diagnosis

of arrhythmias. The use and limitations of each of these techniques will be discussed.

TWELVE-LEAD ELECTROCARDIOGRAPHY

Origin of Electrocardiographic Signals

Electrical signals are generated by the flow of electrically charged particles, a phenomenon that is referred to as an electric current. ECGs record electrical currents occurring in the heart from electrodes located on the surface of the body, the skin. The electrocardiographic signals recorded from the body surface arise from the movement of electrically charged ions (mainly sodium and potassium) across the cell membrane of atrial and ventricular myocytes (as described in Chapter 2).

As the wave of depolarization spreads from the site of initial stimulation toward resting (polarized) regions of the heart, an electrical current is generated. By convention, a skin electrode that is oriented toward an area of positive charge will record an upward deflection. Therefore, as a wave of depolarization moves toward a skin electrode, the positively charged outside surface of the cell will be oriented toward that electrode, and an upward deflection will be recorded. However, once the wave of depolarization passes by the electrode, the deflection abruptly changes from positive to negative, as the current of depolarization is conducted in a direction opposite to the orientation of the surface electrode. Following the period of depolarization, the normal cardiac cell then regenerates the separation of charges across the membrane by shifting the positive charges from the inside to the outside of the cell, reestablishing an excess of positive charges on the outside of the cell. This process results in repolarization of the membrane, which, since it requires the movement of charged ions, generates an electrical current that can be recorded on the ECG.

Since the surface ECG is a composite signal generated from all viable cardiac cells, the electrical signals reflect both the direction of spread of cardiac depolarization and repolarization (manifested as upward or downward deflections). The signals also reflect the time required for each chamber to depolarize (manifested by the width of the QRS complex and P wave) and to repolarize (manifested by the QT interval). Ventricular depolarization is manifested by the QRS complex and atrial depolarization by the P wave. The wave of ventricular repolarization is represented by the T wave where as atrial repolarization is hidden in the QRS. Because (1) the mass of atrial myocardium is relatively small, (2) repolarization occurs more slowly than depolarization, and (3) atrial repolarization usually occurs during ventricular depolarization, the repolarization wave in the atrium does not usually result in a recognizable deflection in the surface ECG.

A 12-lead surface ECG is a graphic recording of the heart's electrical activity transmitted to the body surface from 12 distinct directions. The limb leads reflect the electrical activity in the frontal plane, and the precordial leads record electrical activity in the horizontal plane. Thus the correct diagnosis of arrhythmias can best be facilitated by obtaining a 12-lead ECG during both normal sinus rhythm and the arrhythmia.

Normal Electrocardiographic Patterns

Although a detailed discussion of electrocardiography is not intended here, there are several important clinical rules that can be valuable aids in the diagnosis of arrhythmias. The normal P wave is usually upright in the inferior leads (leads II, III, and aVF) and is virtually always negative in lead aVR, reflecting spread away from the sinus node in the high lateral right atrium toward the inferior aspect of both atria and leftward toward the left atrium. These observations are important clues to remember in the interpretation of ECGs during supraventricular arrhythmias. For example, sinus tachycardia can be excluded as the mechanism of a supraventricular tachycardia if the P wave is inverted in the inferior leads (in which case the atria are activated from low to high) or if the P wave is upright in lead aVR (in which case the right atrium is activated from left to right). However, it should also be recognized that ectopic atrial tachycardias arising in the high right atrium or reentry involving a portion of the sinus node (sinus node reentry) may produce P waves that closely resemble those of normal sinus rhythm.

The normal QRS complex may have an electrocardiographic axis in the frontal plane that varies from -45 to $+110$ degrees, depending in large part on the orientation of the heart within the chest. Thin patients with a vertically oriented heart usually have a vertical QRS axis, whereas obese patients with a more horizontally oriented heart often have a QRS axis that approaches 0 degrees. Thus the electrocardiographic axis reflects the mean direction and magnitude of the electrical forces, or vector, of the heart. The mean QRS vector depicts the overall direction of ventricular depolarization.

Axis analysis can aid in determining the site of origin of tachyarrhythmias in both the atrium and ventricles. The electrocardiographic axis of the QRS complex can be rapidly discerned by examining leads I and aVF. If the QRS is upright in lead I, the axis is leftward. If the QRS is inverted in lead I, the axis is rightward. Similarly, if the QRS is upright in lead aVF, the axis is inferior, and if inverted, the axis is superior. Normally, the axis is oriented toward the left and inferior surface of the heart, resulting in a mean QRS vector that is positive in leads I and aVF.

Since normal activation of the ventricles occurs over the rapidly conducting, branching His-Purkinje system, the right and left ventricles are activated in a relatively uniform and simultaneous manner. Thus normal activation of the ventricles results in a narrow QRS. Normal septal activation proceeds left to right, accounting for the initial r wave in V_1 and its absence in left bundle branch block. The ventricle is activated from the endocardium toward the epicardium. Repolarization, in contrast, usually begins at the epicardium and proceeds toward the endocardium. In addition, the total duration of the action potential (the time from the beginning of depolarization to the end of repolarization) is generally greater for areas of the ventricle activated earliest. Because of this fact, the areas of the ventricle depolarized first are repolarized last, resulting in relatively simultaneous recovery of the heart. This observation has diagnostic value in clinical electrocardiography in that the T wave axis is usually similar to the QRS axis in the normal heart. When depolarization is

abnormal, such as with a bundle branch block, preexcitation, ventricular pacing, or during ventricular tachycardia, the sequence of repolarization is also abnormal. This results in a T wave axis that is often opposite to that of the QRS (Figure 3-1).

The 12-Lead Electrocardiogram for the Diagnosis of Wide QRS Tachycardias

The diagnostic value of the 12-lead ECG in differentiating wide QRS complex supraventricular tachycardias with aberrant conduction from ventricular tachycardia has been extensively studied. Several important features suggesting ventricular tachycardia have been recognized. Most importantly, if AV dissociation or fusion beats are present on the ECG, the tachycardia

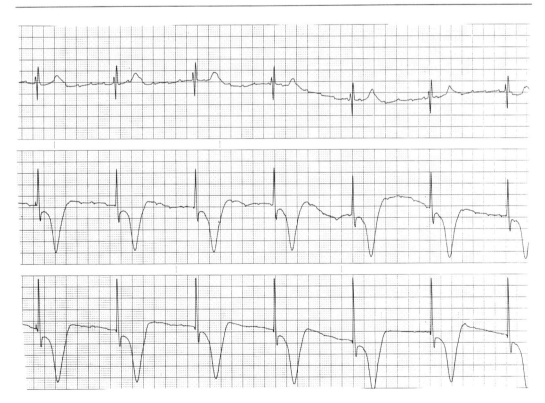

Figure 3-1 Atrial flutter with complete AV block following catheter ablation of the AV conduction system. Note the marked T wave inversion associated with each QRS complex. This represents postpacing T wave changes following temporary inhibition of ventricular pacing. Similar changes in the T wave can be seen following bundle branch block conduction or preexcitation, or with central nervous system disease.

can be confidently classified as ventricular tachycardia (Figure 3-2). Unfortunately, only a minority of wide QRS tachycardias demonstrate these phenomena on the surface ECG. Thus in most cases morphologic criteria are used to differentiate aberrancy from ventricular tachycardia. Wide QRS complex tachycardias are classified as having right bundle branch block or left bundle branch block morphology based on the predominant deflection of the QRS complex in lead V_1. If the predominant QRS deflection is upright in lead V_1, the tachycardia is classified as a right bundle branch block morphology. If the predominant deflection is negative in V_1, the tachycardia is classified as a left bundle branch block morphology. This distinction is of vital clinical importance as the criteria for differentiating aberrant conduction from ventricular tachycardia are different for left bundle branch block than for right bundle branch block tachycardias.

If the tachycardia has a left bundle branch block QRS morphology, four criteria are useful to diagnose the arrhythmia as ventricular tachycardia: (1) duration of the r wave in lead V_1 or V_2 exceeding 30 milliseconds, (2) duration of the S wave in lead V_1 or V_2 exceeding 60 milliseconds, (3) a notch or slur in the downslope of the S wave in leads V_1 or V_2, and (4) any q wave in lead V_6 (Figure 3-3). If any one of these criteria is present with a left bundle branch block, QRS pattern ventricular tachycardia is highly likely.

The criteria for differentiating wide QRS complex tachycardias with right bundle branch block morphology are different from those for left bundle branch block tachycardias (Table 3-1).

If the duration of the QRS with a right bundle branch block morphology exceeds 140 milliseconds, ventricular tachycardia is strongly suggested. Other factors suggesting ventricular tachycardia include a superior frontal plane axis, a ratio of the R wave to the S wave in lead V_6 less than 1, or a biphasic or monophasic QRS complex in lead V_1. If the QRS is triphasic in lead V_1 with the initial upright deflection of greater amplitude than the second upright deflection (R greater than R′), ventricular tachycardia is more likely. If the second upright deflection is greater than the initial deflection of a triphasic

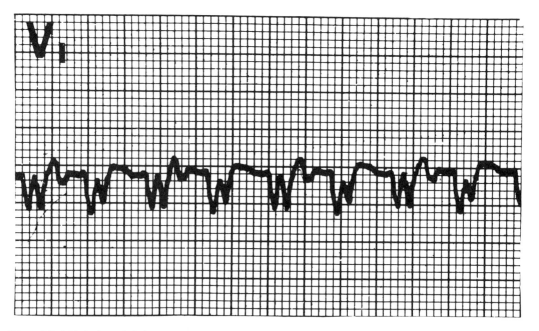

Figure 3-2 A V_1 rhythm strip is demonstrated during ventricular tachycardia. Note that there is a wide QRS complex with a rate of approximately 175 beats per minute. Retrograde P waves are seen after every other QRS complex, demonstrating 2:1 retrograde conduction. The faster ventricular rate compared to the atrial rate is proof that this is a ventricular tachycardia rather than aberrant conduction of a supraventricular rhythm.

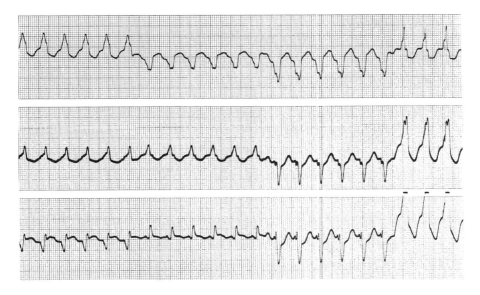

Figure 3-3 Sustained ventricular tachycardia with left bundle branch block morphology and left inferior QRS axis is demonstrated at a rate of 148 beats per minute. Note that in lead V_1 there is a slurred downstroke of the S wave, which also has a notch. This finding, as well as the total duration of the S wave of approximately 100 milliseconds, is quite suggestive of the ventricular origin of this arrhythmia.

Table 3-1 Features Suggesting Ventricular Tachycardia

Left Bundle Pattern	Right Bundle Pattern
r > 30 milliseconds in V_1 or V_2	QRS > 140 milliseconds
S > 60 milliseconds in V_1 or V_2	Superior QRS axis
Notch in S wave downstroke in V_1 or V_2	R:S ratio < 1 in V_6
q in V_6	Mono- or biphasic QRS in V_1

QRS in V_1 (R' greater than R), true right bundle branch block aberrancy is suggested (Figure 3-4).

It should also be emphasized that the patient's clinical history is extremely helpful in the diagnosis of wide QRS complex tachycardias. If a patient has a history of myocardial infarction and the patient's tachycardia began following an infarction, ventricular tachycardia is extremely likely. Asking the patient whether he has suffered a heart attack and, if so, whether the tachycardia began following the heart attack may have diagnostic value at least as great as the ECG. If

the answer to both of these questions is yes, ventricular tachycardia is the likely diagnosis.

The 12-Lead Electrocardiogram for the Diagnosis of Narrow QRS Tachycardias

The surface ECG also has considerable utility in the diagnosis of narrow complex tachycardias. For example, supraventricular tachycardias based on a mechanism of AV nodal reentry can often be distinguished from reentrant tachycardias utilizing a retrogradely conducting accessory bypass pathway by the location of the P wave in relation to the QRS complex during tachycardia. If the P wave is buried within or distorts the terminal portion of the QRS, AV nodal reentry is suggested (Figure 3-5). In contrast, if the P wave is distinct from the QRS complex in the ST segment, a bypass tract can be suspected (Figure 3-6).

Ectopic atrial tachycardias are usually distinguished by an abnormal P wave axis and the frequent association of AV Wenckebach block (Figure 3-7).

The diagnosis of atrial flutter is easily made by the typical sawtooth flutter waves present in the

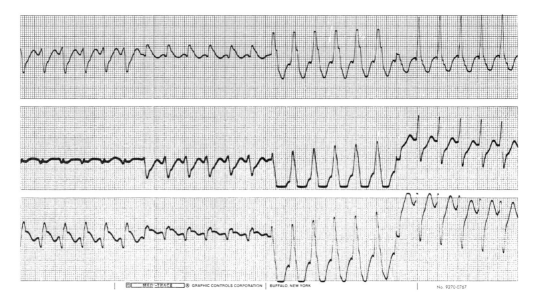

Figure 3-4 Sustained ventricular tachycardia with a right bundle branch block and right superior axis morphology is shown. The ventricular tachycardia has a rate of approximately 145 beats per minute. Note that in lead V_1 there is a monophasic R wave, and in lead V_6 the R:S ratio is less than 1.0. The QRS duration is markedly prolonged at 180 milliseconds, and the axis is quite abnormal. No evidence of AV dissociation is seen on the surface ECG.

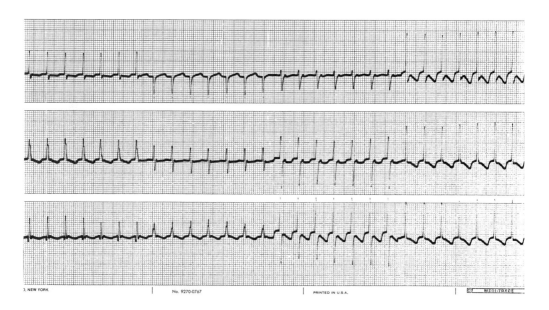

Figure 3-5 AV nodal reentrant tachycardia. Note the regular narrow QRS complex tachycardia at a rate of approximately 160 beats per minute. Also note that in leads III and aVF there is a pseudo–S wave. In leads V_1 and V_2 there is a pseudo–R wave representing a buried P wave that distorts the terminal portion of the QRS. This is very typical of AV nodal reentrant tachycardia.

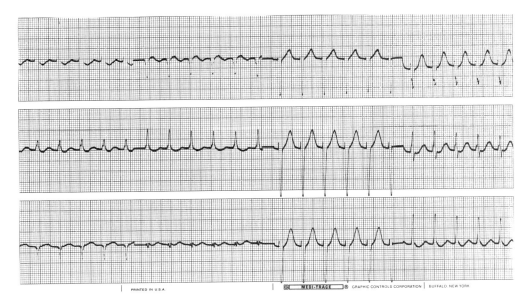

Figure 3-6 Orthodromic reciprocating tachycardia. A narrow QRS tachycardia at a rate of 145 beats per minute is shown. Retrograde P waves can be seen distorting the ST segment in leads I, II, aVL, and aVF. The retrograde P waves distinct from the QRS are helpful in distinguishing this rhythm from AV nodal reentrant tachycardia.

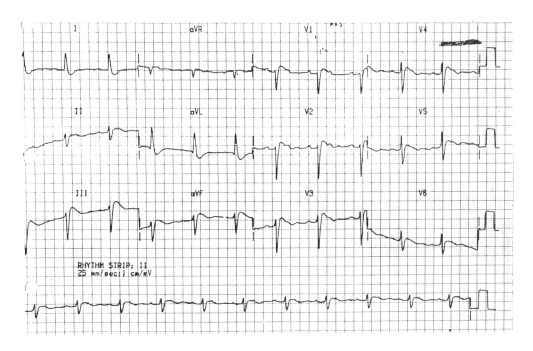

Figure 3-7 Ectopic atrial tachycardia with 2:1 AV conduction. Notice that in lead V₁ there is a regular atrial rate of approximately 115 beats per minute, with 2:1 AV conduction. This tachycardia may be associated with digitalis intoxication.

inferior leads (Figure 3-8). Although there is usually little difficulty distinguishing atrial flutter from atrial fibrillation, large fibrillation waves that are only slightly irregular may be present during atrial fibrillation in lead V_1 and lead to misinterpretation as flutter. Careful inspection will reveal that the rate of these waves is greater than 350 beats per minute and that these waves are not perfectly regular (Figure 3-9).

Multifocal atrial tachycardia, which is usually grossly irregular, is usually associated with very tall, abnormal P waves in the inferior leads with variability in P wave morphology and PR intervals (Figure 3-10).

AMBULATORY ELECTROCARDIOGRAPHIC MONITORING

Since the 12-lead ECG records cardiac activity for only a brief period of time with the patient at rest, it is of limited value for the detection of intermittent arrhythmias. Ambulatory electrocardiography (Holter monitoring) was developed to overcome these limitations of the standard 12-lead ECG. The major advantage of ambulatory monitoring is the capability to record the cardiac rhythm for a longer period while the patient is performing a variety of activities. Ambulatory monitoring has a proven role for documenting the frequency and complexity of arrhythmias. Equally important, the electrocardiographic findings can be correlated with the patient's symptoms. The diagnosis of transient arrhythmias and the assessment of pharmacologic efficacy remain the primary indications for ambulatory monitoring.

Clinical Applications of Holter Monitoring

Holter monitoring is employed in routine clinical practice to evaluate the cause of symptoms, to quantitate the frequency of arrhythmias

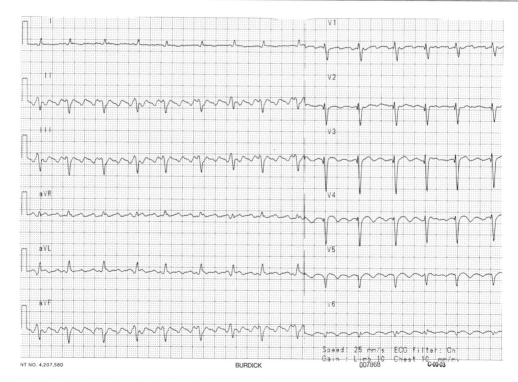

Figure 3-8 Atrial flutter with a 3:1 AV conduction pattern is demonstrated. Notice that in leads II, III, and aVF there is a saw-tooth atrial pattern very typical of atrial flutter. The atrial flutter waves are uniform at a rate of approximately 280 beats per minute.

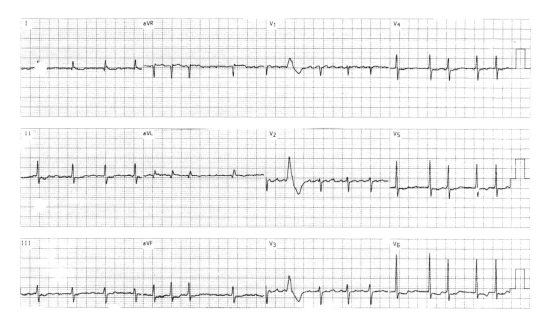

Figure 3-9 Atrial fibrillation. Note the irregularly irregular ventricular rhythm with disorganized fibrillation waves in all leads. A VPD is also demonstrated.

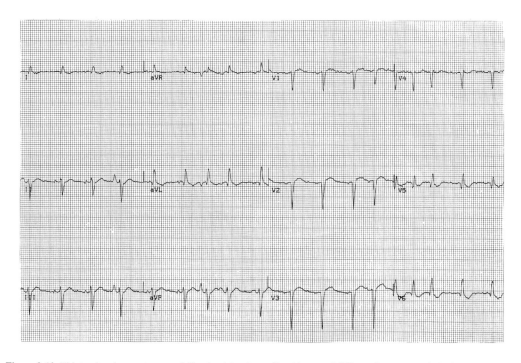

Figure 3-10 This tracing demonstrates multifocal atrial tachycardia with several different P wave morphologies with an irregular ventricular rate. Notice that in leads II, III, and aVF the P waves are tall and peaked, typical of this arrhythmia.

for prognostic stratification, and to assess the efficacy of antiarrhythmic or antianginal therapy. The diagnostic utility of a single 24-hour recording period may be limited in patients with rare clinical symptoms. For example, Holter monitoring of an individual with symptoms that occur once every 1 to 2 months usually provides minimal clinically important information. Other forms of arrhythmia evaluation, such as transtelephonic event recording or invasive electrophysiologic testing, may be more valuable in patients with rare events. It must also be remembered that Holter monitoring is not a substitute for inpatient telemetry in individuals with life-threatening symptoms or arrhythmias. In light of these clinical considerations, Holter monitoring is best used in patients with frequent episodes of symptoms that are probably not life threatening. Over 25% of patients will experience symptoms during a 24-hour Holter recording. The yield of cardiac arrhythmias that correlate with the symptoms is lower, on the order of 5% to 15% of patients. An important function of ambulatory monitoring is the exclusion of cardiac arrhythmias as the cause of the patient's complaints. Approximately one third of patients experiencing symptoms during a 24-hour monitoring period will have no associated cardiac arrhythmia.

The range of normal findings with prolonged ambulatory monitoring needs to be appreciated for accurate assessment of the Holter report. Ventricular premature depolarizations (VPDs) will be recorded in approximately 50% of normal subjects during a 24-hour period. In addition, premature atrial depolarizations, sinus bradycardia during sleep, and AV Wenckebach block may all be recorded in healthy volunteers. The prognosis for each of these arrhythmias in asymptomatic individuals without structural heart disease is excellent, and treatment for these findings is usually unnecessary and even potentially harmful.

The occurrence of more than 6 to 10 VPDs following myocardial infarction is known to be associated with a worsening of long-term prognosis as compared to the prognosis for individuals without these arrhythmias. The combination of ventricular ectopy and poor left ventricular function (left ventricular ejection fraction less than 0.40) carries a substantially increased risk of sudden cardiac death within the first 6 months after myocardial infarction. Despite these findings, the only class of antiarrhythmic drugs that has been shown to decrease mortality in patients following myocardial infarction has been β-blockers. Treatment with class IC drugs in the Cardiac Arrhythmia Suppression Trial has resulted in a significant worsening of mortality risk in patients with ventricular ectopy following myocardial infarction. Thus although Holter monitoring can be used to stratify patients into high and low risk for subsequent mortality following myocardial infarction, the therapeutic value of this information has yet to be demonstrated.

Assessment of Drug Therapy

Assessment of the efficacy of antiarrhythmic drug therapy with ambulatory monitoring requires an understanding of the degree of baseline variability in the occurrence of arrhythmias. Previous studies have demonstrated that the frequency of VPDs may vary as much as 70% from day to day. Because of the wide range of variability in the occurrence of ventricular arrhythmias, at least 70% suppression of single VPDs and at least 90% suppression of repetitive forms during a 24-hour Holter monitoring is required to demonstrate a therapeutic response to antiarrhythmic drug therapy. Extending the monitoring period to 48 hours improves the likelihood that a decrease in ventricular arrhythmia frequency is related to an actual therapeutic effect of a drug rather than simply to spontaneous arrhythmia variability. Whether or not a drug is worsening the frequency of arrhythmias also requires an understanding of spontaneous arrhythmia variability.

The treatment of sustained ventricular tachycardia or ventricular fibrillation with antiarrhythmic drugs has been assessed by serial Holter monitoring. The rationale for this approach is the assumption that suppression of spontaneous VPDs and nonsustained runs of ventricular tachycardia with antiarrhythmic drugs correlates with effective suppression of sustained arrhythmias. Although serial Holter monitoring and treadmill exercise testing are noninvasive and associated with a small inherent risk, ventricular tachycardia may remain inducible with invasive electrophysiologic testing despite the effective suppression of spontaneous VPDs. For a number of years controversy has existed as to which technique, invasive electrophysiologic testing or Holter monitoring, is a better predictor of outcome with antiarrhythmic drug treatment of ventricular tachycardia. Although the results of one randomized clinical trial comparing these approaches demonstrated superior outcome in the invasively assessed group, the controversy has not been completely resolved. The ongoing National Institutes of Health-sponsored ESVEM Trial (Electrophysiologic Study Versus Electrocardiographic Monitoring) for selection of antiarrhythmic therapy of ventricular tachyarrhythmias is comparing the invasive and noninvasive methods of guiding drug therapy for ventricular arrhythmias in a randomized, prospective study. What is clear from the results of previous studies is that Holter monitoring is a useful adjunct to invasive electrophysiologic testing in the assessment of ther-

apy for life-threatening arrhythmias. If frequent arrhythmias persist on Holter monitoring, the likelihood of suppression of inducible arrhythmias with electrophysiologic testing is very low. Therefore, the sensitivity of Holter monitoring for drug ineffectiveness is high. However, the specificity of an apparent therapeutic benefit of drug therapy is probably more difficult to assess with Holter monitoring than with invasive electrophysiologic testing.

Electrode Configurations for Ambulatory Monitoring

Ambulatory monitors usually record one to two electrocardiographic leads simultaneously and require the placement of three to five cutaneous recording electrodes. A light weight, battery-operated, reel-to-reel (Figure 3-11) or cassette (Figure 3-12) recorder allows the patient the flexibility to continue his or her usual physical activities.

Because of the improved diagnostic accuracy of dual-channel recordings, the older single-

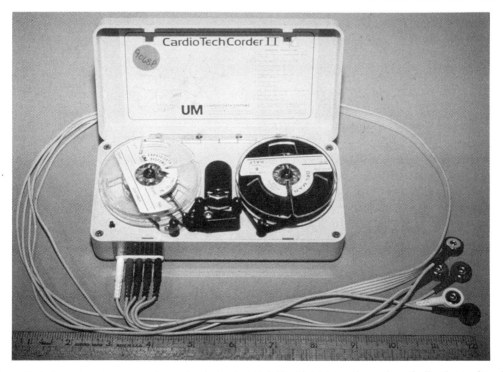

Figure 3-11 A reel-to-reel Holter monitor system is demonstrated. Note that a magnetic tape is gradually taken up from the right to the left. Five electrodes for monitoring are demonstrated. Reprinted with permission from Cardio Data Systems.

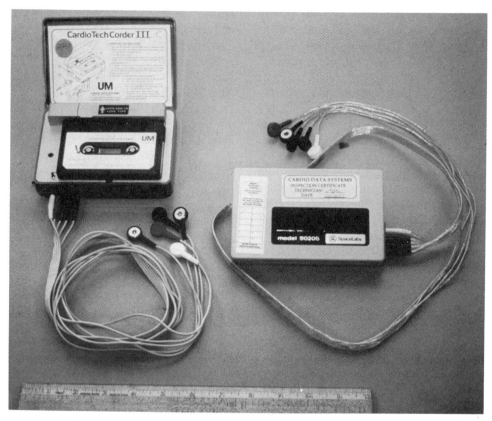

Figure 3-12 A cassette-type Holter monitor system is demonstrated. The cassette recorders have the advantage of a lower incidence of malfunction than reel-to-reel recorders. Reprinted with permission from Cardio Data Systems.

channel systems utilizing a lead II configuration are less commonly used. Two-channel ambulatory monitors decrease the chances of failure to obtain technically adequate signals because of artifacts or loose electrodes and facilitate identification of P waves and QRS morphology. Most presently used ambulatory monitors record modified bipolar V_1 and V_5 leads, though many other lead configurations can be employed. The recordings are obtained by two negative leads, which are placed on the upper sternum or near the clavicles, and two positive leads, which are placed in the V_1 and V_5 positions. The ground electrode is generally placed on the right side of the chest (Figure 3-13).

Patients are also provided with a symptom and activity diary and are instructed to record the time and nature of cardiac symptoms and their physical activities at the time of these events. As patients may be asymptomatic during arrhyth-

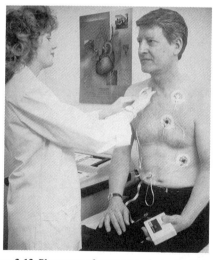

Figure 3-13 Placement of cutaneous electrodes is demonstrated in a patient undergoing Holter monitoring. Notice that electrodes are placed over the clavicles and over the upper quadrant of the abdomen. Other electrodes are placed to the left of the sternum to record modified leads V_2. Reprinted with permission from Cardio Data Systems.

mias, they are also asked to record their activities in the diary.

Other Considerations

The quality of the electrocardiographic recordings is enhanced and artifact minimized by thorough cleansing and preparation of the skin to remove body oils and perspiration. Preparation of the skin for electrode placement may require that areas be shaved and that sandpaper be lightly rubbed over the area to remove nonconductive dry skin. Some electrodes contain sandpaper on the back for this purpose. Skin preparation may also be accomplished with a commercial solution in a prep pad. To minimize motion artifact, the leads are looped on the electrode and then securely taped. The Holter is placed in a pouch with a carrying strap for the shoulder or waist. Advance instruction to the patient to shower and avoid lotions and powders prior to Holter placement will minimize the degree of preparation required.

Patients should be instructed not to immerse the Holter monitor in water and not to bathe, shower, or swim during the monitoring period, to protect the device from becoming wet. Patients are also instructed to periodically listen to the hum of the Holter monitor to verify that it is operating. Holter monitors placed on hospitalized patients should be scrutinized for continued operation by the nursing staff. The evaluation should include listening for the hum of an operating Holter monitor, opening reel-to-reel recorders to verify that the tape is winding correctly, and examining the insertion point of the leads into the recorder to verify that they have not become dislodged. Exposure of the Holter monitors to x-rays should also be avoided to prevent erasing the recording tape. If the clinical condition mandates that x-rays be made during Holter monitoring, the recording leads may be disconnected and the recorder temporarily removed. The disconnect and reconnect times should be recorded in the diary. Radionuclide procedures will not adversely affect Holter recordings. However, the electrodes themselves may interfere with these tests. In this instance it may be best to modify the V_5 electrode, again making a notation in the diary.

Conventional and Real-Time Holter Recordings

Since the Holter tape is scanned hours to days following its recording, this form of arrhythmia detection is not true ambulatory monitoring; rather, it represents continuous ambulatory recording. The electromagnetic recording tape is later electronically scanned for abnormalities of cardiac rhythm, with careful correlation with any symptoms recorded in the patient diary. Although analysis of the tape is performed by a computer employing rule-based logic, operator interaction is essential for accurate interpretation. The Holter report contains a tabular summary of heart rates, quantitation of premature atrial and ventricular depolarizations and nonsustained or sustained atrial and ventricular arrhythmias, and duration of bradycardic events (Exhibit 3-1).

Graphical displays of ST segment shifts, heart rate, and arrhythmic episodes are also presented. The representative electrocardiographic tracings and the interpretation of the reviewing physician are the most important data included in the Holter report (Figure 3-14).

Newer ambulatory monitors offer the capability for real-time analysis and provide improved resolution for shifts in the ST segment. These Holter systems provide beat-by-beat analysis of the ECG. Because the memory in such devices is limited, only a portion of the electrocardiographic record can be stored for later playback and analysis. With further evolution of real-time Holter technology, data compression techniques will allow full disclosure of electrocardiographic events over 24 hours.

TRANSTELEPHONIC EVENT DETECTION

Transtelephonic monitoring has long been used to monitor pacemaker function from the patient's home. Transtelephonic event recorders are also used in patients without pacemakers to record the ECG during intermittent symptomatic episodes of arrhythmias or symptomatic ischemia for later transmission of the recorded arrhythmia via the telephone to a base station. Organized transtelephonic monitoring programs

Exhibit 3-1 An example of a Holter monitor report on a patient with frequent ventricular premature beats (VPB) is demonstrated. In addition, the patient has frequent episodes of both sustained and nonsustained ventricular tachycardia as well as VPB pairs and multiform beats.

VENTRICULAR ECTOPY PROFILE

TIME ENDING	HEART RATE LO	MEAN	HI	VPBs TOTAL	VPBs SINGLE	VPBs PAIRED	VT BEATS	VT EVENTS	VPBs R ON T	MULTI FORM	TIME ANALYZED
8:00.0A1	–	–	–	–	–	–	–	–	–	–	–
9:00.0A1	56	70	90	26	26	0	0	0	0	N	0:57.7
10:00.0A1	55	72	169	851	193	0	658	3	0	N	0:58.8
11:00.0A1	57	67	177	239	156	0	83	2	0	Y	0:57.8
12:00.0P1	55	71	166	533	439	0	94	3	0	Y	0:51.1
1:00.0P1	–	–	–	–	–	–	–	–	–	–	–
2:00.0P1	52	61	75	123	123	0	0	0	0	N	0:59.8
3:00.0P1	52	58	71	0	0	0	0	0	0	N	1:00.0
4:00.0P1	54	61	77	0	0	0	0	0	0	N	1:00.0
5:00.0P1	53	67	177	1673	901	2	770	1	0	Y	0:55.1
6:00.0P1	58	67	112	1836	1834	2	0	0	0	Y	1:00.0
7:00.0P1	55	71	119	2025	2007	12	6	2	0	Y	1:00.0
8:00.0P1	51	70	161	1837	1779	4	54	4	0	Y	0:59.9
9:00.0P1	55	85	154	1588	1562	8	18	23	0	Y	0:57.6
10:00.0P1	56	90	154	5507	1002	2	4503	2	0	Y	0:53.3
11:00.0P1	55	65	90	154	154	0	0	0	0	Y	0:59.2
12:00.0A2	56	68	175	730	578	2	150	1	0	Y	0:59.8
1:00.0A2	58	64	80	700	700	0	0	0	0	Y	1:00.0
2:00.0A2	54	62	76	358	358	0	0	0	0	Y	1:00.0
3:00.0A2	54	65	75	238	238	0	0	0	0	Y	1:00.0
4:00.0A2	51	65	78	1354	1354	0	0	0	0	Y	1:00.0
5:00.0A2	53	62	71	778	778	0	0	0	0	Y	1:00.0
6:00.0A2	55	67	77	542	542	0	0	0	0	Y	1:00.0
7:00.0A2	54	68	90	269	269	0	0	0	0	Y	1:00.0
8:00.0A2	54	70	89	478	478	0	0	0	0	Y	1:00.0
9:00.0A2	55	64	164	1570	1553	2	15	1	0	Y	0:59.8
9:14.5A2	52	65	79	554	554	0	0	0	0	Y	0:14.1
SUMMARY	51	68	177	23963	17578	34	6351	42	0	Y	23:44.0

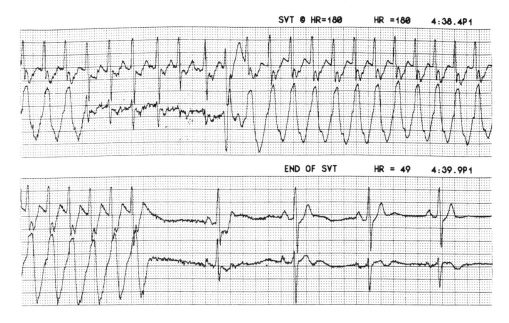

SVT @ HR=180   HR =180   4:38.4P1

END OF SVT   HR = 49   4:39.9P1

Figure 3-14 Representative Holter monitor tracing that demonstrates sustained atrial flutter in a patient with preexcitation. Two electrocardiographic tracings are demonstrated. The top tracing in each panel demonstrates lead V_1 and the bottom tracing lead V_5. Note in the upper panel that a wide QRS morphology is seen for the initial three beats, followed by six beats of a relatively narrow QRS complex. This is subsequently followed by resumption of the wide-complex, preexcited QRS morphology. In the second panel, the atrial flutter terminates, resulting in sinus rhythm with minimal evidence of preexcitation.

for patients may be operated by an individual hospital, an office, or a company specializing in such systems. These specialized base stations offer patients access to a toll-free number, registered nurses and/or trained technicians who answer calls 24 hours a day, immediate arrhythmia interpretation, and physician or emergency medical services notification.

Clinical Applications of Transtelephonic Monitoring

Transient symptomatic event recorders provide a mechanism for patients to record arrhythmias at any place and time, regardless of frequency. These devices are prescribed for persons with symptoms suggestive of arrhythmias that occur too infrequently to be reliably assessed with Holter monitoring. They can be used to diagnose an arrhythmia during a symptomatic event, evaluate the efficacy of a pharmacologic regimen, document the function of antitachycardia pacemakers or implantable defibrillators, or detect ischemic episodes by analysis of the ST segment. Transtelephonic event recorders have increased in popularity as it has become increasingly apparent that consecutive days of Holter recordings may not be sufficient to document rare or sporadic arrhythmias. However, these devices require that the patient perceive an event and be capable of recording the signal during that event. Thus asymptomatic arrhythmias are not well suited to this form of detection. In addition, patients with syncope or those who cannot operate the recorder are not ideal candidates for transtelephonic event recorders. Transtelephonic event recorders can be used in clinical practice to decrease the length of hospitalization for prolonged electrocardiographic monitoring. In some instances the device may serve as an ''umbilical cord,'' providing the patient immediate access to medical personnel from home.

Types and Operation of Transtelephonic Event Recorders

These devices record an electrocardiographic rhythm strip and convert the ECG signal to an audio signal that can be transmitted over the telephone. The audio signals are then transmitted via telephone to a receiver at a base station that converts the signal into an electrocardiographic recording (Figure 3-15).

The duration of an arrhythmia that can be stored is limited by the system memory of the recorder. Virtually all recorders have at least 30 seconds of memory capability, which stores the ECG in the device until it is electronically transmitted by telephone for hard copy recording at a later time. Operation of a standard event recorder requires that the patient place the device on the chest during the symptomatic episode, which allows contact of the electrodes with the skin (Figures 3-16 and 3-17). Alternatively,

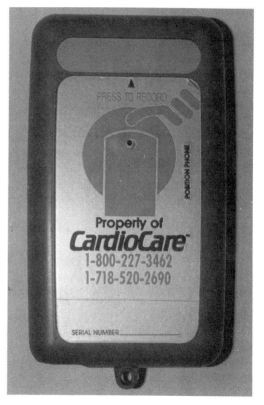

Figure 3-15 A transtelephonic event recorder is demonstrated. In the top portion of the recorder a bar is present that is pressed by the patient to begin recording. This device is used to transmit an electrocardiographic tracing transtelephonically to a central monitoring station. These devices are especially useful for patients with rare episodes of symptoms that may be related to arrhythmias. Reprinted with permission from Medtronic, Inc. © Medtronic, Inc. 1990.

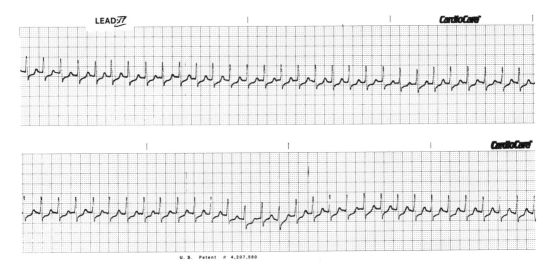

Figure 3-16 Transtelephonic monitoring tracing in a patient with episodic palpitations. The tracing demonstrates a narrow QRS tachycardia at a rate of 170 beats per minute, which was later shown to be AV nodal reentrant tachycardia.

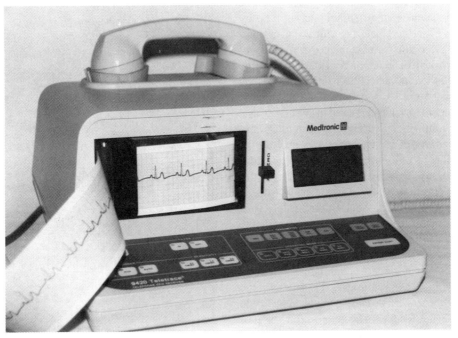

Figure 3-17 Events occurring at a transtelephonic receiving station are depicted. The picture demonstrates a standard telephone placed on the telephone cradle of a telephone ECG receiver. Transtelephonic audiotone signals are converted to electrocardiographic signals that depict both the heart rate and rhythm of the recorded event. Reprinted with permission from Medtronic, Inc. © Medtronic, Inc. 1990.

these devices may use electrodes that are placed under the arms or on the wrists to record the electrocardiographic signal.

However, if the patient is unable to perform the signal recording or if symptoms are very brief, this form of monitoring may prove impractical. In order to address these problems, transtelephonic event recorders have been developed that utilize continuous monitoring with fixed cutaneous electrodes. This looping memory system continuously records the ECG, similarly to a Holter monitor, but overwrites the recording every few minutes. If a symptomatic event occurs, the patient activates the recorder button, which stores the ECG in the recorder for a period of 30 seconds prior to the event and for 45 seconds afterward (Figure 3-18). Thus if the event is very brief or associated with marked symptoms that limit the ability of the patient to operate the recorder, the chances of recording the event are increased (Figure 3-19). Moreover, these devices have demonstrated clinical utility in ST segment monitoring (Figure 3-20). Looping memory devices require that a battery powering the system be maintained, that electrodes be worn 24 hours a day, and that the patient change the electrodes daily.

Other Considerations

Patient education is of paramount importance to obtain maximum benefit from transient event detection services. The cost is usually comparable to that of a Holter monitor but allows monitoring for a period of at least 1 month. Patients are instructed in the operation of the device and are asked to demonstrate its proper operation at the time they are enrolled in the service. Since most companies require a baseline electrocardiographic transmission, this provides an opportunity for patients to demonstrate their understanding and skill in operating the device. Since patients are frequently anxious and often question their competency to operate the equipment, a practice demonstration helps to instill patient confidence. We encourage patients and their family members to practice operation of the recorder at least once a week to maintain familiarity with the equipment. The family members are also encouraged to learn the operation of the device so that transmissions can be accomplished should the patient's symptoms render him or her incapable of transmitting the arrhythmia during the event. Some companies provide videocassettes of the device's operation for the patient and family to have through the enrollment period. Nurses can promote maximum benefit of the transtelephonic event recorder by ascertaining why the device is being prescribed and discussing this information with the patient, emphasizing the important symptoms that should be recorded with the patient and family. Patients are reassured that if they transmit a normal rhythm it may be due to the arrhythmia's brief duration and that they should continue to record their rhythm when they perceive symptoms.

Figure 3-18 A transtelephonic memory trace event recorder is demonstrated in the top panel. The electrodes provide continuous electrocardiographic monitoring. The memory trace monitor automatically stores 30 seconds of memory that is continuously updated. Activation of the patient event recorder located to the right of the electrode cable freezes the previous 30 seconds in memory and records an additional 45 seconds. The bottom panel demonstrates transtelephonic transmission of the event. Reprinted with permission from Medtronic, Inc. © Medtronic, Inc. 1990.

EXERCISE TESTING

Exercise electrocardiography (stress testing) is a method of evaluating the response of the cardiovascular system to increased physical

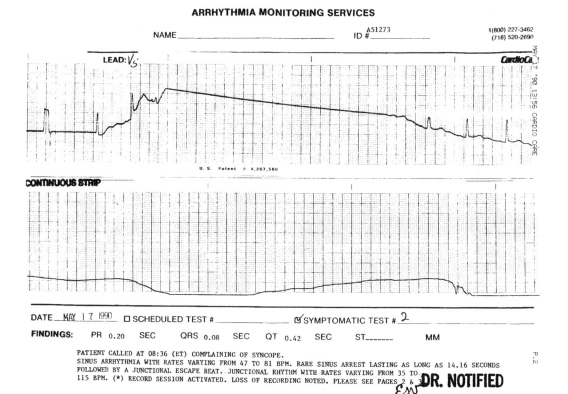

Figure 3-19 A transtelephonic monitor tracing demonstrating a marked sinus pause in a patient who complained of syncope. The patient had a sinus arrest lasting as long as 14 seconds. This tracing demonstrates the usefulness of the Memory Trace Monitor.

demands. Stress testing may be performed during treadmill or bicycle exercise at standardized exercise workloads. Exercise testing has diagnostic value in the detection of coronary artery disease and provides an assessment of prognosis. Exercise testing also allows measurement of functional capacity. While the most common indication for stress testing is the assessment of coronary artery disease, stress testing is vitally important for the assessment of arrhythmias during exercise. Exercise testing may provide useful diagnostic information regarding the diagnosis of arrhythmias, assessment of underlying arrhythmia mechanism, and response to pacemaker or antiarrhythmic drug therapy. Arrhythmias such as exercise-induced ventricular tachycardia may be detected only by this technique. In addition, exercise testing is valuable to assess the efficacy of pharmacologic therapy or nonpharmacologic therapy for tachyar-

rhythmias, to determine the response of the AV conduction system and sinus node to exercise, and to evaluate the function of rate-adaptive pacemakers. Exercise testing is also useful in determining implantable defibrillator high-rate detection criterion.

The cardiopulmonary and neuromuscular systems are the most important determinants of exercise capacity. Exercise testing allows assessment of physiologic adaptation to increased oxygen consumption, myocardial oxygen demand, and sympathetic neural stimulation. Each of these factors may contribute to the production of arrhythmias. Thus exercise testing provides information somewhat different from what is provided by ambulatory monitoring or invasive electrophysiologic testing. For example, in patients with coronary artery disease, the effect of transient myocardial ischemia on the electrical stability of the heart can be

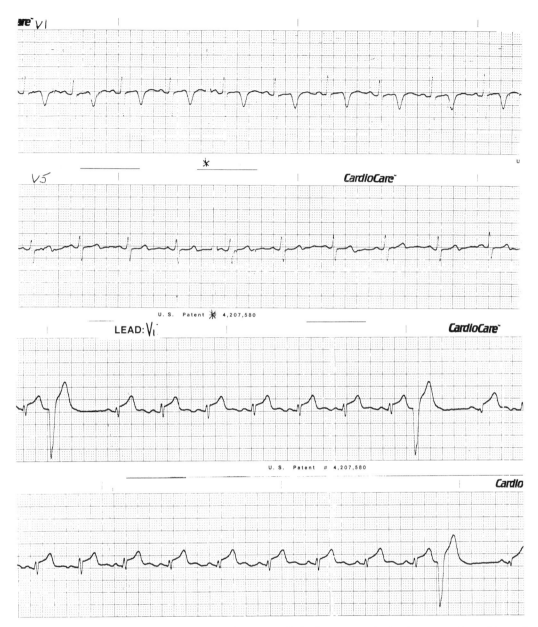

Figure 3-20 Transtelephonic tracings from a Memory Trace transtelephonic event recorder that demonstrate the usefulness of ST segment monitoring. The upper panel demonstrates marked T wave inversion during myocardial ischemia and the notation of chest discomfort (asterisk, upper panel) by the patient. The bottom panel demonstrates ST segment elevation in the same patient. Coronary arteriography studies were performed emergently, and the patient underwent a successful percutaneous transluminal coronary angioplasty of an occluded coronary artery.

studied. Evaluation of sinus node function during exercise has emerged as a separate indication for stress testing and has demonstrated clinical utility in identifying patients who might benefit from a rate-adaptive pacemaker. The diagnostic value of exercise testing can be enhanced in selected individuals by the addition of expired gas exchange analysis. Expired gas exchange analysis involves the measurement of carbon dioxide production and oxygen consumption, precise indices of metabolic function. Other parameters that can be used to assess the metabolic response to exercise include measurements of minute ventilation, respiratory rate, respiratory quotient, and workload at anaerobic threshold.

Evaluation of the Pacemaker Patient— Role of Exercise Testing

The normal sinus node increases its rate linearly in response to external workload in parallel with oxygen consumption. Failure of the sinus node to increase with exercise or to achieve an appropriate heart rate for a given level of activity is referred to as chronotropic incompetence. Exercise testing may be especially useful for evaluating whether patients have abnormal sinus node function. If so, rate-adaptive pacing with an artificial sensor may be indicated. Exercise testing facilitates optimum pacemaker programming postimplantation. Evaluation of exercise capacity and chronotropic response provides an objective indication of whether the heart rate is appropriate for a given level of activity. When evaluating whether an artificial rate-adaptive sensor is functioning appropriately in an individual patient, correlation of heart rate with oxygen consumption during exercise may provide the most useful information. Expired gas exchange can be especially valuable in clinical assessments of this kind.

Evaluation of Ventricular Arrhythmias—Role of Exercise Testing

Ventricular premature depolarizations are relatively common during exercise testing, occurring in up to one third of normal subjects. In these individuals, exercise-induced VPDs are of little prognostic importance. In contrast, those occurring during exercise in approximately 50% of patients with coronary artery disease may portend a worse prognosis. Whether exercise-induced arrhythmias provide prognostic information that is independent of cardiac catheterization data is not certain. In patients suffering from malignant ventricular arrhythmias (sustained ventricular tachycardia or fibrillation),

exercise testing is extremely important. Assessment of the role of myocardial ischemia in the genesis of the patient's arrhythmia is provided by exercise testing, often in conjunction with radionuclide imaging. If a significant ischemic response is demonstrated with exercise, treatment of ventricular arrhythmias may be accomplished by myocardial revascularization rather than by antiarrhythmic drug therapy. In patients with the clinical syndrome of exercise-induced ventricular tachycardia and no structural heart disease, exercise testing before and after β-blocker treatment provides the most important guide to therapy. In addition to these applications of exercise testing, proponents of a noninvasive approach to ventricular tachycardia treatment utilize stress tests in conjunction with ambulatory monitoring to assess drug response. Because of the risk of a serious ventricular arrhythmia during exercise testing, an indwelling intravenous catheter should be placed prior to exercise in patients with a history of malignant ventricular arrhythmias.

Exercise Protocols

A number of exercise protocols have been developed to assess exercise capacity. The exercise protocol selected for each patient depends on the clinical information that needs to be obtained. For example, patients may be exercised using an aggressive treadmill protocol such as the Bruce protocol if the clinical indication is for the diagnosis of coronary artery disease. Similarly, if the indication for exercise testing is to induce catecholamine-dependent arrhythmias in patients without structural heart disease, a high-level exercise protocol may be employed. The patient is asked to exercise until he or she is exhausted or unable to exercise further because of physical symptoms. Submaximal tests are terminated when the patient achieves a target heart rate or a predetermined workload or metabolic equivalent (MET) level.

In contrast, the indication for exercise may not require maximum effort because of safety considerations or because the effect of low-level exercise on chronotropic function needs to be assessed. For the purpose of assessing chronotropic competence, the Chronotropic Assessment Exercise Protocol (CAEP) provides a gradual increase in workload beginning at a very low level. This protocol is designed to assess heart rate response during gradual increments in workload. This slow progression allows a better assessment of sinus node function in elderly patients or those with decreased functional capacity. The CAEP protocol is not as appropriate for trained individuals or those in whom maximal effort needs to be achieved. In these individuals the more aggressive Bruce protocol may be better suited. In both types of testing the procedure is terminated if the patient develops clinically significant arrhythmias, chest pain, marked ischemic ECG changes, or hemodynamic instability.

Other Considerations

The rationale for the exercise testing and the nature of the procedure should be explained to the patient. Patients are requested to fast for a minimum of 2 hours prior to exercise since the postabsorptive state may itself induce ST segment changes. Fasting for longer periods is not recommended since the patient is required to expend considerable energy during exercise. For this reason avoidance of strenuous exercise for the previous 24 hours may be recommended for sedentary individuals. Rubber-soled shoes and comfortable clothes facilitate exercise. Shoes that tie are more likely to prevent the patient from slipping on the treadmill. Patients are also requested to avoid nicotine and caffeine for a minimum of 2 hours prior to the test to avoid the cardiovascular effects of these agents, vessel constriction and increased heart rate. Carbon monoxide also decreases the oxygen-carrying capacity of the blood and may limit exercise. Medications may or may not be continued depending on the purpose of the study. If the purpose of the test is to evaluate the effectiveness of an antiarrhythmic drug, the medication should be continued. If the purpose of the test is to diagnose the presence of coronary artery disease, antianginal drugs are discontinued prior to testing.

Informed consent for the conduct of the exercise test is required. The risks of exercise testing are low, though the mortality rate approaches 0.01%. Preparation of the skin is required to lower skin resistance and improve the quality of the electrocardiographic recording. Preparation of the chest for electrode placement may require that areas be shaved, and sandpaper may be lightly rubbed over the area to remove moisture and improve skin surface conduction. A specialized rotating "drill" often facilitates stable electrode placement. Special electrodes that are resistant to perspiration and motion are used to reduce motion artifact. Heart rate and blood pressure are recorded before, during, and following exercise testing. The ECG is monitored continuously, and 12-lead tracings are obtained at designated intervals or at the time of occurrence of an abnormal response. Elderly patients in particular may not have had prior exercise tests and require assurance that they will be able to walk on the treadmill. It is often helpful to have the patient practice briefly to minimize anxiety and facilitate exercise. Following a brief rest the person may then perform the formal exercise test. Special caution is required to exercise the elderly as their balance may be more precarious and they may become hemodynamically compromised more quickly.

SIGNAL-AVERAGED ELECTROCARDIOGRAPHY

Signal averaging is a noninvasive method of detecting low-amplitude cardiac activation signals (late potentials) that have prognostic information in the presence of coronary artery disease. Late potentials are low-amplitude signals that result from slow conduction through scarred or abnormal regions of the ventricles. Since the presence of slow conduction and abnormal myocardial activation is likely to be the substrate for the development of ventricular arrhythmias, detection of these signals may identify individuals at risk for sudden cardiac death. Low-amplitude signals are masked on the standard 12-lead ECG by noise such as that emitted from the musculoskeletal system, activation that occurs during the ST segment, and electronic artifact. The signal-averaged ECG is generated by recording the surface ECG in three specialized leads for several hundred beats. The QRS from these multiple beats is averaged, a process that eliminates electrocardiographic artifact and noncardiac electrical signals, leaving a relatively pure cardiac signal. Computer processing of identical beats improves the signal-to-noise ratio to generate noise-free or high-resolution ECGs. The QRS can then be filtered and amplified, processes that allow detection of very low amplitude components of ventricular activation.

Clinical Applications of Signal-Averaged Electrocardiography

Late potentials provide prognostic information regarding the development of sustained ventricular tachycardia and sudden death following myocardial infarction. Late potentials also predict the inducibility of ventricular tachycardia during electrophysiologic testing. For example, the presence of late potentials alone carries a risk for sudden death two to three times higher than in patients without late potentials. The risk of sudden death appears to be highest in the first several weeks following myocardial infarction. The combination of poor left ventricular function (ejection fraction less than 0.30), VPDs on Holter monitoring, and late potentials on the signal-averaged ECG allows identification of a group of patients at extremely high risk for malignant ventricular arrhythmias following myocardial infarction. In this subset of individuals, aggressive assessment of ventricular arrhythmias may be warranted. Although the signal-averaged ECG has documented prognostic value following myocardial infarction, the role of this technique in patients with unexplained syncope is less certain. The signal-averaged ECG may predict which patients with syncope are likely to have inducible ventricular tachycardia with invasive electrophysiologic testing. Use of this technique may also allow noninvasive recording of the His bundle potential.

Technique of Signal Averaging

Signal averaging is performed by recording 200 to 300 QRS complexes to discern the presence of late potentials. Premature beats are excluded from the averaging process. Signal averaging is only the first of several steps required to detect late potentials. High-pass frequency filtering is then employed to remove the ST segment and T wave. Filtering at 25 to 40 Hz eliminates signals containing lower frequencies. The ST segment and T wave have lower frequencies than the QRS. Their removal is necessary to unmask the presence of ventricular late potentials. This permits identification of the total QRS duration. The QRS is then amplified 200 to 300 times and converted to digital format. This process produces the filtered, signal-averaged ECG (Figure 3-21).

The three bipolar leads most often used to obtain signal-averaged ECGs are the Frank leads X, Y, and Z, although any of the standard leads would suffice. The Frank lead system records the electrical vector of ventricular depolarization in each of three planes at right angles to each other (horizontal, vertical, and transverse planes). The X, Y, and Z leads are termed orthogonal because they bisect one another to provide a three-dimensional composite picture of ventricular activation. Electrical impulses recorded horizontally from left to right are referred to as the x-axis, similar to standard electrocardiographic lead I. The vertical, or y-axis, records the QRS vector from superior to inferior, similar to the standard electrocardiographic lead aVF. The z-axis records QRS forces moving anteriorly to posteriorly (from sternum to spine).

Criteria for Abnormal Signal-Averaged Electrocardiograms

Criteria for defining the presence of abnormal late potentials include (1) a filtered QRS duration greater than 120 milliseconds, (2) a root mean square voltage of the last 40 milliseconds of the filtered QRS less than 25 μV, and (3) low-amplitude signals (less than 40 μV) for greater than 38 milliseconds (Figure 3-22).

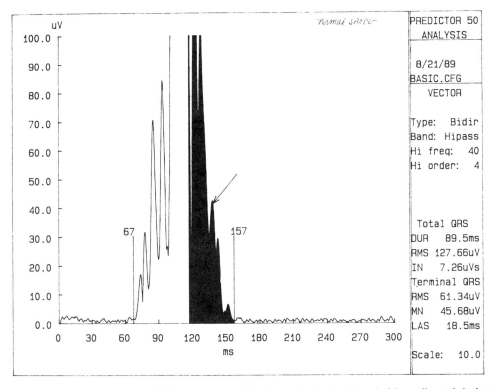

Figure 3-21 A normal signal-averaged ECG is demonstrated. On the x-axis, the time interval of the cardiac cycle is shown in milliseconds. On the y-axis, the amplitude of the cardiac signal is demonstrated in microvolts. The last 40 milliseconds of the QRS (117 to 157 milliseconds) are marked in black. Notice that the end of the QRS is relatively sharp. The total QRS duration is 89.5 milliseconds, well within the normal range. In addition, the root mean squared voltage of the terminal 40 milliseconds of the QRS is 61.34 μV. Low-amplitude signals (less than 40 μV) occupy only 18.5 milliseconds of the cardiac cycle. This normal signal-averaged ECG predicts a low risk of sudden cardiac death in the patient following myocardial infarction.

Since late potentials are low-amplitude signals that are usually not detectable in the QRS complex of a standard 12-lead ECG, the overall duration of the signal-averaged QRS is often longer. The presence of conduction delays such as bundle branch block may mask the presence of a late potential. In addition, the criterion regarding QRS duration is not applicable in the presence of an underlying bundle branch block. The signal-averaged electrocardiographic signal can be processed to display the frequency content of the signal (frequency domain). Patients with ventricular tachycardia have demonstrated higher frequencies in the terminal portion of the QRS than normal controls. High amplitude of the components of the QRS in the frequency range from 25 to 50 Hz is predictive of ventricular tachycardia occurrence. In general, late potentials are not abolished by antiarrhythmic drug therapy. However, surgical or catheter ablation procedures for ventricular tachycardia may eliminate these signals.

Other Considerations

Proper skin preparation and electrode placement are of utmost importance in obtaining the signal-averaged ECG. The time required to obtain a signal-averaged ECG is approximately 10 to 30 minutes, considerably longer than the time required to obtain a standard 12-lead ECG. The patient is encouraged to lie still and not speak during testing. Most patients are familiar with the ECG procedure and demonstrate little anxiety about the procedure. The length of the

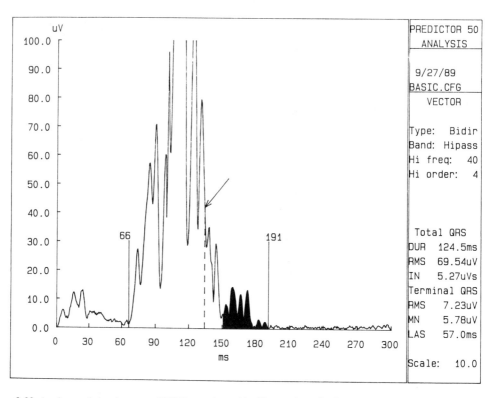

Figure 3-22 An abnormal signal-averaged ECG in a patient with a history of sustained ventricular tachycardia is demonstrated. Note that total QRS duration is 124.5 milliseconds. In addition, the last 40 milliseconds (shaded in black) are low in amplitude, with an RMS voltage of only 7.23 μV. In addition, the low-amplitude signals last 57 milliseconds. The combination of a QRS duration greater than 110 milliseconds, root mean squared voltage less than 25 μV, and low-amplitude signals greater than 38 milliseconds in duration is considered evidence of late potentials and predicts an increased likelihood of ventricular arrhythmias.

procedure should be discussed with the patient and comparisons provided about the similarities and differences to the standard ECG.

ESOPHAGEAL ELECTROCARDIOGRAPHY

The esophagus is separated from the posterior surface of the left atrium by a distance of less than 10 mm. The close proximity of the esophagus to the left atrium permits both the recording of atrial potentials and electrical stimulation of the atrium by pacing from within the esophagus. There are two standard methods of recording the esophageal electrogram, a bipolar "pill" electrode that is swallowed and a bipolar catheter passed via a nare. The recent increased popularity of esophageal recording and pacing is

partially attributed to the esophageal bipolar pill electrode. Both the pill electrode and the transesophageal electrode catheter have made it possible to obtain atrial electrograms at the bedside or in a variety of clinical settings.

Clinical Applications of Esophageal Electrocardiography

The principle value of esophageal recordings is the ability to record atrial activation that is not readily apparent on the surface ECG. Esophageal recordings are useful when an accurate diagnosis of an arrhythmia is required and the 12-lead ECG is not diagnostic. Esophageal electrocardiography can be a valuable semi-invasive diagnostic tool in patients with wide QRS tachycardias in whom ventricular tachycardia must be distinguished from a supraventricular tachycardia with aberrant conduction. Analysis of recordings obtained from the esophagus can indicate whether there is ventriculoatrial dissociation (diagnostic of ventricular tachycardia) or a relationship between ventricular and atrial events. In addition, the esophageal electrogram may be helpful for diagnosing the mechanism of narrow QRS complex arrhythmias. For example, the differentiation of atrial flutter with 2:1 AV conduction and AV nodal reentry tachycardia (Figure 3-23), manifested by simultaneous deflections of the atrial and ventricular components can be made with this technique.

Atrial electrograms obtained from the esophagus may also be used to differentiate supraventricular tachycardia based on a retrogradely conducting accessory pathway from AV nodal reentrant tachycardia. If the ventriculoatrial interval on the esophageal electrogram exceeds 70 milliseconds, an accessory pathway

should be suspected. It should be strongly emphasized that the surface ECG provides an accurate rhythm diagnosis in the vast majority of patients with wide QRS complex tachycardias and that esophageal recordings are not usually necessary.

Pacing of the left atrium from the esophagus, termed transesophageal pacing, is another application of this technique. Both the pill electrode and the transesophageal pacing catheter previously discussed may be readily used to pace the atrium. Transesophageal pacing can be used to both initiate and terminate supraventricular tachycardias. Thus semi-invasive electrophysiologic studies that require tachycardia induction can be performed with esophageal pacing and recording. Esophageal pacing is an effective technique for terminating reentrant supraventricular arrhythmias, including atrial flutter, ectopic atrial tachycardia, AV nodal reentry, and AV reentry utilizing an accessory pathway. This

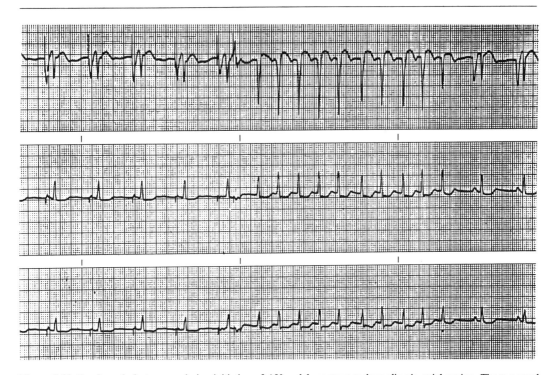

Figure 3-23 Esophageal electrogram during initiation of AV nodal reentrant tachycardia via atrial pacing. The top panel represents a bipolar esophageal electrogram, and the bottom two panels represent surface leads II and III. The complex to the left of the tracing demonstrates atrial pacing with distinct atrial and ventricular deflections. Notice that the PR interval is quite short. Following the fifth QRS of the tracing, a premature atrial stimulus is introduced. This is associated with a long PR interval and a brief run of AV nodal reentrant tachycardia. The esophageal electrogram demonstrates simultaneous activation of the ventricles and the atrium and is highly suggestive of AV nodal reentry.

technique also provides temporary bradycardia pacing support during emergencies, provided that AV conduction is intact. Recently, transesophageal atrial pacing has been employed to simulate stress and substitute for exercise during radionuclide imaging studies of ventricular function and echocardiography in patients who are not able to exercise. Esophageal pacing in these instances may induce myocardial ischemia that can be visualized by radionuclide or echocardiographic recordings. Esophageal pacing has also been used to provide initial localization the bypass tract in individuals with Wolff-Parkinson-White syndrome or to induce atrial fibrillation in patients with Wolff-Parkinson-White syndrome and evaluate the risk for sudden cardiac death.

The advantages of transesophageal pacing include noninvasive access to the atrium and the ease with which the procedure lends itself to a variety of settings such as the bedside or outpatient clinics. Furthermore, the procedure is associated with only minor discomfort and little or no sedation is required.

and pacing the left atrium. The electrodes are attached to thin, Teflon-insulated stainless steel wires. The electrodes are enclosed in a gelatin capsule that dissolves quickly once it is swallowed. The patient is provided with a glass of water and asked to swallow the capsule. The wire is released, allowing the capsule to descend with normal esophageal peristalsis. The two proximal ends of the wires are connected to the right and left arm leads of the ECG machine or filtered esophageal electrogram recorder and displayed on an oscilloscope. The wire is slowly withdrawn until the atrial deflection in the esophageal electrogram exceeds the ventricular deflection and is clearly seen. If the ventricular deflection is larger than the atrial deflection, the wire is pulled back to a higher level in the esophagus where it approaches the left atrium. The esophageal electrogram is then correlated to the surface ECG. If the ECG recorder displays leads I, II, and III simultaneously, lead I will record a bipolar esophageal electrogram and leads II and III will record unipolar electrograms with easily visible surface QRS complexes.

Esophageal Pill Electrode

The pill electrode (Figure 3-24) consists of two electrodes spaced 13 mm apart for recording

Esophageal Catheter

The transesophageal catheter (Figure 3-25) provides several advantages over the pill elec-

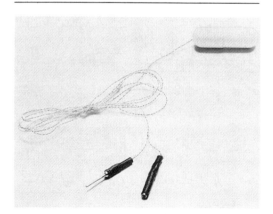

Figure 3-24 An esophageal pill electrode is demonstrated. The pill electrode is encased within a gelatin capsule (top right) that can be swallowed by the patient. Two Teflon-coated wires (bottom) are also illustrated, which can be attached to an electrocardiograph to record bipolar atrial activation from the esophagus. Reprinted with permission from CONMED Corporation.

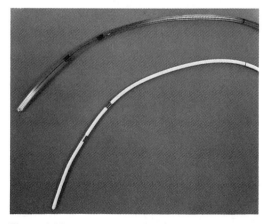

Figure 3-25 Two bipolar esophageal electrode catheters are demonstrated. These catheters are placed via a nare into the esophagus. The poles of these catheters can be used for both recording and pacing of the left atrium from the esophagus. Reprinted with permission from Electro-Catheter Corporation.

trode. In general, the catheter can be passed via a nare in less time than is required to swallow and position the pill electrode. The rounded tip and flexibility of the catheter facilitate insertion, and a variety of sizes is available. Standard 5-mm electrodes are present at the distal end of the catheter. Guide markings are present, though the catheter is positioned in the same manner as that described with the pill electrode to obtain the best esophageal electrograms. Passage of the catheter into the esophagus is facilitated by anesthetizing the nare with lidocaine jelly and the pharynx with benzocaine spray. The catheter approach is easier in patients with impaired consciousness or ability to cooperate.

Other Considerations

It should be emphasized that esophageal pacing requires a special stimulator with a wide pulse duration. Since standard temporary transvenous pacemakers utilize a pulse duration of 2 milliseconds, they are not suited to this purpose. Stimulators used for esophageal pacing must be capable of generating currents from 0 to 30 mA and pulse widths of at least 10 milliseconds. Usually, the patient is connected to a programmable stimulator. Not uncommonly a stimulus amplitude up to 25 mA is required to achieve reliable atrial capture. Patients most frequently complain of a sensation of heartburn during pacing. Pacing is not associated with esophageal erosion, and there is little risk of esophageal injury. Patients may be apprehensive due to a lack of knowledge about the procedure, because of the arrhythmia itself, about swallowing the pacing catheter or pill, or because they do not understand how the procedure will terminate the arrhythmia. Patients are informed that they may experience a sensation similar to heartburn, that they may feel their heart race or flutter, and that sedation is available.

POSTOPERATIVE EPICARDIAL ELECTROCARDIOGRAPHY

Epicardial electrodes provide pacemaker therapy for both bradycardia support and tachycardia termination, electrograms to record atrial activation, and a noninvasive method of performing postoperative electrophysiologic testing to assess the efficacy of surgical intervention for arrhythmias. The clinical use of epicardial wires in conjunction with cardiac surgery dates to the 1960s. Epicardial wires perform the same recording and pacing functions as esophageal and endocardial catheters. The electrograms they provide typically yield more accurate tracings of atrial activation than those visualized on the surface ECG. The proximity of the electrode to the atrial tissue amplifies the atrial signal and decreases the ventricular component (Figure 3-26).

Clinical Applications of Epicardial Wires

Atrial electrograms are useful in differentiating atrial, junctional, and ventricular arrhythmias by depicting the timing of atrial activation and its relationship to ventricular activation (Figures 3-27 and 3-28). Atrial electrograms are valuable in distinguishing the more common type I flutter (Figure 3-29) that can be interrupted by atrial pacing from type II flutter that cannot be terminated by pacing. Tracings can demonstrate whether wide-complex tachycardias are atrial or ventricular in origin.

Epicardial pacing is often effective for managing arrhythmias in the postoperative patient. Postoperative tachyarrhythmias such as atrial flutter may be reliably terminated with pacing when the mechanism is reentry with an excitable gap. Pacing is the treatment of choice for AV block during surgery or postoperatively. Pacing for interruption of atrial flutter is preferable to cardioversion because it does not require additional sedation or anesthesia. Atrial pacing may be preferable to ventricular pacing for postoperative sinus bradycardia because of the ability to improve cardiac output through maintenance of AV synchrony and to reduce the chances of ventricular arrhythmias. Pacing at rates above the intrinsic rate may be employed to augment cardiac output and to suppress both supraventricular and ventricular ectopic beats.

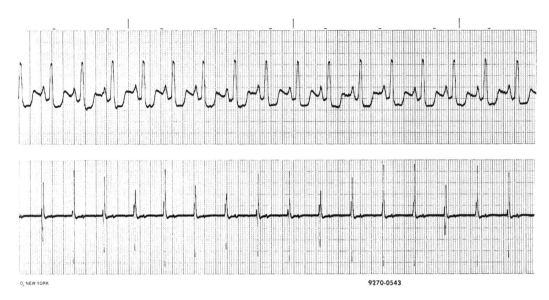

Figure 3-26 In the upper panel a surface electrocardiographic (lead II) is demonstrated, showing normal sinus rhythm. In the lower panel a bipolar epicardial atrial electrogram is demonstrated. Note that atrial activation occurs simultaneously with the P wave in the surface tracing and is a rapid, high-amplitude deflection. The ventricular component of the electrogram is small and broad, and it occurs simultaneously with the QRS on the surface electrogram.

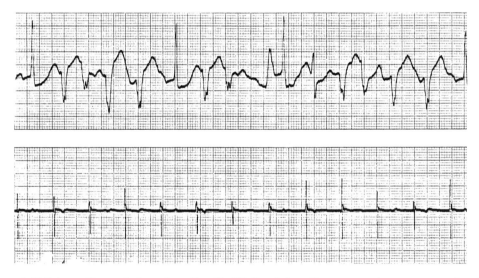

Figure 3-27 Polymorphic ventricular tachycardia with AV dissociation. The upper panel represents a surface lead II electrocardiographic tracing. The lower panel represents a simultaneously recorded bipolar epicardial atrial electrogram. Note that the atrial rate in the lower tracing is approximately 100 beats per minute. There is a bizarre, wide-complex QRS morphology in the upper panel with AV dissociation, proving the ventricular origin of this arrhythmia.

Epicardial Pacing Wires

Epicardial pacing electrodes are usually Teflon-coated stainless steel wires that are anchored to the epicardium of the atria and ven-tricles prior to closure of the thoracic incision during cardiac surgery. The wires are bared at least a centimeter on each end to permit recording and pacing. To anchor the epicardial electrodes, cardiovascular silk is sutured into the

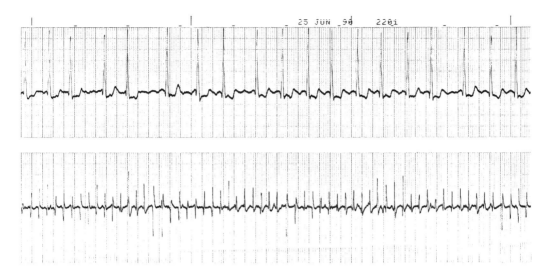

Figure 3-28 Atrial fibrillation is demonstrated with a bipolar epicardial atrial electrogram. In the top panel a surface electrocardiographic lead shows an irregular ventricular rhythm. The lower panel demonstrates the bipolar atrial electrogram, showing complexes at a rate exceeding 350 beats per minute with varying morphology and cycle length. This is typical of atrial fibrillation.

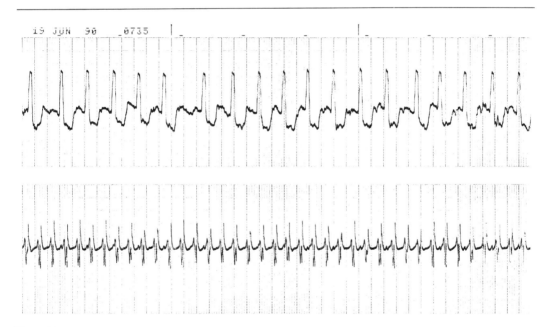

Figure 3-29 Atrial epicardial electrogram demonstrating type I atrial flutter. Note that the atrial electrogram in the lower panel demonstrates a regular and uniform morphology at a rate of approximately 300 beats per minute. The surface ECG in the upper panel demonstrates a slightly irregular ventricular response to atrial flutter.

epicardium, forming a loop, and the bared wire electrode is secured to the epicardium. The wires are subsequently brought through the anterior chest wall, where they are sutured to the skin (Figure 3-30).

Two electrodes are placed on the high right atrium, which by convention exit the skin to the right of the sternum. At least one epicardial wire is placed on the right ventricle, which exits the skin to the left of the sternum. If the patient has

Medtronic 6500 Temporary Myocardial Pacing Lead

The Medtronic Model 6500 temporary myocardial pacing lead is used for short-term pacing after cardiac surgery for the management of any arrhythmias that may occur after the procedure. Pictured is the Model 6500 lead's unique fixation coil and self-contained electrode. The accompanying simplified illustration shows the lead positioned in a bipolar configuration in both the atrium and the ventricle.

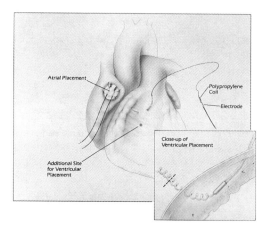

Figure 3-30 Epicardial pacing electrodes placed over the right atrial appendage and the right ventricle are shown. The epicardial wire is attached to the right ventricular epicardial surface by a suture that is used to position the electrode within the myocardium (close-up panel). The atrial wires are secured with the use of a plaque that is sutured to the epicardial surface, allowing the electrodes to contact the epicardium. Reprinted with permission from Medtronic, Inc. © Medtronic, Inc. 1990.

had arrhythmia surgery, additional wires are placed on the left ventricle or left atrium to facilitate postoperative arrhythmia evaluation.

Atrial Electrograms from Epicardial Wires

Atrial electrograms may be obtained from epicardial wires through a standard ECG, bedside monitor, or telemetry unit. Unipolar atrial electrograms represent recordings from a single epicardial wire electrode and a skin electrode that is distant from the atria. Unipolar atrial electrograms may be obtained with the 12-lead ECG

by attaching the epicardial wire to a chest lead with either an alligator clip or a connector cable. The four limb leads are attached to the patient's respective limbs in the usual manner. A rhythm strip of V_1 provides a unipolar electrogram. A second method is to connect the epicardial wire to either arm lead and select a limb lead to provide a measurement of the differences between the atrial electrode and the surface electrode. The disadvantages of unipolar tracings are that atrial activity may be masked within the QRS complex and the amplitude of the P wave and QRS complexes is often similar, which may impede correct diagnosis of the arrhythmia.

Bipolar atrial electrograms use two atrial epicardial electrodes. They are obtained by placing a separate alligator clip or connector on each of the atrial epicardial pacing wires on two of the limb leads (usually the arms) of the surface ECG and attaching the remaining two limb leads in the usual manner. Lead I of the surface ECG then depicts the potential difference in polarity between the two electrodes. Bipolar atrial electrograms eliminate or reduce the size of the QRS complex. P waves are usually biphasic or triphasic and of greater amplitude than the QRS complex, in this mode. Comparison of the electrogram to surface events can then facilitate interpretation of the arrhythmia.

Atrial Epicardial Pacing

The same external pacemaker employed in transvenous pacing may be used with epicardial wires. Termination of atrial tachyarrhythmias may require an atrial pacemaker capable of pacing at rates of up to 750 beats per minute (Figure 3-31). Utmost caution should be exercised when using this pacemaker. It should always be verified that the atrial wires only stimulate the atrium and not the ventricles as ventricular fibrillation could result from inadvertent stimulation of the ventricle at rapid pacing rates. Postoperative patients can have excessively high thresholds, and atrial or ventricular capture may be a problem. The lowest pacing thresholds are usually obtained in the bipolar mode by connecting the wire with the largest atrial electrogram to the negative pole of the pulse generator.

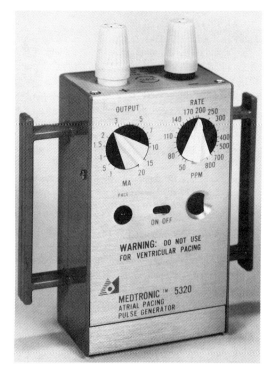

Figure 3-31 A rapid atrial pacemaker that is used for epicardial pacing is demonstrated. Note that the pacing rate can be increased to 800 beats per minute. This device is used for rapid pacing to terminate atrial arrhythmias. Reprinted with permission from Medtronic, Inc., © Medtronic, Inc. 1990.

Other Considerations

Safety precautions require that epicardial wires be covered and protected from potential environmental hazards, but they should remain easily accessible for clinical use. A small rubber grommet is used to insulate and protect the proximal end of the wire, and a gold pin is fixed to the wire with a crimping tool. The pin is then permanently inserted into a nylon connector. The connector is sealed with a removable rubber plug. To use the wire electrodes the plug is removed, and a connector cable is inserted.

Complications associated with epicardial pacing wires are rare. The patient is subject to the same risks and potential environmental hazards encountered with temporary transvenous pacing. Measures to reduce potential complications include prevention of microshock, infection, electrode dislodgement, and, potentially, tam-

ponade. Electrode exit sites should be examined for signs of infection and aseptically cleansed daily. On the day of discharge or the evening prior, the skin suture is removed, and the electrode is pulled from the heart by gentle traction. The electrode is examined to ascertain that it is intact following its removal from the chest, and the patient is observed for possible pericardial tamponade.

CAROTID SINUS MASSAGE

Carotid sinus massage may facilitate cardiac rhythm diagnosis in specific circumstances and provide effective therapy for some arrhythmias. The increased vagal tone produced by carotid sinus massage results in a decrease in the rate of sinus node discharge and prolongation of AV nodal conduction and refractoriness. This increase in vagal tone is a reflex action produced by pressure on the carotid bodies, which triggers a simultaneous withdrawal of sympathetic tone. The techniques should be employed cautiously in monitored patients.

Carotid sinus massage may unmask the presence of flutter or fibrillation waveforms in patients with a rapid ventricular response. AV nodal reentrant tachycardia and AV reentrant tachycardia may terminate abruptly, slow transiently, or not respond. Ventricular tachycardia typically does not respond to carotid massage because it is usually not dependent on the AV node. Sinus tachycardia usually slows with carotid massage and later gradually resumes at the same rate. Individuals with carotid sinus hypersensitivity who may benefit from dual-chamber pacing therapy may be identified by carotid sinus massage. These individuals often have unexplained syncope that can be associated with pivoting of the head and manifest an exaggerated response to carotid massage. Carotid sinus massage is contraindicated in the presence of carotid bruits, history of stroke, or known cerebrovascular disease.

BIBLIOGRAPHY

Akhtar M, Shenasa M, Jazayeri M, et al. Wide QRS complex tachycardia: reappraisal of a common clinical problem. *Ann Intern Med.* 1988;109:905–912.

Akhtar M, Shenasa M, Tchou PJ, et al. Role of surface electrocardiogram in the diagnosis of wide QRS complex tachycardia: a reappraisal of surface electrocardiographic criteria. In: Zipes DP, Rowlands DJ, eds. *Progress in Cardiology*. Philadelphia, Pa: Lea & Febiger; 1988;1–2: 101–113.

Antman EM, Ludmer PL, McGowan N, et al. Transtelephonic electrocardiographic transmission for management of cardiac arrhythmias. *Am J Cardiol*. 1986;58: 1021–1024.

Benditt DG, Pritchett ELC, Gallagher JJ. Spectrum of regular tachycardias with wide QRS complexes in patients with accessory atrioventricular pathways. *Am J Cardiol*. 1978;42:828–838.

Benson DW. Transesophageal electrocardiography and cardiac pacing: state of the art. *Circulation*. 1987;75: III–186-III–90.

Benson DW, Dunnigan A, Benditt DG, et al. Transesophageal cardiac pacing history, application, technique. *Clin Prog Pacing Electrophysiol*. 1984;2:360.

Berbari EJ, Lazzara R. An introduction to high-resolution ECG recordings of cardiac late potentials. *Arch Intern Med*. 1988;148:1859–1863.

Bigger JT, Reiffel JA. Holter versus electrophysiological studies in the management of malignant ventricular arrhythmias. *Am J Cardiol*. 1983;51:1464–1465.

Bjerregaard P. Premature beats in healthy subjects 40–79 years of age. *Eur Heart J*. 1982;3:493–503.

Breithardt G. Recent advances in the identification of patients at risk for ventricular tachyarrhythmias: role of ventricular late potentials. *Circulation*. 1987;75: 1091–1096.

Breithardt G, Borggrefe M, Martinez-Rubio A, et al. Signal averaging. In: Zipes DP, Rowlands DJ, eds. *Progress in Cardiology*. Philadelphia, Pa: Lea & Febiger; 1988;1–2: 257–272.

Brodsky M, Wu D, Denes P, et al. Arrhythmias documented by 24 hour continuous electrocardiographic monitoring in 50 male medical students without apparent heart disease. *Am J Cardiol*. 1977;39:390–395.

Buckingham TA, Chaitman BR. Stress testing. In: Zipes DP, Rowlands DJ, eds. *Progress in Cardiology*. Philadelphia, Pa: Lea & Febiger; 1988;1–2;289–303.

Buckingham TA, Ghosh S, Homan SM, et al. Independent value of signal-averaged electrocardiography and left ventricular function in identifying patients with sustained ventricular tachycardia with coronary artery disease. *Am J Cardiol*. 1987;59:568–572.

Cain ME, Ambos HD, Witkowski FX, et al. Fast-Fourier transform analysis of signal averaged electrocardiograms for identification of patients prone to sustained ventricular tachycardia. *Circulation*. 1984;69:711–720.

Crawford W, Plumb VJ, Epstein AE, et al. Prospective evaluation of transesophageal pacing for the interruption of atrial flutter. *Am J Med*. 1989;86:663–667.

Ezri MD, Huanj SK, Denes P. The role of Holter monitoring in patients with recurrent sustained ventricular tachycar-

dia. An electrophysiologic correlation. *Am Heart J*. 1984;108:1229–1236.

Falk RH, Werner MP. Transesophageal atrial pacing using a pill electrode for the termination of atrial flutter. *Chest*. 1987;92:110.

Fleg JL, Kennedy HL. Cardiac arrhythmias in a healthy elderly population: detection by 24-hour ambulatory electrocardiography. *Chest*. 1982;81:302.

Fleg JL, Lakatta EG. Prevalence and prognosis of exercise-induced nonsustained ventricular tachycardia in apparently healthy volunteers. *Am J Cardiol*. 1984;54: 762–776.

Glasser SP, Clark PI, Appelbaum KJ. Occurrence of frequent complex arrhythmias detected by ambulatory monitoring. Findings in an apparently healthy asymptomatic elderly population. *Chest*. 1979;75:565–568.

Gomes JA, Mehra R, Barreca P, et al. Quantitative analysis of the high-frequency components of the signal-averaged QRS complex in patients with acute myocardial infarction: a prospective study. *Circulation*. 1985;72:105–111.

Hammill SC, Pritchett ELC. Simplified esophageal electrocardiography using bipolar recording leads. *Ann Intern Med*. 1981;95:14–18.

Hilgard J, Ezri MD, Denes P. Significance of ventricular pauses of three seconds or more detected on twenty-four-hour Holter recordings. *Am J Cardiol*. 1985;55: 1005–1008.

Holter NJ. New method for heart studies: continuous electrocardiography of active subjects over long periods is now practical. *Science*. 1961;134:1214.

Jenkins JM, Dick M, Collins S, et al. Use of the pill electrode for transesophageal atrial pacing. *PACE*. 1985;8: 512–527.

Josephson ME, Horowitz LN, Waxman HL, et al. Sustained ventricular tachycardia: role of the twelve-lead electrocardiogram in localizing site of origin. *Circulation*. 1981;64:257–272.

Josephson ME, Wit AL. Fractionated electrical activity and continuous electrical activity: fact or artifact? *Circulation*. 1984;70:529–532.

Kanovsky MS, Falcone RA, Dresden CA, et al. Identification of patients with ventricular tachycardia after myocardial infarction: signal averaged electrocardiogram, Holter monitoring, and cardiac catheterization. *Circulation*. 1984;72:264–270.

Kay GN, Pressley JP, Pritchett ELC, et al. The value of the 12-lead electrocardiogram in discriminating AV nodal reciprocating tachycardia from orthodromic reciprocating tachycardia. *Am J Cardiol*. 1987;59:296–300.

Kennedy HL, Long-term electrocardiographic recordings. In: Zipes DP, Rowlands DJ, eds. *Progress in Cardiology*. Philadelphia, Pa: Lea & Febiger; 1988;1–2;237–256.

Kennedy HL, Wiens RD. Ambulatory (Holter) electrocardiography using real-time analysis. *Am J Cardiol*. 1987;59:1190–1195.

Kindwall KE, Brown J, Josephson ME. Electrocardiographic criteria for ventricular tachycardia in wide complex left bundle branch block morphology tachycardias. *Am J Cardiol.* 1988;61:1279–1283.

Kotis JB, Moreyra AE, Amendo MT, et al. The effect of age on heart rate in subjects free of heart disease. Studies by ambulatory electrocardiography and maximal stress rest. *Circulation.* 1982;65:141–145.

Kuchar DL, Thorburn MB, Sammel NL. Prediction of serious arrhythmic events after myocardial infarction: signal averaged electrocardiogram, Holter monitoring and radionuclide ventriculography. *J Am Coll Cardiol.* 1987; 9:531–538.

Miles WM, Zipes DP. Electrophysiology of wide QRS tachycardia. In: Zipes DP, Rowlands DJ, eds. *Progress in Cardiology.* Philadelphia, Pa: Lea & Febiger; 1988: 77–101.

Miller JM, Marchlinski FE, Buxton AE, Josephson ME. Relationship between the 12-lead electrocardiogram during ventricular tachycardia and endocardial site of origin in patients with coronary disease. *Circulation.* 1988; 77:759–766.

Nalos PC, Gang ES, Mandel WJ, et al. The signal-averaged electrocardiogram as a screening test for inducibility of sustained ventricular tachycardia in high risk patients: A prospective study. *J Am Coll Cardiol.* 1987;9:539–548.

Naughton J. *Exercise Testing Physiological, Biomechanical, and Clinical Principles.* Mt Kisco, NY: Futura Publishing Co; 1988.

Poblete PF, Kennedy HL, Cavales DG. Detection of ventricular ectopy in patients with coronary artery disease and normal subjects by exercise testing and ambulatory electrocardiography. *Chest.* 1978;74:402.

Podrid PJ, Grayboys TB. Exercise stress testing in the management of cardiac rhythm disorders. *Med Clin North Am.* 1984;68:4.

Poll DS, Marchlinski FE, Falcone RA, et al. Abnormal signal-averaged electrocardiograms in patients with non-ischemic congestive cardiomyopathy: relationship to sustained ventricular tachyarrhythmias. *Circulation.* 1985;72:1308–1313.

Prystowsky EN, Pritchett ELC, Gallagher JJ. Origin of the atrial electrogram recorded from the esophagus. *Circulation.* 1981;61:1017–1023.

Ryan M, Horn HR, Lown B. Comparison of ventricular ectopic activity during 24-hour monitoring and exercise testing in patients with coronary heart disease. *N Engl J Med.* 1975;292:224–239.

Sabotka PA, Mayer JH, Bauernfeind RA, et al. The effect of age on heart rate in subjects free of heart disease. Studies by ambulatory electrocardiography and maximal stress rest. *Circulation.* 1982;65:141–145.

Simson MB. Signal-averaged electrocardiography: methods and clinical applications. In: Braunwald E, ed. *Heart Disease—Update 7.* Philadelphia, Pa: WB Saunders Co; 1989:145–156.

Simson MB. The use of signals in the terminal QRS complex to identify patients with ventricular tachycardia after myocardial infarction. *Circulation.* 1981;65:235–242.

Stewart RB, Bardy GH, Green L. Wide complex tachycardia: misdiagnosis and outcome after emergent therapy. *Ann Intern Med.* 1986;104:766–771.

Udall JA, Ellestad MJ. Predictive implications of ventricular premature contractions associated with treadmill stress testing. *Circulation.* 1977;56:985–989.

Vatterott PJ, Hammill SC, Bailey KR, et al. Signal-averaged electrocardiography: a new noninvasive test to identify patients at risk for ventricular arrhythmias. *Mayo Clin Proc.* 1988;63:931–942.

Waldo AL, MacLean WAH. *Diagnosis and Treatment of Cardiac Arrhythmias Following Open Heart Surgery.* Mt Kisco, NY: Futura Publishing Co; 1980.

Weinwe DA, Levine SR, Klein MD, et al. Ventricular arrhythmias during exercise testing: Mechanism, response to coronary artery bypass surgery, and prognostic significance. *Am J Cardiol.* 1984;53:1553–1557.

Wellens HJJ, Bar FW, Lie KI. The value of the electrocardiogram in the differential diagnosis of a tachycardia with a widened QRS complex. *Am J Med.* 1978;64:27–33.

Wellens HJJ, Brugada P, Stevenson WG. Programmed electrical stimulation: its role in the management of ventricular arrhythmias in coronary heart disease. *Prog Cardiovasc Dis.* 1986;29:165–180.

Woelfel A, Foster JR, Simpson RJ, et al. Ventricular arrhythmias during exercise testing: mechanism, response to coronary artery bypass-surgery, and prognostic significance. *Am J Cardiol.* 1984;53:1553–1557.

Zeldis SM, Levine BJ, Michelson EL, et al. Cardiovascular complaints: correlation with cardiac arrhythmias on 24-hour electrocardiographic monitoring. *Chest.* 1980; 78:456.

Chapter 4

Electrophysiologic Testing

INTRODUCTION

Electrophysiologic testing involves the recording of intracardiac electrograms from the atria, ventricles, or AV conduction system and the response to intracardiac electrical stimulation. This technique allows the recording of electrical events that cannot be measured by other methods. It also provides a method for inducing clinical arrhythmias to assess the underlying mechanism of the arrhythmia, to localize the site of the involved reentrant circuits or arrhythmogenic foci, and to evaluate the response of the arrhythmia to treatment with drugs or nonpharmacologic techniques. Electrophysiologic testing may be applied to the study of bradyarrhythmias related to conduction system disease or tachycardias arising in the atria, ventricles, or AV conduction system. In addition to the diagnostic value of electrophysiologic testing and its role in the assessment of the efficacy of antiarrhythmic therapies, invasive catheter techniques may also be used for the nonpharmacologic treatment of arrhythmias.

HISTORY

Although the technique of clinical electrophysiologic testing is frequently credited to Durre and Coumel, who simultaneously introduced the technique of programmed electrical stimulation in 1967, Lenegre and Maurice had previously reported recording electrical activity from the cardiac chambers in humans as early as 1945. A pivotal development in the application of electrophysiologic testing to the study of clinical arrhythmias was the demonstration by Scherlag in 1969 that activation of the His bundle could be recorded in humans. Further acceptance of invasive electrophysiologic testing resulted from the demonstration by Wellens in 1972 that programmed electrical stimulation could be used for the induction of ventricular tachycardia. The clinical utility of this technique became widely appreciated following the demonstration that ventricular tachycardia could be reliably induced and terminated by pacing, observations that allowed serial assessment of antiarrhythmic drug efficacy. Confirmation of this observation led to the formulation of the basic tenets of electrophysiologic testing, namely, that induced arrhythmias replicate spontaneously occurring arrhythmias and that treatment culminating in arrhythmia suppression at the time of electrophysiologic testing is predictive of efficacy.

INDICATIONS FOR INVASIVE ELECTROPHYSIOLOGIC TESTING

The indications for performing an invasive electrophysiologic test are myriad. However, invasive procedures carry an inherent risk of potentially serious complications. Therefore, invasive electrophysiologic procedures are only indicated when the information to be gained is essential for clinical management and cannot be obtained by less invasive means. With this in mind, electrophysiologic studies may be indicated for patients with supraventricular tachycardias that are refractory to medical therapy or markedly symptomatic. For patients with supraventricular tachycardias in whom non-pharmacologic therapy is planned, electrophysiologic testing is essential. For example, some patients with supraventricular arrhythmias cannot tolerate long-term antiarrhythmic therapy because of adverse drug effects, noncompliance, or reproductive considerations. In these individuals nonpharmacologic treatment by antitachycardia pacing, catheter ablation, or surgery may provide optimal management. In selected individuals with the Wolff-Parkinson-White syndrome who present with rapid antegrade conduction (conduction over the accessory pathway rather than the AV node), electrophysiologic testing is indicated to assess the risk of sudden death and to guide proper therapy. Electrophysiologic testing is often essential for patients with preexcitation syndromes who are resuscitated from ventricular fibrillation. Under special circumstances, such as patients engaged in high-risk occupations (pilots, athletes), invasive testing may be necessary to assess the risk of serious arrhythmias in asymptomatic individuals with WPW syndrome.

Electrophysiologic testing is clinically indicated for patients suffering from sustained ventricular tachycardia or ventricular fibrillation in whom a clearly reversible precipitating factor cannot be identified. The benefits of the invasive approach are somewhat controversial, and a noninvasive approach to antiarrhythmic drug therapy for serious ventricular arrhythmias has been advocated by some authors. However, the invasive approach to management of this group of patients is likely to offer an improved long-term prognosis. Invasive electrophysiologic testing is also indicated for all patients in whom nonpharmacologic therapy for ventricular arrhythmias (implantable defibrillators, antitachycardia pacing, catheter ablation) is consid-

ered. Electrophysiologic studies may also be indicated to evaluate the function of implantable antitachycardia devices in patients with ventricular tachycardia or fibrillation. The role of invasive programmed stimulation in the evaluation of nonsustained ventricular arrhythmias has yet to be clearly defined. In addition, routine electrophysiologic testing for patients with late potentials on the signal-averaged ECG following myocardial infarction remains an investigational strategy. The usefulness of electrophysiologic testing in this subset of patients is strengthened in the presence of left ventricular dysfunction and nonsustained ventricular tachycardia.

The role of electrophysiologic testing for the evaluation of bradyarrhythmias has evolved to a position of less importance. Initially, His bundle recordings in patients with second-degree AV block were shown to be helpful in elucidating the site of impaired AV conduction (i.e., in the AV node or His bundle). However, these levels of AV block can usually be clinically distinguished by analysis of the electrocardiographic PR interval, QRS morphology, escape QRS rate, and response to exercise, in the vast majority of patients. In addition, the value of invasive measurements of sinus node function is uncertain, with most clinical decisions being made on the basis of noninvasive testing.

Electrophysiologic studies may be indicated for selected individuals with syncope that remains unexplained despite a complete evaluation using noninvasive testing. In patients with an abnormal ECG and/or a positive signal-averaged ECG, evidence of structural heart disease, or abnormalities of ambulatory electrocardiography, electrophysiologic testing may provide useful diagnostic information. Invasive testing has a low yield in the evaluation of syncope in patients with no structural heart disease and a normal ECG. Noninvasive diagnostic tests may be more useful in this clinical setting.

CONTRAINDICATIONS TO INVASIVE ELECTROPHYSIOLOGIC TESTING

In order for electrophysiologic testing to be meaningful, the patient must be stable and free of reversible precipitating factors at the time programmed electrical stimulation is performed. Acute factors such as ischemia, electrolyte imbalance (including sodium, potassium, calcium, and magnesium), and drug toxicity are contraindications to electrophysiologic testing. In addition, congestive heart failure should be adequately compensated prior to testing. Underlying structural heart disease such as critical outflow tract obstruction in hypertrophic cardiomyopathy, severely symptomatic aortic stenosis, and unstable angina pectoris is likely to increase the risk of electrophysiologic testing and represents important contraindications. These conditions may compromise patient safety because of the potential for irreversible hemodynamic impairment.

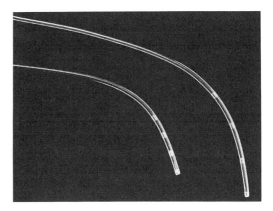

Figure 4-1 Quadripolar electrode catheters are demonstrated with different electrode spacings. A quadripolar electrode catheter with a 1 cm interelectrode distance is shown on the right. A quadripolar electrode catheter with 0.5 cm electrode spacing is shown on the left. *Source*: Courtesy of Bard electróphysiology, Billerica, MA.

TECHNIQUE OF ELECTROPHYSIOLOGIC TESTING

Electrophysiologic testing requires placement of catheters within the heart under fluoroscopic guidance. The catheters generally contain four to eight electrodes that are used to record intracardiac electrograms and to deliver pacing stimuli to the heart. The interelectrode distance ranges from approximately 1 mm to 1 cm. Catheters are named for the type of curve or shape they hold, the number of electrodes they contain, and the diameter of their shaft (Figures 4-1 and 4-2).

A bipolar catheter has two electrodes, a tripolar three, a quadripolar four, and so on. The electrodes are numbered so that the most distal (near the tip) electrode is number 1. Pacing is usually performed using the distal electrode as the cathode (negative pole) and pole number 2 as the anode (positive pole). If a quadripolar catheter is used, recordings can be made from the more proximal pair of electrodes (poles 3 and 4). Recordings of intracardiac electrical activity are confined to the area distal to the recording electrode. Most catheters have an external diameter of 6F and can be placed through a vascular sheath that has a diameter of 7F. Specialized catheters may have larger or smaller diameters and require sheaths of different sizes.

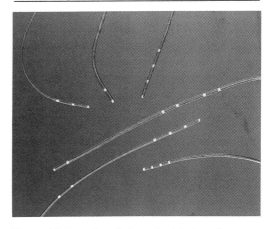

Figure 4-2 Examples of electrophysiologic catheters are demonstrated. Electrophysiologic catheters have varying numbers of electrodes for pacing and recording and widely varying interelectrode intervals. Also note that the curve of the catheters ranges from none to quite pronounced. Each catheter is designed for a specific application. *Source*: Courtesy of Bard electróphysiology, Billerica, MA.

The site of vascular access for the introduction of electrode catheters is determined by the intracardiac chamber that will be assessed, the desired site of stimulation, the accessibility of the vessel in each individual, and whether the catheter will be left in place after the study. The most common sites for introduction of catheters include the femoral vein, the internal jugular or subclavian veins, and the femoral artery. The femoral artery catheter is often omitted for routine studies. Subclavian or jugular catheters may be left in place for follow-up studies.

A comprehensive baseline electrophysiologic study involves placement of two to four electrode catheters in the heart (Figure 4-3). A quadripolar electrode catheter is advanced from the femoral, subclavian, or internal jugular vein and positioned at the right ventricular apex or right ventricular outflow tract. Traditionally, the right ventricular apex is stimulated first, and the catheter then repositioned to the outflow tract if necessary. A catheter, generally tripolar or quadripolar, is introduced via a femoral vein to record activation of the His bundle. The His bundle catheter is positioned across the superior margin of the tricuspid valve, abutting the right side of the interventricular septum in close proximity to the His bundle. The catheter must often be pulled back toward the right atrium until a large biphasic or triphasic His deflection is obtained. The His bundle electrogram (HBE) also contains both atrial and ventricular deflections (Figure 4-4). Precise catheter position is crucial for accurate determination of the cardiac rhythm and the measurement of conduction intervals.

A third catheter is typically positioned in the high right atrium (HRA) in close proximity to the sinus node (Figure 4-3). Electrophysiologic studies for supraventricular tachycardia usually require placement of a fourth catheter in the coronary sinus to record activation of the left

atrium and basal portion of the left ventricle (Figure 4-3). This catheter is crucial to accurately localize left-sided accessory pathways. The ostium of the coronary sinus is located in the right atrium posterior to the tricuspid valve annulus. The coronary sinus catheter is advanced from the subclavian or internal jugular vein into the coronary sinus using the electrogram recorded from the distal electrodes for guidance. Correct placement in the coronary sinus is confirmed by obtaining a recording of a large atrial deflection with a brisk upstroke and a low amplitude, broad ventricular deflection.

The left ventricle may be accessed via the femoral or axillary arteries if recordings or stimulation of this chamber is essential. This is usually performed when ventricular tachycardia is not induced by programmed electrical stimulation at either the right ventricular apex or the outflow tract of the right ventricle, or when left ventricular mapping is required to determine the site of origin of ventricular tachycardia in preparation for surgery or catheter ablation.

RECORDING EQUIPMENT

Intracardiac electrograms and surface electrocardiographic tracings are recorded simultaneously during the study. One to four surface electrocardiographic leads and each intracardiac electrogram recorded from the electrode catheters are processed by separate amplifiers for display (Figure 4-5). Organization of multiple intracardiac electrograms from multiple poles on several catheters is accomplished by a switching box that allows the signals to be sent to specific amplifier channels. The switching box also allows individual poles on the intracardiac catheters to be selected for pacing. The intracardiac electrograms are amplified and filtered to remove unwanted frequencies and to improve the signal-to-noise ratio. Standard filtering of the intracardiac signals removes frequencies below 30 to 50 Hz and frequencies above 500 Hz. The electrocardiographic leads and intracardiac electrogram signals are continuously displayed on an oscilloscope, and hard copy paper output of selected portions of the study is provided by a physiologic recorder. The electrical signals are

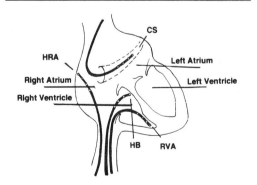

Figure 4-3 Intracardiac electrode catheter placement for a standard supraventricular tachycardia study. Notice that one catheter is placed in the coronary sinus (CS) extending in the AV ring between the left atrium and left ventricle. Other catheters are placed in the high right atrium (HRA) across the tricuspid valve for recording of the His bundle (HB), and into the right ventricular apex (RVA).

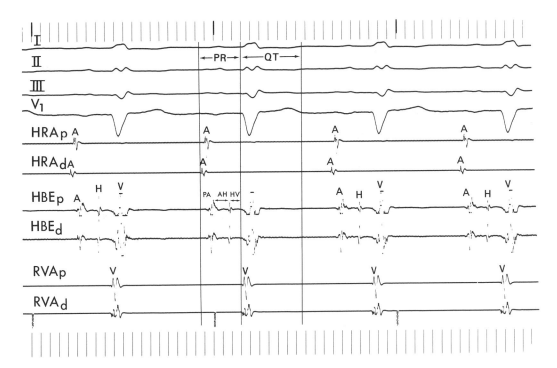

Figure 4-4 Intracardiac conduction intervals. Surface electrocardiographic leads I, II, III and V₁ are shown simultaneously with bipolar electrograms from the high right atrium proximal (HRAp) and distal (HRAd) electrode pairs, His bundle electrograms from the proximal (HBEp) and distal (HBEd) electrode pairs, and electrograms from the right ventricular apex proximal (RVAp) and distal (RVAd) electrode pairs. A solid line drawn at the onset of the P wave on the surface ECG is shown. Note that the HRA electrode pairs record atrial activation at the onset of the P wave. This is consistent with catheter positioning close to the sinus node. In the His bundle electrogram the first deflection represents atrial activation. The interval from the onset of the P wave to atrial activation in the HBE is known as the PA interval and reflects conduction within the right atrium. The interval from the atrial deflection to the His bundle deflection in the HBE is known as the AH interval and reflects conduction through the AV node. The interval from the onset of His bundle activation to the onset of ventricular activation (solid black line) is known as the HV interval and reflects conduction through the His bundle and bundle branch system. The end of the T wave (solid black line) represents the approximate end of the relative refractory period of the ventricle.

also recorded on magnetic tape for later playback and analysis. A standard 12-lead ECG is also recorded at the start of the study, following induction of arrhythmias, and after administration of medications.

Pacing and programmed electrical stimulation are performed using a programmable stimulator that provides delivery of stimuli of known current amplitude and pulse duration (Figure 4-6). The stimulator also allows the electrical stimuli to be delivered in precisely timed sequences that are timed to the patient's intracardiac or electrocardiographic signals.

Other essential equipment for the electrophysiology laboratory includes an external defibrillator for termination of induced arrhythmias that fail to respond to pacing tech-

niques (Figure 4-7). Most laboratories use adhesive electrode patches that are placed on the patient's skin prior to the electrophysiologic testing and connected to the defibrillator. When an induced arrhythmia cannot be terminated with pacing techniques, the arrhythmia may be cardioverted or defibrillated immediately. Pressure transducers to allow recording of hemodynamics, intravenous infusion pumps for the delivery of medications, oxygen and wall suction, and a fluoroscope for guiding the placement of intracardiac catheters are also essential equipment. Many laboratories have the capability for tilt table testing, bicycle exercise stress testing, and transcutaneous oxygen saturation monitoring. Other equipment that must be available includes pericardiocentesis and thoracotomy

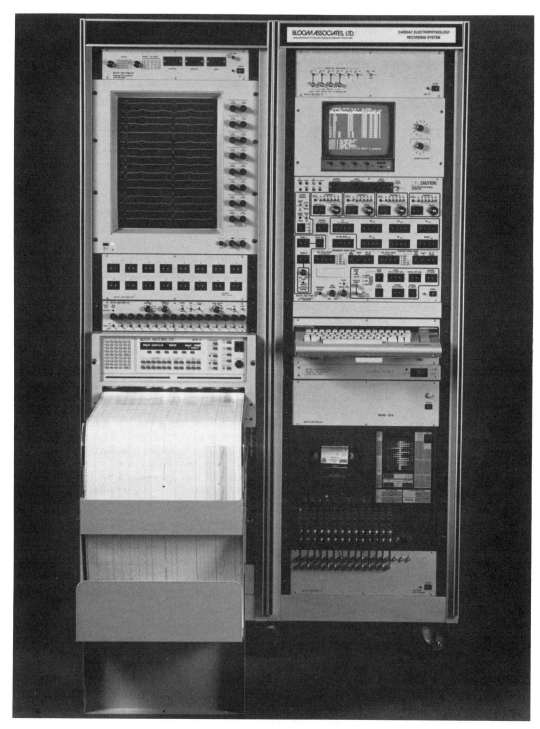

Figure 4-5 Integrated electrophysiologic recording system. This system provides inputs for up to 30 intracardiac recording electrodes and standard ECG leads. The oscilloscope, shown in the upper left corner, can display up to 16 channels simultaneously including any combination of surface ECG and intracardiac electrograms. Multiple banks of amplifiers are shown beneath the oscilloscope and allow for individual filtering and amplification of cardiac signals. All selected channels can be displayed on a chart recorder shown on the bottom left. At the top right is a switched beam oscilloscope for measuring intracardiac activation intervals. Immediately beneath the switched beam oscilloscope is a programmable stimulator. On the lower right a multichannel tape deck that interfaces with the amplifiers is shown. Reprinted with permission from Bloom Associates Ltd.

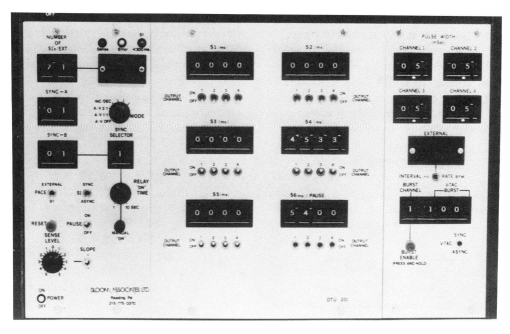

Figure 4-6 A programmable stimulator is demonstrated that is capable of delivering up to five premature extrastimuli as well as burst pacing. The stimulator can be used to pace both the atrium and ventricle and to stimulate up to four channels. The intervals of S1, S2, S3, S4, S5, and S6 (see text for discussion of terminology) are programmable to within 1 millisecond. This stimulator is used for the induction of arrhythmias with standard programmed electric stimulation. Reprinted with permission from Bloom Associates Ltd.

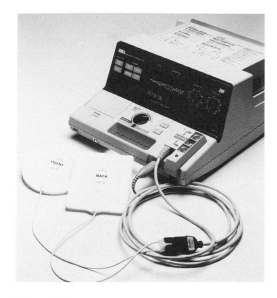

Figure 4-7 An external cardiac defibrillator capable of transthoracic pacing as well as defibrillation/cardioversion is demonstrated. Patch electrodes that can be placed on the front and the back of the chest can be used for continuous monitoring of the ECG as well as for pacing and defibrillation. Reprinted with permission from ZMI.

trays, endotracheal tubes and laryngoscopes, and a wide variety of emergency medications.

Essential personnel for the performance of electrophysiologic studies include an experienced cardiac electrophysiologist, a technician knowledgeable in the operation of the recording and stimulating equipment, and an electrophysiology nurse. The electrophysiology nurse must be a highly skilled professional capable of assessing, managing, and evaluating patient care throughout the procedure in an interdependent manner with the physician. The nurse continually assesses and evaluates the patient's responses, particularly the hemodynamic response, to electrical stimulation and assists with the management of complications and emergencies that may arise.

TECHNIQUE OF PROGRAMMED ELECTRICAL STIMULATION

Programmed electrical stimulation involves the introduction of precisely timed electrical stimuli into the patient's spontaneous cardiac rhythm or following a sequence of paced beats. Programmed stimulation may be performed in either the atrium or the ventricle and is used to assess refractory periods and evaluate the conduction characteristics of the AV node, His bundle, bundle branches, or accessory AV connections. Programmed stimulation is also used to induce atrial or ventricular arrhythmias.

The intensity of the electrical stimulus is usually set to twice the pacing threshold, with a uniform pulse duration (usually 2 milliseconds). Programmed stimulation is often performed beginning with single extrastimuli (atrial or ventricular premature depolarizations) that are delivered during sinus rhythm. The coupling interval between the sinus beats and the extrastimuli is progressively decreased until an arrhythmia is induced or the stimulus fails to capture the atrium or ventricle because the tissue is refractory. The longest coupling interval that does not result in a propagated response is defined as the effective refractory period. Double extrastimuli may be delivered, with the coupling interval of the first stimulus set 20 milliseconds longer than the effective refractory period. This sequence of scanning the diastolic

interval until an arrhythmia is induced or the refractory period is reached is continued for double and triple extrastimuli.

If no arrhythmias are induced by delivery of electrical stimuli during sinus rhythm, extrastimuli are then delivered following atrial or ventricular pacing at a constant cycle length (RR interval) for eight beats. This eight-beat pacing train is referred to as the S1 drive. The first extrastimulus is termed S2, the second extrastimulus is termed S3, and the third S4 (Figure 4-8). Programmed stimulation for the induction of ventricular tachycardia is usually performed using two or three cycle lengths of S1 (generally 600, 500, and 400 milliseconds) using up to three extrastimuli at the right ventricular apex and right ventricular outflow tract. Burst pacing, generally a train of eight beats at rates of 160 to 250 beats per minute, is also frequently employed to facilitate arrhythmia induction. Programmed stimulation can also be performed during the infusion of isoproterenol (at an infusion rate that increases the heart rate by 20%). In selected individuals, programmed stimulation in the left ventricle may be added in an attempt to induce ventricular tachycardia.

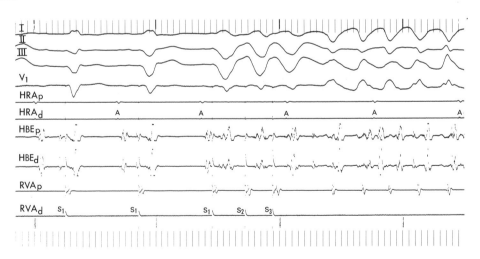

Figure 4-8 Initiation of ventricular tachycardia by programmed electrical stimulation. Leads I, II, III, and V_1 are shown simultaneously with bipolar electrograms from the high right atrium proximal (HRAp) and distal (HRAd) electrode pairs, His bundle electrograms from the proximal (HBEp) and distal (HBEd) electrode pairs, and electrograms from the right ventricular apex proximal (RVAp) and distal (RVAd) electrode pairs. Programmed stimulation is performed using a constant pacing rate (S1) followed by premature extrastimuli (S2 and S3). Following the S3 extrastimulus, sustained ventricular tachycardia is induced. Note that the atrial activation in the high right atrium (A) is dissociated from ventricular activation.

Pacing techniques that induce the arrhythmia may also be effectively utilized to terminate arrhythmias. Usually burst pacing techniques are employed to rapidly terminate the arrhythmia. A detailed explanation of the rationale for employing pacing techniques is provided in Chapter 10.

The other major method of electrical stimulation that is employed during electrophysiologic testing involves pacing the atria or ventricles at progressively faster rates (incremental pacing). This technique is used to determine the function of the AV conduction system and the conduction characteristics of accessory AV connections. The technique may induce clinically relevant tachycardias.

BASIC ASSUMPTIONS INHERENT TO ELECTROPHYSIOLOGIC STUDIES FOR EVALUATION OF VENTRICULAR ARRHYTHMIAS

Central to the clinical utility of electrophysiologic testing are four basic assumptions related to the technique: (1) In the absence of its spontaneous occurrence, ventricular tachycardia is rarely induced by programmed stimulation; (2) arrhythmias induced by programmed electrical stimulation duplicate the spontaneously occurring arrhythmia; (3) the induced arrhythmias can be safely and reliably terminated; and (4) the efficacy of a treatment may be predicted by suppression of the inducible arrhythmia. The rationale for employing electrical stimulation techniques to induce cardiac arrhythmias is the assumption that arrhythmias that are induced in the electrophysiology laboratory are representative of spontaneously occurring arrhythmias. Since life-threatening arrhythmias usually occur in a random and unpredictable pattern, the ability to induce these arrhythmias in a controlled setting allows the efficacy of antiarrhythmic treatment to be evaluated more safely than is possible in empiric trials. The initiation and termination of arrhythmias that a controlled situation provides are especially important for evaluating the efficacy of treatment modalities in patients at high risk for sudden cardiac death. Repeated

induction of the spontaneously occurring cardiac arrhythmia improves the level of confidence that the technique can be relied upon as a measure of the therapeutic efficacy of antiarrhythmic drugs.

Baseline electrophysiologic studies are usually performed in a drug-free (five drug half-lives), postabsorptive state. The function of the normal AV conduction system is defined at rest and during pacing, and the mechanism and location of abnormal conduction pathways are assessed. The requirements for induction and termination of the arrhythmia are also defined. Repeat electrophysiologic tests are generally performed to evaluate the effects of specific interventions such as drug therapy, surgery, or ablation.

During a baseline study, failure to induce an arrhythmia with programmed electrical stimulation is considered a negative study and may indicate that the mechanism of the arrhythmia is not reentry, that the specific factors precipitating the spontaneously occurring arrhythmia are no longer present, or that the technique is not a reliable method of assessing antiarrhythmic therapy in a given individual. The correct interpretation depends on evaluation of the total clinical picture, though that may be difficult to accurately judge. If programmed electrical stimulation cannot elicit an arrhythmia, follow-up studies are not usually performed.

Induction of the clinical arrhythmia with programmed electrical stimulation is indicative of a positive study. Several viable treatment alternatives may be suggested by a positive study, depending on the patient's clinical scenario. For example, in the setting of inducible sustained ventricular tachycardia, it is common to administer intravenous antiarrhythmics to categorize the patient's response to types of antiarrhythmic agents. Typically, an antiarrhythmic drug such as procainamide is infused, and programmed stimulation is repeated to determine the patient's response. If the arrhythmia is suppressed on the intravenous preparation of this drug, therapy is assumed to be efficacious. The patient is then placed on oral therapy, and testing is repeated when steady-state drug levels are achieved to be certain that the oral preparation adequately protects the patient from arrhythmia recurrence. Should the oral preparation fail to suppress arrhythmia induction, a different antiarrhythmic agent will be selected and tested.

If, however, the arrhythmia was induced following intravenous administration of a class IA antiarrhythmic drug, it is highly likely that the agent will not protect the patient from an arrhythmia recurrence. Lidocaine, a IB agent, may then be administered intravenously to evaluate combination therapy. Testing is again repeated before the patient leaves the laboratory. Evaluations such as these done in conjunction with the baseline study minimize trauma and reduce patient costs by decreasing the number of electrophysiologic procedures required.

Definitions of Induced Ventricular Arrhythmias

Numerous investigators have developed and refined the criteria for assessing the characteristics of ventricular arrhythmias induced by programmed electrical stimulation. Their efforts to achieve standardized definitions have been aided by the North American Society of Pacing and Electrophysiology (NASPE). The term "repetitive ventricular response" (RVR) refers to a short run (two to five beats) of ventricular premature depolarizations. Repetitive ventricular responses may be related to reentry within the bundle branches, intraventricular reentry in areas of scarred myocardium or the distal Purkinje network, or triggered activity. Nonsustained ventricular tachycardia (NSVT) has been defined as a ventricular rhythm greater than 100 beats per minute lasting from six beats to 29 seconds. Both RVR and NSVT can be commonly induced in patients with heart disease. Induction of either response is less specific than reproduction of the clinical arrhythmia. The incidence of these responses depends to an extent on the aggressiveness of the stimulation protocol (i.e., the number of extrastimuli employed). Sustained ventricular tachycardia has been defined as a ventricular rhythm greater than 100 beats per minute lasting for at least 30 seconds or resulting in hemodynamic compromise requiring termination by pacing or cardioversion.

Induction of sustained monomorphic ventricular tachycardia in patients without clinical arrhythmias is relatively rare. Induction of sustained monomorphic ventricular tachycardia is an abnormal response that is highly specific and usually indicates a fixed substrate for the arrhythmia. In the presence of coronary artery disease, monomorphic ventricular tachycardia can be reliably reproduced by programmed electrical stimulation in over 90% of patients. In contrast, polymorphic ventricular tachycardia or ventricular fibrillation can be induced in up to 10% of subjects without a history of these arrhythmias if three or more premature extrastimuli are delivered during programmed electrical stimulation. Induction of polymorphic ventricular tachycardia or fibrillation is often a nonspecific response to an aggressive stimulation protocol. If these arrhythmias can be induced with one or two extrastimuli, their clinical relevance is increased.

ELECTROPHYSIOLOGIC TESTING FOR SUPRAVENTRICULAR ARRHYTHMIAS

The reliability of electrophysiologic testing in paroxysmal supraventricular tachycardias has also been well documented. The assumptions that form the basis for the validity of electrophysiologic testing of supraventricular arrhythmias are the same as for ventricular arrhythmias. Evaluation of supraventricular tachycardias with electrophysiologic testing requires analysis of intracardiac activation in the right atrium, coronary sinus, His bundle, right ventricle, and, occasionally, the left ventricle. The specific location and functional characteristics of the reentrant circuit are identified by mapping techniques and the response to atrial and ventricular programmed stimulation. Precise localization of the reentrant circuit is essential for surgical or catheter ablation of the foci of supraventricular tachycardias. Prospective pharmacologic testing may be employed with supraventricular tachycardias to ascertain the efficacy of antiarrhythmic treatment to prevent tachycardia induction or slow antegrade conduction over accessory AV connections. The effect of antiarrhythmic drugs on the refractory period of each component of the reentrant circuit is routinely measured. The effectiveness of antitachycardia pacing for termination of the tachycardia can also be assessed.

Measurements routinely made during electrophysiologic testing for supraventricular arrhythmias include characterization of the response of the AV conduction system to programmed electrical stimulation, with identification of the presence of dual AV nodal pathways; response of the AV node to progressively faster atrial pacing and quantitation of the rate at which AV Wenckebach block occurs; determination of atrial, ventricular, and AV nodal refractory periods; and characterization of retrograde conduction characteristics of the AV node. If an accessory AV connection is present, the antegrade and retrograde refractory periods are measured, as well as the maximum pacing rate sustaining 1:1 conduction over the pathway. The sequence of antegrade ventricular activation during atrial pacing and the sequence of retrograde atrial activation during ventricular pacing are also mapped. The sequence of atrial and ventricular activation during atrial and ventricular pacing and supraventricular tachycardia is also determined by catheter mapping, and the response to premature atrial and ventricular pacing stimuli is characterized. The response to induced atrial fibrillation is routinely quantitated if an accessory AV connection is present, to determine the risk of sudden cardiac death. These measurements are repeated following the administration of antiarrhythmic drugs.

Selected patients evaluated with supraventricular tachycardias may receive catheter ablative treatment at the time of their baseline electrophysiologic procedure. For example, if noninvasive diagnostic tests such as the 12-lead ECG, ambulatory monitoring, or transtelephonic monitoring suggest the presence of an accessory pathway, ablative therapy should be discussed with the patient in advance and consent elicited for both procedures.

ELECTROPHYSIOLOGIC EVALUATION OF THE CONDUCTION SYSTEM

Electrophysiologic testing may be employed to evaluate the function of the sinus node, or the AV conduction system in selected patients with suspected or confirmed bradyarrhythmias. Evaluation of the sinus node by invasive techniques is rarely performed as the primary indication for electrophysiologic testing. Rather, invasive evaluation of the sinus node is usually performed during testing for the diagnosis of syncope or is performed as a routine part of the comprehensive electrophysiologic study for other clinical indications. Sinus node dysfunction is usually detected by noninvasive recordings of the ECG with symptomatic correlation. The electrophysiologic evaluation of sinus node function consists of three tests. First, atrial pacing is performed at a rate slightly faster than the spontaneous atrial rate for 45 seconds, then abruptly terminated. The duration of the pause following the last paced beat to the first spontaneous sinus beat is termed the sinus node recovery time (SNRT) (Figure 4-9). The sinus node recovery time can be corrected for the underlying sinus rate prior to pacing (corrected sinus node recovery time, or CSNRT). Longer sinus node recovery times have been demonstrated to correlate with other signs of sinus node dysfunction.

The sino atrial conduction time is the second measurement of sinus node function. Timed, premature atrial extrastimuli are introduced during sinus rhythm to evaluate the time required for an extrastimulus to travel into and out of the sinus node. The interval between the premature extrastimulus and the next spontaneous sinus beat is plotted against the sinus cycle length. The SACT is approximately one half of this interval assuming that conduction time into the sinus node equals conduction time out of the sinus node. Longer sinoatrial conduction times correlate with sinus node dysfunction.

The third test of sinus node function is referred to as the intrinsic sinus rate and is measured during autonomic blockade with atropine and propranolol. Slower intrinsic sinus rates may indicate sinus node dysfunction. Because of the day-to-day variability in the results of these sinus node tests and their relatively poor sensitivity and specificity, clinical decisions regarding the need for permanent cardiac pacing are rarely based on these data alone.

Electrophysiologic testing may also be done to define the site of block (whether in the AV

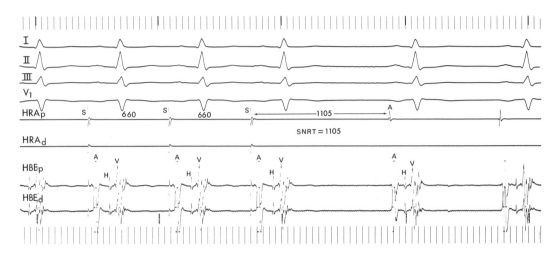

Figure 4-9 Sinus node recovery time. Surface leads I, II, III, and V_1 are shown simultaneously with bipolar electrograms from the high right atrium proximal (HRAp) and distal (HRAd) electrode pairs and His bundle electrograms from the proximal (HBEp) and distal (HBEd) electrode pairs. Note that atrial pacing is performed in the high right atrium with pacing stimuli that are clearly identified (S). In this example, pacing is performed at a cycle length of 660 milliseconds. Following termination of atrial pacing, the interval from the last extrastimulus (S) to the first spontaneous atrial activation (A) in the high right atrial electrogram is measured. The sinus node recovery time is thus 1105 milliseconds in this example.

node or bundle of His) in persons who demonstrate AV block on the surface ECG. Electrophysiologic testing in the absence of ECG-documented AV block may be also be done, especially if antiarrhythmic drugs will be administered that may impair AV conduction. In the setting of documented symptomatic high-degree AV block, invasive testing is not required prior to permanent pacemaker implantation (Figure 4-10). However, His bundle recordings may be useful in asymptomatic patients with second-degree AV block to assess the functional integrity of the AV node and His bundle. Since block in the AV node is associated with a relatively stable escape rhythm and a good prognosis, recording of AV block above the level of the His bundle may obviate the need for permanent pacing. In patients with block within the His bundle (manifested by a "split" His potential) or below the His bundle, the prognosis without permanent pacing is poor. Thus His bundle recordings may provide useful information in patients with AV block or syncope of undetermined etiology. It should be reemphasized that the vast majority of clinical decisions regarding the indications for permanent pacemaker implantation can be made without invasive procedures.

The response of the AV conduction system to programmed atrial stimulation may also allow recognition of dual AV nodal pathways, the substrate for AV nodal reentry. The normal response to incremental atrial pacing at gradually increasing rates is gradual prolongation of the time required to traverse the AV node (the atrium to His bundle, or AH, interval) until AV Wenckebach block occurs. Pacing is started at a rate just faster than that of the sinus node. The pacing rate is progressively increased every 30 seconds, which allows stabilization of conduction properties and refractory periods. Because the AV node exhibits the property of decremental conduction (progressive conduction delay at increasing pacing rate), its response to rapid atrial pacing differs from the response of other parts of the conduction system. Whereas Purkinje fibers develop shorter refractory periods and improved conduction at a faster heart rate, the refractory period of the AV node lengthens with increasing pacing rate.

Ventricular pacing provides information about ventriculoatrial conduction and is usually done from the right ventricular apex catheter. Incremental pacing is done in a similar manner until retrograde ventriculoatrial Wenckebach

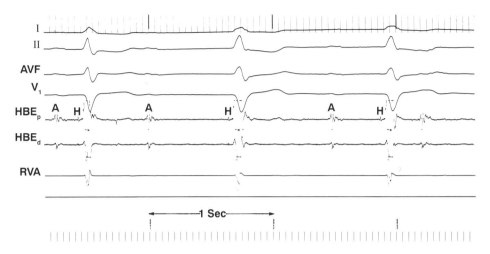

Figure 4-10 Complete AV block following catheter ablation of the AV node with intracoronary infusion of alcohol. Surface leads I, II, aVF, and V_1 are demonstrated simultaneously with electrograms from the His bundle proximal (HBEp) and (HBEd) distal electrode pairs and from the right ventricular apex (RVA). Notice that with complete AV block there is dissociation of the atrial and ventricular deflections. The escape rhythm originates in the His bundle with a clearly defined His bundle deflection before each QRS.

block occurs. Retrograde ventriculoatrial activation normally proceeds from the center of the heart at the AV node and spreads laterally to the left and right atria. The clinical significance of this information is its value in determining the location of accessory AV connections during studies to evaluate supraventricular tachycardias.

Assessment of the refractory periods of cardiac tissue is an integral part of the complete electrophysiologic study. Refractory periods are measured with the programmed electrical stimulation technique. The premature stimuli are introduced at progressively shorter S1-S2 coupling intervals until the tissue is not able to conduct an impulse. The effective refractory period (ERP) is defined as the longest coupling interval that fails to elicit a propagated response. The functional refractory period (FRP) is the shortest interval between two consecutively conducted impulses that can be achieved. The FRP is always longer than the ERP. Refractoriness of the cardiac tissue is dependent upon the pacing cycle length, with almost all structures except the AV node demonstrating shorter refractory periods at shorter pacing cycle lengths. The refractory period of the AV conduction system or accessory AV connections often differs in the antegrade and retrograde directions.

INTRACARDIAC CONDUCTION INTERVALS

Routine measurements during baseline electrophysiologic tests include those derived from the surface ECG (the RR, PR, QRS, and QT intervals). Intracardiac conduction times that are also routinely measured include those involving the His bundle electrogram and involve the intervals between the atrial, His, and ventricular deflections (Figure 4-3). AV conduction requires that the propagating wavefront traverse the AV node (the atrium to His bundle, or AH interval) and the His-Purkinje system (the His bundle to ventricle, or HV, interval). The resting AH interval is normally 60 to 125 milliseconds. This measurement can fluctuate depending on the autonomic state of the individual. The HV interval reflects conduction from the proximal His bundle to the ventricular myocardium and is normally 35 to 55 milliseconds. Unlike the AH interval, the HV interval is not significantly influenced by sympathetic or parasympathetic tone. The normal His bundle deflection is recognized as a sharp biphasic or triphasic signal. However, under diseased conditions the His deflection may be split or fragmented. If AV block occurs in the AH interval, the site of the block is localized to the AV node. If AV block occurs in the HV interval, disease of the His bundle or bundle branches is confirmed.

The intra-atrial conduction time is measured from the onset of the P wave in the surface ECG to the atrial component of the His bundle electrogram (Figure 4-11). This reflects conduction within the right atrium between the sinus and AV nodes. Interatrial conduction may be measured between the right and left atria if a coronary sinus catheter has been placed. This interval may be of clinical value for optimal programming of the AV delay with dual-chamber pacemakers.

INTRACARDIAC ACTIVATION MAPPING

Nonpharmacologic treatment of atrial or ventricular arrhythmias by catheter ablation or surgery requires accurate localization of the reentrant pathways or arrhythmogenic foci. The sequence of intracardiac activation is determined by recording local electrograms from multiple sites in the heart. The site of earliest activation usually corresponds to the site of origin of the tachycardia or the conduction path involved in a reentry circuit. An activation map is constructed by measurement of local activation at each site in relation to a fixed reference, usually on the surface ECG. Ventricular mapping is most commonly performed to localize the site of origin or reentrant circuit during monomorphic ventricular tachycardia. Ventricular tachycardia is induced by programmed electrical stimulation, and several multipolar catheters are moved to predetermined sites in both the right and left ventricles. These data are used to direct catheter ablation or surgery for ventricular tachycardia. Ventricular mapping requires that the patient be relatively stable during ventricular tachycardia so that the procedure can be completed, and that the tachycardia have a uniform morphology.

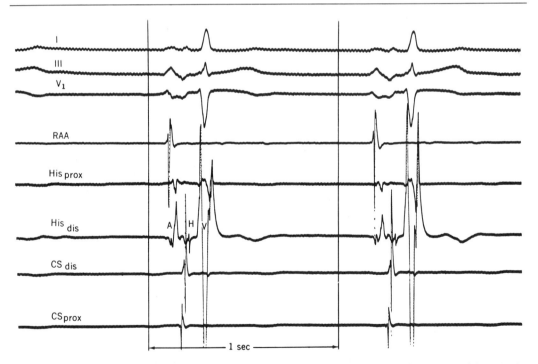

Figure 4-11 Surface electrocardiographic leads and intracardiac electrograms in a patient with an interatrial conduction abnormality. Surface leads I, III, and V₁ are demonstrated simultaneously with bipolar electrograms from the right atrial appendage (RAA), His bundle proximal (His prox) and distal (His dis) electrode pairs, and coronary sinus proximal (CS prox) and distal (CS dis) electrode pairs. Note that the P wave on the surface electrocardiographic leads is bizarre, with a prolonged deflection and fragmentation. Also note that there is a delay in activation from the right atrial appendage to the distal coronary sinus electrode, suggesting that conduction between the right and left atria is impaired.

Mapping during ventricular fibrillation or polymorphic ventricular tachycardia is not possible. Ventricular mapping is also useful in patients with Wolff-Parkinson-White syndrome in order to localize the site of ventricular insertion of an accessory pathway.

Atrial mapping is routinely performed during complete electrophysiologic studies of supraventricular tachycardias in an attempt to localize the reentrant circuit or ectopic atrial focus. During tachycardias related to Wolff-Parkinson-White syndrome, the site of earliest atrial activation usually indicates the location of the accessory pathway. Ectopic atrial tachycardias may arise in either atrium or the interatrial septum. Mapping is important to localize the ectopic focus prior to surgery or catheter ablation.

COSTS AND LIMITATIONS OF ELECTROPHYSIOLOGIC TESTING

Despite its important role in the diagnosis and management of many clinical arrhythmias, electrophysiologic testing is both invasive and costly. The risk of severe complications is low, with most laboratories experiencing a mortality rate approaching 0.01%. Morbidity arising from invasive electrophysiologic testing is approximately 1%. Rare complications include venous thrombosis, arterial injuries, bleeding, pneumothorax, hemothorax, pulmonary embolism, cardiac perforation with pericarditis or cardiac tamponade, myocardial infarction, exacerbation of congestive heart failure, induction of incessant tachycardias, and death. These risks can be minimized by the use of experienced operators, exclusion of unsuitable patients, and careful monitoring during the procedure. Most laboratories use intravenous heparin for studies involving venous access from the femoral vein. The use of low-dose subcutaneous heparin following the procedure may further diminish thrombotic complications.

PATIENT PREPARATION

Several important factors must be considered prior to electrophysiologic testing. Serum electrolytes, especially potassium, sodium, and magnesium, should be normalized, and other metabolic abnormalities such as acid/base disturbances or hyperthyroidism corrected. Patients with coronary artery disease should be on stable anti-ischemic regimens. Since many patients with ventricular tachycardia have poor left ventricular function, even subtle signs of heart failure should be sought and corrected. Any proarrhythmic drugs or exacerbating medical conditions should be eliminated.

Baseline electrophysiologic testing usually requires that pharmacologic therapy be discontinued for five drug half-lives (some labs use four half-lives). However, treatment is continued if the intent of the procedure is to assess the efficacy of the medication. Sedation may be given to some individuals but is avoided in others because it may alter the response to programmed electrical stimulation. Food and fluids are withheld for a minimum of 6 to 8 hours.

Physical preparation for the procedure is similar to that for a heart catheterization. The skin is sterilized with antiseptic agents, and the patient is draped with sterile sheets. The groin area is left exposed. The area surrounding the femoral vein is infiltrated with a local anesthetic, usually mepivacaine because of its relatively long duration of action. Percutaneous cannulation of the femoral vein is achieved with a thin-walled 18-gauge needle, and a flexible guide wire is passed through the needle into the vein. A small stab wound is made at the entrance site to facilitate introduction of a venous sheath. The electrode catheters are then advanced via the sheath to the desired intracardiac recording site. This procedure is repeated until all necessary catheters have been inserted. A similar procedure is performed if the internal jugular vein or subclavian vein is to be used. Positioning of the catheters is guided by fluoroscopy. If the electrophysiologic test involves induction of a tachycardia, particular attention is given to how the patient tolerates the arrhythmia. An antiarrhythmic drug may be administered intravenously during the procedure with repeat attempts to induce the clinical arrhythmia. Following completion of the procedure, the catheters and sheaths are usually removed, and hemostasis is achieved by manual pressure.

Supine bed rest with elevation of the head of the bed (30 degrees) is required following the procedure for approximately 6 hours if a femoral venous catheter was used. If the femoral artery was cannulated, patients are allowed to log roll after 8 hours but may be required to remain in bed for up to 24 hours. The artery should be auscultated for the development of a bruit, which, if present, requires physician notification. Although a number of centers are performing same-day heart catheterizations, most electrophysiologic procedures will require an overnight hospital stay if the patient has had an arterial puncture or if multiple venous sheaths were used. Prolonged flexion associated with sitting is discouraged until a minimum of 24 hours have elapsed. The patient's ECG is continuously monitored after the procedure. The nursing assessment of the patient poststudy varies but typically includes vital signs, the quality of peripheral pulses distal to the vascular access site, and visual inspection of the catheter introduction site. Assessing the patient for bleeding, hematoma formation, and perfusion distal to the vascular access site is done to determine if the patient has experienced procedural complications evidenced by an alteration in tissue perfusion or cardiac output. Customarily, the patient is evaluated every 15 minutes for the first hour at a minimum, every half hour for 2 hours, and then every hour for 4 hours.

Preparing the patient for electrophysiologic testing is of paramount importance. Nursing interventions prior to the procedure are directed toward education of the patient and family about the arrhythmia, the rationale for electrophysiologic testing, and the testing procedure. Explanations that include how electrophysiologic testing might influence treatment alternatives and arrhythmia recurrence may minimize anxiety and provide psychologic support of the patient and family. Verbal explanations are facilitated with supplemental written materials that explain the electrical and mechanical properties of the heart, their relationship to the arrhythmia, and the electrophysiologic procedure. Presenting the procedure in a positive manner and adjusting information to the coping style and level of patient comprehension may markedly reduce anxiety.

A patient's anxiety may be multifaceted. Patients may verbalize several fears, including fear of recurrence of the arrhythmia, fear of memory loss experienced with a previous arrhythmia event, fear that treatment associated with a prior arrhythmia occurrence (such as endotracheal intubation or cardioversion) may be required, or fear that the results of testing will influence their life-style.

Patients are usually informed by their physician that all medications will be stopped prior to electrophysiologic testing, and fear of arrhythmia recurrence is especially prevalent during this washout period. Particularly vulnerable during this time are patients who recount being "shocked" while awake. Lidocaine may be administered during a prolonged washout time due to its brief half-life. However, if the physician anticipates that there is a high likelihood of arrhythmia recurrence during drug washout, a temporary pacing catheter may be inserted to permit pacing for tachycardia termination. Assessment of the hemodynamic response of the patient, should the arrhythmia recur, is of paramount importance. Countershock should be avoided while the patient is conscious.

Initial information about the procedure is presented by the cardiac electrophysiologist. Often, for simplicity and clarity of explanation, the term "pacing" is substituted for cardiac electrical stimulation. Initial information given by the physician and nurse typically include the length of the procedure, a description of the room and its equipment and personnel, the procedure itself, and postprocedure care. It is crucial to emphasize that reproducing the arrhythmia in the laboratory is safe because the arrhythmia can be terminated using the same techniques that elicited it.

Accurate assessment of a patient's comprehension of electrophysiologic testing may be facilitated by asking the patient to describe in his or her own words what the procedure involves and why it is being performed. Thus misconceptions can be clarified and understanding can be verified. Anxiety may be further alleviated by describing the sensations that the patient might experience. It should be remembered that some patients cope with anxiety by limiting their knowledge acquisition to a minimum; such persons will indicate that detailed information is not desired. A patient's desire to have only limited information should be respected, as this may be an effective coping mechanism.

Sensations associated with the procedure that patients may experience include the burning or stinging that accompanies a local anesthetic prior to venipuncture, pressure sensations associated with vessel cannulation, application of cold solutions for sterile skin preparation, and the degree of coolness of the room. Explanations that include ways to prevent inadvertent contamination of the sterile field, catheter dislodgement, and musculoskeletal artifact or ECG dislodgement reinforce explanations about the necessity of lying still and avoiding arm movements. Informing the patient of what to expect assists the patient to comply with expected behaviors. The patient is also instructed to inform the physician of any sensations of chest pain, dizziness, or palpitations. Post-procedure, the patient is instructed to report any occurrences of bleeding, pain, or other discomfort.

Often patients may not comprehend the rationale for electrophysiologic testing. The following explanation may be helpful in such cases. Most episodes of arrhythmias occur as random, unpredictable events. Electrophysiologic testing removes the uncertainty and permits the effectiveness of a treatment to be assessed prior to hospital discharge. The best place to assess efficacy is in a fully prepared environment such as the electrophysiology laboratory.

BIBLIOGRAPHY

Akhtar M, Mahmud R, Tchou P, et al. Normal electrophysiologic responses of the human heart. *Cardiology Clinics*. 1986;4(3):365–386.

Amat-y-Leon F, Rosen KM. Catheter mapping of retrograde atrial activation: Observations during ventricular pacing and AV nodal re-entrant paroxysmal tachycardia. *Br Heart J*. 1976;38:355.

Bardy GH, Packer DL, German LD, et al: Utility of electrophysiologic studies in the management of tachycardia, sudden death, and syncope. Clinical aspects of life-threatening arrhythmias. *Univ New York Acad Sci*. 1984; 427:16–38.

Bauernfeind RA, Wyndham CR, Dhingra RC, et al. Serial electrophysiologic testing of multiple drugs in patients

with atrioventricular nodal reentrant paroxysmal tachycardia. *Circulation*. 1980;62:1341–1349.

Brugada P, Abdollah H, Heddle B, et al. Results of a ventricular stimulation protocol using a maximum of 4 premature stimuli in patients without documented or suspected ventricular arrhythmias. *Am J Cardiol*. 1983;52:1214–1218.

Cassidy DM, Vassallo JA, Klein AM, et al. The use of programmed electrical stimulation in patients with documented or suspected ventricular arrhythmias. *Heart Lung*. 1984;13:602–607.

Cobb LA, Werner JA, Trobaugh GB. Sudden cardiac death, II. outcome of resuscitation, management, and future directions. *Mod Concepts Cardiovasc Dis*. 1980; 49:37–41.

Denes P, Wu D, Dhingra R, et al. The effects of cycle length on the cardiac refractory period in man. *Circulation*. 1974;49:32.

DiMarco JP, Garan H, Ruskin JN. Complications in patients undergoing cardiac electrophysiologic procedures. *Ann Intern Med*. 1982;97:490–493.

Dreifus L, ed. *Cardiac Arrhythmias: Electrophysiologic Techniques and Management*. Philadelphia, Pa: FA Davis Co; 1985.

Durrer D, Schoo L, Schuilenburg RM, et al. The role of premature beats in the initiation of supraventricular tachycardia in the Wolff-Parkinson-White syndrome. *Circulation*. 1967;36:644–662.

Freedman RA, Mason JW. Invasive electrophysiologic study. In: Zipes DP, Rowlands DJ, eds. *Progress in Cardiology*. Philadelphia, Pa: Lea & Febiger; 1988; 1–2:215–236.

Garan H, Stavens CS, McGovern B, et al. Reproducibility of ventricular tachycardia suppression by antiarrhythmic drug therapy during serial electrophysiologic testing in coronary artery disease. *Am J Cardiol*. 1986;58:977–980.

Greenspan AM. Indications for electrophysiologic studies. *Cardiology Clinics*. 1986;4(3):387–400.

Higgins J, Scheinman NM, Morady F, et al. Electrophysiologic evaluation of patients with bundle branch block and syncope. *Circulation*. 1982;66(suppl 2):II-147.

Horowitz LN, Kay HR, Kutalek SP, et al. Risks and complications of clinical cardiac electrophysiologic studies: a prospective analysis of 1,000 consecutive patients. *J Am Coll Cardiol*. 1987;9:1261–1268.

Josephson ME, Horowitz LN. Electrophysiologic approach to therapy for recurrent sustained ventricular tachycardia. *Am J Cardiol*. 1979;43:631–641.

Josephson ME, Scharf DL, Kastor JA, et al. Atrial endocardial activation in man. Electrode catheter technique for endocardial mapping. *Am J Cardiol*. 1977;39:972–981.

Josephson ME, Seides SF. *Clinical Cardiac Electrophysiology Techniques and Interpretations*. Philadelphia, Pa: Lea & Febiger; 1979.

Kim SG. The management of patients with life-threatening tachyarrhythmias: programmed stimulation or Holter monitoring (either or both)? *Circulation*. 1987;76:1–5.

Kim SG. Is programmed stimulation of value in predicting the long-term success of antiarrhythmic therapy of ventricular tachycardias? *N Engl J Med*. 1986;315:356–362.

Kowey PR, Friehling TD. Uses and limitations of electrophysiology studies for the selection of antiarrhythmic therapy. *PACE*. 1986;9:231–247.

Livelli FD, Bigger JT, Reiffel JA, et al. Response to programmed ventricular stimulation: sensitivity, specificity, and relation to heart disease. *Am J Cardiol*. 1982;50: 452–458.

Mason JW, Winkle RA. Electrode-catheter arrhythmia induction in the selection and assessment of antiarrhythmic drug therapy for recurrent ventricular tachycardia. *Circulation*. 1978;58:971–985.

Rae AP. Proarrhythmic responses during electrophysiologic testing. *Cardiol Clin*. 1986;4:487–496.

Rae AP, Kay HR, Horowitz LN, et al. Proarrhythmic effects of antiarrhythmic drugs in patients with malignant ventricular arrhythmias evaluated by electrophysiologic testing. *J Am Coll Cardiol*. 1988;12:131–139.

Reddy CP, Damato AN, Akhtar M. Time dependent changes in the functional properties of the atrioventricular conduction system in man. *Circulation*. 1975;52:1012–1022.

Ruskin JN, DiMarco JP, Garan H. Out-of-hospital cardiac arrest: electrophysiologic observations and selection of therapy. *New Engl J Med*. 1980;303:607–613.

Scherlag BJ, Lau S, Helfant RH, et al. Catheter technique for recording His bundle activity in man. *Circulation*. 1969;39:13–18.

Tyndall A. A nursing perspective of the invasive electrophysiologic approach to treatment of ventricular tachycardia. *Heart Lung*. 1983;12:620–629.

Vanderpol CJ, Farshidi A, Spielman SR, et al. Incidence and clinical significance of induced ventricular tachycardia. *Am J Cardiol*. 1980;45:725–731.

Vlay S. Electrophysiologic testing. In Vlay S, ed. *Manual of Cardiac Arrhythmias*. Boston, Mass: Little, Brown Co; 1988.

Wellens HJJ, Schuilenburg RM, Durrer D. Electrical stimulation of the heart in patients with ventricular tachycardia. *Circulation*. 1972;46:216–226.

Pharmacologic Treatment of Arrhythmias

INTRODUCTION

Antiarrhythmic drugs are the initial therapy chosen for most clinical arrhythmias. Except for bradyarrhythmias, nonpharmacologic treatment is usually reserved for patients with arrhythmias that are refractory to medical management. Although increased recognition of the potential adverse effects of antiarrhythmic drugs and technical advances in antiarrhythmic devices are likely to decrease reliance on medications, pharmacologic agents will continue to be the dominant therapy for tachyarrhythmias. The optimal clinical benefit from the use of antiarrhythmic drugs can only be obtained by understanding the pharmacology of these agents and the mechanism of the arrhythmia to be treated. The currently available antiarrhythmic medications have effects on excitability, refractoriness, and conduction. These effects vary in different regions of the conduction system. For example, some agents affect the sinus and AV nodes to a greater extent than working atrial and ventricular myocardium. Antiarrhythmic drugs may have quantitatively greater effects on abnormal reentrant circuits than on normal regions of myocardium.

For clinical purposes, antiarrhythmic drugs can be broadly characterized by whether their predominant effects are on the inward sodium or calcium currents. Drugs that block the inward calcium current tend to have predominant effects on the sinus and AV nodes, whereas drugs that affect the inward sodium current tend to act on the His-Purkinje system to a greater extent. However, since antiarrhythmic drugs are not selective for arrhythmogenic foci or reentrant pathways, they may have undesirable effects on other regions of the heart. For example, while drugs such as quinidine may suppress atrial fibrillation effectively, they may worsen AV conduction or induce other arrhythmias such as torsades de pointes. In addition, antiarrhythmic agents may have other adverse effects on myocardial contractility and interact with the function of devices to raise pacing and defibrillation thresholds. These potential adverse drug effects are often related to the underlying structural cardiac disease. Deleterious effects on normal cardiac conduction are much more likely to be manifest in patients with clinical evidence of conduction system disease. Likewise, the negative inotropic effects of a medication may produce no clinical signs or symptoms in patients with structurally normal hearts but precipitate overt congestive heart failure in patients with impaired left ventricular function. Thus the use of antiarrhythmic drugs requires an understanding of their widespread effects and an appreciation that the desired effects must be weighed against the potential for adverse complications.

Effective clinical use of antiarrhythmic medications requires that the narrow range between therapeutic effects and drug toxicity be appreciated and that serum concentrations and electrophysiologic manifestations be carefully monitored. Since the common adverse effects of these drugs are known, specific patient physical signs, symptoms, and laboratory values must be periodically measured. The ECG should be monitored regularly, and serum levels quantitated when appropriate. It must always be remembered that the balance between therapeutic and toxic effects may change in an individual with changes in the arrhythmic substrate and structural heart disease and changes in the individual's physiology. In this chapter the principles of antiarrhythmic drug absorption, distribution, metabolism, and elimination will be reviewed. The specific properties of each of the commonly used antiarrhythmic drugs will also be discussed.

REVIEW OF BASIC PHARMACOLOGIC PRINCIPLES

Bioavailability

Bioavailability is the extent to which a drug is available in the various tissues of the body following administration. Pharmacologic agents exhibit individual characteristics of absorption, distribution, metabolism, and elimination. Drug absorption is influenced by a variety of factors including the route of administration, physiochemical properties of the drug, and the biologic characteristics of the sites of absorption and metabolism. Intravenous preparations of drugs are administered directly into the systemic circulation and produce clinical effects more rapidly than when administered orally. Orally administered drugs are absorbed in the gastrointestinal tract and enter the portal circulation. Many drugs are extensively metabolized in the liver prior to reaching the systemic circulation, so that only a fraction of the drug that is absorbed is delivered to the rest of the body. This effect is

known as first-pass metabolism and is observed with drugs such as verapamil. The drug that reaches the systemic circulation may be extensively altered by hepatic metabolism producing a metabolite that exerts effects different from those of the parent compound. Drugs such as lidocaine may have their bioavailability so markedly reduced by extensive liver metabolism that only a negligible amount of drug reaches the systemic circulation, rendering an oral preparation useless. Thus hepatic extraction influences the degree of bioavailability through elimination or alteration prior to the drug reaching the systemic circulation.

The bioavailability of drugs subject to first-pass metabolism may change with chronic treatment. With repeated doses the binding sites in the liver may become saturated, so that the drug is no longer extracted with the same degree of efficiency. This accounts for the marked change in a drug's action that can occur with small changes in doses, as is seen with the use of propafenone. The extent of absorption is determined by the drug's physiochemical properties, gastrointestinal tract function, and hepatic metabolism. Therefore, disease or dysfunction in the gastrointestinal tract or liver may markedly alter the effects of a drug. For example, if severe congestive heart failure is present, the intestine is often edematous and may absorb medications poorly. Since the liver is also congested, drugs requiring hepatic metabolism may accumulate. Following treatment of the congestive heart failure, the effects of a drug may change dramatically.

The two major determinants of drug concentration in the body are its distribution and elimination characteristics. Factors that influence the distribution of a drug include the perfusion of a specific organ, the degree of protein and/or tissue binding of the drug, the solubility of the drug in lipid and water, the water volume, and the physiologic state of the patient. The percentage of a drug that is bound to plasma protein and tissue varies with each drug. Usually drugs that are acidic bind to plasma proteins, and drugs that are alkaline (such as most antiarrhythmic agents) bind to the acute phase-reactive protein α-1-acid glycoprotein (AAG). AAG is manufactured in the liver, and hepatic dysfunction can cause marked variation in the amount of AAG available in the circulation. AAG binding is increased post myocardial infarction, post CABG, and after other stressful conditions, such as burns. Since only the "free" or unbound portion of the drug is available to diffuse into tissue, drugs that are highly bound to plasma proteins are highly influenced by the concentration of proteins in the blood. Disease states may alter the bioavailability of a drug at different times within a given individual because of changes in the binding affinity of the drug or the number of binding sites available. The desired antiarrhythmic response to a drug is derived from the amount of drug that is free and available to interact at receptor sites in the tissues. If the clinical laboratory report of a drug level reflects combined bound and free drug concentrations, the same measured level may produce widely varying clinical effects depending on the concentration of plasma proteins that bind to the drug. For example, quinidine and lidocaine levels may increase following myocardial infarction or surgery due to increased AAG binding. However, the free fraction of the drug may actually decline since more of the drug is in the unusable, protein-bound phase. Therefore, although a lidocaine level may be increased because of increased binding to plasma proteins, the antiarrhythmic efficacy may decline because less of the drug is in the free state. Thus higher than normal drug levels may need to be achieved to produce desired antiarrhythmic effects.

Following absorption into the systemic circulation, drugs are distributed to the plasma and to tissues with high rates of blood flow, such as the brain, kidneys, and heart. These areas are collectively referred to as the central compartment. The concentration of a drug in central compartment tissues rapidly equilibrates with the plasma concentration. Distribution of the drug occurs more slowly into poorly perfused tissue, termed the peripheral compartment. Both physiochemical properties of the drug and the physiologic state of the patient influence the extent of distribution. In the setting of congestive heart failure, fluid from the central compartment is shifted to varying degrees to the peripheral compartment. There is also reduced blood flow in both compartments in congestive heart failure, accounting for an increased frequency of side effects and elimination time.

Cellular Effects of Antiarrhythmic Drugs

The pharmacologic actions of a drug at the tissue level are usually related to the interaction of the drug with specific binding sites. The response is attributed to stimulation or inhibition of cellular enzymes, blockade of the interaction of a naturally occurring substance with its specific receptor, blockade of ion transport within membrane-bound channels, or direct actions on the cell membrane. Drugs that are soluble in lipid have greater penetration into the endoplasmic reticulum through the cell membrane. Drug receptor sites are believed to be protein molecules that are most likely situated within the lipoprotein structure of the cell membrane.

Drug Metabolism

Generally, metabolism of a drug is accomplished by the action of specific liver enzymes. During metabolism, the drug undergoes chemical alteration or biotransformation. Most antiarrhythmic drugs are metabolized by hepatic biotransformation and eliminated from the body in the bile or by renal excretion. Metabolism may render a drug more water soluble and facilitate renal excretion. The results of metabolism may be transformation of a pharmacologically active drug into an inactive metabolite devoid of pharmacologic effects, or into one or more pharmacologically active metabolites, each of which may exert different effects. For example, procainamide, encainide, and propafenone undergo transformation of the parent drug into pharmacologically active metabolites with specific effects of their own. Drug metabolism is dependent on the functions of the heart, liver, and kidneys. Primary dysfunction or secondary alteration of any of these organs may significantly alter drug metabolism.

The metabolic fate of a drug is also affected by the genetically determined metabolic enzymes that each individual possesses. Individuals may be classified as "poor metabolizers" or "extensive metabolizers" depending on the activity of their genetically determined set of metabolic enzymes. Patients who rapidly convert the parent compound of a drug to a metabolite will often experience drug effects different from those experienced by individuals who generate the metabolite more slowly. The hepatic cytochrome P-450 pathway is a common enzyme pathway that is used to metabolize several antiarrhythmic agents. Persons with the poor metabolizer phenotype have a genetic deficiency in this enzyme pathway and experience impaired metabolism of a number of drugs; they are estimated to constitute 7% of the United States population. Poor metabolizers maintain a high ratio of the parent compound to its metabolites in the serum, whereas extensive metabolizers maintain a low serum ratio of parent drug to its metabolites. Thus the pharmacologic effects of a drug may vary depending on the activity of the patient's cytochrome P-450 pathway. For example, a poor metabolizer who receives propafenone may maintain high levels of propafenone and low levels of its principal metabolite, 5-hydroxy propafenone. Since the P-450 enzymatic pathway is shared by a number of drugs, drug-drug interactions are possible. Concomitant medications that utilize the same enzyme pathway may change an extensive metabolizer to a poor metabolizer. Drugs such as quinidine that inhibit the cytochrome P-450 pathway will convert an extensive metabolizer to a poor metabolizer, resulting in high concentrations of the parent compound and low concentrations of the metabolite. Concomitant administration of drugs that utilize the same enzyme pathway may result in several drug interactions. The interaction may be one-sided only, altering the concentration of one of the drugs, or two-sided, altering the concentration of both drugs.

Concomitant administration of drugs that increase hepatic metabolism, such as phenobarbital, dilantin, and rifampin, may result in a decreased serum concentration of the antiarrhythmic agent. Conversely, drugs that inhibit or decrease hepatic metabolism may result in an increased serum concentration of the antiarrhythmic agent. It should be emphasized that not all drugs are metabolized. In some cases the drug may be excreted unchanged in the urine.

Elimination

Following metabolism of a drug, the remaining parent compound and its metabolites are excreted from the body. Clearance is determined by the perfusion and function of the organ of excretion. Elderly patients or those with congestive heart failure are particularly vulnerable to changes in the elimination of a drug because of reduced blood flow to the liver or kidneys. Patients with congestive heart failure have reduced blood flow to the central compartment tissues and a greater volume of pooled blood in their extremities and interstitial spaces, the peripheral compartment. The extent to which this occurs may be markedly influenced by the use of other medications. For example, peripheral pooling is augmented by drugs such as venodilators that are used to decrease preload or relieve ischemia. The greatest potential for the development of toxicity occurs in drugs that require both hepatic metabolism and renal excretion.

The rate of elimination of a drug is defined as the percent of the drug removed from the body per unit of time, usually hours. The half-life of a drug is a reciprocal function of the elimination rate constant. It is defined as the amount of time required for an amount of drug in the bloodstream to be reduced by 50%. The elimination half-life is dependent on drug clearance and the volume of distribution of the drug. Although estimates of a drug's half-life are derived from studies in normal volunteers and patients with relatively normal renal and hepatic function, the half-life of a drug when used in a patient with impaired hepatic or renal function may be considerably different from that observed in reference populations. The half-life is actually an exponential term, so that after one half-life 50% of the drug is removed, after two half-lives 25% of a drug remains, and after three half-lives 12.5% is present. By five half-lives, approximately 97% of the drug has been excreted. The half-life is also used to determine the length of time that is required to attain steady-state concentrations of a drug. Steady state refers to a state of equilibrium such that uptake and elimination of the drug are equal. Over 90% of the steady-state serum concentration is achieved after four half-lives. Drugs that have long half-lives, such as digoxin or amiodarone, require a very long period of drug administration to reach a steady state. Rapid loading of these drugs by a large initial dosing regimen is frequently used to produce a therapeutic concentration more quickly. Although there is an increase in the initial plasma concentration of the drug, the loading regimen does not shorten the time to steady state.

The half-lives of antiarrhythmic drugs assume particular importance in patients who have altered metabolism and elimination due to renal, hepatic, or cardiac impairment. In these patients, the time to reach steady state or to eliminate the drug may be greatly prolonged due to altered distribution and clearance. Marked accumulation of the drug with attendant toxicity may occur unless the dose is slowly titrated and adjusted. The diagnostic value of electrophysiologic testing and Holter monitoring directly relates to the issue of drug half-lives. Since the baseline electrophysiologic test or Holter monitoring should be done in a drug-free state, an interval of approximately five half-lives should be allowed for between the last dose of a drug and performance of these studies. Similarly, testing of the therapeutic efficacy of a drug should not be performed until the drug has been administered for at least four to five half-lives.

Proarrhythmia

Proarrhythmia refers to aggravation of an existing arrhythmia or the development of a new arrhythmia attributable to an antiarrhythmic agent. The electrophysiologic effects of pharmacologic agents that alter properties of conduction and refractoriness to abolish an arrhythmia may also initiate or sustain an arrhythmia. Mechanisms of proarrhythmia include inhomogeneity of repolarization and refractoriness, decreased conduction velocity, decreased ventricular fibrillation threshold, reduced excit-

ability, induction of triggered activity, and augmented automaticity. The extent of underlying heart disease, particularly the status of left ventricular function, may influence the risk of proarrhythmia. Patients at greatest risk for developing a proarrhythmic response with an antiarrhythmic drug are those with structural heart disease, left ventricular dysfunction, and congestive heart failure.

Proarrhythmic responses may be manifested as an increase in the frequency, duration, or response of the arrhythmia. A proarrhythmic response may be manifested as a bradycardia or a tachycardia. Arrhythmia aggravation may be seen in a variety of patterns. For example, an increased incidence of ventricular premature depolarizations compared to baseline or the new onset of sustained ventricular tachycardia may be due to an antiarrhythmic drug. Antiarrhythmic drugs may slow the rate of both supraventricular or ventricular tachyarrhythmias but dramatically increase their frequency. The most serious proarrhythmic responses include the development of torsades de pointes related to excessive prolongation of the QT interval and the spontaneous occurrence of hemodynamically unstable sustained ventricular tachycardia or fibrillation in patients who do not have a clinical history of these arrhythmias. Other life-threatening proarrhythmic responses include the development of complete AV block, prolonged sinus arrest, or extreme bradycardia.

The class IA drugs are noted for their risk of producing torsades de pointes. Careful attention to the QT interval is required when these drugs are used. In most instances, excessive QT prolongation occurs as an idiosyncratic response and is unpredictable. Torsades de pointes is most likely to develop within the first 2 days of therapy. Because of this, class IA drugs are best initiated in a monitored inpatient setting. The class IC drugs are also noted for their propensity to induce sustained ventricular tachycardia. This is unrelated to the QT interval but is more common in the presence of impaired left ventricular function. These arrhythmias are often precipitated by exercise. Because of this, treadmill exercise testing is often useful to predict an adverse outcome. The use of digoxin serum concentrations to guide therapy has sharply reduced the incidence of severe digitalis toxicity. However, digoxin toxicity remains a frequent occurrence in patients with impaired renal function.

ANTIARRHYTHMIC DRUG CLASSIFICATION

At least three mechanisms are thought to be responsible for the action of antiarrhythmic agents: (1) suppression of automaticity due to an increase in the threshold membrane potential or a slower rate of spontaneous diastolic depolarization; (2) depression of phase 0 of the action potential, which is carried by the inward sodium current; and (3) prolongation of the effective refractory period of the tissue. Thus drugs may affect excitability, conduction, or refractoriness. The Vaughn-Williams classification of antiarrhythmic agents developed in 1970 and Harrison's subsequent modification classify drugs by the effect that they exert on the cardiac action potential. This classification scheme is widely used and has important clinical value. However, the Vaughn-Williams system has several limitations. One drawback is that it was based on observations of isolated Purkinje fibers even though antiarrhythmic agents may exert differing effects on normal and diseased myocytes. Moreover, pharmacologic agents in one class may manifest properties of several classes. Although these limitations have been recog-

nized, we will use the Vaughn-Williams classification (Table 5-1) to discuss the individual antiarrhythmic drugs.

CLASS I AGENTS

Class I antiarrhythmic drugs are known for their local anesthetic properties. Commonly referred to as fast sodium channel blockers and membrane-stabilizing agents, class I drugs function primarily by decreasing sodium conductance across the cell membrane during phase 0 of the action potential, or depolarization. Class I drugs are further divided into three subgroups based on the effect that they exert on action potential duration and refractoriness. Although the resting membrane potential is not altered by class I drugs, they cause a depressed slope of phase 4 leading to a decreased rate of automaticity in Purkinje fibers and increased threshold for inducing ventricular fibrillation. Despite the sensitivity and specificity that antiarrhythmic sodium channel blockers have for cardiac cells at the cellular level, they may also affect sodium conductance in nerve and noncardiac muscle cells. These effects on noncardiac tissue account for some of the toxic side effects associated with class I agents. The ECG may manifest slowed conduction with an increased PR interval and QRS duration. Prolongation of

Table 5-1 The Vaughn-Williams Classification of Antiarrhythmic Drugs

Class I		Class II		Class III	Class IV	Class V
Moricizine	(I)	Propanolol	(NS)	Sotalol (+ II)	Verapamil	Digoxin
Quinidine	(IA)	Esmolol	(CS)	Amiodarone	Diltiazem	Atropine
Procainamide	(IA)	Acebutolol	(ISA)	Bretylium tosylate		Adenosine
Disopyramide	(IA)					
Lidocaine	(IB)					
Mexiletine	(IB)					
Tocainide	(IB)					
Phenytoin	(IB)					
Flecainide	(IC)					
Encainide	(IC)					
Propafenone	(IC)					

Note: Example of Vaughn-Williams classification of antiarrhythmic agents based on their dominant mechanism of action. Class I agents are categorized as IA, IB, or IC with the exception of moricizine. Representative class II agents are categorized as nonselective cardiac β receptors (NS), cardioselective (CS), or possessing intrinsic sympathomimetic activity (ISA). Sotalol contains properties representative of both class II and class III.

the action potential duration (typical of class IA and III drugs) is manifested as increased QT and JT intervals. The overall efficacy rate of class I drugs to prevent inducible ventricular tachycardia in patients with this clinical arrhythmia is approximately 20% to 30%.

Class IA agents such as procainamide, quinidine, and disopyramide decrease conduction velocity to a moderate degree and prolong refractoriness by increasing the action potential duration. They exert a more pronounced effect on conduction in the setting of tachycardias, decreased pH, and hyperkalemia. Pirmenol, an investigational class IA drug, is not affected by serum potassium concentration. Class IA drugs have a minimal effect on the AV node; thus the PR interval is usually unchanged. Class IA drugs are most notable for their prolongation of the QT interval, primarily in the JT segment.

The most worrisome adverse effect associated with class IA drugs is the development of torsades de pointes ventricular tachycardia; this arrhythmia is highly associated with class IA antiarrhythmic agents (see discussion in Chapter 7). It occurs in approximately 1% to 2% of individuals, usually following the first several doses of the drug. Most patients who develop torsades de pointes have low or therapeutic levels of the drug, so this adverse effect is usually an idiosyncratic reaction. Patients who receive toxic concentrations may also develop torsades de pointes. The incidence of torsades de pointes is increased in the setting of hypokalemia, preexisting prolongation of the QTC, and bradycardia. Frequent measurement of the QT interval at the start of therapy with a class IA drug is essential to its safe use. If a patient develops torsades de pointes on quinidine, he or she should not receive the other class IA drugs. However, class IC drugs have been shown to be safe in patients who have developed torsades de pointes with the class IA agents. Because of the unpredictable nature of torsades de pointes at the start of therapy with the class IA drugs, patients are routinely hospitalized for monitoring during the first 24 hours of therapy. QTC prolongation beyond 550 milliseconds in the presence of a normal QRS duration requires discontinuation of therapy. Serum drug levels should be closely monitored as well.

Class IB agents such as lidocaine, tocainide, mexiletine, and phenytoin increase potassium conductance across the cell membrane, depressing the rate and height of the depolarizing current, but in a potassium-dependent fashion. These drugs decrease action potential duration and shorten refractoriness. Because the magnitude of the IB agents' effects is directly related to the concentration of extracellular potassium, these antiarrhythmic agents are particularly useful in situations where arrhythmias arise because of cell injury. Class IB agents also differ from other class I agents in that conduction is depressed to a greater degree at low membrane potentials. Thus while they exert virtually no effect in normal tissue, they exert marked effects on ischemic Purkinje fibers with a relatively depolarized membrane potential. This observation may explain why the class IB drugs are especially effective in arrhythmias associated with acute ischemia but are less useful for chronic ventricular arrhythmias. These agents exert minimal effects on sinus node automaticity and virtually no effects on atrial arrhythmias. Thus they have no role in the clinical treatment of atrial arrhythmias. Minimal ECG changes are associated with the use of these agents.

The class IC drugs, such as encainide, flecainide, and propafenone, markedly slow conduction by their effect on phase 0 of the action potential. They specifically decrease the rate of rise and the amplitude of the depolarizing current carried by sodium ions. Unlike IA agents, they do not appreciably alter the action potential duration or prolong refractoriness. These agents are primarily associated with prolongation of the PR interval and QRS duration because of their marked effects on conduction. The QT prolongation that occurs with IC agents is secondary to an increased QRS duration, while the JT segment remains relatively stable. Thus frequent measurement of the PR and QRS intervals should be used to guide therapy with class IC drugs. Increases in the QRS duration by 50% may require discontinuation of therapy, and QRS durations of 200 milliseconds necessitate discontinuation. Proarrhythmic effects may also occur with these medications. Torsades de pointes ventricular tachycardia does not occur with class IC drugs. Rather, proarrhythmia with these drugs is often manifest by ventricular tachycardia that is incessant in nature and is extremely difficult to manage. Widened, bizarre QRS complexes of 200 to 300 milliseconds are not uncommon with class IC drugs. In our experience, the incessant ventricular tachycardia that is caused by class IC drugs may be suppressed by intravenous boluses of hypertonic saline or sodium bicarbonate.

The class IC drugs are extremely effective for the suppression of ventricular premature depolarizations, especially in the presence of minimal left ventricular dysfunction. However, since the preliminary Cardiac Arrhythmia Suppression Trial (CAST) findings have been published, the IC antiarrhythmic agents have been restricted to the treatment of life-threatening ventricular arrhythmias. CAST was designed to test the hypothesis that suppression of ventricular arrhythmias with antiarrhythmic drugs in patients following myocardial infarction prevents sudden cardiac death. In CAST, patients with spontaneous VPDs and recent myocardial infarction were randomly assigned to therapy with encainide, flecainide (if the ejection fraction was ≥ 0.3), moricizine, or a matching placebo. After a mean follow-up period of 10 months, the rate of sudden death was 2.5 to 3.6 times higher in the encainide and flecainide groups than in the group receiving placebo. Since all patients had demonstrated at least 80% suppression of ventricular premature depolarizations and 90% suppression of nonsustained ventricular tachycardia by these antiarrhythmic drugs prior to randomization, the overall results demonstrate a striking deleterious effect of encainide and flecainide on survival in this population. Whether other drugs have similar adverse effects when prescribed in this way is not known. The moricizine arm of the trial (CAST II) has been discontinued because of a trend toward higher mortality in the moricizine treatment group. Whether these findings can be generalized to other antiarrhythmic drugs is unknown. The CAST findings have also influenced the development of new antiarrhythmic drugs for use in the United States. For example, clinical trials of the IC drugs diprafenone, lorcainide, and cibenzoline were discontinued following the preliminary CAST results.

Propafenone, a IC drug with β-blocking activity, and indecainide, another IC agent, were approved in late 1989. Both drugs carry the same restrictions as flecainide and encainide and are indicated for the treatment of life-threatening ventricular arrhythmias only. Indecainide will not be available commercially but will remain available for treatment of patients with life-threatening arrhythmias who have responded to this drug during clinical trials.

Class IA and IC drugs are effective for the treatment of both atrial and ventricular arrhythmias. The class IB agents exert little effect on atrial tissue and are only used in the treatment of ventricular arrhythmias. Both class IA and IC drugs block accessory bypass pathway conduction. Because of their marked effect on conduction, the class IC drugs should be used with extreme caution in patients with impaired AV conduction.

Class IA Agents

Quinidine

Quinidine is approved for treatment of atrial and ventricular arrhythmias including premature ventricular and atrial depolarizations, ventricular tachycardia, atrial fibrillation, and atrial flutter, and intraatrial reentrant tachycardia. Quinidine is also indicated for selected patients with AV nodal reentrant tachycardia or with Wolff-Parkinson-White syndrome. Quinidine is frequently used in combination with digoxin to maintain normal sinus rhythm following cardioversion from atrial flutter or fibrillation. Quinidine decreases conduction velocity in the Purkinje system and ventricular myocardium. Quinidine prolongs both action potential duration and refractoriness, which are reflected on the ECG as increases in the QRS duration and QT interval. Quinidine's depressant effects on the sinus and AV nodes are counteracted by its vagolytic action. The net effect of quinidine on the sinus and AV nodes is relatively neutral. In some patients with atrial flutter, quinidine and the other class IA drugs may actually speed the ventricular response. This effect is primarily due to slowing of the atrial flutter rate, with little or no effect on AV conduction. Thus the ventricular response to atrial flutter may change from a 2:1 to a 1:1 ratio. It is for this reason that when quinidine is used to treat atrial flutter, prior blocking of the AV node with digoxin is recommended. Since the class IA drugs have minimal effects on the AV node, the PR interval is usually unchanged.

Quinidine is most commonly administered in tablet or capsule form as a sulfate, gluconate, or polygalacturonate salt with 100 to 330 mg of quinidine base. Sulfate salts are generally the least expensive, are absorbed the most rapidly, and produce the shortest duration of action. However, quinidine sulfate may be less well tolerated than other preparations due to its side effects (discussed below). Sustained-release preparations are available that decrease the frequency of dosing and encourage compliance. Oral dose requirements typically range from 800 to 2400 mg/d. While sulfate preparations often require an every 6-hour dosing frequency, gluconate preparations may be administered to most patients every 8 hours. Quinidine sulfate is 82% quinidine, while the gluconate preparation is 62% quinidine. These differences should be considered when preparations are changed so that the patient remains on the same dose of quinidine base. Quinidine gluconate may be administered intravenously at a rate of 10 mg/min in doses of 200 to 400 mg. A single loading dose of 10 mg/kg is often used during electrophysiologic testing. It should be emphasized that intravenous quinidine administration may be associated with profound hypotension. Blood pressure should be monitored every 2 to 3 minutes during intravenous infusion.

Quinidine is highly protein bound and is not significantly affected by first-pass hepatic metabolism. Following oral ingestion of quinidine, approximately 90% of the drug is available in the systemic circulation. Blood levels peak within 60 to 90 minutes after ingesting oral quinidine sulfate, with quinidine gluconate preparations producing slightly later peak levels. Quinidine has a mean half-life of 6 to 7 hours and is extensively metabolized by the liver. Dosage adjustment is required in patients who have reduced hepatic flow or hepatic dysfunction. Dose reductions of approximately one third are required in patients with renal failure. Two types

of quinidine assays are available. Therapeutic total quinidine concentrations generally range from 3 to 6 mg/L (direct assay). The direct quinidine assay measures quinidine plus its major metabolites. Extractable quinidine assays measure only the parent quinidine compound, with therapeutic levels ranging from 2 to 5 mg/L.

Concomitant administration of quinidine and digoxin is known to increase digoxin levels due to displacement of digoxin from binding sites and decreased renal clearance of digoxin. Thus when quinidine is given to a patient receiving digoxin, a 50% reduction in digoxin dosage is generally required. Enhanced anticoagulant effects are also present with concomitant warfarin administration because of displacement of warfarin from protein-binding sites. Cimetidine and propranolol may increase quinidine levels due to decreased hepatic metabolism, whereas concomitant administration of nifedepine, rifampin, phenytoin, and barbiturates such as phenobarbital is known to decrease the serum quinidine concentration due to increased hepatic metabolism. Quinidine potentiates the effects of muscle relaxants and should be avoided in the immediate postoperative period when the effects of muscle relaxants may still be present. While its anticholinergic properties antagonize the effects of cholinergic drugs such as pilocarpine and may antagonize the effects of neostigmine and edrophonium, an additive effect with other anticholinergics such as atropine occurs. Quinidine should be used with caution in patients with myasthenia gravis.

The most common adverse effects associated with quinidine therapy are gastrointestinal. The incidence and severity of side effects may be reduced by using nonsulfate preparations. Neurologic complaints of vertigo, headaches, and visual disturbances, referred to as cinchonism, have been reported with high-dose quinidine therapy. Blood dyscrasias such as thrombocytopenia are rare but potentially life-threatening. Quinidine may also produce unexplained fever, known clinically as "quinidine fever," which is associated with a rash. Quinidine is also associated with hepatotoxicity, heart block, hypotension, and a negative inotropic effect in persons with impaired ventricular function. Prolongation of the QT interval for the development of torsades de pointes ventricular tachycardia is monitored for a minimum of 24 hours, for all patients. QT interval measurements from a 12-lead ECG should be obtained prior to therapy, at 6 hours, and at 18 hours after initiation of therapy.

Procainamide

Procainamide is approved for the treatment of atrial and ventricular arrhythmias, with the same indications as detailed for quinidine. Procainamide exerts electrophysiologic actions that are very similar to those of quinidine. Its efficacy in electrophysiology guided therapy of life-threatening ventricular arrhythmias in preventing induction of ventricular tachycardia is generally less than 30%. Although it may be used in circumstances comparable to those requiring quinidine, quinidine has traditionally been preferred for the long-term treatment of arrhythmias because of the possibility of procainamide-induced lupus. In the short term, procainamide is associated with fewer side effects than quinidine. Therefore, procainamide is more likely to be used to maintain sinus rhythm if the duration of drug therapy is anticipated to be short—for example, following open heart surgery.

Procainamide readily lends itself to the emergency treatment of both supraventricular and ventricular arrhythmias because the intravenous preparation is usually well tolerated, and there are very few side effects. However, intravenous procainamide may produce hypotension if the rate of infusion exceeds 25 mg/min. Procainamide is effective for the emergency treatment of atrial fibrillation and flutter. For the reasons discussed with quinidine, the AV node should be blocked with digoxin if procainamide is to be used for atrial flutter. Procainamide is probably the drug of choice for wide-complex tachycardias of uncertain origin. In patients with preexcitation syndromes with antegrade conduction over a bypass pathway during atrial fibrillation or antidromic reciprocating tachycardia, procainamide will slow conduction in the accessory pathway and is the treatment of choice. Although procainamide primarily prolongs the QT interval, the QRS duration may also be prolonged, particularly in instances of toxicity. QRS widening is particularly associated with intravenous administration. If a 50% increase in the QRS duration over baseline occurs, the drug should be stopped. Treatment with procainamide has been associated with the development of torsades de pointes ventricular tachycardia and heart block. As with other IA antiarrhythmic agents, initiation of therapy requires a minimum of 24 hours of hospitalization.

The duration of action of procainamide is very short, on the order of 3 to 4 hours. Because of its short duration of action, sustained-release preparations have been made available, which permits a decreased dosing frequency of every 6 to 8 hours. Sustained-release preparations are available in doses ranging from 250 to 1000 mg. Daily doses of procainamide range from 2 to 6 g/d. Procainamide is administered intravenously in loading doses of 10 to 17 mg/kg, followed by a maintenance infusion of 2 to 6 mg/min to maintain plasma levels.

The major differences between quinidine and procainamide relate to their pharmacokinetics, drug interactions, and adverse effects. Procainamide is only slightly less bound to plasma proteins than quinidine and has a bioavailability of greater than 75%, achieving peak blood levels approximately 1 hour following oral administration. Procainamide is metabolized in the liver to N-acetyl procainamide (NAPA). NAPA is an active metabolite with class III properties. Both procainamide and NAPA are eliminated by renal excretion; therefore, procainamide is a poor choice for patients with impaired renal function. If procainamide is used in the presence of impaired renal function, the dosage must be dramatically reduced. The half-life of procainamide is usually considered to be 3 to 4 hours, while the half-life of NAPA is 4 to 6 hours. Therapeutic procainamide levels are generally 4 to 10 μg/L, while NAPA levels are 10 to 20 μg/mL. The ratio of procainamide to NAPA serum levels is determined by the metabolic phenotype of the person and is dictated by the activity of the N-acetyl transferase enzyme. As with other enzyme systems, persons can be divided into two groups based on the degree of activity exhibited by the enzyme; in this instance they are referred to as slow acetylators and rapid acetylators. Population studies indicate that 50% to

65% of whites, blacks, Mexicans, and South Indians are slow acetylators. In contrast, approximately 80% to 95% of Eskimos, Japanese, and Chinese are rapid acetylators. Rapid acetylators exhibit high levels of NAPA and low levels of procainamide. In most patients with adequate renal function, procainamide and NAPA levels will be roughly the same. However, in patients with renal failure, NAPA will accumulate. In this setting, the dose is reduced so that procainamide levels are very low, while NAPA levels are adjusted to be within the therapeutic range.

While procainamide may produce nausea, vomiting, and hypotension (if given intravenously), the most common reason for discontinuation in long-term therapy is the development of drug-induced lupus. Approximately 50% of patients on procainamide will develop a positive antinuclear antibody (ANA) titer within the first year of treatment, while 30% will develop symptoms of lupus. The acetylator phenotype may be a prognostic indicator of the propensity to develop lupus. Slow acetylators are more likely than rapid acetylators to develop lupus, and to develop it on lower levels of procainamide. The drug-induced lupus-like syndrome is characterized by arthralgias, fever, erythema, pleuritis, pericarditis, hepatomegaly, and skin rash. Although discontinuation of therapy reverses the disease process, the patient will continue to have a positive ANA titer. The onset of drug-induced lupus in patients with positive ANA titers may be differentiated from the development of spontaneous systemic lupus erythematosus by a positive antihistone antibody titer, which is negative in the absence of a drug-induced lupus. Although drug-induced lupus usually resolves within a few days after stopping the drug, this syndrome can be difficult to diagnose. In addition, patients who develop pleuritis or pericarditis may have persistent effusions for months. A short course of corticosteroids may help to relieve the symptoms of drug-induced lupus.

Procainamide has several quinidine-like drug interactions, including enhancing the effects of other anticholinergic drugs and antagonizing cholinergic drugs. Procainamide may also potentiate neuromuscular blocking drugs and

should be avoided in myasthenia gravis. Barbiturates may decrease the effect of procainamide due to augmented hepatic metabolism, while cimetidine and propranolol may increase its effects. Overall, procainamide is an extremely useful drug for the acute management of arrhythmias.

Disopyramide

Disopyramide is approved for the treatment of ventricular arrhythmias including VPDs and ventricular tachycardia and demonstrates comparable efficacy to quinidine and procainamide in the treatment of VPDs and an efficacy rate of 20% to 30% in the treatment of life-threatening arrhythmias. Disopyramide is also useful for the treatment of atrial fibrillation, atrial flutter, and arrhythmias associated with Wolff-Parkinson-White syndrome. Despite its efficacy, the use of disopyramide is limited by two major adverse effects: a marked anticholinergic effect and a potent negative inotropic action. Disopyramide is the most negatively inotropic antiarrhythmic drug yet approved. The negative inotropic effect is more marked in patients with pre-existing left ventricular dysfunction, often the very group that could most use its beneficial antiarrhythmic actions. As with other drugs, the hemodynamic depression is usually unnoticeable in persons with normal ventricular function. However, congestive heart failure may be precipitated in patients with only moderate left ventricular dysfunction when they are given disopyramide. This effect is especially likely to occur when patients are treated with both disopyramide and a β-blocker.

Disopyramide has a high bioavailability and achieves peak plasma concentrations within 2 hours following oral administration. Dosage adjustments are required with hepatic and renal dysfunction since renal clearance accounts for 50% of its elimination and hepatic metabolism the remainder. It cannot be emphasized too strongly that treatment with disopyramide should be avoided in persons with congestive heart failure. Therapeutic serum concentrations range from 2 to 5 µg/mL. The half-life varies within a range of from 4 to 10 hours, due to the drug's unique binding characteristics. Disopyramide exhibits its greatest binding affinity when plasma concentrations are low and a decreased degree of binding as plasma levels increase. This results in a marked increase in free or unbound disopyramide levels as the plasma concentration increases and is most likely responsible for the occurrence of toxicity seen with small dose changes.

Oral disopyramide is available in 100- and 150-mg capsules in both the regular formulation and a controlled-release preparation. The controlled-release preparation usually permits twice-a-day dosing rather than an every-6-hour regimen. The side effects associated with disopyramide are related to its anticholinergic effects and include blurred vision, dry mouth, urinary hesitancy, and constipation. Because of its anticholinergic effects, disopyramide should not be used with other anticholinergic agents or in patients with glaucoma, urinary retention, or urinary tract obstruction. This effect also limits its use in older men with benign prostatic hypertrophy. Concomitant administration with β-blockers or calcium blockers can further depress sinus node automaticity and myocardial function. Decreased serum levels occur with concomitant use of phenytoin and rifampin. The anticoagulant effect of warfarin is increased with concomitant disopyramide administration. There is no interaction with digoxin.

Class IB Agents

Lidocaine

Lidocaine is the prototype class IB agent and remains the drug of choice for ventricular arrhythmias during and following myocardial infarction. Lidocaine exhibits moderate protein binding but is only available in parenteral form because of a significant degree of first-pass metabolism. Intravenous administration is accompanied by a rapid onset of action, with cardiac effects occurring within 1 minute following administration. Lidocaine demonstrates two phases of elimination kinetics. Following an intravenous bolus, lidocaine is rapidly cleared from the bloodstream, with a half-life of 15 to 20 minutes. The half-life prolongs to at least

3 hours following chronic infusion. For this reason lidocaine is usually administered in several intravenous boluses, followed by an intravenous infusion. To achieve steady-state levels, several bolus regimens have been devised. One method is to administer lidocaine intravenously in a dose of approximately 75 mg given slowly over 3 to 5 minutes. After a 5-minute interval, 50 mg of lidocaine is again given over 3 to 5 minutes. Two further boluses of 50 mg each are given over 5 minutes, separated by 5 minutes. Thus the total loading dose of lidocaine for an average adult man is approximately 225 mg, given over 30 minutes. This bolus regimen is then followed by an infusion of lidocaine in a dose of 0.10 to 0.40 mg/kg/min. Side effects are related to the total dose administered and, more importantly during bolus injection, the rate of administration. Lidocaine levels are useful for guiding therapy. Typically, lidocaine concentrations rise following the first 12 hours of infusion and may require subsequent dosage adjustment. Therapeutic concentrations of lidocaine are 1.5 to 5 μg/mL. To achieve therapeutic concentrations with intramuscular injections, doses of 200 to 300 mg (4 mg/kg) are required.

Lidocaine, in contrast to other agents, exerts little effect on blood pressure or myocardial contractility. Since it is eliminated through hepatic metabolism, persons with myocardial or hepatic impairment require a 50% reduction in dosage to prevent toxicity. Decreased doses are also recommended in the elderly. Patients with renal failure do not require a dosage adjustment. Although side effects are brief in nature, they are primarily neurologic and may be severe. Side effects include drowsiness, paresthesia, muscle twitching, slurred speech, hallucinations, and drowsiness and progress to seizures and respiratory arrest. Conversely, lidocaine may also cause agitation, particularly in the elderly. These side effects are particularly unpleasant for the patient since they are long remembered. Because the half-life of lidocaine is short, the infusion may be interrupted and resumed at a decreased rate if high serum levels accumulate during infusion.

Since other class IB agents manifest similar neurologic side effect profiles, concomitant administration of lidocaine with these drugs should be avoided. Lidocaine concentrations are increased in the presence of cimetidine and drugs that decrease hepatic blood flow, such as β-blockers. Reduced lidocaine levels may occur in the presence of drugs such as phenobarbital due to augmented hepatic metabolism.

Mexiletine

Originally developed as an anticonvulsant agent, mexiletine is a congener of lidocaine that is used to treat ventricular arrhythmias including VPDs and ventricular tachycardia. Its hemodynamic and electrophysiologic profile is similar to that of lidocaine, and it also demonstrates negligible ECG effects. The efficacy of mexiletine for the suppression of ventricular tachycardia is generally less than that observed with the class IA drugs. As with the other class IB drugs, mexiletine has no role in the management of atrial arrhythmias. Although it suppresses VPDs and ventricular tachycardia in some patients when used alone, mexiletine is most useful when combined with a class IA drug. Mexiletine has been demonstrated to have a synergistic therapeutic effect when given with quinidine for the suppression of ventricular arrhythmias.

Mexiletine is available as 150-, 200-, and 250-mg capsules and is administered in doses of 150 to 400 mg orally every 8 hours. Approximately 90% of oral mexiletine reaches the systemic circulation, with peak blood levels occurring 1 to 2 hours following administration. Typically, mexiletine has a half-life of 10 to 12 hours, although it may range from 6 to 16 hours. Therapeutic serum concentrations range from 0.5 to 2.0 μg/mL. Although mexiletine is metabolized in the liver, unlike most other antiarrhythmic agents it is absorbed in the small intestine, has an initial distribution to organs with high blood flow (central compartment), such as the brain, heart, liver, and kidneys, and a subsequent large volume of distribution to less richly perfused organs, such as skeletal muscle (peripheral compartment). While renal impairment does not significantly prolong the half-life, hepatic dysfunction and decreased hepatic flow do. Drugs that delay gastric emptying, such as narcotics, will also decrease the absorption rate of mexiletine. Interactions of mexiletine with other medications are the same as described for lidocaine.

Mexiletine is associated with a 30% to 60% incidence of side effects, most of which are gastrointestinal or neurologic. The gastrointestinal side effects include nausea, anorexia, and epigastric distress, all of which can be minimized or eliminated by taking mexiletine with food or antacids. Neurologic side effects include paresthesia, dizziness, tremors, diplopia, drowsiness, confusion, sleep disturbances, personality changes, dysarthria, and, infrequently, seizures. The occurrence of side effects necessitates dosage reduction or discontinuation in approximately 30% of patients treated with mexiletine. Rarely, liver function abnormalities and the development of antinuclear antibodies may occur. In general, the side effects are not life threatening, and the incidence of proarrhythmia is very low.

Tocainide

Tocainide is an oral congener of lidocaine that is indicated for the treatment of life-threatening ventricular arrhythmias; its efficacy is somewhat less than that of quinidine or procainamide. Initially released for the treatment of symptomatic ventricular arrhythmias, the Food and Drug Administration (FDA)-approved indications for treatment with tocainide were subsequently modified to the treatment of life-threatening ventricular arrhythmias following recognition of the incidence of serious and sometimes fatal pulmonary fibrosis and hematologic disorders with tocainide use.

Tocainide is available in 400- and 600-mg tablets; 200 to 800 mg is usually administered every 8 to 12 hours, with peak plasma levels occurring approximately 1 hour after oral administration. While the half-life of tocainide is approximately 15 to 17 hours, a range of 9 to 37 hours has been reported. Therapeutic serum concentrations of tocainide are 4 to 10 μg/mL. Tocainide is metabolized by the liver, although approximately 40% is excreted through the kidneys. Its bioavailability is nearly 100%, and dosage adjustment is required in instances of hepatic and renal impairment. Unlike other drugs that undergo hepatic metabolism, tocainide plasma concentrations do not vary with concomitant administration of drugs that affect hepatic enzymes; therefore, there are negligible drug interactions.

The potentially fatal pulmonary fibrosis and hematologic disorders including leukopenia, agranulocytosis, or aplastic anemia necessitate careful follow-up care. Hematologic disorders are most commonly manifest during the first 3 months of therapy. Weekly hematology profiles are indicated during the first 3 months of therapy and subsequently every 3 months. Patients should be taught the signs and symptoms of impaired hematologic and respiratory function and instructed to notify their physician promptly should any symptoms occur. Laboratory profiles and chest x-rays are clinically indicated to evaluate whether discontinuation of treatment is advisable. Tocainide's neurologic side effects profile is similar to that of other class IB agents. Unlike other IB agents, however, tocainide may produce important negative inotropic effects, especially when given with β-blockers. Use of this drug in the presence of congestive heart failure is probably unwise.

Phenytoin

Phenytoin does not have an FDA-approved indication for arrhythmias and is not commonly administered. Although this drug has limited efficacy, it may suppress ventricular arrhythmias that do not respond to conventional therapy and has been used particularly in the treatment of digitalis-induced ventricular arrhythmias. Phenytoin is given intravenously in doses of 250 mg every 5 minutes up to a maximum of 1 g or 100 mg every 15 minutes until arrhythmias subside or 1 g has been given. Intravenous boluses of the drug may produce atrial and ventricular asystole; therefore, the drug should be given slowly when used intravenously. Phenytoin crystallizes in dextrose solutions and should only be administered with normal saline. Phenytoin may be administered orally in doses of 100 mg every 6 to 8 hours for chronic suppression of ventricular arrhythmias. The half-life of oral phenytoin is approximately 22 to 30 hours. Therapeutic serum levels range from 10 to 20 μg/mL. The adverse effects of phenytoin include ataxia, slurred speech and nystagmus, and gum hyperplasia with chronic therapy.

Class IC Agents

Flecainide

Flecainide was the first class IC agent approved for the treatment of ventricular arrhythmias. Initially used to suppress symptomatic VPDs and nonsustained ventricular arrhythmias, it is now approved only for life-threatening ventricular arrhythmias. Flecainide is known to be highly efficacious in suppressing VPDs and nonsustained ventricular tachycardia. Although it may suppress spontaneous ventricular arrhythmias, flecainide has limited efficacy in the treatment of sustained ventricular tachycardia as assessed with electrophysiologic testing. Application for a supraventricular tachycardia indication, to include AV nodal reentrant tachycardia, AV reentrant tachycardia, and paroxysmal atrial fibrillation and flutter, is pending FDA approval. It has a significant negative inotropic effect in the presence of impaired ventricular function. It may induce or exacerbate heart failure and should be used with caution in patients with left ventricular dysfunction. The electrophysiologic effects and electrocardiographic manifestations of flecainide administration are typical of the IC class. The clinical effects relate mainly to its ability to slow conduction of the inward sodium current. Mean increases in QRS duration that may approach 50% are directly linked to plasma levels. Flecainide has a high bioavailability, is moderately bound to plasma proteins, and reaches peak plasma levels 2 to 4 hours following oral administration. The mean half-life is approximately 20 hours, with elimination being via both hepatic metabolism and renal excretion. Flecainide is available in doses of 100 mg and is routinely administered every 12 hours. Daily doses are usually 100 to 400 mg/d. Therapeutic concentrations of flecainide range from 0.2 to 1.0 mg/L. The most common side effects related to flecainide are neurologic symptoms including dizziness, blurred vision, headache, nausea, and memory impairment. Like the other class IC drugs, flecainide may induce ventricular tachycardia in patients without a prior history of these arrhythmias. The ventricular tachycardia that is characteristic of the class IC drugs is often precipitated by exercise. Many centers perform routine exercise testing of patients who are receiving flecainide to evaluate the risk of proarrhythmia. Flecainide may raise pacing and defibrillation thresholds.

Encainide

Encainide remains approved for the treatment of life-threatening ventricular arrhythmias. Its efficacy in the treatment of sustained ventricular tachycardia is comparable to that of other class I agents. The efficacy of encainide in suppressing VPDs is significantly greater than that of quinidine, whereas its efficacy in treating sustained ventricular tachycardia is probably similar to that of quinidine. However, the vast majority of patients with sustained ventricular tachycardia will continue to have inducible arrhythmias on encainide therapy. Encainide gained widespread popularity following its clinical release for its high effectiveness in suppressing VPDs and nonsustained ventricular tachycardia. However, since the CAST results have become available, encainide use has dramatically declined. The drug is effective for atrial arrhythmias in many patients, though it is not approved for this indication.

In early controlled trials, encainide appeared to have only a mild negative inotropic action. However, later experience demonstrated that patients with impaired ventricular function are at risk for the development of congestive heart failure if given encainide. The incidence of proarrhythmia has been reported to be about 10% in the presence of poor left ventricular function. Encainide shares the same potential for proarrhythmia as described for flecainide. Similarly to flecainide, it can significantly suppress sinus node function in persons with preexisting sinus node dysfunction. While it is acknowledged that many antiarrhythmic agents increase pacing threshold to a small degree, encainide is also known to increase the ventricular defibrillation threshold.

Encainide has a high degree of bioavailability, achieving peak plasma concentration 1 to 2 hours following oral administration. It is available in 25-, 35-, and 50-mg capsules. Dosing is usually every 8 hours, but it may be administered as frequently as every 6 hours, or as infrequently as every 12 hours. Dose increases should be made after a minimum of 48 hours on a given dose because of the gradual increase in the levels of encainide's metabolites. Daily doses range from 50 to 200 mg/d. The variability in total daily doses of encainide given during chronic therapy is due to the presence of two metabolites that are more active than the parent compound: o-demethyl encainide (ODE), which is a more potent sodium channel blocker than encainide, and 3-methoxy-o-demethyl encainide (MODE), which is also active. Both metabolites are potent antiarrhythmic agents. The cytochrome P-450 pathway is utilized in encainide metabolism. In poor metabolizers the biotransformation of encainide to the MODE and ODE metabolites is markedly diminished, and levels of the parent encainide compound accumulate. The half-life of encainide in the poor metabolizer phenotype is increased to 6 to 11 hours. Extensive metabolizers with low encainide levels and high ODE and MODE levels demonstrate greater increases in QRS duration than do poor metabolizers, who have high encainide and low ODE and MODE levels. While the mean half-life of encainide is approximately 2 hours, the half-life of the ODE metabolite is approximately 3.5 hours, and the half-life of the MODE metabolite is 6 to 12 hours. While food delays absorption of encainide, its bioavailability is not changed. Therapeutic levels of encainide and its metabolites are generally considered to be 60 ng/mL for encainide, 200 ng/mL for the ODE metabolite, and 200 ng/mL for the MODE metabolite.

Adverse neurologic effects associated with encainide are dose related and include blurred vision, dizziness, and ataxia. Less frequently, patients may develop headache tremors. There have been rare reports of elevated liver enzymes and the occurrence of hyperglycemia and increased insulin requirements.

Propafenone

Propafenone possesses the electrophysiologic and electrocardiographic characteristics of IC drugs, but, unlike other IC agents, it prolongs refractoriness and exhibits both β-blocking and calcium-blocking activity. Its β-blocking effect is approximately a 40th that of propranolol, and its calcium-blocking effect is a 100th that of verapamil. Propafenone is approved in the United States for the treatment of life-threatening ventricular arrhythmias. It has been used extensively worldwide for the treatment of atrial arrhythmias and for the Wolff-Parkinson-White syndrome. Although propafenone is also associated with a negative inotropic effect in patients with preexisting left ventricular dysfunction, in our experience, propafenone has not depressed myocardial function to the same degree as flecainide or encainide.

Propafenone is available in 150- and 300-mg tablets, which are taken in divided doses three to four times daily for a cumulative dose of 450 to 900 mg. The dose of propafenone should not be increased at intervals more frequent than every 4 days. Doses in excess of 900 mg/d are not recommended. Limited safety and efficacy data on the 1200 mg/d dose have indicated a higher frequency of dose-related side effects and congestive heart failure. Propafenone is approximately 95% protein bound and demonstrates a high degree of bioavailability, which is increased when it is taken with food. Its bioavailability also increases with higher doses, probably due to saturation of first-pass hepatic metabolism, and accounts for the nonlinear dose-to-plasma level relationship seen with the drug. Thus significant increases in antiarrhythmic effect may occur with small increments in dosage. Elimination characteristics also exhibit variance, which is probably due to decreased hepatic extraction at higher doses. Propafenone achieves peak plasma concentrations with visible antiarrhythmic effects within 2 hours of administration. Propafenone is extensively metabolized in the liver, and at least three metabolites have been identified. The principal metabolite, 5-hydroxypropafenone (5-OHP), demonstrates antiarrhythmic activity and exerts a myocardial depressant effect in excess of that of the parent compound. A second major metabolite is N-depropylpropafenone (NDPP). The half-life of propafenone varies considerably but is generally acknowledged to be 6 to 7 hours; its principal metabolite 5-OHP is thought to have a longer half-life. Therapeutic plasma concentra-

tions of propafenone range from 200 to 1500 ng/mL. The 5-OHP metabolite level is usually measured and generally present in amounts equal to 25% to 30% of propafenone levels.

As mentioned with other drugs, propafenone is metabolized by the cytochrome P-450 hepatic enzyme pathway. Poor metabolizers maintain a high serum concentration of propafenone and a low level of the 5-OHP metabolite, whereas extensive metabolizers maintain a low propafenone level and a high 5-OHP concentration. Despite the higher doses of propafenone required for arrhythmia suppression in poor metabolizers, the degree of observed ECG changes, such as QRS widening and PR prolongation, is less than that observed with extensive metabolizers. The degree of β-blockade associated with propafenone is also subject to genetic factors, with poor metabolizers demonstrating significantly more β-blockade than extensive metabolizers.

Propafenone is known to increase digoxin levels in a dose-dependent manner. Digoxin levels are increased by approximately 35% with propafenone doses of 450 mg/d and by 85% with 900 mg/d. Drugs that compete with α-1 acid glycoprotein may alter free levels of propafenone. Concomitant administration of propafenone potentiates warfarin and enhances its anticoagulant effect, although concentrations of propafenone are not affected. Conversely, in the presence of cimetidine both propafenone and cimetidine levels are increased. However, in both instances the increased levels are not accompanied by increases in conduction intervals.

Propafenone is generally well tolerated. Side effects are limited in the vast majority of cases to gastrointestinal and neurologic symptoms including nausea, constipation, metallic taste, dizziness, and fatigue. Since propafenone undergoes such extensive hepatic metabolism, dosage adjustment is required in instances of impaired hepatic blood flow or hepatic dysfunction. For example, a 10% reduction in hepatic blood flow may double systemic bioavailability.

Moricizine

Moricizine is a phenothiazine derivative that is classified as a class I membrane-stabilizing drug because it has local anesthetic activity. It is not clearly identified with any one subgroup because it shares characteristics of the IB and IC subgroups. Moricizine (also known as ethmozine) shortens action potential duration and the effective refractory period, decreases phase 0 conduction velocity in a dose-dependent manner, and is not thought to significantly affect repolarization. Like IC agents, increases in the QTC with moricizine are primarily due to increases in the QRS duration with minimal change in the JT interval. Moricizine is approved for the treatment of life-threatening ventricular arrhythmias. In clinical trials, moricizine has demonstrated efficacy in the suppression of VPDs not only in manufacturer-sponsored trials but also in the National Institutes of Health (NIH)-sponsored Cardiac Arrhythmia Pilot Study. However, the preliminary results of CAST II (the moricizine vs. placebo arm of the trial) demonstrated that the treatment of VPDs with moricizine worsened mortality. Data on its use in ventricular tachycardia are more limited; its efficacy rate appears comparable to other class I agents. It has proven difficult to terminate and has responded to the administration of sodium bicarbonate.

Moricizine undergoes significant first-pass metabolism, is highly protein bound, and achieves peak plasma levels within 2 hours following oral administration. Two active metabolites, moricizine sulfoxide and phenothiazine-2-carbamic acid ethyl ester sulfoxide, have been identified but represent only a small portion of the total dose and have a mean half-life of 3 hours. The generally accepted mean half-life of moricizine is 3.5 hours, though limited data are available on half-life with chronic therapy. The elimination half-life in patients with arrhythmias ranges from 6.4 to 13.1 hours, with a mean of 10 hours, and is further prolonged in the presence of cimetidine. Moricizine is administered every 8 hours, and daily doses range from 450 to 900 mg.

Moricizine has not been demonstrated to increase digoxin levels, though it does have additive effects on the PR interval. Concomitant administration with phenothiazines and monoamine oxidase inhibitors is contraindicated. Moricizine is also contraindicated in patients with moderate to severe obstructive pulmonary disease and is thought to lower theophylline levels. Hemodynamically, moricizine appears to be well tolerated and does not significantly affect intracardiac pressures, stroke volume, or cardiac index when administered to patients with impaired left ventricular function. Reported adverse effects with moricizine are primarily related to its gastrointestinal and central nervous system effects and include dry mouth, dyspepsia, nausea, vomiting, diarrhea, abdominal discomfort, headache, fatigue, dyspnea, dizziness, lightheadedness, anxiety, euphoria, hyperesthesia, and sweating. Two reports of drug fever were confirmed (drug rechallenge) to be due to moricizine; liver enzyme elevation has also occurred.

Other Class I Agents

Class I agents currently under investigation include pirmenol, recainam, ajamaline, and bidisomide. Imipramine, a tricyclic antidepressant, exhibits class IA antiarrhythmic effects but was significantly less efficacious than flecainide, encainide, and moricizine in the Cardiac Arrhythmia Pilot Study, with only a 37% efficacy for suppression of VPDs.

CLASS II AGENTS

Class II drugs (β-blockers) are effective for the treatment of arrhythmias, angina, hypertension, and a variety of other conditions. A number of multicenter postinfarction trials have demonstrated the β-blocking drugs significantly decrease mortality following myocardial infarction, principally by preventing sudden cardiac death. β-Blockade may be protective by antagonizing the effects of β-adrenergic receptor stimulation of the heart, including increased automaticity, and shortening of the refractory period of atrial and ventricular muscle. Class II drugs slow conduction, prolong refractoriness, and decrease the rate of discharge of cardiac pacemaker cells. β-Blockers are an effective means of suppressing ectopic pacemaker activity and may be useful in the treatment of ectopic atrial tachycardia. β-Blockers reduce the ventricular response to atrial tachyarrhythmias by slowing AV nodal conduction. Thus these drugs enjoy a predominant role in the treatment of AV nodal reentrant tachycardia and orthodromic reciprocating tachycardia based on an accessory pathway. Class II drugs are also effective in a minority of patients for the suppression of both ventricular premature depolarizations and sustained ventricular tachycardia, particularly exercise-induced ventricular tachycardia. Prevention of ventricular fibrillation is thought to be due to the increased fibrillation threshold that occurs with β-blockade. Class II drugs exert a more homogeneous action on the heart than class I drugs and vary principally by whether they are selective for β_1 receptors in the heart, are lipid or water soluble, have membrane-stabilizing properties, or possess intrinsic sympathomimetic activity.

A complex relationship exists between β-blocking agents and their central nervous system activity. Type II drugs block sympathetic-mediated responses in the heart through β_1- and β_2-adrenergic receptor blockade. β_1 Receptors are located primarily in the heart, while β_2 receptors are located throughout the bronchopulmonary and peripheral vascular systems. Cardioselective β-blockers exert their action primarily on the β_1 receptors, with only a minimal effect on β_2 receptors. In addition to their cardiac effect, β_2 receptors increase airway resistance and peripheral vasoconstriction. Thus nonselective β-blockers such as propranolol may exacerbate asthma. Metoprolol, a cardioselective β-blocker, may be administered more safely. However, since the selectivity of β-blockers seen at lower doses is lost at high doses, they are contraindicated for patients known to have bronchospasm. β-Blockers that also possess β_2 receptor stimulation activity are referred to as having intrinsic sympathetic activity and may prevent the peripheral vasoconstriction observed with β_2 blockade.

The electrocardiographic manifestations of β-blockers include a decrease in both the resting and peak exercise heart rate and an increase in the PR interval. β-Blockers may have synergistic effects with the cardiac glycosides on the sinus and AV nodes. The most common side effect of β-blockers is sinus bradycardia. They may also potentiate the action of insulin and oral hypoglycemic agents and may mask sympathetically mediated signs of hypoglycemia. Treatment with nonselective β-blockers may be problematic due to associated increased airway resistance and peripheral vascular resistance. In terms of overall safety and efficacy, β-blocking drugs are probably associated with the lowest incidence of severe adverse effects of any of the antiarrhythmic agents. Adverse reactions are primarily caused by its effects on the sympathetic nervous system and commonly include decreased libido, impotence, fatigue, and depression. Impotence is more common with concurrent cardiovascular disorders associated with atherosclerosis of the peripheral vascular system. Since the β-blockers are metabolized in the liver, impaired hepatic function may require drug dosage adjustment. Lipid-soluble β-blockers undergo extensive hepatic metabolism and may be preferred in renal insufficiency.

β-Blockers with an FDA-approved indication for the treatment of both supraventricular and ventricular arrhythmias are limited to propranolol (a nonselective agent). Acebutolol (an agent with intrinsic sympathomimetic activity) is approved for ventricular arrhythmias, and esmolol (a cardioselective agent) is approved for supraventricular tachycardias, specifically atrial fibrillation and atrial flutter. Acebutolol's principal metabolite, diacetolol, manifests similar properties to acebutolol, but its half-life is three times that of acebutolol. Both propranolol and acebutolol are subject to significant first-pass hepatic metabolism.

Esmolol is an ultra-short-acting β-blocker that is only available in the intravenous form. Its half-life is approximately 9 minutes. When administered in doses of 50 to 300 μg/kg/min, at concentrations not to exceed 10 mg/mL, steady-state plasma levels are achieved within 5 minutes. Esmolol is indicated for the treatment of atrial fibrillation and atrial flutter when there is rapid ventricular response. In instances where conversion to sinus rhythm does not occur, treatment with esmolol permits short-term rate control that can be maintained for an extended period with a continuous infusion until other therapies achieve therapeutic effects.

CLASS III AGENTS

Class III agents such as amiodarone and sotalol selectively block sodium channels to prolong all phases of the action potential. The duration of refractoriness is prolonged, automaticity is reduced, excitability is decreased, and conduction is slowed by amiodarone. Torsades de pointes ventricular tachycardia is associated with these drugs and occurs because of prolongation of refractoriness. The QT interval is prolonged in a dose-dependent manner with class III drugs, as it is with class IA drugs.

Sotalol

Sotalol is a class III antiarrhythmic drug with important β-blocking properties. The oral and intravenous preparations of sotalol at the time of this writing remain investigational in the United States, although it has been available in Europe since the 1960s. Sotalol also manifests nonselective β-adrenergic blocking properties of approximately 50% the strength of propranolol's and without intrinsic sympathomimetic activity. Sotalol decreases the resting heart rate and blunts the peak heart rate achieved with exercise.

Daily oral doses of sotalol generally range from 160 to 480 mg administered in divided doses; however, daily doses of 640 mg have been reported. Peak plasma levels occur 2 to 3 hours following administration. Sotalol should be taken prior to meals, and dose increases should not be sooner than 3 to 4 days apart for patients with arrhythmias. The half-life of sotalol is usually 7 to 18 hours, with reported increases to 24.2 hours in the presence of decreased renal clearance. Patients with impaired conduction may experience AV block. In the presence of left ventricular dysfunction, sotalol further decreases cardiac output and may aggravate or precipitate congestive heart failure. Dosage adjustments are required when there is reduced elimination, which occurs in the setting of impaired left ventricular function or impaired renal function and in elderly patients who demonstrate a prolonged elimination time (as compared to younger patients). Sotalol has a bioavailability approaching 100%, a negligible

first-pass effect, and is not affected by impaired hepatic function. Electrocardiographic changes associated with sotalol are primarily related to an increased QT interval and PR prolongation. Torsades de pointes ventricular tachycardia has been observed with sotalol administration.

Common side effects associated with sotalol are due to its β-blocking effects and include lethargy, fatigue, decreased libido, and impotence. Potential adverse effects caused by nonselective β-blockade may occur, and the patient should be carefully monitored. These adverse effects are described in the section on class II antiarrhythmic drugs.

Amiodarone

Amiodarone is the most effective antiarrhythmic available to treat refractory ventricular and supraventricular arrhythmias. Initially marketed as an antianginal agent, the marked antiarrhythmic properties of amiodarone were only appreciated later. Although amiodarone has only been commercially available in the United States since 1986, it has been used in Europe for over 25 years. Despite its marked antiarrhythmic efficacy, the severity and frequency of its side effects limit its application to the setting of life-threatening ventricular arrhythmias that are refractory to other pharmacologic agents. The use of amiodarone has been shown to be associated with control of ventricular arrhythmias in most patients treated with the drug. While class I antiarrhythmic agents typically have an efficacy rate of 20% to 30% for life-threatening ventricular arrhythmias, numerous investigators have reported an efficacy rate associated with amiodarone in excess of 50%. However, only a minority of individuals can be maintained on amiodarone throughout a follow-up period of 5 years, an observation that is primarily related to the development of serious toxicity.

Amiodarone in combination with another antiarrhythmic agent in the class I category may suppress an arrhythmia when neither agent alone is effective. The role of electrophysiologic testing in guiding amiodarone therapy is not as clear as with other antiarrhythmic agents. For example, the induction of sustained ventricular tachycardia on a predischarge electrophysiologic test in a patient receiving amiodarone does not necessarily predict spontaneous recurrence of the arrhythmia. In fact, the available evidence suggests that despite persistent arrhythmia inducibility, many patients will have a favorable clinical outcome. However, electrophysiologic testing may provide a means to stratify patients into high, intermediate, and low risk for sudden death. For example, if ventricular tachycardia is not inducible on amiodarone, the risk of sudden death due to arrhythmia recurrence is decreased. If the cycle length of the tachycardia is increased by at least 100 milliseconds and is hemodynamically well tolerated, the risk of sudden death is lower than if a rapid or poorly tolerated ventricular tachycardia remains inducible.

Amiodarone is absorbed and metabolized by the liver. Abundantly distributed in adipose and muscle tissue at concentrations up to 30 times greater than the plasma concentration, amiodarone has a half-life of 16 to 65 days. Typically, amiodarone and N-desethylamiodarone levels fall significantly 30 to 45 days after discontinuation of therapy; however, the therapeutic effects of amiodarone may persist for up to 6 months after therapy has been discontinued. Adverse effects are generally dose dependent. Hemodynamically, amiodarone is well tolerated and is associated with no significant negative inotropic effect. Amiodarone is known to decrease coronary and peripheral vascular resistance, resulting in a decrease in myocardial oxygen consumption and an increase in coronary blood flow.

Electrocardiographic manifestions of amiodarone include QT prolongation, depression of sinus node automaticity, and increases in the PR interval and QRS duration. These changes occur because amiodarone prolongs the duration of the action potential and of refractoriness due to a decrease in potassium conductance across the cell membrane during the plateau phase (phase 2). Both the atrial and ventricular refractory periods are markedly increased. Amiodarone affects depolarization to a smaller extent and does not alter the amplitude of the action potential or the resting membrane potential. As with other antiarrhythmic agents that prolong the QT interval, the development of torsades de pointes ventricular tachycardia is

possible. However, monitoring the QT interval is less predictive of torsades de pointes in patients receiving amiodarone than in patients treated with class IA drugs. Amiodarone depresses automaticity of the sinus node and may be associated with sinus bradycardia, sinoatrial block, and sinus arrest. The bradycardia associated with amiodarone usage is often resistant to treatment with atropine. The striking depression of sinus node function results in the requirement for permanent pacemaker implantation in up to 10% of patients treated with amiodarone.

The extremely long half-life and propensity for tissue binding of amiodarone result in a very long interval from initiation of therapy to achievement of steady-state concentrations. This is managed clinically by the use of high initial loading doses, with gradual reduction of the dose over time. A common loading regimen is 400 mg every 6 hours for 7 days. A repeat electrophysiologic test is usually performed between 10 to 14 days. Unless the patient demonstrates hemodynamically unstable ventricular tachycardia that requires additional drug or device therapy, he or she is discharged from the hospital on the drug. If the arrhythmia is life threatening, most patients require 600 mg/d of amiodarone for the first month of therapy. Outpatient dosage adjustments are guided by serum concentrations, Holter monitoring, and patient examination. At 6 weeks the dose can usually be decreased to 400 mg/d. Most patients treated with amiodarone for life-threatening ventricular arrhythmias can be maintained on a dose of 300 mg/d. If the arrhythmia being treated is not life threatening, a lower dose of amiodarone is usually used, sometimes as low as 100 mg/d. Patients who receive implantable defibrillators may be managed with low doses of amiodarone therapy to prevent repeated defibrillation shocks.

Meticulous, comprehensive follow-up of patients receiving amiodarone is required to recognize the development of toxic side effects. This follow-up is time consuming and financially burdensome. Upon initiating therapy, a baseline laboratory profile for the patient is established. A battery of tests, including laboratory analysis of renal, liver, and thyroid function, a chest x-ray, ECG, pulmonary function tests, Holter recording, and a radionuclide gated ejection fraction (MUGA) study, is performed. Repeat tests at the time of scheduled follow-up include laboratory analysis of renal, liver, and thyroid function, an ECG, and a chest radiograph at 1 month and then every 3 months following discharge. At each follow-up visit the patient receives a thorough history and physical. The patient is specifically questioned for symptoms suggesting the recurrence of arrhythmias, the development of respiratory impairment, altered levels of energy or fatigue, neurologic symptoms, or altered hepatic function. If properly educated, the patient or the patient's family can often recognize symptoms associated with the side effects of amiodarone, so that they can be reported in a timely fashion. The ECG is monitored for changes indicative of a pharmacologic effect, and serum drug levels are used to guide dosing. Laboratory profiles are monitored for the development of a chemical hepatitis or abnormalities of thyroid function.

Neurologic toxicity is manifested as tremors, ataxia, or paresthesias. Patients frequently manifest increased sun sensitivity and are encouraged to avoid unnecessary exposure, wear protective clothing, and use sun screens. A bluish skin discoloration, clearly related to sun exposure, may develop during extended treatment. Bilateral corneal microdeposits are a frequent occurrence associated with amiodarone therapy. However, these deposits do not usually impair vision. Patients may complain of a sense of dryness of the eyes or may see halos around bright lights. These side effects usually respond to dosage reduction. Routine chest x-rays often demonstrate the early phase of potentially fatal pulmonary infiltrates that may necessitate discontinuation of the drug and corticosteroid treatment. The pulmonary infiltrates are characterized pathologically by interstitial fibrosis, foamy macrophages in the alveolar spaces, and hyperplasia of type II pneumocytes. Pulmonary function tests demonstrate a decreased diffusion capacity for carbon monoxide.

Amiodarone interferes with the metabolism of numerous compounds, thereby enhancing their pharmacologic effects. The combined use of digoxin and amiodarone has been associated with marked increases in digoxin levels. Generally, upon initiation of amiodarone therapy the digoxin dose is decreased by 50%. Concomitant administration of amiodarone and anticoagulants increases the prothrombin time by 50% to 100%. The recommended decrease in warfarin dose is approximately 50%. Amiodarone also increases procainamide, quinidine, flecainide, aprindine (no longer commercially available in the U.S.), and phenytoin levels. In contrast, cholestyramine use typically decreases amiodarone levels.

While not generally used for the management of preexcitation syndromes because of its side effects profile, amiodarone prolongs the effective refractory periods of accessory bypass tracts in both the antegrade and retrograde directions.

Bretylium Tosylate

Bretylium is employed in the short-term management of ventricular tachycardia and ventricular fibrillation. The drug is especially useful for ventricular arrhythmias resulting from acute coronary ischemia or infarction. Bretylium has minimal effects on conduction velocity or refractory periods. The major action of the drug appears to involve an increase in the ventricular fibrillation threshold. Bretylium may be administered as a bolus in doses of 5 mg/kg and may be increased to 10 mg/kg followed by an infusion of 1 to 2 mg/min. Intramuscular injections of bretylium are also possible. Intravenous bretylium exhibits a rapid onset of action, usually within 5 minutes, and a variable half-life ranging from 4 to 17 hours. Bretylium is not metabolized and is excreted unchanged by the kidneys. The most common side effect associated with bretylium is hypotension. Prolonged orthostatic hypotension develops in most patients receiving an intravenous infusion of bretylium that is related to the depletion of norepinephrine from postganglionic nerve terminals. This may also lead to an increased sensitivity to exogenous catecholamines.

INVESTIGATIONAL CLASS III AGENTS

Sematilide, an analogue of procainamide, is an investigational class III agent. The electrophysiologic action of sematilide is similar to that of N-acetyl procainamide. Sematilide has been associated with the potential for development of torsades de pointes ventricular tachycardia. It appears to exert a minimal negative inotropic effect, and its oral and intravenous preparations are well tolerated. Sematilide has been associated with the development of a drug-induced lupus syndrome in one patient who had previous developed lupus on procainamide therapy. Allergic reactions to procainamide are considered contraindications to sematilide therapy. Other investigational class III agents include dofetilde, risotilide, tedisamil, and clofilium.

CLASS IV AGENTS

Class IV agents, referred to as calcium channel blockers, block the slow inward calcium current. Calcium channel blockers, in contrast to other categories of antiarrhythmic agents, exhibit heterogenous electrophysiologic properties. Calcium blockers such as verapamil and diltiazem exert an antiarrhythmic effect by depressing the automaticity of slow-response fibers such as the sinus node, AV node, and injured cells by slowing conduction and decreasing the slope of phase 4 of the action potential. Their principal antiarrhythmic usefulness lies in the degree to which they slow AV nodal conduction or block impulse transmission through the AV node. Supraventricular tachycardias utilizing the sinus or AV nodes as part of a reentrant circuit, or those based on automaticity related to the slow calcium current, may be markedly slowed or interrupted by the administration of calcium channel blockers.

Administration of verapamil is contraindicated in most episodes of ventricular tachycardia. In patients with atrial fibrillation and rapid antegrade conduction over an accessory bypass tract, administration of calcium blockers can cause the impulse to block in the AV node and increase the ventricular rate by preventing retrograde concealed conduction in the accessory pathway. Since the ventricles are activated by an accessory pathway that is freed of the retrograde

concealed conduction imposed by activation over the AV node, ventricular fibrillation may ensue. Unfortunately, this scenario continues to occur by the improper use of intravenous verapamil. A more common adverse effect of verapamil administration occurs when the drug is given to patients in sustained ventricular tachycardia. In these patients, verapamil produces vasodilatation, resulting in hypotension and shock. Thus verapamil should be used with extreme caution in patients with a wide QRS complex tachycardia unless it is certain that the arrhythmia is supraventricular with a bundle branch block.

Calcium blockers effectively terminate AV nodal reentrant tachycardia. The drug may be safely administered to patients with AV nodal reentry or orthodromic reciprocating tachycardia. Although verapamil depresses the ventricular response to atrial fibrillation or flutter by its action on the AV node, the drug is only rarely used for this purpose. Verapamil is especially useful in patients with multifocal atrial tachycardia and some instances of ectopic atrial tachycardia. In patients with these arrhythmias, an intravenous infusion of verapamil in a dose of 0.1 to 0.2 mg/min is often effective. The intravenous preparation of diltiazem is pending FDA approval at the time of this writing. Nifedepine and nicardipine have few electrophysiologic properties and are not useful as antiarrhythmic agents.

Verapamil and diltiazem share many similarities. Both are 90% protein bound, are extensively metabolized in the liver, and have a half-life of 3 to 5 hours. Both drugs are available in a sustained-release preparation, which facilitates compliance. Intravenous verapamil has a rapid onset of action, usually within 2 to 3 minutes, with effects subsiding after approximately 20 minutes. Verapamil is administered intravenously in increments of 5 to 10 mg given every 2 minutes until the tachycardia is terminated. The bolus may be repeated 30 minutes later if required. Monitoring of the ECG and blood pressure response is necessary following each bolus. When there is no significant change in the arrhythmia following administration of an intravenous calcium channel blocker, the clinical situation should be reevaluated.

CLASS V AGENTS

Class V agents include digitalis glycosides and anticholinergic drugs that affect membrane responsiveness, action potential, and refractoriness.

Digoxin

Digoxin is indicated for the treatment of atrial fibrillation and flutter, supraventricular tachycardias whose mechanism of conduction involves the AV node, and atrial tachycardias. Digoxin may be used alone or in combination therapy with β-blockers, calcium blockers, or with type I or III antiarrhythmic drugs to control the ventricular response, decrease ectopic automaticity, and maintain sinus rhythm following cardioversion. Digoxin slows conduction and increases the refractory period in the AV node but causes a slight increase in conduction

velocity in atrial and ventricular tissue. The effects of digitalis are enhanced in the setting of hypokalemia. Thus caution should be used when this drug is administered to patients receiving concomitant therapy with diuretics. Hypercalcemia and hypoxia may also enhance the effect of digoxin and lead to toxicity. These states enhance excitability of latent pacemaker and ectopic pacemaker cells by altering the slope of phase 4. More pronounced effects of enhanced automaticity occur due to sympathetic stimulation in the presence of high serum concentrations. Digoxin is known to have a narrow window between its therapeutic and toxic effects, which decreases in size in a linear manner with age. Digitalis toxicity may produce a wide variety of arrhythmias, often based on triggered activity and delayed afterdepolarizations. Unusual cardiac arrhythmias such as bidirectional ventricular tachycardia (Figure 5-1), fascicular tachycardia, or ectopic atrial tachycardia may occur as a result of digitalis toxicity. Ven-

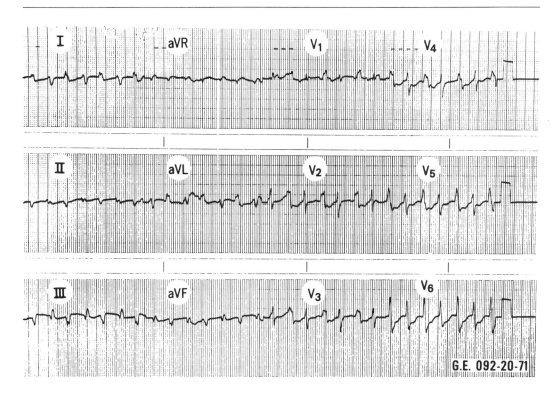

Figure 5-1 Bidirectional ventricular tachycardia related to digitalis intoxication. There is an alternating axis of the QRS morphology from one beat to the next. This patient had digitalis intoxication and developed ventricular fibrillation. This patient was successfully treated with antidigitalis antibodies.

tricular fibrillation that is incessant and resistant to treatment may result from digitalis toxicity.

Therapeutic digoxin levels range from 0.5 to 2.0 ng/mL. Digoxin is eliminated through the kidneys, and dosage adjustments are required when there is congestive heart failure or renal failure due to an increased elimination time. Dosage reductions are also required with the concomitant administration of drugs that interact with digoxin to increase serum digoxin levels, which may result in toxicity at normal doses. Digoxin levels are increased in the presence of amiodarone, flecainide, propafenone, quinidine, verapamil, and aminoglycosides. The half-life of digoxin is approximately 35 to 40 hours, and loading regimens are required to achieve rapid therapeutic effects. A variety of loading regimens for intravenous and oral dosing may be employed, with consideration given to the body surface area and age of the person. A common intravenous loading regimen is the delivery of a total dose of 1.25 mg administered in boluses of 0.75 mg initially, followed by 0.25 mg 2 hours later, and an additional dose of 0.25 mg repeated at 4 hours. Therapeutic effects with intravenous administration are observed at approximately 1 to 2 hours.

Early signs of digitalis toxicity include gastrointestinal effects and visual disturbances. Common gastrointestinal complaints include anorexia, nausea, vomiting, and abdominal discomfort. Reported visual disturbances include flickering lights, blurred vision, yellow borders around objects, and colored dots in the visual field. Patients may also complain of restlessness, irritability or fatigue, and headaches; elderly patients may become confused or disoriented. Acute digitalis intoxication is best treated with antidigoxin antibodies.

Atropine

Atropine is an anticholinergic agent that increases the heart rate by blocking parasympathetic stimulation of the sinus and AV nodes. Atropine shortens the action potential duration and the effective refractory period without altering membrane responsiveness. In the presence of bradycardia and hypotension, atropine may increase the cardiac output and blood pressure. Failure of the heart rate to increase with atropine administration may be due to either an insufficient dosage, too slow administration, or the site of heart block. While atropine improves block in the AV node, it can worsen block occurring in the His bundle or bundle branches. Atropine should not be administered to patients with narrow-angle glaucoma since it increases intraocular pressure. Atropine also causes urinary retention, dry mouth, and blurred vision.

Adenosine

Adenosine is highly efficacious for terminating AV nodal reentrant tachycardia or orthodromic reciprocating tachycardia utilizing an accessory pathway, due to its effects on AV nodal conduction. Adenosine significantly decreases the velocity of conduction through the AV node. In AV nodal reentrant tachycardia adenosine is believed to block conduction in the slow antegrade pathway, and in supraventricular tachycardia due to a concealed retrograde accessory pathway, to block antegrade conduction in the AV node. Adenosine will not terminate atrial flutter, but because adenosine slows conduction in the AV node, flutter waves may be observed that had been obscured at faster ventricular rates.

At this point, adenosine is the treatment of choice for AV nodal reentrant tachycardia and orthodromic reciprocating tachycardia. Its ultrashort half-life (approximately 10 seconds) allows interruption of these arrhythmias without a persistent hemodynamic effect. Adenosine is administered intravenously in a dose of 6 mg initially. If the tachycardia is not terminated, a repeat bolus of 12 mg is administered. Adenosine should be administered as rapidly as possible because of its short half-life, so that sufficient concentrations are present to achieve a therapeutic effect.

Adenosine causes sinus bradycardia due to its negative chronotropic response on the sinus node and may cause sinus arrest, AV block, and reflex sinus tachycardia secondary to vasodilatation. Other side effects include headache, flushing, malaise, nausea, and coughing. Reflex tachycardia is associated with slow administration. Aminophylline is a competitive antagonist of adenosine, and its concurrent administration effectively inhibits the action of adenosine.

BIBLIOGRAPHY

Arnsdorf MF, Wasserstrom JA. Mechanism of action of antiarrhythmic drugs: A matrical approach. In: Fozzard HA, Haber E, Jennings RB, et al, eds. *The Heart and Cardiovascular System Scientific Foundations*. New York, NY: Raven Press; 1986:1259–1316.

β-blocker Heart Attack Trial Research Group: A randomized trial of propanolol in patients with acute myocardial infarction 1. mortality results. *JAMA*. 1982;247(12): 1707–1714.

Borgeat A, Gay J, Maendly R. Flecainide versus quinidine for conversion of atrial fibrillation to sinus rhythm. *Am J Cardiol*. 1986;58:496–498.

The CAPS Investigators. Effects of encainide, flecainide, imipramine and moricizine on ventricular arrhythmias during the year after acute myocardial infarction: The CAPS. *Am J Cardiol*. 1988;61:501–509.

The Cardiac Arrhythmia Suppression Trial Investigators. Preliminary report: effect of encainide and flecainide on mortality in a randomized trial of arrhythmia suppression after myocardial infarction. *N Engl J Med*. 1989; 321:406–412.

Chobanian AV, Taylor SH. A symposium: beta blockade, cardioselectivity, and intrinsic sympathomimetic activity. *Am J Cardiol*. 1987;59:1F–54F.

Connolly SJ, Kates RE, Lesback CS, et al. Clinical pharmacology of propafenone. *Circulation*. 1983;68: 589–596.

DiMarco JP, Sellers TD, Berne RM, et al. Adenosine: electrophysiologic effects and therapeutic use for terminating paroxysmal supraventricular tachycardia. *Circulation*. 1983;68:1254–1263.

DiMarco JP, Sellers TD, Lerman BB, et al. Diagnostic and therapeutic use of adenosine in patients with supraventricular tachyarrhythmias. *J Am Coll Cardiol*. 1985;6:417–425.

Epstein AE, Kay GN, Plumb VJ. Considerations in the diagnosis and treatment of arrhythmias in patients with end-stage renal disease. *Semin Dialysis*. 1989;2:31–37.

Falk RA, Knowlton AA, Bernard SA, et al. Digoxin for converting recent onset atrial fibrillation to sinus rhythm. *Ann Intern Med*. 1987;106:503–506.

Fogoros RN. Amiodarone-induced refractoriness to cardioversion. *Ann Intern Med*. 1984;100:699–700.

Funck-Brentano C, Kroemer HK, Lee JT. Drug therapy: propafenone. *New Engl J Med*. 1990;332A:518–525.

Gilman AG, Goodman LS, Rall TW, Murad F. *The Pharmacologic Basis of Therapeutics*. 7th ed. New York, NY: MacMillan Publishing Co; 1985.

Gundersen T. Secondary prevention after myocardial infarction: Subgroup analysis of patients at risk in the Norwegian timolol multicenter study. *Clin Cardiol*. 1985; 8:253–265.

Heger JJ, Prystowsky EN, Miles WM, et al. Clinical use and pharmacology of amiodarone. *Med Clin North Am*. 1984;68:1339–1365.

Horowitz LN. Drugs and proarrhythmia. In: Zipes DP, Rowlands DJ, eds. *Progress in Cardiology*. Philadelphia, Pa: Lea & Febiger; 1988;1–1:109–125.

Kay GN, Epstein AE, Kirklin JK, et al. Fatal postoperative amiodarone pulmonary toxicity. *Am J Cardiol*. 1988;62:490–492.

Kay GN, Plumb VJ, Arciniegas JG, et al. Torsades de pointes: the long-short initiating sequence and other observations in 32 patients. *J Am Coll Cardiol*. 1983;2:806.

Kennedy JI, Myers JL, Plumb VJ, et al. Amiodarone pulmonary toxicity. *Arch Intern Med*. 1987;147:50–55.

Kunze KP, Schluter M, Kuck KH. Sotalol in patients with Wolff-Parkinson-White syndrome. *Circulation*. 1987; 75:1050–1057.

Lee JT, Kroemer HK, Silberstein DJ, et al. The role of genetically determined polymorphic drug metabolism in the beta-blockade produced by propafenone. *New Engl J Med*. 1990;322:1764–1768.

Lichstein E. Why do beta-receptor blockers decrease mortality after myocardial infarction? *J Am Coll Cardiol*. 1985;6:973–975.

Ludmer PL, McGowan NE, Antman EM, et al. Efficacy of propafenone in Wolff-Parkinson-White syndrome: electrophysiologic findings and long-term follow-up. *J Am Coll Cardiol*. 1987;9:1357–1363.

Mann DL, Maisel AS, Atwood JE, et al. Absence of cardioversion-induced ventricular arrhythmias in patients with therapeutic digoxin levels. *J Am Coll Cardiol*. 1985;5:882–888.

Marchlinski FE, Gansler TS, Waxman HL, et al. Amiodarone pulmonary toxicity. *Ann Intern Med*. 1982;97:839–845.

Mason JW. Amiodarone. *N Engl J Med*. 1987;316:455–466.

McGovern B, Garan H, Ruskin JN. Precipitation of cardiac arrest by verapamil in patients with Wolff-Parkinson-White syndrome. *Ann Intern Med*. 1986;104:791–793.

Multicenter International Study: Improvement in prognosis of myocardial infarction by long-term beta-adrenoreceptor blockade using practolol. *British Med J*. 1975;3:735–740.

Myerburg RJ, Kessler KM, Zaman L. Pharmacologic approaches to management of arrhythmias in patients with cardiomyopathy and heart failure. *Am Heart J*. 1987; 114:1273–1279.

Nordin C. Basic relationships between congestive heart failure and ventricular arrhythmias. *Heart Failure*. 1986, pp. 256–269.

Norwegian Multicenter Study Group: Timolol-induced reduction in mortality and reinfarction in patients surviving acute myocardial infarction. *N Engl J Med*. 1981; 304:801–807.

Parmley WW. Factors causing arrhythmias in chronic congestive heart failure. *Am Heart J*. 1987;114:1267–1272.

Pratt C, Lichstein E. Ventricular antiarrhythmic effects of beta-adrenergic blocking drugs: a review of mechanism and clinical studies. *J Clin Pharmacol*. 1982;22:335–347.

Prystowsky EN, Greer GS, Packer DL, et al. Beta blocker therapy in the Wolff-Parkinson-White syndrome. *Am J Cardiol*. 1987;60:460.

Prystowsky EN, Klein GJ, Rinkenerger RL, et al. Clinical efficacy and electrophysiologic effects of encainide in patients with Wolff-Parkinson-White syndrome. *Circulation*. 1984;69:278–287.

Rae AP, Kay HR, Horowitz LN, et al. Proarrhythmic effects of antiarrhythmic drugs in patients with malignant ventricular arrhythmias evaluated by electrophysiologic testing. *J Am Coll Cardiol*. 1988;12:131–139.

Roth A, Harrison E, Mitani G, et al. Efficacy and safety of medium- and high-dose diltiazem alone and in combination with digoxin for control of heart rate at rest and during exercise in patients with chronic atrial fibrillation. *Circulation*. 1986;73:316–324.

Sellers TD, Campbell RW, Bashore TM, et al. Effects of procainamide and quinidine sulfate in the Wolff-Parkinson-White syndrome. *Circulation*. 1977;55:15–22.

Singh BN, Venkatesh N. Prevention of myocardial reinfarction and of sudden death in survivors of acute myocardial infarction: role of prophylactic β-adrenoreceptor blockade. *Am Heart J*. 1984;107:189–200.

Smith WM, Lubbe WF, Whitlock RM, et al. Long-term tolerance of amiodarone treatment for cardiac arrhythmias. *Am J Cardiol*. 1986;57:1288–1293.

Steinberg JS, Katz RJ, Bren GB, et al. Efficacy of oral diltiazem to control ventricular response in chronic atrial fibrillation at rest and during exercise. *J Am Coll Cardiol*. 1987;9:405–411.

Velebit V, Podrid P, Lown B, et al. Aggravation and provocation of ventricular arrhythmias by antiarrhythmic drugs. *Circulation*. 1982;65:886–894.

Wellens HJJ, Braat S, Brugada P, et al. Use of procainamide in patients with the Wolff-Parkinson-White syndrome to disclose a short refractory period of the accessory pathway. *Am J Cardiol*. 1982;50:1087–1089.

Woosley Raymond L. Pharmacokinetics and pharmacodynamics of antiarrhythmic agents in patients with congestive heart failure. *Am Heart J*. 1987;114:1280–1290.

Yusuf S, Petro R, Lewis J, et al. Beta blockade during and after myocardial infarction: an overview of the randomized trials. *Prog Cardiovasc Dis*. 1985;27:335–71.

Chapter 6

Supraventricular
Tachycardias

INTRODUCTION

Supraventricular tachycardias are common arrhythmias that are encountered in both inpatient and outpatient settings. These arrhythmias may occur at any stage in life, with many demonstrating characteristic ages of onset. Although usually not life threatening, supraventricular tachycardias are often markedly symptomatic and can interfere with both life-style and overall sense of well-being. These arrhythmias are usually characterized by a narrow QRS complex, but they may be conducted aberrantly, leading to their common misinterpretation as ventricular tachycardia. The treatment of supraventricular tachycardias has evolved with advances in catheter ablation and surgery. In this chapter the mechanisms, diagnostic evaluation, and current management of these arrhythmias will be discussed in detail. In keeping with current trends in the management of supraventricular tachycardias, we will emphasize nonpharmacologic approaches to treatment.

OVERVIEW OF MECHANISMS INVOLVED IN SUPRAVENTRICULAR TACHYCARDIAS

Supraventricular tachycardias may arise in the atrium, in the AV node and perinodal tissues, or

involve both the atria and the ventricles with conduction over an accessory AV connection. The careful characterization of the mechanism and conduction pathways involved in the genesis of these arrhythmias is crucial to their effective management. Arrhythmias that involve only the atrial myocardium without a requirement for intact AV conduction can be grouped as primary atrial arrhythmias. These tachycardias include ectopic atrial tachycardia, multifocal atrial tachycardia, atrial fibrillation, and atrial flutter. Primary atrial arrhythmias may arise from a single focus in the atrial myocardium or involve reentrant conduction pathways that are confined to the atria. For practical purposes, primary atrial tachycardias are diagnosed when the atrial rate is faster than the ventricular rate. This usually occurs because of physiologic AV nodal block related to the pathologically rapid atrial rate.

Tachycardias that have been traditionally referred to as paroxysmal atrial tachycardia (PAT) are characterized by episodic rapid palpitations and include AV nodal reentrant tachycardia and reentrant arrhythmias involving accessory AV pathways. Arrhythmias utilizing accessory AV pathways as part of the reentrant circuit are characterized by the requirement that both the atria and ventricles be involved in the tachycardia, with sequential activation of these chambers. In many, but not all, patients with accessory AV connections, a characteristic short PR interval and widened QRS with a slurred onset known as a delta wave may be present during sinus rhythm.

SINUS TACHYCARDIA

Sinus tachycardia is usually observed as a physiologic response to increased sympathetic stimulation and parasympathetic withdrawal. The mechanism of this rhythm is enhanced automaticity of the sinus node. Sinus tachycardia occurs with exercise, anxiety or emotional stimulation, or as a consequence of abnormal metabolic demand such as fever, hypovolemia, anemia, thyrotoxicosis, drugs, or peripheral AV shunting. Sinus tachycardia may be slowed slightly by carotid massage but rapidly returns to its spontaneous rate. Pacing or cardioversion does not terminate sinus tachycardia. Because it is a normal physiologic response, sinus tachycardia itself should rarely be treated. The primary therapy for this rhythm is correction of the underlying clinical disorder.

In unusual patients, sinus tachycardia may be a manifestation of a disordered autonomic nervous system, a condition known as dysautonomia. In this disorder, the sinus tachycardia is inappropriate for the patient's metabolic demands and may be a source of symptomatic palpitations. Patients with dysautonomia often exhibit other manifestations of exaggerated sympathetic tone such as diaphoresis and anxiety, or may demonstrate inappropriate responses to changes in posture with orthostatic hypotension. Treatment with β-blockers may be appropriate for those rare individuals with inappropriate sinus tachycardia.

A pathologic form of sinus tachycardia based on the mechanism of reentry involving the sinus node may also occur. In contrast to physiologic sinus tachycardia, which is based on enhanced automaticity, sinus node reentry involves a circuit within or around the sinus node. This tachycardia utilizes the sinus node and perinodal atrial fibers as components of a reentrant circuit. It is a very rare arrhythmia that is manifested by paroxysmal episodes of rapid palpitations, with abrupt onset and offset of the tachycardia. Sinus node reentry can be distinguished from physiologic sinus tachycardia by its faster rate, abrupt onset and offset, termination by carotid sinus massage or intravenous adenosine, and inducibility and termination by pacing. The ECG demonstrates a P wave morphology identical to that of sinus rhythm. However, the PR interval may lengthen during sinus node reentrant tachycardia, and AV Wenckebach block may be observed. Treatment of sinus node reentry involves the use of antiarrhythmic drugs that affect either the sinus node itself (calcium blockers, β-blockers, digoxin) or the perinodal atrial myocardium (class I antiarrhythmic agents).

ECTOPIC ATRIAL TACHYCARDIA

Ectopic atrial tachycardias may arise from foci anywhere in the atrial myocardium (Figure 6-1). The distinguishing feature of ectopic atrial tachycardia from analysis of the 12-lead ECG is an abnormal P wave morphology. This P wave axis depends on where the abnormal focus is located within the atria. Tachycardias arising in the right atrium are usually associated with a P wave that is inverted in lead aVR and upright in leads I and aVL (Figure 6-2).

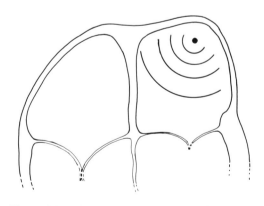

Figure 6-1 A diagrammatic representation of an ectopic atrial tachycardia focus arising in the high left atrium is shown. Note that the focus does not involve the ventricles or the AV conduction system but is a primary arrhythmia arising in the atrium. The tachycardia focus is usually quite small and results in a wavefront of activation that spreads radially from the site of origin.

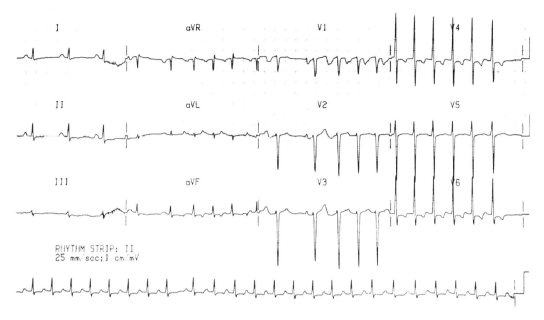

Figure 6-2 The figure demonstrates bursts of ectopic atrial tachycardia with a P wave morphology that is similar though not identical to the sinus P wave morphology. Note that in lead aVR the P wave is inverted, suggesting that the axis of activation is from the right toward the left atrium. Also, note that in lead aVL the P wave is upright. However, in lead aVF the P wave is inverted, suggesting inferior to superior activation of the atrium. This patient was subsequently found to have a right atrial ectopic tachycardia focus that was successfully ablated with surgery.

Tachycardias arising in the left atrium usually manifest a P wave that is inverted in leads I and aVL and that has an upright deflection in lead aVR (Figure 6-3).

Since the atrial rate exceeds the physiologic demands of the patient, AV Wenckebach block is commonly observed during ectopic atrial tachycardia (Figure 6-4). Ectopic atrial tachycardia may be confidently diagnosed when there is an abnormal P wave axis and evidence of AV block during the tachycardia. A distinct clinical syndrome may occur as a consequence of incessant atrial tachycardia that is manifested by development of a dilated cardiomyopathy and congestive heart failure. This tachycardia-induced cardiomyopathy is completely reversible upon control of the arrhythmia.

Two distinct clinical forms of ectopic atrial tachycardia are observed, depending on the age of the individual. The most common presentation of ectopic atrial tachycardia is that of an incessant arrhythmia beginning in childhood or young adult life. The mechanism of this arrhythmia is most likely to be related to abnormal automaticity (or triggered activity). The atrial rate demonstrates a gradual acceleration with exercise and emotion, and it may slow during sleep. A wide range of tachycardia rates is possible throughout a 24-hour period. Carotid sinus massage often produces AV block with little change in the atrial rate.

Treatment of automatic ectopic atrial tachycardia with antiarrhythmic drugs is notoriously ineffective. Pacing and cardioversion are ineffective for treating ectopic atrial tachycardia in most children and young adults because of the automatic mechanism. Occasional patients may respond to β-blockers or verapamil, though usually these drugs produce only a slowing of the atrial rate and enhanced AV block. Flecainide has been effective in some children with this arrhythmia. Many if not most patients with automatic ectopic atrial tachycardias will not be effectively managed with medications, and non-pharmacologic therapy will need to be considered. We have successfully used catheter ablation and open heart surgery to destroy the abnormal atrial focus and permanently cure these arrhythmias, with uniform success. With these procedures, the abnormal atrial focus is

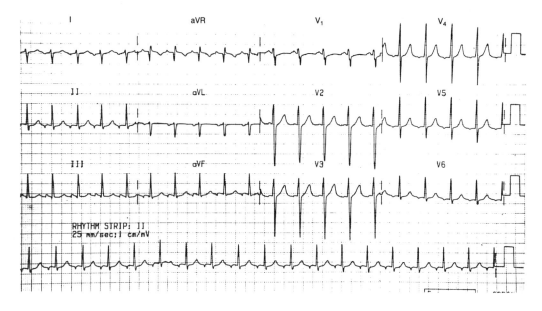

Figure 6-3 An ectopic atrial tachycardia arising in the left atrium is demonstrated. The ectopic atrial tachycardia is associated with an unusual P wave morphology and a P wave axis that is inverted in leads I and aVL and upright in lead aVR. This suggests that the P wave vector is from the left atrium toward the right atrium. Also notice that in leads II and aVF the P wave is predominantly negative, suggesting an inferior to superior vector in the atrium. This tachycardia was successfully ablated by cardiac surgery with the removal of a focus in the lateral left atrium.

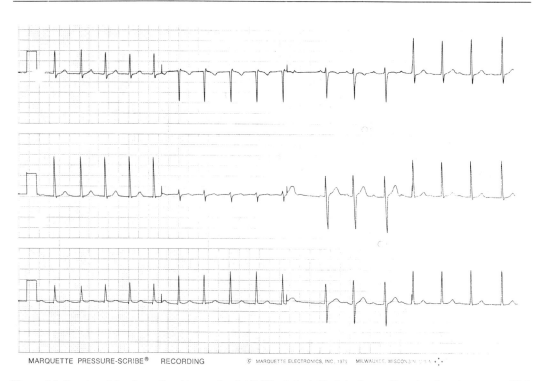

Figure 6-4 Ectopic atrial tachycardia with occasional AV Wenckebach block is shown. Note that there is a narrow QRS complex tachycardia. In leads V_1 and V_2, clear P waves can be seen in AV Wenckebach conduction. AV block during the tachycardia is proof that the AV conduction system and ventricle are not integral parts of the tachycardia.

either destroyed or removed, allowing the sinus node to resume control of the atrial rhythm. For young patients facing lifelong drug therapy, these definitive nonpharmacologic treatments may be the preferred therapy. Electrophysiologic studies are crucial to define the mechanism of the tachycardia and to localize the automatic focus with atrial mapping. Preoperative mapping of the tachycardia is critical for a successful outcome of either catheter ablation or surgery. For patients with a left atrial focus, mapping of the left atrium usually requires transseptal catheterization with puncture of the interatrial septum with a Brockenbrough needle and passage of a long sheath from the right atrium to the left atrium. At surgery, the epicardial and endocardial surfaces of the atria are mapped during tachycardia. The abnormal focus is then resected by sharp dissection and cryolesions are placed around the border of the resected area.

A second clinical form of ectopic atrial tachycardia may be observed in older patients with evidence of structural heart disease. In these individuals, the atrial tachycardia can be terminated by cardioversion or pacing and is likely to be based on intra-atrial reentry. This arrhythmia is more responsive to drug therapy than the automatic form of ectopic atrial tachycardia in children. Class IA antiarrhythmic drugs such as quinidine or procainamide have proven effective in many patients with intra-atrial reentrant tachycardia. Class IC drugs may also provide satisfactory suppression. In addition to suppressing atrial reentry, concomitant therapy with an AV nodal blocking drug such as digoxin is usually needed to slow the ventricular rate during the tachycardia. Catheter ablation of the AV conduction system has also been widely used to successfully manage older patients with drug-refractory ectopic atrial tachycardia. Following catheter ablation of the AV conduction system, complete AV block is induced, and a permanent, rate-adaptive ventricular pacemaker is required.

ATRIAL FIBRILLATION

Atrial fibrillation is the most common atrial arrhythmia encountered in clinical practice (Figure 6-5). This arrhythmia may complicate the

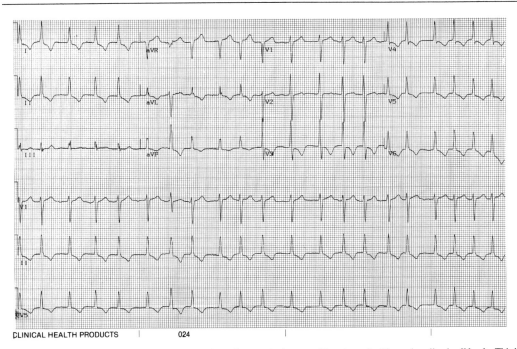

Figure 6-5 Atrial fibrillation. Note the irregularly irregular ventricular rate with an irregular bizarre baseline in all leads. This is typical of atrial fibrillation.

course of virtually all forms of structural heart disease, including hypertension, coronary artery disease, cardiomyopathies, valvular heart disease, pericardial disorders, and congenital cardiac abnormalities. It is a common sequela of chronic obstructive lung disease and pulmonary embolism. Atrial fibrillation is extremely common following open heart surgery, occurring in up to one third of patients in the first several weeks postoperatively. In addition to the association of atrial fibrillation with these structural heart disorders, atrial fibrillation can occur as a consequence of thyrotoxicosis, drugs, or alcohol abuse. It may also occur in patients with no clear precipitating factor as a primary electrical abnormality of the heart. Patients with primary atrial fibrillation (also known as lone atrial fibrillation) often manifest signs of abnormal sinus node function, suggesting a diffuse abnormality of the atrium and sinus node. In patients demonstrating both atrial fibrillation (or atrial flutter) and sinus node dysfunction, the clinical terms "tachybrady" or sick sinus syndrome may be applied. This is a very common abnormality of older patients, with a progressive increase in frequency with age.

Atrial fibrillation is probably based on the mechanism of micro–reentry, that is, reentry without an anatomic obstacle (Figure 6-6).

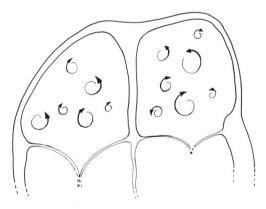

Figure 6-6 Diagrammatic representation of multiple wavefronts of micro–reentry circuits during atrial fibrillation. Note that multiple wavefronts occur simultaneously in the atrium, with all parts of the atrium being involved. This rhythm cannot be terminated by pacing but requires cardioversion with simultaneous depolarization of both atria for termination.

Atrial mapping studies performed at the time of open heart operations have demonstrated multiple wavefronts of activation spreading in a chaotic manner over the right and left atria. Atrial fibrillation does not respond to overdrive pacing. Carotid sinus massage simply slows the ventricular rate without affecting the atrial rhythm. In contrast, electrical cardioversion is usually effective in terminating atrial fibrillation as it simultaneously entirely depolarizes both atria, allowing the multiple wavelets of reentry to be extinguished.

Standard therapy for atrial fibrillation involves slowing the ventricular response with medications that suppress AV conduction, especially digoxin, calcium blockers such as verapamil or diltiazem, or β-blockers. With the exception of β-blockers, these drugs usually do not affect the underlying atrial rhythm. β-blockers have been demonstrated to decrease the frequency of atrial fibrillation when given prophylactically to patients following open heart surgery. Class I medications such as quinidine and procainamide are usually given to both terminate atrial fibrillation and maintain normal sinus rhythm. The drugs will convert atrial fibrillation to sinus rhythm in approximately 40% of patients, with a higher conversion rate in the setting of acute postoperative atrial fibrillation.

For patients who do not convert to sinus rhythm with class I antiarrhythmic medications, electrical cardioversion is commonly used. However, since restoration of the normal rhythmic contraction of the atria with electrical or chemical cardioversion may expel thrombi that have developed in the stagnant, noncontractile atrium during the period of atrial fibrillation, patients with atrial fibrillation of more than 1 week's duration are usually anticoagulated for 3 to 4 weeks prior to attempts to restore sinus rhythm. Anticoagulation is usually continued for an additional 3 to 4 weeks following cardioversion to reduce the risk of systemic embolization. Patients at high risk for systemic emboli, such as those with rheumatic valvular disease or with a prior history of emboli, are usually chronically anticoagulated. Growing evidence that both paroxysmal and chronic atrial fibrillation are associated with an increased risk of stroke has led many clinicians to chronically anticoagulate all patients with atrial fibrillation who do not have a contraindication. Other clinicians offer patients at relatively low risk for systemic emboli drugs that inhibit platelet function, such as aspirin.

The natural history of paroxysmal atrial fibrillation is usually that of a gradual increase in the frequency of this arrhythmia. For patients with rapid atrial fibrillation and marked symptoms who fail to be controlled with antiarrhythmic drugs, catheter ablation of the AV conduction system may be warranted. Following ablation, a rate-adaptive pacemaker is implanted. This approach has been demonstrated to improve the quality of life and the exercise capacity of selected patients with highly symptomatic and medically refractory atrial fibrillation. In addition, patients with the tachy-brady syndrome may develop worsening of sinus node function when treated with antiarrhythmic drugs for atrial fibrillation. Effective therapy in these patients may require implantation of a permanent pacemaker prior to treatment of the tachyarrhythmia with medications.

ATRIAL FLUTTER

Atrial flutter has virtually the same natural history and association with structural heart disease as that described for atrial fibrillation. Indeed, atrial flutter and atrial fibrillation are often observed in the same patient at different times. Despite its similarities to atrial fibrillation, there are some important functional differences. Classical atrial flutter demonstrates an atrial rate ranging from approximately 260 to 320 beats per minute in the absence of antiarrhythmic drugs. The atrial rate is generally very regular in atrial flutter, with intracardiac and esophageal electrograms demonstrating a constant morphology of the atrial complexes (Figure 6-7).

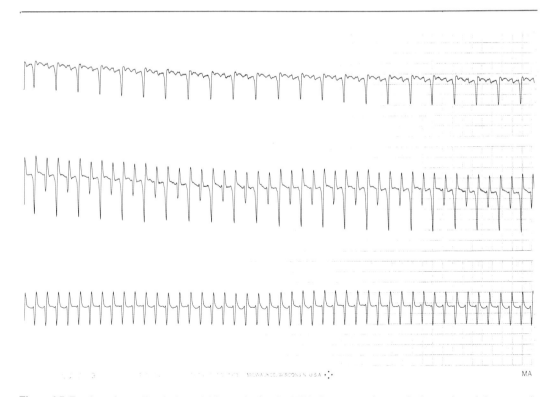

Figure 6-7 Esophageal recording during atrial flutter. Surface lead III in the upper tracing, a unipolar esophageal electrogram in the middle tracing, and a bipolar esophageal electrogram in the bottom tracing—depict atrial flutter. Note that in the bottom tracing there is a regular uniform morphology atrial electrogram at the rate of approximately 300 beats per minute. This is typical of atrial flutter.

The ventricular rate is usually an exact fraction of the atrial rate; 2:1 conduction is typical. In some individuals, typical AV Wenckebach conduction may be present, with grouped beating of the ventricular complexes and a regularly irregular ventricular rhythm. The diagnosis of atrial flutter can almost always be made by careful inspection of the 12-lead ECG for sawtooth flutter waves in leads II, III, and aVF (Figure 6-8). In instances where the QRS complex is wide, carotid sinus massage may be required to enhance AV block and allow recognition of flutter waves.

The mechanism underlying classical atrial flutter (termed type I flutter) is probably reentry with an excitable gap (Figure 6-9). The reentrant circuit has been demonstrated to involve the right atrium with rapid conduction from the high to the low right atrium lateral to the crista terminalis and slow conduction between the inferior vena cava and the ostium of the coronary sinus in the low, medial right atrium. The left atrium is generally activated in a counterclockwise direction from the low left atrium to the high left atrium. This inferior to superior activation of the left atrium produces the inverted flutter waves in leads II, III, and aVF in the surface ECG. Because classical atrial flutter is based on a mechanism of reentry with a gap of excitability within the circuit, it can be interrupted with rapid atrial pacing in most individuals. The excitable gap provides a window of opportunity for pacing stimuli to enter the circuit and terminate the rhythm.

Cardioversion with low-energy shocks (less than 50 J) is also an effective method for interrupting atrial flutter. A faster variety of atrial flutter (type II flutter) occurs, with an atrial rate in the range of 320 to 360 beats per minute. Although this rhythm is likely to be based on reentry, an excitable gap is not present in the circuit, and atrial pacing is not effective for its interruption. The presence of an excitable gap provides the essential link in the tachycardia

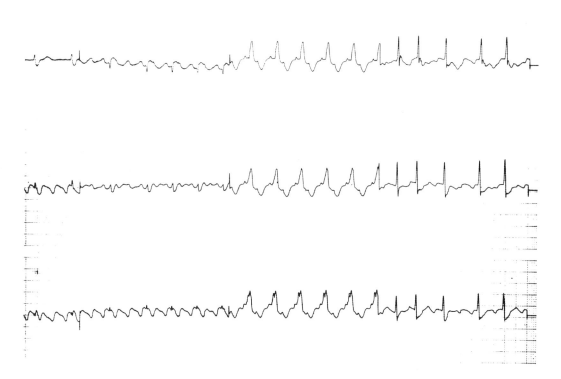

Figure 6-8 Classical atrial flutter. Note that in leads II, III, and aVF a classic sawtooth atrial pattern is demonstrated. The atrial flutter waves are of a constant morphology at a rate of approximately 280 beats per minute. There is a right bundle branch block QRS morphology with 2:1 AV conduction.

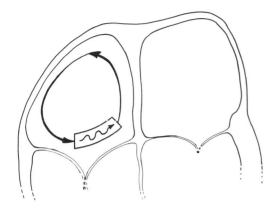

Figure 6-9 Diagrammatic representation of an atrial flutter reentrant circuit. The reentrant loop of atrial flutter in most patients involves a region of slow conduction near the orifice of the coronary sinus in the low medial right atrium. Reentry occurs in the right atrium, with the left atrium being activated as an innocent bystander in most cases. There is often an excitable gap in the reentrant circuit that allows termination of the rhythm by rapid pacing.

circuit for pacing termination. Type II atrial flutter does respond to cardioversion, however.

Standard antiarrhythmic drug therapy for atrial flutter involves slowing AV nodal conduction by the use of digoxin, calcium blockers, or β-blockers, followed by the use of class I antiarrhythmic drugs. Class I drugs are effective in converting atrial flutter to sinus rhythm in 30% to 50% of patients. It is always prudent to block the AV node prior to the addition of a class I drug when treating atrial flutter. Class I antiarrhythmic drugs slow the atrial rate in atrial flutter, with little effect on AV conduction. If class I antiarrhythmic drugs are administered to patients with atrial flutter in the absence of AV node blocking agents, the atrial flutter rate may be slowed enough so that the atrial rhythm may be conducted through the AV node in a 1:1 ratio to the ventricles. For example, if the atrial rate during atrial flutter is 300 beats per minute with 2:1 conduction through the AV node, the ventricular rate will be 150 beats per minute. If procainamide or quinidine are given, the atrial rate may slow to 240 beats per minute. At the slower atrial rate, the AV node may be capable of 1:1 conduction, resulting in a ventricular rate of 240 beats per minute. This scenario may be

prevented by first blocking the AV node with digoxin. Other drugs that have proven effective for atrial flutter include the Class IC drugs, though they are not yet approved for this indication.

The risk of systemic emboli during atrial flutter is less than the risk during atrial fibrillation. This is probably explained by the observation that atrial contraction continues during flutter but not during fibrillation. Since the atria continue to eject, atrial stasis and intracardiac thrombi are less likely to occur. For this reason, systemic anticoagulants are often not given to patients with isolated atrial flutter. However, since patients may experience both atrial fibrillation and flutter, the nature of the arrhythmia history should be clarified before cardioversion or rapid pacing is used to interrupt atrial flutter without prior anticoagulation.

As with atrial fibrillation, atrial flutter may be refractory to management with antiarrhythmic drugs. In patients with medically refractory atrial flutter with rapid ventricular rates and severe symptoms, catheter ablation of the AV conduction system with permanent pacemaker implantation may be indicated. In selected individuals with atrial flutter, atrial antitachycardia pacemakers may provide an effective method of long-term control.

MULTIFOCAL ATRIAL TACHYCARDIA

Multifocal atrial tachycardia is most commonly observed in patients with severe chronic obstructive pulmonary disease. It is associated with exacerbations of pulmonary dysfunction, including bronchospasm or infection. The typical patient with multifocal atrial tachycardia is receiving theophylline preparations and β-agonist bronchodilators. This arrhythmia may be easily diagnosed by the 12-lead ECG, which typically demonstrates tall, peaked P waves in leads II, III, and aVF with at least three different P wave morphologies in an irregular pattern (Figure 6-10). The ventricular rhythm is irregularly irregular, with rates ranging from 100 to 200 beats per minute.

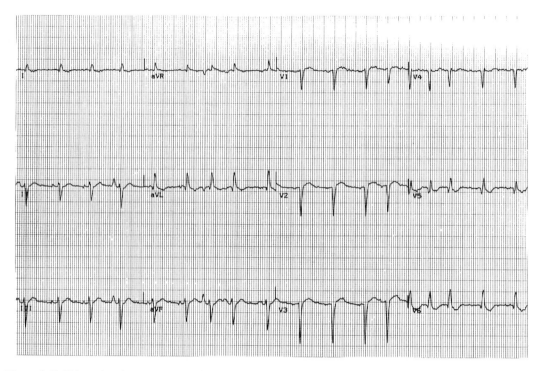

Figure 6-10 This tracing demonstrates multifocal atrial tachycardia with several different P wave morphologies with an irregularly irregular ventricular rate. Notice that in leads II, III, and aVF, the P waves are tall and peaked, typical of this arrhythmia.

The mechanism of multifocal atrial tachycardia is uncertain but is likely to be based on triggered activity and delayed afterdepolarizations. β-Agonists, theophylline, and digoxin are potential factors exacerbating delayed afterdepolarizations and triggered activity. Thus the treatment of multifocal atrial tachycardia is often complicated by the therapy required for the patient's underlying pulmonary disease. Fortunately, most patients with multifocal atrial tachycardia have minimal symptoms from their arrhythmia, and the balance of clinical priorities favors aggressive treatment of the pulmonary disorder. Indeed, most patients require no specific therapy for well-tolerated multifocal atrial tachycardia, and treatment is provided only for the underlying medical problems. For patients with symptomatic multifocal atrial tachycardia, verapamil has been demonstrated to suppress this arrhythmia without causing bronchospasm. β-Blockers are also effective for multifocal atrial tachycardia but are contraindicated for patients with bronchospasm and therefore seldom used.

Intravenous infusion of verapamil is an effective treatment for symptomatic multifocal atrial tachycardia in critically ill patients and is probably the therapy of choice for individuals needing acute suppression of this arrhythmia. Rapid pacing and cardioversion are ineffective and should not be used. In addition, digoxin therapy is usually ineffective and is probably best avoided.

AV NODAL REENTRANT TACHYCARDIA

As its name implies, AV nodal reentrant tachycardia is based on a reentrant mechanism within the AV node (Figure 6-11). Although the reentrant circuit during this arrhythmia has been demonstrated to involve the AV node, it is possible that perinodal tissue in the right atrium forms a critical part of the circuit. Because catheter ablation may permanently cure AV nodal reentrant tachycardia without the need for permanent pacing, there has been a resurgence of

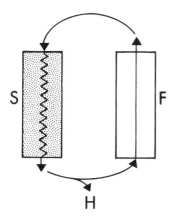

S   F

H

Figure 6-11 Schematic representation of dual AV nodal pathways and AV nodal reentrant tachycardia. A slow AV nodal pathway (S; shaded rectangle) and a fast AV nodal pathway (F; open rectangle) are shown. AV nodal reentrant tachycardia of the usual variety begins with antegrade conduction over a slow AV nodal pathway and retrograde conduction over a fast AV nodal pathway. The tachycardia circuit is confined to the AV node and/or perinodal tissues.

interest in the nonpharmacologic treatment of this arrhythmia.

AV nodal reentry is the most common mechanism of paroxysmal atrial tachycardia that is seen in outpatient practice. The tachycardia usually begins in young adulthood, though onset of symptoms in middle age is not uncommon. Patients typically experience an abrupt onset of rapid palpitations, often accompanied by dyspnea and lightheadedness. Although syncope is possible with this arrhythmia, it is relatively uncommon. The episodes of tachycardia are precipitated by exercise in many individuals, but in some patients the arrhythmia may occur more commonly at rest. Patients often learn that they can interrupt the tachycardia by performing a Valsalva maneuver, lying down, holding their breath, or performing other maneuvers that enhance vagal tone.

The ECG usually demonstrates a regular narrow QRS complex tachycardia at rates ranging from approximately 110 to 250 beats per minute. The rate of the tachycardia may vary from episode to episode in the same individual, depending on the patient's autonomic tone and medication regimen. The 12-lead ECG typically reveals no clearly discernible P waves, though atrial activity may be seen to distort the terminal part of the QRS. Thus pseudo–S waves may occur in leads II, III, and aVF and pseudo–R waves may be seen in lead aVR. Careful comparison of the ECG during tachycardia to that during sinus rhythm may allow recognition of retrograde P waves at the end of the QRS complex. At very rapid heart rates (over 200 beats per minute), the phenomenon of QRS alternation may be observed. Esophageal recordings demonstrate a 1:1 ratio of atrial and ventricular deflections, usually with simultaneous activation of both chambers.

Electrophysiologic studies in patients with AV nodal reentrant tachycardia have demonstrated that this arrhythmia depends on the presence of two pathways for conduction within the AV node. One pathway is characterized by fast conduction, but with a long refractory period. The other pathway conducts impulses slowly through the AV node but has a shorter refractory period. The presence of these two conduction pathways in an individual is referred to as "dual AV nodal pathways." Although dual AV nodal pathways are probably critical for the development of AV nodal reentrant tachycardia, not all patients with dual pathways develop this arrhythmia. Thus dual pathways may be discovered as an isolated finding at the time of electrophysiologic testing. In addition, it is not always possible to demonstrate the presence of dual AV nodal pathways in individuals with AV nodal reentrant tachycardia.

The method of demonstrating dual AV nodal pathways is by programmed atrial stimulation with delivery of timed, premature atrial stimuli. As the coupling interval of the premature atrial stimuli is decreased, a gradual lengthening of the AH interval normally occurs. If dual pathways are present, the premature stimulus may encounter the fast pathway in its refractory period, and conduction will shift to the slow pathway. This shift from the fast to the slow pathway with small changes in the coupling interval of the extrastimuli results in a sudden "jump" in the AH interval. Dual AV nodal pathways are diagnosed when there is a prolongation in the AH interval greater than 50 milliseconds with a small decrement (10 milliseconds) in the extrastimulus coupling intervals (Figure 6-12). This sudden

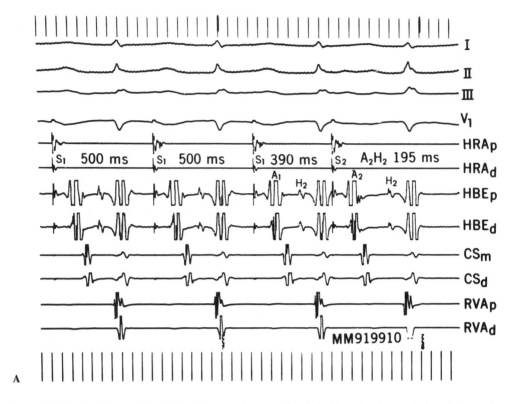

Figure 6-12 A discontinuous AV nodal function curve demonstrating dual AV nodal pathways. Surface electrocardiographic leads I, II, III, and V_1 are shown simultaneously with bipolar electrograms from the high right atrium proximal (HRAp) and distal (HRAd) electrode pairs, His bundle electrogram proximal (HBEp) and distal (HBEd) electrode pairs, coronary sinus mid (CSM) and distal (CSD) electrodes, and right ventricular apex proximal (RVAp) and distal (RVAd) electrode pairs. Programmed stimulation from the high right atrium is performed at an S1 drive at 500 milliseconds. In panel A, with an S1-S2 coupling interval of 390 milliseconds, the A2-H2 interval measures 195 milliseconds.

lengthening of the AH interval is also referred to as a discontinuous AV nodal function curve. Dual AV nodal pathways may also be suspected by the presence of two distinct PR intervals in the surface ECG.

AV nodal reentrant tachycardia usually begins when a premature atrial depolarization enters the AV node and finds the fast pathway refractory. It then conducts over the slow pathway to the ventricles. However, since the conduction time through the slow pathway is long, the impulse may encounter the distal portion of the fast pathway when it is no longer refractory. The impulse may then return to the atrium by conducting over the fast pathway in the retrograde direction. As the retrograde impulse reaches the proximal portion of the AV node, it may then reenter the slow pathway and conduct to the ventricles. A sus-

tained tachycardia is generated by antegrade conduction over the slow pathway and retrograde conduction over the fast pathway. Since the conduction time from the lower portion of the AV node to the atrium is short, the P wave will occur nearly simultaneously with the QRS complex in the surface ECG (Figure 6-13). The shortest interval between ventricular and atrial activation will typically be less than 45 milliseconds during the usual "slow-fast" form of AV nodal reentry. Atrial mapping during AV nodal reentrant tachycardia reveals that the earliest site of retrograde atrial activation occurs adjacent to the AV node in the His bundle catheter. In rare patients, the reentrant circuit can be reversed so that there is antegrade conduction over the fast pathway and retrograde conduction over the slow pathway. This "fast-slow" form of AV

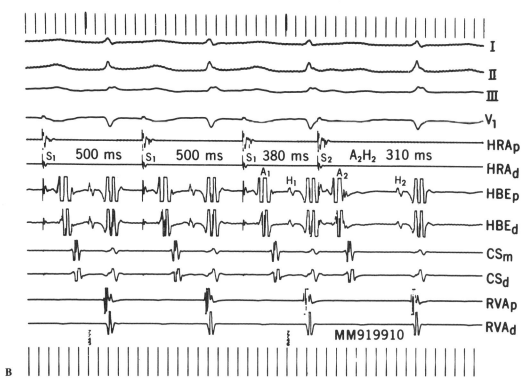

Figure 6-12 continued In panel B, when the S1-S2 interval is decreased to 380 milliseconds, the A2-H2 interval prolongs to 310 milliseconds. This "jump" in the A2-H2 interval from 195 milliseconds in panel A to 310 milliseconds in panel B is caused by a shift of conduction through the AV node from a fast pathway to a slow pathway. This "jump" in the A2-H2 interval exceeds 50 milliseconds and is indicative of dual AV nodal pathways, the substrate for AV nodal reentrant tachycardia.

nodal reentry is also known as the "unusual" form of AV nodal reentrant tachycardia. In unusual AV nodal reentry, the RP interval exceeds the PR interval, and retrograde P waves are clearly identifiable in the 12-lead ECG.

The acute treatment of AV nodal reentrant tachycardia usually begins with the Valsalva maneuver or carotid sinus massage. Standard antiarrhythmic drug therapy for an acute episode of AV nodal reentry involves the intravenous administration of agents that block the slow antegrade pathway. Drugs such as verapamil, β-blockers, or adenosine interrupt the tachycardia by slowing conduction in the slow pathway. These drugs are virtually always effective in interrupting AV nodal reentry, provided a sufficient dose is administered. Adenosine is particularly well suited for the termination of AV nodal reentry because it has an ultrarapid duration of action and is a powerful blocker of the slow AV

nodal pathway, usually producing transient Wenckebach or complete heart block that lasts for several seconds.

Chronic, prophylactic antiarrhythmic drug therapy is indicated for patients with frequent or severely symptomatic tachycardia. If long-term therapy is required, agents such as digoxin, verapamil, or β-blockers are usually given as initial treatment. If these agents are not effective, the class I antiarrhythmic drugs that may produce block in the fast retrograde pathway are usually prescribed. In general, patients with AV nodal reentrant tachycardia that is precipitated by exercise are likely to respond to therapy with β-blockers or verapamil. Patients who develop tachycardia predominantly at rest usually respond poorly to these drugs, and class I agents may be preferable. In patients with rare episodes of tachycardia, prophylactic antiarrhythmic therapy is probably not warranted. These

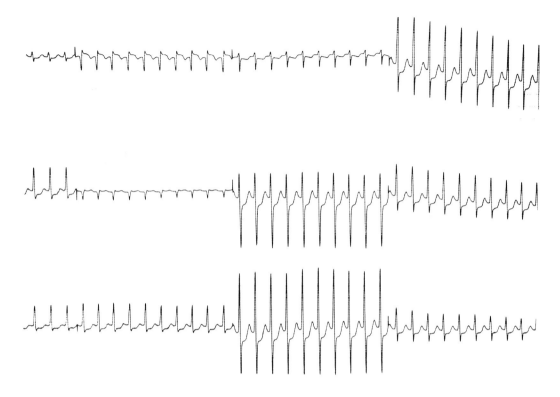

Figure 6-13 A 12-lead ECG demonstrating AV nodal reentrant tachycardia is demonstrated. Notice that there is a regular, narrow QRS complex tachycardia at a rate of 210 beats per minute. A retrograde P wave is seen to distort the terminal part of the QRS with a pseudo–S wave in leads II, III, and aVF and a pseudo–R' wave in lead aVR. This reflects simultaneous activation of the ventricles and the atrium by reentry within the AV node.

patients may be given verapamil or β-blockers to take orally at the onset of tachycardia and are taught the appropriate use of vagal maneuvers. This approach has proven satisfactory in less-symptomatic individuals.

Although most patients with AV nodal reentrant tachycardia respond to medical therapy, occasional patients develop intolerable side effects to medications or prove to be refractory. Other patients may simply prefer nonpharmacologic therapy to long-term drug treatment. In these individuals, antitachycardia pacing is an effective therapy. Antitachycardia pacemakers continuously monitor the cardiac rhythm and are programmed to deliver a burst of rapid pacing stimuli at the onset of tachycardia. Although these devices do not prevent AV nodal reentrant tachycardia, they usually promptly interrupt it and provide effective long-term control. Antitachycardia pacemakers allow most patients

freedom from the side effects of antiarrhythmic drugs and confidence that they are protected from prolonged episodes of their arrhythmia.

Catheter ablation offers patients with AV nodal reentrant tachycardia a chance at permanent cure. Selective ablation of the fast retrograde or slow antegrade AV nodal pathway may be accomplished with either radiofrequency or direct current energy. The radiofrequency technique uses radiofrequency energy delivered from a special electrode catheter with a large surface area to produce destruction of a portion of the AV node or the perinodal tissues. Considerable experience with this technique suggests that radiofrequency energy produces long-term cure of AV nodal reentrant tachycardia in the majority of patients. Catheter ablation of the slow pathway may be the preferred technique as it is associated with a lower risk of AV block. Currently, radio frequency catheter ablation of the slow AV pathway may be considered the therapy of choice for symptomatic patients with AV nodal reentrant tachycardia. Direct current shocks have also been used to selectively modify AV nodal conduction and permanently prevent AV nodal reentry. Both of these techniques have been successfully used for this arrhythmia, without the need for permanent pacemaker implantation.

Many patients with AV nodal reentrant tachycardia have undergone successful catheter ablation of the His bundle with induction of permanent complete AV block and subsequent permanent pacemaker implantation. This earlier technique is a more drastic but effective non-pharmacologic treatment for medically refractory AV nodal reentrant tachycardia. The selective infusion of ethanol into the AV nodal artery has also been successfully used to produce complete heart block and control AV nodal reentry. Open heart surgery has also been used for the modification of AV nodal conduction and cure of AV nodal reentrant tachycardia. During surgery, cryothermal lesions are placed around the AV

node to ablate perinodal fibers. The risk of AV block has been low, and selective ablation of either the slow or fast pathways has been observed. Although the long-term follow-up has been excellent with this procedure, the newer catheter ablation techniques are likely to make this therapy obsolete.

PREEXCITATION SYNDROMES

Wolff-Parkinson-White Syndrome

Preexcitation refers to any abnormality of AV conduction that results in earlier activation of the ventricles than would be expected if the AV node-His Purkinje system were the sole pathway of electrical activation. Patients with the Wolff-Parkinson-White syndrome manifest (1) a short PR interval, (2) a slurred onset of the QRS complex known as a delta wave, and (3) a history of supraventricular arrhythmias (Figures 6-14, 6-15, and 6-16). As discussed in Chapter 1, Wolff-Parkinson-White syndrome is related to

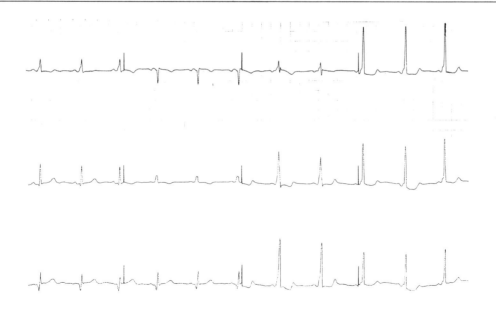

Figure 6-14 Wolff-Parkinson-White syndrome with a left posterior accessory pathway. Notice that the delta wave is upright in leads V_1 to V_6, which is typical of a left-sided accessory pathway. The delta wave is inverted in leads II, III, and aVF, with Q waves that could be confused with those of an inferior myocardial infarction. This represents preexcitation and is typical of a left posterior accessory pathway.

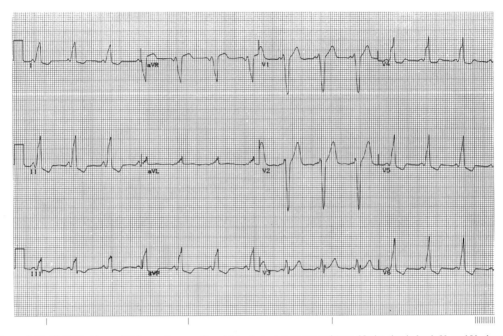

Figure 6-15 Wolff-Parkinson-White syndrome with a right anterior accessory pathway. Notice that in leads V₁ and V₂ there is a biphasic QRS with a delta wave that is predominantly inverted. This is typical of a right-sided accessory pathway. The delta wave is upright in leads II, III, and aVF, which is suggestive of the right anterior location of this accessory pathway.

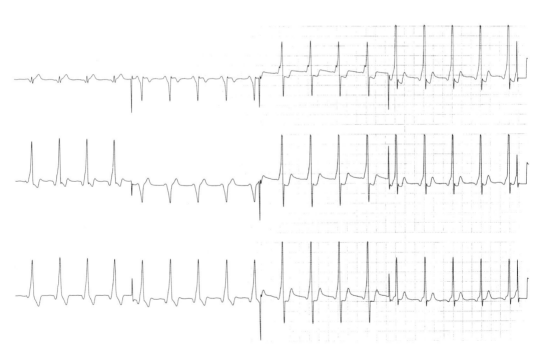

Figure 6-16 Wolff-Parkinson-White syndrome with a left lateral accessory pathway. Notice that in leads V₁ to V₆, there is an upright delta wave. In leads I and aVL, the delta wave is inverted.

the presence of an accessory AV connection that joins the atria to the ventricles, bypassing the AV node. Since the normal delay in AV conduction imposed by the AV node is bypassed in patients with Wolff-Parkinson-White syndrome, the PR interval is shorter than normal. The QRS is widened and slurred since ventricular activation begins at the base of the heart along the AV rings and spreads slowly through ventricular myocardium, without the specialized Purkinje fiber conduction system network. The AV connections found in Wolff-Parkinson-White syndrome have also been called "Kent bundles."

In some individuals, accessory AV connections may conduct only in the retrograde direction. Since antegrade conduction is absent in these patients, the PR and QRS complexes are normal. However, the accessory pathway may participate in reentrant tachycardias that use the accessory pathway as the retrograde limb of the circuit and the AV node as the antegrade limb. Since antegrade conduction is not present, Wolff-Parkinson-White syndrome is not manifest on the 12-lead ECG.

The preexcitation syndromes are actually a form of congenital heart disease, with Wolff-Parkinson-White syndrome occurring in approximately 1 of 2000 persons in the general population. Although the incidence of Wolff-Parkinson-White syndrome is usually sporadic, approximately 1 in 50 patients will have an affected first-degree relative. Although most patients with this condition have structurally normal hearts, there is an association of this condition with a congenital anomaly of the tricuspid valve, Ebstein's anomaly, in which the tricuspid valve is displaced into the right ventricle below the right AV ring. Other conditions associated with Wolff-Parkinson-White syndrome are corrected transposition of the great arteries and hypertrophic cardiomyopathy.

Patients with Wolff-Parkinson-White syndrome typically develop supraventricular arrhythmias in childhood or as young adults. However, up to 30% of patients with the electrocardiographic pattern of Wolff-Parkinson-White syndrome never develop arrhythmias. Arrhythmias may first appear as early in life as in utero or as late as in old age. The severity of symptoms and the frequency of arrhythmias vary widely, from complete absence of symptoms to life-threatening arrhythmias and sudden death. Sudden death from arrhythmias related to Wolff-Parkinson-White syndrome is usually due to the development of atrial fibrillation with rapid antegrade conduction from the atria to the ventricles over the accessory pathway. Since impulses may be conducted from the atria to the ventricles over the accessory pathway without the conduction delay that is normally imposed by the AV node, the ventricular rate may exceed 300 beats per minute. Ventricular fibrillation may be precipitated by these very rapid ventricular rates. The AV node itself may be protective for patients with Wolff-Parkinson-White syndrome who develop atrial fibrillation by the phenomenon of concealed retrograde conduction. Since impulses that travel to the ventricles over the AV node may collide with impulses traversing the accessory pathway, the overall ventricular rate may be slowed. Ventricular fibrillation may be induced during atrial fibrillation with rapid antegrade conduction over an accessory pathway if patients are treated with agents that block the AV node. In this setting, drugs such as digoxin or verapamil inhibit the protective effect of concealed retrograde conduction and speed the ventricular rate by allowing more impulses to travel over the accessory pathway. Patients having accessory pathways with short antegrade refractory periods and patients with multiple accessory pathways are at highest risk for sudden death. The best estimate of the risk of sudden death in Wolff-Parkinson-White syndrome is the response to atrial fibrillation. Atrial fibrillation is intentionally induced during electrophysiologic studies to record the shortest RR interval. The risk of ventricular fibrillation is highest for patients with RR intervals less than 220 milliseconds.

The most common arrhythmia associated with Wolff-Parkinson-White syndrome is orthodromic reciprocating tachycardia (Figure 6-17). During this arrhythmia, antegrade conduction from the atria to the ventricles occurs over the normal AV node-His conduction system. Retrograde conduction from the ventricles to the atria occurs over the accessory pathway (Figure 6-18). Since antegrade conduction is normal, the QRS is usually narrow. Orthodromic reciprocating

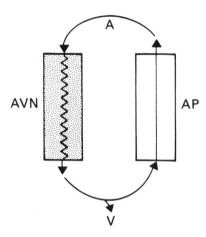

Figure 6-17 Schematic representation of the reentrant circuit in orthodromic reciprocating tachycardia. Orthodromic reciprocating tachycardia is based on antegrade conduction over the AV node (AVN; shaded rectangle) with activation over the His bundle to the ventricle. The activation pattern then spreads through the ventricle and retrogradely over an accessory pathway (AP; open rectangle) from the ventricle to the atrium. Thus both the AV node and an accessory pathway, as well as the ventricle and the atrium, are integral parts of the reentrant circuit.

tachycardia may be initiated by a premature ventricular depolarization that fails to conduct in the retrograde direction from the ventricles to the atria through the AV node. If the premature ventricular beat blocks retrogradely in the AV node but travels to the atria over an accessory pathway, the impulse may then travel through the atrium to the AV node and conduct antegradely over the node and His bundle to reenter the ventricles. In this way, a sustained reentrant tachycardia is induced that conducts from the ventricles to the atria over the accessory pathway and from the atria to the ventricles over the AV node.

At the rapid tachycardia rates of orthodromic reciprocating tachycardia, functional left or right bundle branch block may occur (Figure 6-19). It is common for patients with orthodromic reciprocating tachycardia to demonstrate both a narrow and a wide bundle branch block QRS morphology at different times. Unlike AV nodal reentry, in which the atria and ventricles are activated simultaneously, orthodromic reciprocating tachycardia requires that the atria

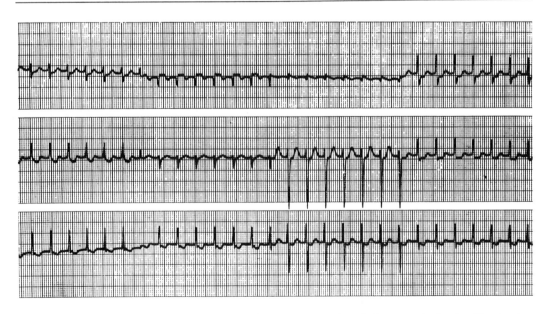

Figure 6-18 Orthodromic reciprocating tachycardia utilizing an accessory pathway in the retrograde direction. Note that there is a narrow QRS complex tachycardia that is regular, at a rate of approximately 160 beats per minute. Note that in leads II, III, and aVF an inverted P wave is seen in the ST segment. The retrograde P wave distinguishes this tachycardia from AV nodal reentry. Orthodromic reciprocating tachycardia utilizes the AV node and His bundle as the antegrade limb of the circuit and an accessory pathway as the retrograde limb.

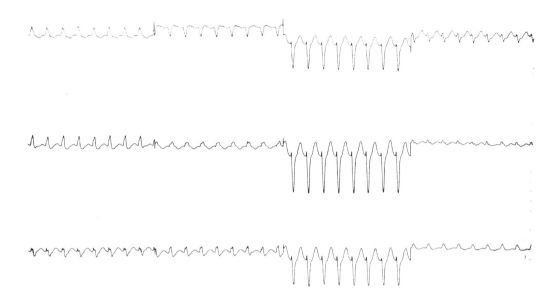

Figure 6-19 Orthodromic reciprocating tachycardia with left bundle branch block QRS morphology is demonstrated. Notice that there is a typical left bundle branch block QRS morphology with a narrow and sharp R wave in leads V_1 and V_2, with a sharp downstroke of the S wave in each of these leads. Also note that there is no Q wave in lead V_6. This tachycardia involves conduction over the AV node and right bundle branch in an antegrade direction, with block in the left bundle. The retrograde limb of the circuit is provided by an accessory pathway conducting from the ventricle to the atrium.

and ventricles be activated sequentially. Thus the P wave is usually clearly visible between QRS complexes in the 12-lead ECG. The esophageal electrogram may also help to differentiate orthodromic reciprocating tachycardia using a concealed accessory pathway from AV nodal reentrant tachycardia. If the ventriculoarterial conduction interval on the esophageal electrogram exceeds 70 milliseconds, an accessory pathway is probably present. In addition, there must be a 1:1 relationship between the atria and ventricles during orthodromic reciprocating tachycardia. Since the earliest site of retrograde atrial activation occurs along the AV rings by conduction over the accessory pathway, the P wave axis is inverted (i.e., runs from inferior to superior). The P wave morphology is therefore inverted in leads II, III, and aVF.

Antidromic reciprocating tachycardia is an arrhythmia involving an accessory AV pathway and results from a reentrant circuit that operates in a direction opposite to that of the more common orthodromic reciprocating tachycardia. In

antidromic reciprocating tachycardia, antegrade conduction from the atria to the ventricles occurs via the accessory pathway, and retrograde conduction occurs over the AV node (or a second accessory pathway) (Figure 6-20). Since activation of the ventricles is eccentric and does not involve the normal specialized Purkinje network, the QRS is slurred and widened (Figure 6-21). In fact, the QRS complex during antidromic reciprocating tachycardia represents a pure delta wave. Because of the very broad QRS, retrograde P waves may not be easily discernible on the 12-lead ECG. Antidromic reciprocating tachycardia is an unusual arrhythmia. When it is observed, suspicion should be high that more than one accessory pathway is present.

The treatment of Wolff-Parkinson-White syndrome depends on the conduction characteristics of the accessory pathway, the frequency and severity of symptoms, and the preference of the patient. Other factors such as the patient's occupation or desire for pregnancy enter into the

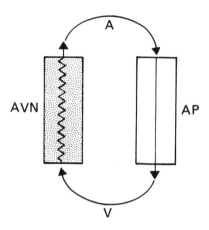

Figure 6-20 Schematic representation of the reentrant circuit during antidromic reciprocating tachycardia. The reentrant circuit is shown, with antegrade conduction from the atrium to the ventricle over an accessory pathway (AP; open rectangle) and with retrograde conduction from the ventricle to the atrium over the AV node (AVN; shaded rectangle). Note that the tachycardia circuit is reversed as compared to orthodromic reciprocating tachycardia and that both the ventricle and the atrium are integral parts of the reentrant circuit.

decision as to whether or not antiarrhythmic drugs or nonpharmacologic treatment should be considered. For acute episodes of narrow QRS complex orthodromic reciprocating tachycardia, carotid massage, intravenous adenosine, verapamil, or β-blockers will usually terminate the arrhythmia. However, when the QRS is preexcited during tachycardia (atrial fibrillation with antegrade conduction or antidromic tachycardia) (Figure 6-22), class I drugs are preferable. The acute management of atrial fibrillation or antidromic tachycardia in patients with Wolff-Parkinson-White syndrome usually involves intravenous procainamide, cardioversion, or both. Severely symptomatic patients or those in shock should be sedated and promptly cardioverted. Patients who are more stable are best treated with intravenous procainamide, with cardioversion being reserved for failure of drug therapy. As previously mentioned, drugs such as verapamil or digoxin may precipitate ventricular fibrillation if there is antegrade conduction over an accessory pathway during atrial fibrillation, and they should be avoided. When in doubt, choose procainamide.

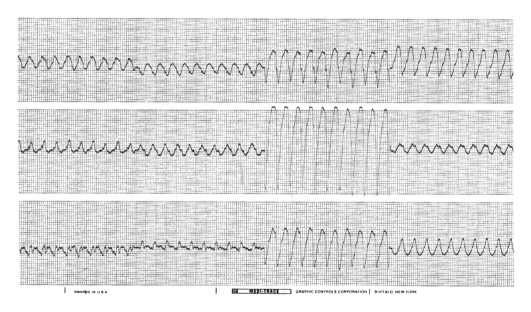

Figure 6-21 Antidromic reciprocating tachycardia. This arrhythmia involves antegrade conduction over an accessory pathway to the ventricles, with retrograde conduction over the AV node. Notice that the QRS is extremely wide, representing a pure delta wave. The QRS is negative in leads V_1 and V_2, upright in lead II, negative in lead III, and biphasic in lead AVF, suggesting a right free wall pathway. This arrhythmia is easily confused with ventricular tachycardia.

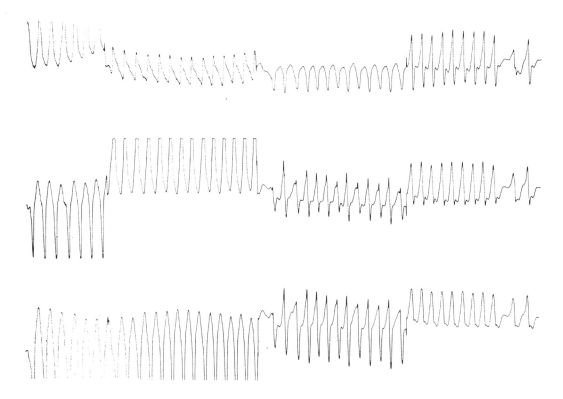

Figure 6-22 Atrial fibrillation with antegrade conduction over an accessory pathway in a patient with Wolff-Parkinson-White syndrome. This figure represents atrial fibrillation with preexcitation in a patient with a posteroseptal accessory pathway. Notice that there is an irregular, wide QRS complex tachycardia at a rate of approximately 300 beats per minute. The QRS is inverted in lead V_1 and predominantly upright in leads V_2 to V_6. In addition, there is an inverted QRS complex in leads II, III, and aVF, suggesting a posteroseptal accessory pathway. This tachycardia has life-threatening potential and can degenerate into ventricular fibrillation.

Long-term therapy for Wolff-Parkinson-White syndrome involves antiarrhythmic drug therapy, surgery, antitachycardia pacing, or catheter ablation. Patients with very rapidly conducting accessory pathways in the antegrade direction (refractory period less than 250 milliseconds, heart rate greater than 240 beats per minute) are best treated with either surgery or catheter ablation. Patients with concealed retrograde-only accessory pathways may be effectively managed by either drugs that block the AV node (digoxin, β-blockers, verapamil) or by class I drugs that slow conduction in the accessory pathway. Many patients respond to therapy with quinidine, procainamide, disopyramide, encainide, flecainide, or propafenone. The class I antiarrhythmic agents act to slow conduction in the accessory pathway. If

the refractory period of the accessory pathway is short (less than 270 milliseconds), class I drugs are less likely to be effective. However, accessory pathways with relatively long refractory periods may demonstrate marked prolongation of refractoriness with these drugs. The electrophysiologic study is often useful to predict the response to drug therapy in Wolff-Parkinson-White syndrome. It should be emphasized that a possible response to class IC drug therapy is retarded conduction over the accessory pathway resulting in slower but incessant orthodromic reciprocating tachycardia. It should also be emphasized that exercise or catecholamines may antagonize the therapeutic effects of class I drugs and shorten refractoriness in the accessory pathway. Thus isoproterenol is often infused during the electrophysiologic assessment of class I drug therapy for Wolff-Parkinson-White syndrome. Although amiodarone is very effective in slowing conduction over accessory pathways, it is indicated for Wolff-Parkinson-White syndrome only in very unusual circumstances because of its side effect profile. In some individuals with orthodromic reciprocating tachycardia, a combination of an AV nodal blocking drug and a class I agent may be especially effective.

Antitachycardia pacemakers may be useful for patients with concealed or poorly conducting accessory pathways in the antegrade direction. Since precipitation of atrial fibrillation by antitachycardia pacing is possible, patients with accessory pathways capable of rapid antegrade conduction should not receive antitachycardia pacemakers. The advances in catheter ablation will likely decrease the role of antitachycardia pacing.

Until recently, surgery has been the mainstay of nonpharmacologic therapy for Wolff-Parkinson-White syndrome in patients with life-threatening accessory pathways. Patients surviving ventricular fibrillation are best managed by surgery or catheter ablation. Surgery may also be used for patients desiring to avoid lifelong anti-arrhythmic drug therapy or those who wish to become pregnant. The surgical approach to Wolff-Parkinson-White syndrome generally requires a median sternotomy, often with cardiopulmonary bypass. The epicardial surface of the heart is mapped to determine the precise location of the accessory pathway prior to either sharp dissection or cryoablation of the AV ring at the involved site. The surgical cure rate is very high, on the order of 95% to 99%. The mortality of the surgery is low, generally less than 1%. As in other open heart operations, the convalescence period can be prolonged in occasional patients.

A new and promising approach to the treatment of Wolff-Parkinson-White syndrome involves the use of catheter ablation with radiofrequency energy directed at the accessory pathway. With this technique, a catheter is placed at the ventricular insertion site of the accessory pathway in the right or left ventricle, and radiofrequency energy electrically destroys the tissue. Early results with this technique have demonstrated a high success rate and a low incidence of complications. Indeed, catheter ablation may be the treatment of choice for most patients with symptomatic Wolff-Parkinson-

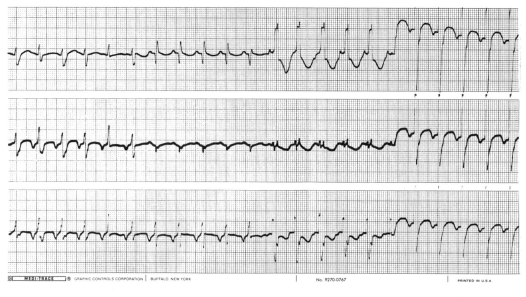

Figure 6-23 Twelve-lead ECG demonstrating the permanent form of junctional reciprocating tachycardia. Note the inverted P waves in leads II, III, and aVF, with long RP and short PR intervals. There is a right bundle branch block QRS morphology.

White syndrome. The effectiveness of radiofrequency ablation is higher for left-sided than for right-sided or septal accessory pathways.

Other Forms of Preexcitation

Besides Wolff-Parkinson-White syndrome, reentrant arrhythmias may be associated with nodofascicular (Mahaim) fibers, or atriohisian (Brechenmacher) fibers. These rare anomalies may produce reentrant supraventricular tachycardias producing clinical manifestations similar to the Wolff-Parkinson-White syndrome. The permanent form of junctional reciprocating tachycardia is characterized by a very slowly conducting accessory pathway that is located in the posterior septal region. This tachycardia is usually found in children and has a long RP and a short PR interval (Figure 6-23). These arrhythmias may respond to the same therapies discussed above.

BIBLIOGRAPHY

Akhtar M, Shenasa M, Jazayeri M, et al. Wide QRS complex tachycardia: reappraisal of a common clinical problem. *Ann Intern Med.* 1988;109:905–912.

Atwood JE, Sullivan M, Forbes S, et al. Effect of beta-adrenergic blockade on exercise performance in patients with chronic atrial fibrillation. *J Am Coll Cardiol.* 1987;10:314–320.

Benditt DG, Benson DW. *Cardiac Preexcitation Syndromes: Origins, Evaluation and Treatment.* Boston, Mass: Martinus Nijhoff; 1986.

Benditt DG, Pritchett ELC, Gallagher JJ. Spectrum of regular tachycardias with wide QRS complexes in patients with accessory atrioventricular pathways. *Am J Cardiol.* 1978;42:828–838.

The Boston Area Anticoagulation Trial for Atrial Fibrillation Investigators. The effects of low-dose warfarin on the risk of fibrillation. *N Engl J Med.* 1990;323:1505–1511.

Chesbro JH, Fuster V, Halperin JL. Atrial fibrillation-risk marker for stroke. *N Engl J Med.* 1990;323:1556–1558.

Critelli C, Gallagher JJ, Monda V, et al. Anatomic and electrophysiologic substrate of the permanent form of junctional reciprocating tachycardia. *J Am Coll Cardiol.* 1984;4:601–610.

Critelli G, Gallagher JJ, Perticone F, et al. Evaluation of noninvasive tests for identifying patients with preexcitation syndrome at risk of rapid ventricular response. *Am Heart J.* 1984;108:905–909.

David D, Segni ED, Klein HO, et al. Inefficacy of digitalis in the control of the heart rate in patients with chronic atrial

fibrillation: beneficial effect of an added beta adrenergic blocking agent. *Am J Cardiol.* 1979;44:1378–1382.

Denes P, Wu D, Dhingra RC, et al. Demonstration of dual A-V nodal pathways with paroxysmal supraventricular tachycardias. *Circulation.* 1973;48:549–555.

Dunn M, Alexander J, De Silva R, et al. Antithrombotic therapy in atrial fibrillation. *Chest.* 1986;89:685.

Durrer D, Schoo L, Schuilenburg RM, et al. The role of premature beats in the initiation and the termination of supraventricular tachycardia in the Wolff-Parkinson-White syndrome. *Circulation.* 1967;36:644–662.

Gallagher JJ, Sealey JL, German LD, et al. In: Josephson ME, Wellens HJJ, eds. *Tachycardias: Mechanism, Diagnosis, Treatment.* Philadelphia, Pa: Lea & Febiger; 1984.

Henthorn RW, Plumb VJ, Arciniegas JG, et al. Entrainment of "ectopic atrial tachycardia": evidence for reentry. *Am J Cardiol.* 1982;49:920.

Huycke EC, Sung RJ. Atrial tachycardias. In: Zipes DP, Rowlands DJ, eds. *Progress in Cardiology.* Philadelphia, Pa: Lea & Febiger; 1988;1–1:313–325.

Josephson ME, Seides SF. Supraventricular tachycardias. In: *Clinical Cardiac Electrophysiology.* Philadelphia, Pa: Lea & Febiger; 1979:147–190.

Kannel WB, Abbott RP, Savage DD, et al. Epidemiologic features of chronic atrial fibrillation: the Framingham study. *N Engl J Med.* 1982;306:1018–1022.

Kastor JA. Multifocal atrial tachycardia. *New Engl J Med.* 1990;322:1713–1717.

Kay GN, Bubien RS, Epstein AE, et al. Effect of catheter ablation of the atrioventricular junction on quality of life and exercise tolerence in patients with paroxysmal atrial fibrillation. *Am J Cardiol.* 1988;62:741–744.

Kay GN, Pressley JC, Packer DL, et al. Value of the 12-lead electrocardiogram in discriminating atrioventricular nodal reciprocating tachycardia from circus movement atrioventricular tachycardia utilizing a retrograde accessory pathway. *Am J Cardiol.* 1987;59:296–300.

Keefe DL, Miura D, Somberg JC. Supraventricular tachyarrhythmias: their evaluation and therapy. *Am Heart J.* 1986;111:1150–1161.

Klein GJ, Bashore TM, Sellers TD, et al. Ventricular fibrillation in the Wolff-Parkinson-White syndrome. *N Engl J Med.* 1979;301:1080–1085.

Mann DL, Maisel AS, Atwood JE, et al. Absence of cardioversion-induced ventricular arrhythmias in patients with therapeutic digoxin levels. *J Am Coll Cardiol.* 1985;5:882–888.

Morady F, Sledge C, Shen E, et al. Electrophysiologic testing in the management of patients with the Wolff-Parkinson-White syndrome and atrial fibrillation. *Am J Cardiol.* 1983;51:1623–1628.

Morris JJ, Peter RH, McIntosh HD. Electrical conversion of atrial fibrillation: immediate and long-term results. *Ann Intern Med.* 1966;65:216–231.

Packer DL, Bardy GH, Worley SJ, et al. Tachycardia-induced cardiomyopathy: a reversible form of left ventricular dysfunction. *Am J Cardiol.* 1986;57:563–570.

Packer DL, Prystowsky EN. Wolff-Parkinson-White syndrome: further progress in evaluation and treatment. In: Zipes DP, Rowlands DJ, eds. *Progress in Cardiology*. Philadelphia, Pa: Lea & Febiger; 1988;1–1:147–187.

Panidis JP, Morganroth J, Baessler C. Effectiveness and safety of oral verapamil to control exercise-induced tachycardia in patients with atrial fibrillation receiving digitalis. *Am J Cardiol*. 1983;52:1197–1201.

Reddy GV, Schamroth L. The localization of bypass tracts in the Wolff-Parkinson-White syndrome from the surface electrocardiograms. *Am J Heart*. 1987;113:984–993.

Sharma AD, Yee R, Guiraudon GM, et al. AV nodal reentry—current concepts and surgical treatment. In: Zipes DP, Rowlands DJ, eds. *Progress in Cardiology*. Philadelphia, Pa: Lea & Febiger; 1988;1–1:129–145.

Sharma AD, Yee R, Guiraudon G, et al. Sensitivity and specificity of invasive and noninvasive testing for risk of sudden death in Wolff-Parkinson-White syndrome. *J Am Coll Cardiol*. 1987;10:373–381.

Shea MJ, Morady F. Atrial flutter/fibrillation. In: Zipes DP, Rowlands DJ, eds. *Progress in Cardiology*. Philadelphia, Pa: Lea & Febiger; 1988;1–1:189–204.

Steinberg JS, Katz RJ, Bren GB, et al. Efficacy of oral diltiazem to control ventricular response in chronic atrial fibrillation at rest and during exercise. *J Am Coll Cardiol*. 1987;9:405–411.

Waldo AL, Akhtar M, Benditt DG, et al. The minimally appropriate electrophysiologic study and treatment of patients with the Wolff-Parkinson-White syndrome. *PACE*. 1988;11:536–544.

Waldo AL, Plumb VJ, Arciniegas JG, et al. Transient entrainment and interruption of A-V bypass pathway type paroxysmal atrial tachycardia. A model for understanding and identifying reentrant arrhythmias in man. *Circulation*. 1983;67:73–83.

Wellens HJJ, Durrer D. Effect of digitalis on atrioventricular conduction and circus-movement tachycardia in patients with Wolff-Parkinson-White syndrome. *Circulation*. 1973;47:1229–1233.

Chapter 7

Ventricular Arrhythmias

INTRODUCTION

Each year over 400,000 Americans die suddenly, most from ventricular tachycardia or fibrillation. In Western countries ventricular tachycardia and fibrillation are most commonly a consequence of coronary artery disease. However, ventricular arrhythmias may complicate the course of virtually all forms of structural heart disease. These arrhythmias may produce a range of clinical manifestations, from complete absence of symptoms to sudden cardiac death. In addition to the most malignant forms of ventricular arrhythmias (sustained ventricular tachycardia or ventricular fibrillation), ventricular arrhythmias associated with a benign clinical course may also occur. The distinction between benign and malignant ventricular arrhythmias is vitally important to proper clinical management. In this chapter the diagnosis of ventricular arrhythmias and the therapeutic options available for their treatment will be reviewed.

CLASSIFICATION OF VENTRICULAR ARRHYTHMIAS

The discussion of a complex topic requires that certain terms be defined so that the subject can be approached in an organized manner. Ventricular premature depolarizations are categorized by the Lown classification as single, multiform, R-on-T, and repetitive forms. Although this classification system is quite useful for evaluating the risk of developing more malignant arrhythmias in the first several days following acute myocardial infarction, it has limited value in the setting of chronic arrhythmias. For practical purposes, VPDs may be classified as either single or repetitive forms (two to four beats). Nonsustained ventricular tachycardia is defined as five or more consecutive ventricular complexes at a rate greater than 100 beats per minute lasting less than 30 seconds. Sustained ventricular tachycardia is defined as lasting at least 30 seconds or resulting in hemodynamic collapse requiring termination by pacing or cardioversion. It is extremely useful to subdivide sustained ventricular tachycardia as either monomorphic (a constant QRS morphology) or polymorphic (a changing QRS morphology). This distinction has important implications for understanding the mechanisms and treatment of ventricular tachycardia.

Ventricular arrhythmias may also be categorized by their prognostic implications as either benign, potentially lethal, or lethal. The benign ventricular arrhythmias include VPDs in the setting of no structural heart disease. Potentially lethal arrhythmias include nonsustained ventricular arrhythmias in a wide variety of structural cardiac disorders and some cases of sustained ventricular tachycardia in otherwise normal hearts. Lethal ventricular arrhythmias include sustained ventricular tachycardia and ventricular fibrillation. Although it is usually not a problem to identify patients with benign ventricular arrhythmias and those with lethal arrhythmias, major difficulties arise when considering the intermediate category of potentially lethal arrhythmias. Distinguishing those patients in this intermediate group who should be aggressively treated from those who are best left untreated remains problematic. The use of several techniques, such as signal-averaged electrocardiography and invasive electrophysiologic studies, may offer some improvements for defining prognosis in this group.

VENTRICULAR PREMATURE DEPOLARIZATIONS RELATED TO SUDDEN DEATH FOLLOWING MYOCARDIAL INFARCTION

Several large, randomized, multicenter studies have demonstrated that the presence of frequent VPDs (over six per hour) is associated with a 1.5- to 3-fold increase in the risk of sudden death following myocardial infarction. For example, the Myocardial Infarction Limitation of Infarct Size (MILIS) study reported that over an 18-month period following myocardial infarction, sudden death occurred in over 12% of patients with VPDs. Similarly, the Cardiac Arrhythmia Supression Trial (CAST) reported that patients with over 6 VPDs per hour had a 7% risk of sudden or arrhythmia-induced death over a period of 12 months post myocardial infarction. Virtually all of these studies have suggested that the presence of VPDs after myocardial infarction portends an increased risk of sudden death. The prognostic significance of VPDs has been shown to be further increased in the presence of impaired left ventricular function; the worse the left ventricular function, the greater the effect that VPDs have on the risk of sudden death. The presence of VPDs in the setting of relatively normal left ventricular function following myocardial infarction adds little to the

risk of subsequent sudden death. However, in the first 6 months following myocardial infarction, patients with both frequent VPDs and a left ventricular ejection fraction less than 0.40 have repeatedly been shown to be at higher risk for sudden death than those with either factor alone. Although it has been suggested that VPDs may imply a worse prognosis simply because they occur in patients with the worst cardiac function, multivariate statistical techniques that attempt to control for other clinical factors have demonstrated that the presence of ventricular arrhythmias adds important prognostic information that is independent of other clinical variables.

VENTRICULAR PREMATURE DEPOLARIZATIONS AND OTHER CARDIAC DISORDERS

Despite the adverse effect that ventricular arrhythmias have on prognosis after myocardial infarction, the presence of VPDs in patients with no evidence of heart disease does not predict an adverse clinical course. For example, untreated VPDs in otherwise healthy individuals have been shown to have no association with either sudden death or development of more malignant arrhythmias in long-term follow-up studies spanning up to 30 years. Because of the observed benign nature of asymptomatic ventricular arrhythmias in patients with structurally normal hearts, no treatment is needed for patients in this category. Indeed, antiarrhythmic drugs are likely to be detrimental to the health of these individuals because of the inherent risk of proarrhythmia. The presence of VPDs in patients with dilated or hypertrophic cardiomyopathy has not been conclusively shown to worsen prognosis. However, since many patients with cardiomyopathy die suddenly, the optimal management of asymptomatic VPDs in this group of patients remains uncertain. A newly appreciated group of patients at risk for sustained ventricular tachycardia is long-term survivors of congenital heart surgery, especially those following repair of the tetralogy of Fallot. These individuals may experience sustained ventricular tachycardia years to several decades following surgery. Although VPDs are common following this operation, the value of VPDs to predict more serious arrhythmias in this setting is not clearly defined. Whether prophylactic treatment should be initiated for patients following repair of tetralogy of Fallot is uncertain at this point.

RISK STRATIFICATION: PATIENTS WITH POTENTIALLY LIFE-THREATENING VENTRICULAR ARRHYTHMIAS

As mentioned in the preceding discussion, many patients with structural heart disease can be demonstrated to be at increased risk for sudden cardiac death. The clinical management of patients in this large group would be optimized if those patients destined to develop more malignant arrhythmias could be discriminated from those who would have a benign clinical course. To this end, several techniques have been developed. The concept of signal-averaged electrocardiography was discussed in Chapter 3. The signal-averaged ECG allows detection of low-amplitude, fractionated electrical activity related to slow conduction of activation in areas of scarred myocardium. These regions of slow conduction may be involved in the genesis of re-entrant ventricular tachycardia or fibrillation. The signal-averaged ECG produces a relatively pure QRS complex that is devoid of artifact related to muscle activity or electrical noise. This signal is then amplified and filtered to detect these areas of slow conduction and delayed activation, termed late potentials.

Late potentials in the signal-averaged ECG have been shown to enhance the ability to predict which patients are at risk for malignant ventricular arrhythmias. Signal-averaged ECG's recorded between 1 and 6 weeks post myocardial infarction have correctly identified greater than 90% of patients who subsequently developed ventricular tachycardia or ventricular fibrillation. However, the specificity for predicting the occurrence of arrhythmias is less, approaching only 60% to 70%. More importantly, this technique has demonstrated that a normal signal-averaged ECG identifies an extremely low-risk group of patients having a

risk for life-threatening ventricular arrhythmias to be less than 1%. When the results of radionuclide angiography to assess left ventricular ejection fraction are combined with the findings of the signal-averaged ECG, the positive predictive value of these techniques increases. The presence of a normal signal-averaged ECG and a left ventricular ejection fraction greater than 0.40 defines a low-risk population. A signal-averaged ECG demonstrating late potentials with an ejection fraction less than 0.40 places patients with frequent VPDs at a substantially higher risk for the development of sustained ventricular tachycardia or sudden death. The techniques of the radionuclide angiogram, the signal-averaged ECG, and Holter monitoring provide independent prognostic information. Therefore, strategies combining these tests to determine which patients should undergo programmed electrical stimulation or receive drug therapy are being developed, in hopes of reducing the subsequent risk of sudden death. It should be emphasized that the effectiveness of these treatment strategies has yet to be proven.

EVALUATION AND TREATMENT OF VENTRICULAR ARRHYTHMIAS RELATED TO CORONARY ARTERY DISEASE

Although frequent VPDs following myocardial infarction are associated with an increased risk for arrhythmic events, especially when there is significant impairment of left ventricular function, treatment of this with antiarrhythmic drugs has not been shown to improve long-term survival. In fact, CAST has convincingly demonstrated that antiarrhythmic drugs may worsen survival in this setting. The CAST study is an ongoing multicenter trial that addresses the issue of whether suppression of ventricular arrhythmias in patients with impaired left ventricular function following myocardial infarction decreases the risk of sudden cardiac death. In the study, patient selection for participation was based on the occurrence of a myocardial infarction within the 2 years preceding the study and the persistence of frequent VPDs (six or more per hour) with a left ventricular ejection fraction less than 0.55 if the myocardial infarction occurred within 90 days of the start of the study, or less than 0.40 if the myocardial infarction occurred within 90 days to 2 years prior to the start of the study. Patients were treated with either flecainide (if their ejection fraction was ≥ 0.3), encainide, or moricizine, with Holter monitoring. The dose of these drugs was titrated to achieve greater than 80% suppression of VPDs and more than 90% suppression of nonsustained ventricular tachycardia runs on a 24-hour episode of Holter monitoring. Patients demonstrating suppression of their ventricular arrhythmias were then randomly assigned to receive the effective drug or placebo. By an average of 10 months of follow-up, the overall mortality in the flecainide and encainide groups was 2.5 times higher than that in the placebo group. Thus class IC drugs given to patients demonstrating suppression of ventricular arrhythmias post myocardial infarction worsen prognosis. The moricizine arm of the study, CAST II, compared treatment with moricizine to that of placebo in patients with left ventricular ejection fractions (≤ 0.40 post myocardial infarction). CAST II was also discontinued due to higher mortality rates.

The CAST results are striking when one considers that only patients demonstrating suppression of their arrhythmias were entered into the randomized phase of the trial. One criticism of the CAST study has been that the mortality rate for patients entered into the randomized phase of the study was lower than expected. The actuarial (Kaplan-Meier) estimated mortality rate for all patients enrolled in CAST, including patients not randomized, was 10.3%, similar to the reported incidence in previous studies examining the mortality rate postinfarction. As postulated by Epstein and other CAST investigators, the lower mortality rate of the randomized population may reflect a favorable prognosis for patients whose arrhythmias are suppressed by antiarrhythmia drug therapy, regardless of whether such therapy is actually administered. Thus patients who have suppressible arrhythmias have a good prognosis even with placebo therapy.

It should be emphasized that other class I antiarrhythmic drugs have not been shown to improve survival in this population. Whether these drugs demonstrate a deleterious effect on survival similar to the CAST results is uncertain, as randomized trials have not been performed with these agents. The summary of our current knowledge regarding asymptomatic VPDs after myocardial infarction is that class I antiarrhythmic drugs have not been shown to favorably influence survival. Considering that the only adequate randomized trial demonstrated a deleterious effect of class I drugs and in the absence of any favorable information about their use, these drugs should not be administered for asymptomatic VPDs. In contrast to class I drugs, β-blockers have been shown to favorably influence postinfarction survival. These agents do have a role to play in routine postinfarct management.

The proper management of nonsustained ventricular tachycardia in patients with coronary artery disease remains unsettled. In the absence of definitive studies, the following comments regarding nonsustained ventricular tachycardia are based on the authors' current practice. For patients with asymptomatic nonsustained ventricular tachycardia in the presence of coronary artery disease, the only antiarrhythmic treatment that is routinely prescribed is β-blocking drugs. Class I antiarrhythmic medications are not used in this population. However, for patients with symptomatic nonsustained ventricular tachycardia with coronary artery disease, a more aggressive approach is taken. In light of the CAST results, standard Holter-guided antiarrhythmic drug trials are probably no longer warranted. Rather, these patients are likely to be more accurately assessed with invasive electrophysiologic studies to determine if sustained ventricular arrhythmias are inducible. If sustained ventricular tachycardia can be induced by programmed stimulation, chronic therapy is guided by the results of electrophysiologic testing. In patients without inducible arrhythmias, therapy is individualized depending on the frequency and severity of symptoms and the response to β-blockers (if no contraindications to this treatment exist). While such an approach is not universally accepted, we believe that it is reasonable based on our current level of incomplete information.

MECHANISM OF VENTRICULAR TACHYCARDIA RELATED TO CORONARY ARTERY DISEASE

The mechanism underlying ventricular tachycardia in acute ischemia is unknown. However, it is known that acute ischemia produces loss of the normal resting membrane potential, resulting in relatively depolarized myocytes. The refractory period decreases during early ischemia, a fact that correlates with the clinical observation of shortening of the QT interval and short coupling intervals for VPDs that initiate polymorphic ventricular tachycardia in this setting (Figure 7-1).

In addition, excitability is increased in the early phase of ischemia. Later in the course of ischemia, the refractory period lengthens, and excitability is depressed. There also develops a marked inhomogeneity in the refractoriness of ischemic myocardium, with areas having a relatively short action potential duration being in close proximity to areas of a longer action potential duration. This loss of the normal closely controlled synchronization in action potential duration and ventricular refractory periods has been referred to as dispersion of refractoriness. This dispersion in refractoriness may serve as fertile ground for the development of micro–reentrant circuits. Experimental studies of acute ischemic ventricular arrhythmias have demonstrated multiple wavelets of reentry of changing diameter and size.

A second mechanism that may produce arrhythmias during acute ischemia involves the flow of injury current between depolarized ischemic cells and neighboring normal areas of myocardium. Since the ischemic areas demonstrate a depolarized resting membrane potential during diastole (the current of injury), the passive flow of electrical current between these cells and normal cells may initiate propagated impulses in the normal myocardium (Figure 7-2).

Other factors that may play a role in acute ischemic arrhythmias include acidosis, localized accumulation of potassium ions, inhibition of the sodium-potassium exchange pump as ATP is

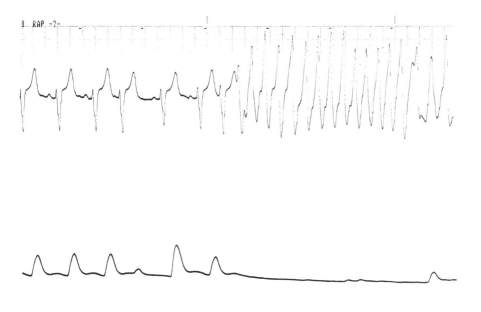

Figure 7-1 Ischemic polymorphic ventricular tachycardia is demonstrated. In the upper panel surface lead II demonstrates sinus rhythm with atrial premature depolarizations. The seventh beat initiates a polymorphic ventricular tachycardia at a rate of approximately 300 beats per minute. Notice that the initiating coupling interval is approximately 300 milliseconds. Note that the QT interval is normal. This is quite typical of ischemic polymorphic ventricular tachycardia. In the bottom panel a radial artery pressure tracing is demonstrated. Notice that during ventricular tachycardia there is no effective blood pressure.

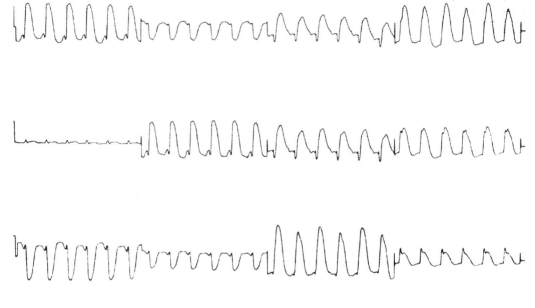

Figure 7-2 Acute anterior myocardial infarction masquerading as ventricular tachycardia. Note that this tracing represents sinus rhythm with ST segment elevation in leads V_2 to V_6 as well as in leads I and aVL. This patient had an occlusion of the left anterior descending coronary artery, with massive acute anterior injury. There are reciprocal changes of ST segment depression in leads III and aVF.

lost, and accumulation of lipids, which may depolarize the membrane and influence refractoriness. The reflex increase in sympathetic nervous tone and circulating catecholamines may also worsen arrhythmias in acute myocardial infarction. Experimental studies have demonstrated that blockade of the left stellate ganglion decreases the frequency of ventricular arrhythmias.

The mechanism of ventricular tachycardia during the chronic, healed phase following myocardial infarction is likely to be very different from that of acute ischemic arrhythmias. Ventricular tachycardia remote from acute myocardial infarction tends to be monomorphic, have a stable, regular rate, and persist for minutes to many days (Figures 7-3, 7-4, 7-5, and 7-6).

Chronic recurrent ventricular tachycardia tends to recur with the same QRS morphology over a period of years. It is usually easily inducible by programmed electrical stimulation and can usually be terminated by rapid ventricular pacing. It can usually be transiently entrained by rapid pacing, a technique that strongly suggests reentry with a gap of excitability as the mechanism of the tachycardia. Each of these features of chronic recurrent ventricular tachycardia points to a mechanism of reentry around an anatomic obstacle (described in Chapter 2). The use of ventricular mapping studies in clinical ventricular tachycardia has also suggested that a stable reentrant circuit is present, with the expected features of a region of slow conduction and unidirectional block. Recent experimental studies utilizing the technique of transient entrainment in patients with ventricular tachycardia have suggested that antiarrhythmic drugs may have preferential effects on the region of slow conduction in the reentrant circuit and act to slow conduction in the circuit of ventricular tachycardia to a greater extent than in other areas of the myocardium. Human studies of ventricular tachycardia in the operating room have indicated that most of these arrhythmias originate in subendocardial areas of scarring, often at the border of infarcted regions and normal myocardium, and typically occur with ventricular aneurysms.

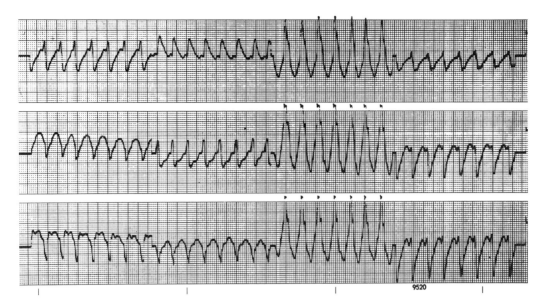

Figure 7-3 Sustained right bundle branch block left superior axis QRS morphology ventricular tachycardia. A wide QRS complex tachycardia at a rate of approximately 200 beats per minute is demonstrated, with a monophasic R wave in lead V_1 and an R:S ratio in lead V_6 of less than 1.0. Notice that the QRS duration is approximately 200 milliseconds and that the axis is superior, with the predominant QRS deflection in lead aVF being negative. These factors are suggestive of a ventricular origin for this tachycardia.

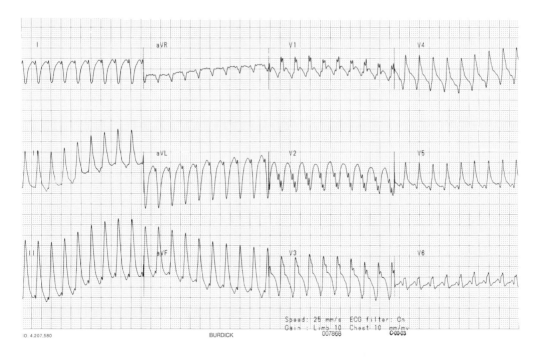

Figure 7-4 Right bundle branch block right inferior axis QRS morphology ventricular tachycardia. Note that the predominant deflection in V_1 is upright, with a RSR' pattern. The QRS duration is 180 milliseconds, which is strongly suggestive of ventricular tachycardia. Also note the bizarre transition between leads V_1 and V_2 from a predominantly upright QRS to a predominantly negative QRS. These features are also suggestive of ventricular tachycardia.

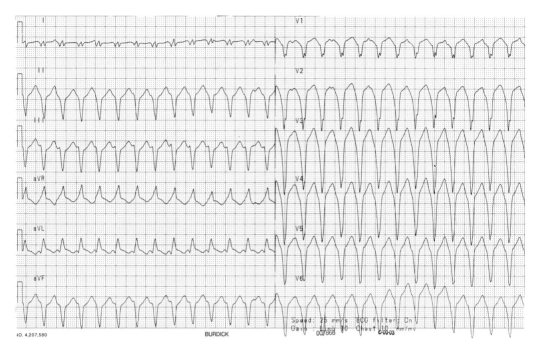

Figure 7-5 Sustained left bundle branch block and right superior axis QRS morphology ventricular tachycardia is demonstrated at a rate of 165 beats per minute. Notice that in leads V_1 and V_2 there is a slurred downstroke of the S wave. The period from the onset of the QRS to the nadir of the S wave is approximately 120 milliseconds. Also note that in lead V_6 there is a prominent Q wave. These features are highly suggestive of a ventricular origin for this arrhythmia. Also notice that in lead V_1, AV dissociation is clearly seen, with P waves that are dissociated.

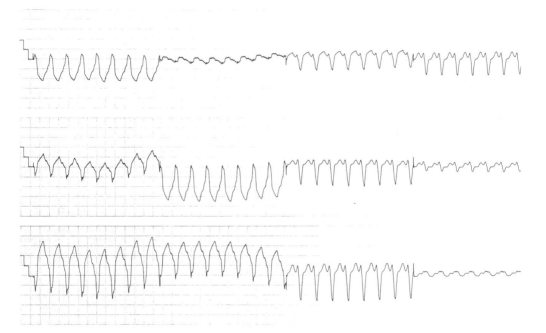

Figure 7-6 Sustained left bundle branch block, left superior axis QRS morphology ventricular tachycardia at approximately 185 beats per minute is shown. Note in V_1 and V_2 that the R wave is greater than 30 milliseconds in duration, that there is a notch in the S wave in V_1, and that the duration of the S wave is greater than 60 milliseconds.

EVALUATION AND TREATMENT OF SUSTAINED VENTRICULAR ARRHYTHMIAS RELATED TO CORONARY ARTERY DISEASE

Sustained ventricular arrhythmias in the presence of coronary artery disease may be an acute response to infarction or ischemia or may represent a chronic, recurrent problem. The management of ventricular tachycardia or fibrillation complicating the first several hours of myocardial infarction is quite different from the management of chronic, recurrent sustained ventricular tachycardia. Patients who experience sustained ventricular arrhythmias within hours of a myocardial infarction generally have a low risk of arrhythmia recurrence and subsequent sudden death. In this setting, ventricular fibrillation is usually a response to partially depolarized, ischemic myocardium. Once the acute injury is over, these arrhythmias are unlikely to recur. The acute ischemic ventricular arrhythmias usually constitute either a rapid, polymorphic ventricular tachycardia that promptly degenerates to ventricular fibrillation or the direct development of ventricular fibrillation. These arrhythmias require defibrillation and are usually treated with intravenous lidocaine, β-blockers, and possibly bretylium. Long-term therapy is rarely required.

The onset of acute ischemic polymorphic ventricular tachycardia is usually marked by a short-coupled VPD in an R-on-T pattern (Figure 7-1). The QT interval is typically short, a factor that distinguishes the ischemic nature of this rhythm from that of torsades de pointes. The rate of ischemic polymorphic ventricular tachycardia is usually greater than 240 beats per minute, and syncope is typical. This arrhythmia rapidly degenerates to ventricular fibrillation. Fortunately, ischemic polymorphic ventricular tachycardia usually does not recur after the first 48 hours post myocardial infarction. This arrhythmia may complicate the course of patients with severe myocardial ischemia in the setting of unstable angina. The proper treatment of patients with polymorphic ventricular tachycardia or ventricular fibrillation in the presence of a normal QT interval involves prompt coronary arteriography and relief of ischemia.

Lidocaine and bretylium are often effective agents prior to the performance of definitive coronary revascularization procedures.

Sustained ventricular tachycardia that occurs remote from acute myocardial ischemia represents a chronic, recurrent problem with a very high recurrence rate. Early studies of the survival of patients resuscitated from sudden death have consistently shown an arrhythmia recurrence rate of 30% to 40% over the subsequent 1 to 2 years. More recent studies of patients in whom an implantable cardioverter defibrillator has been implanted have shown similar rates of defibrillator discharge, episodes that presumably would have resulted in sudden death. Thus ventricular tachycardia or ventricular fibrillation that does not occur during acute ischemia is associated with a very high rate of recurrence. In fact, there are few if any chronic diseases with as high a mortality rate.

The initial approach to the treatment of sustained ventricular tachycardia associated with chronic coronary artery disease usually begins with an assessment of left ventricular function and coronary artery anatomy. Cardiac catheterization and coronary arteriography are indicated for almost all patients with sustained ventricular arrhythmias. If there is a clear, identifiable precipitating factor for the arrhythmia (marked electrolyte abnormality, proarrhythmic drug therapy, thyrotoxicosis, ischemia), these factors are corrected. Patients with evidence of critical coronary artery stenoses, unstable angina, and electrocardiographic or radionuclide evidence of severe ischemia are treated with antianginal drugs, coronary artery bypass grafting, or percutaneous transluminal coronary angioplasty. This approach is especially useful if the clinical arrhythmia was polymorphic ventricular tachycardia. However, most patients with monomorphic ventricular tachycardia will not have a readily correctable precipitating cause, and myocardial revascularization alone will rarely eliminate the arrhythmia. In this majority of patients, a direct approach to the arrhythmia is necessary.

Although early studies suggested that empiric antiarrhythmic drug therapy with achievement of therapeutic serum concentrations is effective for preventing recurrent ventricular tachycardia, this approach has been discredited because of a very high rate of failure. The two competing approaches to the management of sustained ventricular arrhythmias have involved a noninvasive, Holter monitor-guided approach to drug therapy and an invasive, electrophysiologically guided approach. Although there has been a debate regarding the overall merits of these treatment strategies, there has been only one prospective randomized study addressing this issue. Mitchell et al. randomized patients with sustained ventricular tachycardia to treatment guided by either invasive electrophysiologic testing or noninvasive monitoring (Holter monitoring and exercise testing). The results of this study suggest that the noninvasive strategy is associated with a higher rate of arrhythmia recurrence. A prospective randomized study, the ESVEM Trial (Electrophysiologic Study Versus Electrocardiographic Monitoring) involving multiple centers is now going on to further define the role of each of these techniques.

The noninvasive approach to ventricular tachycardia is based on the hypothesis that suppression of spontaneous VPDs and nonsustained ventricular tachycardia predicts suppression of sustained arrhythmias. Patients are evaluated in the baseline, drug-free state with prolonged Holter monitoring and treadmill or bicycle exercise testing to quantitate their level of spontaneous ventricular arrhythmias. If significant ventricular ectopy is present during the baseline evaluation, patients are treated with an antiarrhythmic drug to achieve a steady-state serum level, and the Holter monitor and exercise tests are repeated. Effective suppression with this approach is considered to have occurred with a 90% reduction in single VPDs and complete suppression of nonsustained ventricular tachycardia.

Although early results suggested a high rate of arrhythmia control with the noninvasive approach, subsequent studies have suggested a sudden cardiac death rate of 5% to 12% within the first year with this approach. A limitation of the noninvasive approach is that a significant minority of patients with a history of malignant ventricular arrhythmias do not have sufficient ventricular ectopy to permit adequate assessment of therapeutic efficacy by noninvasive

means. The strategy of suppressing spontaneous VPDs as a means to reduce the risk of sudden cardiac death has been further questioned by the preliminary report of CAST, which showed a higher mortality in patients treated with drugs that suppressed ambient ectopy than in patients treated with placebo. Since the CAST trial excluded patients with sustained ventricular arrhythmias, it is not certain that the results can be generalized to a Holter-guided strategy for these more malignant arrhythmias. Regardless, the CAST results are not supportive of this approach. It should also be emphasized that failure to suppress VPDs and nonsustained ventricular tachycardia during a drug trial is highly predictive of failure of that drug to prevent induction of sustained ventricular arrhythmias with programmed stimulation. The major limitation of the noninvasive approach is the tendency of this method to falsely predict drug efficacy. Although noninvasive testing for ventricular tachycardia suppression has these important limitations, patients may decline invasive electrophysiologic studies or may be poor candidates for these procedures for other clinical reasons. Because of this, noninvasive testing will continue to be a reasonable strategy for selected patients and an adjunct to more aggressive approaches.

Electrophysiologic testing has gained widespread popularity as a method for evaluating the effectiveness of antiarrhythmic drugs to suppress sustained ventricular arrhythmias. The rationale for this technique has been that the effect of antiarrhythmic drugs on this arrhythmia could be tested under controlled conditions. Patients are typically evaluated by programmed electrical stimulation in the baseline, drug-free state. If sustained ventricular tachycardia is inducible at baseline, programmed stimulation is repeated after treatment with antiarrhythmic drugs. An electrode catheter may be left in place for serial testing of drugs on subsequent days.

Several early reports of the invasive electrophysiologic-guided approach for management of the malignant ventricular arrhythmias suggests that lack of arrhythmia inducibility during drug therapy with an antiarrhythmic agent predicted a very low spontaneous recurrence rate of ventricular arrhythmias. Despite these initial results, later reports of the long-term survival of patients whose treatment with antiarrhythmic medications was guided by electrophysiologic testing have been less encouraging. Mortality rates as high as 17% in the first year after therapy for malignant ventricular arrhythmias directed by electrophysiologic studies have been reported. It should be emphasized that accurate comparison of the invasive and noninvasive approaches to ventricular arrhythmia management is limited by the sparcity of controlled trials of these methods. The varying results that have been reported may reflect differences in patient populations, including the nature and severity of ventricular arrhythmias, the degree of functional impairment and the inclusion of patients with amiodarone. It is likely that differences in these parameters markedly influences the overall mortality of the trials and the probability of arrhythmia recurrence.

In addition to these limitations of drug therapy guided by programmed stimulation, the rate of sudden death among patients without inducible ventricular arrhythmias at baseline electrophysiologic study is relatively high, ranging from 12% to 17% over a period of up to 24 months. It remains clear that persistence of inducibility is associated with an increased probability of recurrent cardiac arrest. The electrophysiologic-guided approach identifies only 25% to 30% of patients with sustained ventricular arrhythmias as being responsive to standard antiarrhythmic drugs (not including amiodarone). It has been demonstrated that the response to intravenous procainamide is highly predictive of the response to other standard antiarrhythmic drugs. For example, Josephson and colleagues found that an effective drug regimen could be identified in only 5% of patients failing to respond favorably to intravenous procainamide. The relatively low success rate for drug therapy predicted by invasive electrophysiologic testing has resulted in a growing enthusiasm for treatments that are nonpharmacologic, especially implantable cardioverter defibrillators, and catheter ablation.

Our standard approach to programmed electrical stimulation is to deliver one, two, or three extrastimuli from the right ventricular apex and outflow tract at basic S1 drive cycle lengths of 500 and 400 milliseconds. Rapid ventricular burst pacing is also used if standard extrastimuli are not effective in the induction of ventricular tachycardia. Over 95% of patients with sustained monomorphic ventricular tachycardia related to chronic coronary artery disease will have inducible arrhythmias with this approach. If ventricular tachycardia is not inducible with this stimulation, isoproterenol is infused in a dose sufficient to increase the sinus rate by 20%, and programmed stimulation is continued using one, two, or three extrastimuli. If ventricular tachycardia has not been induced and there is a clearly documented clinical episode of monomorphic ventricular tachycardia, programmed stimulation will then be performed from the left ventricle. Any arrhythmias that are induced are recorded on a 12-lead ECG. In approximately 75% of patients, rapid ventricular pacing will result in termination of the induced arrhythmia. In the remaining 25%, synchronized cardioversion will be required for termination. In the baseline study, it is important to reproduce the induced arrhythmia to confirm that programmed stimulation will be a valid guide to arrhythmia management.

The initial electrophysiologic study will usually test the response to intravenous procainamide or quinidine. For patients responding to either of these agents, programmed stimulation will then be repeated on an oral preparation of these drugs after achievement of steady-state serum concentrations. In patients who are not suppressed by either procainamide or quinidine, a decision will be made either to pursue serial drug testing with other, standard agents, to proceed to investigational antiarrhythmic drugs, to begin amiodarone therapy, or to pursue nonpharmacologic therapy with catheter ablation, the implantable cardioverter defibrillator with or without antitachycardia pacing, or ventricular tachycardia surgery. If the ventricular tachycardia remains inducible but is slowed significantly (cycle length prolonged by over 100 milliseconds), we often proceed to other drugs or combinations of drugs (typically lidocaine to evaluate a 1/A 1/B combination in the laboratory). The addition of mexiletine to a class IA drug is often effective in these partial responders. Although class IC agents may be effective for selected individuals with sustained ventricular tachycardia in whom class IA drugs have failed, the usefulness of testing these drugs in these patients is very small. Because of this, flecainide, encainide, and propafenone are rarely chosen in patients failing to have suppression of ventricular tachycardia with intravenous procainamide.

Treatment with amiodarone is associated with control of ventricular arrhythmias in approximately 70% of patients. Many patients who have a favorable clinical response to amiodarone continue to demonstrate inducible ventricular arrhythmias by programmed electrical stimulation while receiving the drug. Follow-up electrophysiologic testing may be useful, however, as a very low risk group may be identified by the absence of inducible arrhythmias on this agent. If rapid, poorly tolerated ventricular tachycardia remains inducible on amiodarone, a second drug may be added, or another therapy may be considered. Although amiodarone is an extremely effective antiarrhythmic drug, its clinical use is limited by its long-term side effects. Approximately 10% of patients will develop significant bradycardia on amiodarone and require permanent pacemaker implantation. Furthermore, approximately 7% of patients receiving amiodarone in doses effective for the suppression of ventricular tachycardia will develop pulmonary toxicity. Overall, at 5 years of follow-up, only 20% to 30% of patients initially treated with amiodarone will remain alive and on the drug. The majority will either have died or have developed an important side effect requiring discontinuation of the medication. The 1-year mortality rate for patients treated with amiodarone for sustained ventricular tachycardia is approximately 20% to 25%. It has been demonstrated that this mortality rate is similar to that expected in other patients without arrhythmias, matched for similar levels of left ventricular dysfunction, congestive heart failure, and coronary artery stenoses.

Patients with clinical episodes of ventricular tachycardia or ventricular fibrillation related to coronary artery disease who do not have arrhythmias inducible with programmed electrical stimulation pose difficult clinical management problems. Since the sensitivity of programmed stimulation for sustained monomorphic ventricular tachycardia in the presence of coronary artery disease is high (more than 95%), evidence for acute, reversible precipitating factors is sought. If the clinical arrhythmia is polymorphic ventricular tachycardia or ventricular fibrillation, the precipitating factor is likely to be related to acute ischemia. In this situation, primary therapy should be directed toward relieving ischemia. However, if the clinical arrhythmia is sustained monomorphic ventricular tachycardia, an easily reversible precipitating factor is usually not found. This group of patients is usually managed by implantation of an automatic defibrillator if otherwise clinically appropriate.

MAPPING OF VENTRICULAR TACHYCARDIA TO LOCALIZE THE SITE OF ORIGIN

Localization of the site of origin of ventricular tachycardia is not required if pharmacologic treatment is planned. However, nonpharmacologic therapies directed at the reentrant circuit of ventricular tachycardia require that the circuit be accurately localized. Mapping of ventricular tachycardia is performed with the use of endocardial catheters in the electrophysiology laboratory. Ventricular tachycardia is induced by programmed electrical stimulation, and the activation sequence of the right and left ventricles is recorded at multiple sites. The standard electrode catheters are manipulated in an organized manner over the endocardial surface of both ventricles. The onset of local activation at each recording site is compared to the surface QRS complex. Areas recording local ventricular activation prior to the onset of the surface QRS are activated early and are closer to the site of origin of the tachycardia than are areas activated later. The accuracy of mapping may be enhanced by techniques of resetting and transient entrainment that seek to localize the region of slow conduction in the reentry circuit. In order for ventricular mapping to be completed, the tachycardia must be relatively well tolerated to allow time to record at multiple sites. Neither polymorphic ventricular tachycardia nor ventricular fibrillation can be mapped, as a stable reentrant circuit is not present. These arrhythmias are probably best managed with other techniques. For tachycardias that are poorly tolerated, pacing at multiple sites in the ventricles is performed, with comparison of the paced QRS morphology on the 12-lead ECG to the QRS morphology during induced ventricular tachycardia.

NONPHARMACOLOGIC TREATMENTS FOR SUSTAINED VENTRICULAR ARRHYTHMIAS

The first nonmedical therapy for ventricular tachycardia demonstrated to have a high rate of success was direct surgical resection of the arrhythmogenic substrate. Surgery for ventricular tachycardia generally requires a preoperative catheter mapping study to localize the site of origin of the tachycardia. Mapping is also performed in the operating room over the epicardial surface of the heart and following opening of the ventricle. In the presence of coronary artery disease, the vast majority of ventricular tachycardias arise in the subendocardial layer of the left ventricle or interventricular septum. Thus endocardial mapping is most accurate in localizing the site of earliest ventricular activation during ventricular tachycardia.

Following endocardial mapping in ventricular tachycardia, the site of earliest activation is resected by peeling the scarred endocardial layer from more healthy regions of myocardium (subendocardial resection) or by freezing this region with a liquid nitrogen cryoprobe to a temperature of $-60°C$ for 2 to 3 minutes. Left ventricular aneurysms, which are frequently present, are also resected. In some cases, an incision is made around the site of origin of the tachycardia (encircling endocardial ventriculotomy) to isolate it from the remainder of the ventricle. Other techniques include blind resection of all scarred myocardium without mapping and use of laser energy to destroy the areas involved in the tachycardia. These surgical approaches can be performed with the heart warm and beating or during cold cardioplegia. Following these techniques, programmed electrical stimulation is

performed in an attempt to reinduce ventricular tachycardia. If the tachycardia can still be induced, further mapping and surgery are done to destroy the tachycardia focus.

Most centers report that 80% to 90% of patients will no longer have inducible ventricular tachycardia following surgery for ventricular tachycardia. However, there is a significant operative mortality rate, approaching 10% at most centers. This is related to the relatively poor left ventricular function that is found in most patients with these arrhythmias. In addition to the early mortality rate, long-term survival of these patients is on the order of only 35% to 50% at 5 years. The most common cause of late death following surgery for ventricular tachycardia involves congestive heart failure. The late recurrence of arrhythmias is much less likely. Despite these limitations, primary surgery is often a very good solution for patients with ventricular tachycardia if the left ventricle will not be severely impaired postoperatively.

The most promising nonpharmacologic techniques for management of ventricular tachycardia involve use of the implantable cardioverter defibrillator. When combined with antitachycardia pacing to terminate relatively slow and well-tolerated ventricular tachycardias are terminated by pacing and to terminate more rapid or less well-tolerated arrhythmias are terminated by direct current shocks. Devices combining the features of both antitachycardia pacing and defibrillation are now becoming available for clinical studies. The implantable cardioverter-defibrillator has been demonstrated to provide the best chance of freedom from arrhythmic death for patients with sustained ventricular arrhythmias. Although the current generation of implantable cardioverter defibrillators requires that a thoracotomy be performed to implant the defibrillation patch electrodes, nonthoracotomy devices are being evaluated in clinical trials. In many centers, the implantable cardioverter defibrillator has replaced drug therapy as primary treatment for malignant ventricular arrhythmias. It should be emphasized that the implantable cardioverter defibrillator does not protect patients from congestive heart failure or recurrent myocardial infarction, and long-term mortality related to these factors remains relatively high. For patients with severe congestive heart failure and ventricular arrhythmias, cardiac transplantation may be the best long-term solution.

Catheter ablation techniques have been developed for the treatment of ventricular tachycardia related to coronary artery disease. Catheter ablation for ventricular tachycardia has generally involved use of high-energy direct current shocks delivered to the site of origin, although the technique of radiofrequency catheter ablation has recently been applied with limited success. Mapping of ventricular tachycardia with localization of the region of slow conduction has been shown to improve the success of this technique. The overall results have been only modestly encouraging, with most centers experiencing a success rate of approximately 30%. A newer technique involving the intracoronary infusion of ethanol to destroy the tachycardia focus has shown some initial promise, though it has so far had less than 50% overall success.

VENTRICULAR TACHYCARDIA IN SETTINGS OTHER THAN CORONARY ARTERY DISEASE

Ventricular tachycardia may complicate the course of many structural heart disorders other than coronary artery disease. In these other clinical settings, the mechanism of ventricular tachycardia may be related to reentry, enhanced automaticity, or triggered activity based on early or late after depolarizations. Because of the variable tachycardia mechanisms, the response to programmed stimulation, to drug therapy, and to such factors as exercise or catecholamines may differ. In general, programmed stimulation is less sensitive in these other clinical settings than in coronary artery disease. However, electrophysiologic studies may be important for many of these forms of ventricular tachycardia.

Cardiomyopathies

Cardiomyopathies may be classified as dilated, restrictive, or hypertrophic. Ventricular tachycardia or ventricular fibrillation may develop during the clinical course of any of these disorders, and sudden death is a major cause of mortality. Dilated cardiomyopathies commonly demonstrate VPDs, nonsustained ventricular tachycardia, and ventricular fibrillation. The initial approach to therapy is similar to that outlined above for coronary artery disease. At this point, there is no evidence that asymptomatic arrhythmias should be treated. Evaluation of the survivors of sustained ventricular tachycardia or ventricular fibrillation requires that the structural heart disease be carefully defined. Therefore, cardiac catheterization is performed, and reversible causes of cardiomyopathy are sought (myocarditis, iron overload, incessant atrial arrhythmias). The sensitivity of electrophysiologic studies for induction of sustained ventricular tachycardia in dilated cardiomyopathy has been found to be approximately 60% to 80%. In those patients with inducible sustained monomorphic ventricular tachycardia, serial drug testing may be approached in the same way as with coronary artery disease. A fairly common mechanism of ventricular tachycardia in patients with cardiomyopathies is known as bundle branch reentry. In this arrhythmia, a sustained ventricular tachycardia may develop that involves conduction in the antegrade direction over either the right or left bundle branch, with retrograde conduction over the other bundle branch. The reentry circuit is thus confined to the specialized conduction system. Because unidirectional block and slow conduction are required for reentry, virtually all patients with bundle branch reentry demonstrate a bundle branch block during sinus rhythm. Catheter ablation of either the right or left bundle branch has proven to be highly successful for patients with bundle branch reentry.

For patients with dilated cardiomyopathy and no inducible arrhythmias, empiric amiodarone, implantable cardioverter defibrillator implantation, and cardiac transplantation are likely to be the best options. If the ventricular function is poor and congestive heart failure is present, cardiac transplantation should be strongly considered. Our experience with use of the implantable cardioverter defibrillator in patients with dilated cardiomyopathy has been very encouraging, especially if patients have relatively well-compensated ventricular function and can tolerate β-blocker therapy. The presence of atrial arrhythmias can complicate use of the implantable cardioverter defibrillator in these individuals, and concomitant drug therapy is commonly required.

Hypertrophic cardiomyopathy may be accompanied by a high risk of sudden death, usually in the setting of physical exertion. β-Blockers and amiodarone have been the mainstays of therapy for this disorder. If congestive heart failure is absent or relatively well compensated, patients with hypertrophic cardiomyopathy and sustained ventricular arrhythmias may be well served by implantable cardioverter defibrillator implantation. A more controversial issue involves the proper management of asymptomatic individuals with hypertrophic cardiomyopathy and nonsustained ventricular tachycardia. These patients have an increased risk of sudden death. The empiric use of amiodarone for nonsustained ventricular tachycardia has been advocated and may improve survival. Although this approach has not been definitively proven, we have adopted the use of amiodarone for nonsustained ventricular tachycardia in patients with hypertrophic cardiomyopathy.

Restrictive cardiomyopathies involve infiltration of the myocardium with fibrous tissue, abnormal proteins (amyloid), or inflammatory cells (e.g., as in sarcoidosis). The presenting manifestation of sarcoidosis may be sudden death or sustained ventricular tachycardia. Ventricular tachycardia has been monomorphic in some individuals and polymorphic in others. Our experience with ventricular tachycardia related to sarcoidosis has indicated that this condition may be very difficult to treat, with an unpredictable response to drug therapy. For many patients, the implantable cardioverter defibrillator may provide the best long-term survival, provided that pulmonary function is adequate to tolerate thoracotomy. In other patients, combined heart-lung transplantation has been successful.

Right Ventricular Dysplasia

Right ventricular dysplasia is a disorder characterized by replacement of the right ventricular myocardium with an abnormal combination of fibrous and fatty tissue. This disorder typically involves the right ventricular apex, right ventricular outflow tract, and right ventricular inflow tract. This diagnosis is confirmed by echocardiography or right ventriculography, either of which will demonstrate enlargement of the right ventricle with abnormal outpouchings in the ventricular myocardium. Patients often are called to medical attention by the development of syncope or recurrent sustained ventricular tachycardia with a left bundle branch block QRS morphology. Although the prognosis is generally good, some patients suffer sudden cardiac death. Sustained monomorphic ventricular tachycardia is usually inducible by programmed electrical stimulation and can be terminated by rapid ventricular pacing. The tachycardia may respond to standard antiarrhythmic drug therapy and can often be managed by serial drug testing. This condition may be treated by catheter ablation with high-energy shocks or by surgery. The combination of antitachycardia pacing and automatic defibrillator implantation may be very effective for arrhythmogenic right ventricular dysplasia.

Exercise-Induced Ventricular Tachycardia in Structurally Normal Hearts

Ventricular tachycardia may develop in otherwise healthy young persons without evidence of structural cardiac abnormalities. These arrhythmias are often induced by exercise or clinical situations wherein serum catecholamine concentrations are high. The ventricular tachycardia tends to be monomorphic and associated with variable cardiac symptoms, ranging from completely asymptomatic to syncope or even sudden death. The mechanism of these arrhythmias is likely to vary, with most patients having no arrhythmias inducible with programmed electrical stimulation. Ventricular tachycardia is usually provoked by infusions of isoproterenol or exercise stress testing, suggesting abnormal automaticity as the underlying mechanism. In a minority of patients, programmed stimulation is effective for the induction of ventricular tachycardia, suggesting that reentry is the probable mechanism.

The naturally occurring substance adenosine is often used to probe the properties of ventricular tachycardia in the setting of no structural heart disease. Tachycardias responding to adenosine are likely to have arrhythmias that can be managed by β-blockers or verapamil. Patients who do not respond to adenosine are usually not responsive to calcium or β-blockers. Proof of effective therapy for exercise-induced ventricular tachycardia is provided by repeat exercise testing during oral drug therapy (usually β-blockers).

Two clinical syndromes of ventricular tachycardia occurring in otherwise healthy individuals should be mentioned. Patients with monomorphic ventricular tachycardia with left bundle branch block and inferior axis may be classified as having right ventricular outflow tract tachycardia (Figure 7-7). This arrhythmia is often inducible with programmed stimulation and is mapped to the outflow tract of the right ventricle. It carries a good prognosis and usually responds well to class I antiarrhythmic drugs. We have had excellent results with high-energy direct current shocks with this arrhythmia. The second clinical syndrome involves sustained right bundle branch block, superior axis ventricular tachycardia in healthy young individuals. This arrhythmia may be induced by either atrial or ventricular pacing and is responsive to verapamil.

It should be emphasized that rare patients with no obvious structural heart disease may develop polymorphic ventricular tachycardia or ventricular fibrillation. The malignant nature of these arrhythmias and their typical noninducibility demand that the implantable cardioverter defibrillator be considered. These patients usually have little else wrong with them and can live normal lives if their arrhythmia is effectively managed. It is probably unwise to trust the life of these patients to antiarrhythmic drugs when such an effective nonpharmacologic treatment is available.

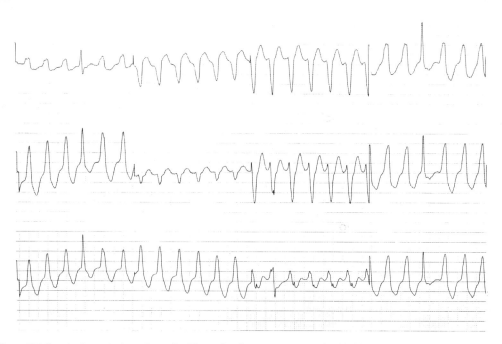

Figure 7-7 Sustained ventricular tachycardia. The tracing demonstrates a sustained left bundle branch block left inferior axis ventricular tachycardia at 150 beats per minute with fusion beats. The fusion beat seen in the fourth beat from the left is evidence of AV dissociation and is proof of the ventricular origin of this tachycardia. This tachycardia morphology is typical of tachycardias of right ventricular outflow tract origin.

Congenital Heart Disease

As more and more patients have undergone total repair for the tetralogy of Fallot, it has become clear that they are at risk for sudden death and recurrent ventricular tachycardia. Patients may develop malignant ventricular arrhythmias at any time following surgery, though usually after 10 years of follow-up. The factors predicting an increased risk of ventricular tachycardia include frequent VPDs, pulmonary hypertension, and bifascicular block. Sustained ventricular tachycardia can usually be induced by programmed ventricular stimulation in tetralogy of Fallot, and electrophysiologically guided therapy is useful for management. Electrophysiologic testing is indicated for patients following repair of tetralogy of Fallot with unexplained syncope and a history of sustained ventricular tachycardia, and probably for patients with symptomatic nonsustained ventricular tachycardia. Whether or not asymptomatic individuals with frequent VPDs or nonsustained ventricular tachycardia should undergo invasive studies is not certain at the present time. The reason that patients develop postoperative ventricular tachycardia is probably related to the use of a right ventriculotomy during the repair.

Other congenital diseases associated with late sudden death include transposition of the great vessels (corrected by Mustard repair) and transposition. Congenital anomalies of the coronary arteries, especially origin of the left main coronary artery from the right sinus of Valsalva, may be associated with sudden death, usually during exercise.

Congenital and Acquired Long QT Syndromes

The congenital long QT syndromes involve genetically transmitted abnormalities with (Jervell and Lange-Neilson syndrome) or without (Romano-Ward syndrome) congenital deafness. Patients with these disorders manifest bizarre T wave and U wave abnormalities in the surface ECG, marked prolongation of the QT interval, and recurrent syncope or sudden death. Sudden death and syncope have been demonstrated to be due to a specific variety of polymorphous ventricular tachycardia, torsades de pointes. This arrhythmia may be provoked by exercise or emotional stress in patients with the congenital long QT syndromes. Although the syndromes may be transmitted with autosomal dominant or autosomal recessive patterns, apparently many spontaneous mutations may occur.

The pathogenesis of the congenital long QT syndrome probably relates to an abnormality of the sympathetic innervation of the heart. In experimental animals, stimulation of the left stellate ganglion produces QT prolongation and may induce ventricular tachycardia. In contrast, stimulation of the right stellate ganglion may shorten the QT interval. This observation has been applied clinically with the use of surgical left stellate ganglionectomy to treat the congenital long QT syndromes. Although initial results were promising, reliable protection from torsades de pointes has not been provided by this procedure for all patients. Catecholamines may also lengthen the QT interval in these syndromes and trigger ventricular arrhythmias. β-Blockers have long been used successfully to manage patients with congenital QT prolongation. For patients failing these treatments, implantable cardioverter defibrillator implantation may be required.

The QT interval may be prolonged by a great number of drugs, toxins, electrolyte abnormalities, or medical illnesses, with resultant torsades de pointes (Figure 7-8). The most common cause of acquired torsades de pointes is antiarrhythmic drug treatment with the class IA and class III drugs. Quinidine, procainamide, NAPA, disopyramide, satalol, and amiodarone have all been repeatedly demonstrated to induce this arrhythmia. This adverse response usually occurs in an unpredictable manner, usually following the first several doses of these drugs. Although very high serum levels of quinidine or procainamide may induce torsades de pointes in almost any patient, the most common clinical scenario is an idiosyncratic reaction to the drugs with a low or therapeutic blood level.

Torsades de pointes may occur with phenothiazine drugs (especially Thioridazine HCl), antidepressants, erythromycin, hypokalemia, hypomagnesemia, arsenic poisoning, liquid pro-

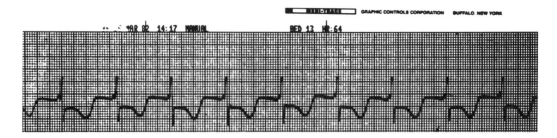

Figure 7-8 Drug-induced QT prolongation. This patient demonstrates a markedly prolonged QT interval following three doses of quinidine sulfate. The patient developed torsades de pointes ventricular tachycardia. Note that the T waves are bizarre and biphasic.

tein diets, complete AV block, and increased intracranial pressure. The mechanism of this arrhythmia is related to early afterdepolarizations arising in phase 3 of a markedly prolonged action potential. These early afterdepolarizations may result in triggered activity and polymorphic ventricular tachycardia. In experimental animals, marked QT prolongation and torsades de pointes can be produced by administration of cesium chloride, which blocks the outward potassium channel.

The electrocardiographic features that allow diagnosis of torsades de pointes include (Figure 7-9) (1) a prolonged QT interval (usually greater than 0.55 seconds); (2) long coupling intervals between the last normal sinus beat and the first beat of the tachycardia; (3) a long-short cycle length sequence with a pause preceding initiation of the tachycardia; (4) a twisting, polymorphic arrhythmia; (5) bradycardia; and (6) episodes of self-terminating tachycardia preceding sustained runs of tachycardia. Several treatments for torsades de pointes have been proposed, including isoproterenol infusion, phenytoin, intravenous magnesium, and overdrive pacing. Intravenous magnesium sulfate can be administered quickly and results in shortening of the QT interval. Definitive therapy involves atrial or ventricular pacing at a rate of at least 90 beats per minute. Pacing is continued as long

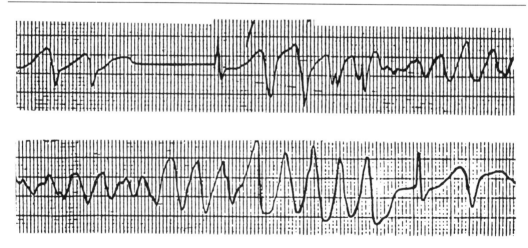

Figure 7-9 Continuous rhythm strip showing typical torsades de pointes ventricular tachycardia. Note the characteristic long-short initiating sequence with a pair of ventricular beats, followed by a long pause that ends with a junctional escape beat. This is followed by a marked prolongation of the QT interval and the initiation of a nonsustained run of ventricular tachycardia with twisting QRS morphology. Also note that the coupling interval between the junctional beat and the first beat of the ventricular tachycardia is quite long, on the order of 600 milliseconds. The self-termination of this tachycardia is also typical of this arrhythmia.

as the QT interval remains prolonged. Obviously, the precipitating factor should be corrected. If torsades de pointes has developed with one class IA drug, all drugs in this class should be avoided.

BIBLIOGRAPHY

Adhar GC, Larson LW, Bardy GH, et al. Sustained ventricular arrhythmias: differences between survivors of cardiac arrest and patients with recurrent sustained ventricular tachycardia. *J Am Coll Cardiol*. 1988;12:159–165.

Akhtar M, Shenasa M, Jazayeri M, et al. Wide QRS complex tachycardia: reapprisal of a common clinical problem. *Ann Intern Med*. 1988;109:905–912.

Bigger JT Jr, Fleiss JB, Kleiger R, et al. The relationship between ventricular arrhythmias, left ventricular dysfunction and mortality in the two years after myocardial infarction. *Circulation*. 1984;69:250–258.

Buxton AE, Waxman HL, Marchlinski FE, et al. Right ventricular tachycardia: clinical and electrophysiologic characteristics. *Circulation*. 1983;68:917–927.

The CAPS Investigators. The Cardiac Arrhythmia Pilot Study. *Am J Cardiol*. 1986;57:91–95.

CAPS Investigators. Effects of encainide, flecainide, imipramine and moricizine or ventricular arrhythmias during the year after acute myocardial infarction: The CAPS. *Am J Cardiol*. 1988;61:501–509.

The Cardiac Arrhythmia Suppression Trial Investigators. Preliminary report: effect of encainide and flecainide on mortality in a randomized trial of arrhythmia suppression after myocardial infarction. *N Engl J Med*. 1989;321:405–412.

Coromilas J. Electrolytes and cardiac arrhythmias. In: Zipes DP, Rowlands DJ, eds. *Progress in Cardiology*. Philadelphia, Pa: Lea & Febiger; 1988;1–2:39–58.

Deal BJ. Ventricular tachycardia in a young population without overt heart disease. *Circulation*. 1986;73:1111–1118.

Echt DS, Liebson PR, Mitchell LB, et al. Mortality and morbidity in patients receiving encainide, flecainide, or placebo. The Cardiac Arrhythmia Supression Trial. *N Engl J Med*. 1991;324:781–788.

Epstein AE, Bigger T, Wyse DG, et al. Events in the Cardiac Arrhythmia Supression Trial (CAST): Mortality in the entire population enrolled. *J Am Coll Cardiol*. 1991;18:14–19.

The ESVEM Investigators. The ESVEM trial: electrophysiologic study versus electrocardiographic monitoring for selection of antiarrhythmic therapy of ventricular tachyarrhythmias. *Circulation*. 1989;79:1354–1360.

Frame LH. Ischemia and infarction: The evolving substrate for arrhythmias. In: Zipes DP, Rowlands DJ, eds. *Progress in Cardiology*. Philadelphia, Pa: Lea & Febiger; 1988;1–1:87–109.

Furgerg CD, Friedewald WT, Eberlein KA, eds. Proceedings of the workshop on implications of recent betablocker trials for post-myocardial infarction patients. *Circulation*. 1983;67:1–111.

Gettes LS. Effect of ischemia on cardiac electrophysiology. In: Fozzard HA, Haber E, Jennings RB, et al, eds. *The Heart and Cardiovascular System Scientific Foundations*. New York: Raven Press; 1986:1317–1342.

Gomes JA, Winters SL, Steward D, et al. A new noninvasive index to predict sustained ventricular tachycardia and sudden death in the first year after myocardial infarction: signal-averaged electrocardiogram, radionuclide ejection fraction and Holter monitoring. *J Am Coll Cardiol*. 1987;10:349–357.

Haluska EA, Whistler SJ, Calfee RJ. A hierarchical approach to the treatment of ventricular tachycardias. *PACE*. 1986;9:1320–1324.

Herre JM, Sauve MJ, Malone P, et al. Long-term results of amiodarone therapy in patients with recurrent sustained ventricular tachycardia or ventricular fibrillation. *J Am Coll Cardiol*. 1989;13:422–449.

Huang SK, Meser JV, Denes P. Significance of ventricular tachycardia in idiopathic dilated cardiomyopathy: observations in 35 patients. *Am J Cardiol*. 1983;51:507–512.

Janse MJ, van Capelle FJL, Morsink H, et al. Flow of ''injury'' current and pattern of excitation during early ventricular arrhythmias in acute regional myocardial ischemia in isolated procine and canine hearts: evidence for two different arrhythmogenic mechanisms. *Circ Res*. 1980;47:151–165.

Josephson ME, Almendral JM, Buxton AE. Mechanisms of ventricular tachycardia. *Circulation*. 1987;75:41–47.

Kadish AH, Buxton AE, Waxman HL, et al. Usefulness of electrophysiologic study to determine clinical tolerance of arrhythmia recurrences during amiodarone therapy. *J Am Coll Cardiol*. 1987;10:90–96.

Kastor JA, Horowitz LN, Harken AH, et al. Clinical electrophysiology of ventricular tachycardia. *New Engl J Med*. 1981; 304:1004–1020.

Kay GN, Plumb VJ, Arciniegas JG, et al. Torsades de pointes: the long-short initiating sequence and other clinical features: observations in 32 patients. *J Am Coll Cardiol*. 1983;2:806–817.

Kay GN, Pryor DP, Lee KL, et al. Comparison of survival of amiodarone-treated patients with coronary artery disease and malignant ventricular arrhythmias with that of a control group with coronary artery disease. *J Am Coll Cardiol*. 1987;9:877–881.

Kim SG. Is programmed stimulation of value in predicting the long-term success of antiarrhythmic therapy of ventricular tachycardias. *N Engl J Med*. 1986;315:356–362.

Kuchar DL, Thornburn CW, Sammel NL. Prediction of serious arrhythmic events after myocardial infarction: signal-averaged electrocardiogram, Holter monitoring and radionuclide ventriculography. *J Am Coll Cardiol*. 1987;9:531–538.

Lavie CJ, Gersh BJ. Mechanical and electrical complications of acute myocardial infarction. *Mayo Clin Proc*. 1990;65:709–730.

Lerman BB. Ventricular tachycardia unassociated with coronary artery disease. In: Zipes DP, Rowlands DJ, eds. *Progress in Cardiology*. Philadelphia, Pa: Lea & Febiger; 1988;1–1:255–279.

Lima JAC, Weiss JL, Guzman PA, et al. Incomplete filling and incoordinate contraction as mechanisms of hypotension during ventricular tachycardia in man. *Circulation*. 1983;68:928–938.

Little RE, Kay GN, Cavendar JB, et al. Torsades de pointes and T-U wave alternans associated with arsenic poisoning. *PACE*. 1990;13:164–170.

Lown B, Axelrod P. Implanted standby defibrillators. *Circulation*. 1972;46:637–639.

Marchlinski FE. Ventricular tachycardia associated with coronary artery disease. In: Zipes DP, Rowlands DJ, eds. *Progress in Cardiology*. Philadelphia, Pa: Lea & Febiger; 1988;1–1:231–253.

Mason JW, Winkle RA. Electrode-catheter arrhythmia induction in the selection and assessment of antiarrhythmic drug therapy for recurrent ventricular tachycardia. *Circulation*. 1978;58:971–985.

McGovern B, Garan H, Malacoff RF, et al. Long-term clinical outcome of ventricular tachycardia or fibrillation treated with amiodarone. *Am J Cardiol*. 1984;53:1558–1563.

Miller JM, Josephson ME. Malignant ventricular arrhythmias early after myocardial infarction: brighter prospects. *J Am Coll Cardiol*. 1985;6:769–771.

Mitchell LB, Duff HJ, Manyari DE, et al. A randomized clinical trial of the noninvasive and invasive approaches to drug therapy of ventricular tachycardia. *N Engl J Med*. 1987;317:1681–1687.

Moss AJ, Davis HT, DeCamilla J, et al. Ventricular ectopic beats and their relation to sudden and nonsudden cardiac death after myocardial infarction. *Circulation*. 1978; 60:998–1003.

Nalos PC, Gang ES, Mandel WJ, et al. The signal-averaged electrocardiogram as a screening test for inducibility of sustained ventricular tachycardia in high risk patients: a prospective study. *J Am Coll Cardiol*. 1987;9:539–548.

Platia EV, Reid PR. Comparison of programmed electrical stimulation and ambulatory electrocardiographic monitoring in the management of ventricular tachycardia and fibrillation. *J Am Coll Cardiol*. 1984;4:493–500.

Poll DS, Marchlinski FE, Buxton AE, et al. Sustained ventricular tachycardia in patients with idiopathic dilated cardiomyopathy: electrophysiologic testing and lack of response to antiarrhythmic drug therapy. *Circulation*. 1984;70:451–456.

Rae AP, Spielman SR, Kutalek SP. Electrophysiologic assessment of antiarrhythmic drug efficacy for ventricular tachyarrhythmias associated with dilated cardiomyopathy. *Am J Cardiol*. 1987;59:291–295.

Romeo F, Pelliccia F, Cianfrocca C, et al. Predictors of sudden death in idiopathic dilated cardiomyopathy. *Am J Cardiol*. 1989;63:138–140.

Roy D, Waxman HL, Kienzle MG, et al. Clinical characteristics and long-term follow-up in 119 survivors of cardiac arrest: relation to inducibility at electrophysiologic testing. *Am J Cardiol*. 1983;52:969–974.

Ruskin JN, DiMarco JP, Garan H. Out-of-hospital cardiac arrest. Electrophysiologic observations and selection of long-term antiarrhythmic therapy. *N Engl J Med*. 1980;303:607–613.

Schaffer WA, Cobb LA. Recurrent ventricular fibrillation and modes of death in survivors of out-of-hospital ventricular fibrillation. *N Engl J Med*. 1975;293:259–262.

Schechter E, Freeman CI, Lazzara R. Afterdepolarizations as a mechanism for the long QT syndrome: electrophysiological studies of a case. *J Am Coll Cardiol*. 1984;3:1556–1561.

Scherlag BJ, El-Sherij N, Hope RR, et al. Characterization and localization of ventricular arrhythmias resulting from myocardial ischemia and infarction. *Circ Res*. 1974;35:372–383.

Skale BT, Miles WM, Hegger JJ, et al. Survivors of cardiac arrest: prevention of recurrance by drug therapy as predicted by electrophysiologic testing or electrocardiographic monitoring. *Am J Cardiol*. 1986;57:113–119.

Smith WM, Lubbe WF, Whitlock RM, et al. Long-term tolerance of amiodarone treatment for cardiac arrhythmias. *Am J Cardiol*. 1986;57:1288–1293.

Spielman SR, Schwartz JS, Untereker WJ, et al. Chronic recurrent sustained ventricular tachycardia: anatomic hemodynamic and electrophysiologic substrates. In: Josephson ME, ed. *Ventricular Tachycardia: Mechanisms and Management*. Mt Kisco, NY: Futura Publishing Co; 1982:21–32.

Stamato NJ, Marchlinski FE. Role of Holter monitoring in the management of patients with ventricular tachycardia treated with amiodarone. *Clin Prog Electrophysiol Pacing*. 1986;4:395.

Sung RJ, Shen EN, Morady F, et al. Electrophysiologic mechanism of exercise-induced sustained ventricular tachycardia. *Am J Cardiol*. 1983;51:525–530.

Swerdlow CD, Peterson J. Prospective comparison of Holter monitoring and electrophysiologic study in patients with coronary artery disease and sustained ventricular tachyarrhythmias. *Am J Cardiol*. 1985;56:577–580.

Swerdlow CD, Winkle RA, Mason JW. Determinants of survival in patients with ventricular tachyarrhythmias. *N Engl J Med*. 1983;308:1436–1442.

Tzivone D, Banai S, Schuger C, et al. Treatment of torsades de pointes with magnesium sulfate. *Circulation*. 1988;77:392–397.

Vanderpol CJ, Farshidi A, Spielman SR, et al. Incidence and clinical significance of induced ventricular tachycardia. *Am J Cardiol*. 1980;45:725–731.

Vincent GM. Long QT Syndromes. In: Zipes DP, Rowlands DJ, eds. *Progress in Cardiology*. Philadelphia, Pa: Lea & Febiger; 1988;1–2:115–130.

Waller TJ, Kay HR, Spielman SR, et al. Reduction in sudden death and total mortality by antiarrhythmic therapy evaluated by electrophysiologic drug testing: criteria of efficacy in patients with sustained ventricular tachyarrhythmia. *J Am Coll Cardiol*. 1987;10:83–89.

Waxman HL, Buxton AE, Sadowski LM, et al. The response to procainamide during electrophysiologic study for sustained ventricular tachyarrhythmias predicts the response to other medication. *Circulation*. 1983;67:30–37.

Woelfel A, Foster JR, Simpson RJ, et al. Reproducibility and treatment of exercise-induced ventricular tachycardia. *Am J Cardiol*. 1984;53:751–756.

Wud KHC, Hung JS. Exercise triggered paroxsysmal ventricular tachycardia. A repetitive rhythmic activity possibly related to afterdepolarization. *Ann Intern Med*. 1981;95:410–414.

Chapter 8

Evaluation and Management of Bradyarrhythmias

INTRODUCTION

Abnormal functioning of the conduction system is a common cause of a wide variety of cardiac symptoms, ranging from fatigue to sudden death. Prior to the development of permanent cardiac pacemakers in 1958, the occurrence of complete AV block was associated with a very high mortality. Although permanent cardiac pacing has dramatically changed the prognosis for patients with complete heart block, this therapy has also been applied to the treatment of bradycardias that are not associated with a high risk for life-threatening complications. For these less malignant cardiac rhythm disorders, permanent pacemakers offer the possibility of an improved quality of life. A basic overview of permanent cardiac pacing will be presented in this chapter. In addition, the causes, clinical manifestations, and treatment of bradyarrhythmias will be reviewed.

OVERVIEW OF PERMANENT PACING

The first permanent cardiac pacemaker was implanted in 1958 for complete heart block in a patient who is still alive at the time of this writing. The initial pacemakers functioned by asynchronously stimulating the ventricle; they did not have the capability to sense intrinsic ventricular activity. Soon thereafter, atrial and ventricular pacemakers that could both pace and sense were introduced. Further developments in pacemaker technology have included pacing in both the atrium and the ventricles (Figure 8-1) and ventricular pacing in response to atrial activation. Newer generations of permanent pacemakers have allowed the pacing rate to vary in response to the output of artificial sensors that monitor physiologic variables of metabolic demand (Figure 8-2). With these advances in pacemaker technology there have been tremendous improvements in the options that are available for pacing in a variety of clinical circumstances. These advances have also produced a marked increase in the complexity of these devices.

A permanent cardiac pacing system consists of a pulse generator and leads. The pulse generator includes the battery, an output circuit for generating the stimulating pulse, a sensing circuit that amplifies the heart's intrinsic electrical signals, and a telemetry coil that allows communication between the pacing system and an external programmer. The pulse generator is hermetically sealed inside a titanium case that prevents the ingress of tissue fluids. The power source for permanent pacemakers consists of batteries, virtually all of which are lithium iodide in the present generation of pulse generators.

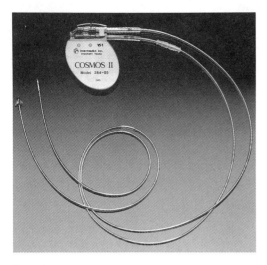

Figure 8-1 A dual chamber pacing system is demonstrated. Pacing leads are required for both the atrium and ventricle. Notice that the ventricular lead is a passive fixation (tined) electrode, which is positioned in the right ventricle. The atrial lead is an active fixation lead with a helical screw for fixation to the atrial endocardium. Reprinted with permission from Intermedics, Inc.

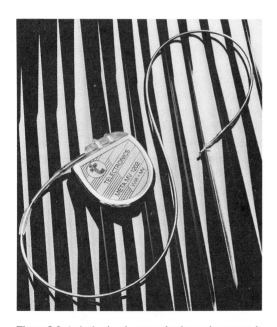

Figure 8-2 A single-chamber rate-adaptive pacing system is demonstrated. A bipolar electrode emerges from the connector block on the top of the pulse generator. The distal electrode of the lead is used as the cathode, and the proximal electrode is used as the anode. Reprinted with permission from Telectronics Pacing Systems, Inc.

Lithium iodide provides a long battery life, a consistent pattern of voltage decline at end of service life, does not require a liquid electrolyte solution, and emits no gases that need to be vented from the pulse generator. These properties make lithium iodide an ideal battery chemical for permanent pacemakers. The electronic "brains" of the pulse generator are located in an integrated circuit that determines the logic that the device will use to respond to sensed events and store diagnostic patient information. Newer pulse generators incorporate a microprocessor that can be programmed to function in a wide variety of modes, store information in memory, and be updated with further functional properties following implantation. The term "telemetry" refers to the functional capability for transmitting information regarding the function of the pacing system from the pulse generator to an external programmer. The development of telemetry has facilitated programming of pacemakers to optimize settings for an individual patient, display diagnostic information, and allow temporary adjustments for testing.

Pacing systems also require the implantation of leads that deliver electrical information to and from the heart. The pacing leads conduct the pacing stimulus from the pulse generator to the atrial or ventricular myocardium, resulting in contraction of the cardiac chamber. The leads also transmit the electrical signal originating in the atrium or ventricle to the sensing amplifier of the pulse generator. Pacing leads are composed of a metal conductor, an electrode that lies in contact with the heart, and an insulating material that surrounds the conductor. Most pacing systems are currently implanted in the pectoral region, with the pacing leads introduced into the heart via the cephalic, subclavian, or jugular veins. The pulse generator is usually placed in a subcutaneous pocket overlying the fascia of the pectoralis major muscle. Transvenous pacing leads may be attached to the heart with passive fixation devices such as flexible tines, fins, or hooks that wedge the electrode between trabeculae (Figures 8-3 and 8-4). These fixation devices are later covered by endothelium and become firmly fixed to the endocardium.

Transvenous pacing leads may also be attached to the endocardium by a metal screw

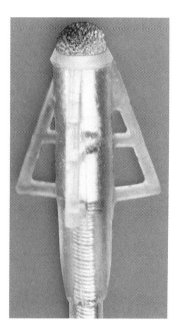

Figure 8-3 A passive fixation lead utilizing fins. Permanent pacing leads utilize tines, fins, or conical shapes as mechanisms for passive fixation. Reprinted with permission from Telectronics Pacing Systems, Inc.

that penetrates the myocardium. These leads are referred to as active fixation leads (Figures 8-5 and 8-6).

Alternatively, pacing leads may be placed directly on the epicardial surface of the heart. This technique is used primarily when a concomitant open heart operation is to be performed or when transvenous pacing is not possible because of abnormalities of the tricuspid valve that do not permit access to the right ventricle. The electrodes used for permanent pacing leads are composed of platinum, platinum-iridium, activated carbon, or alloys of steel. These materials are designed to be relatively biologically inert, that is, to incite minimal inflammatory and fibrotic reaction at the site of contact with the endocardium. The material used to insulate the conductor is usually either silicone rubber or polyurethane. These materials are designed to be thin and flexible yet possess adequate tear and

Figure 8-5 An active fixation pacing lead is shown. The distal end of the lead has a ring-shaped electrode made of porous platinum miridium. A helical screw extends from within the electrode to anchor the lead to the endocardial surface. The screw helix is retractable so that the lead can be passed atraumatically through the vasculature. The helix is extended once the lead is positioned against the endocardial surface. Reprinted with permission from Telectronics Pacing Systems, Inc.

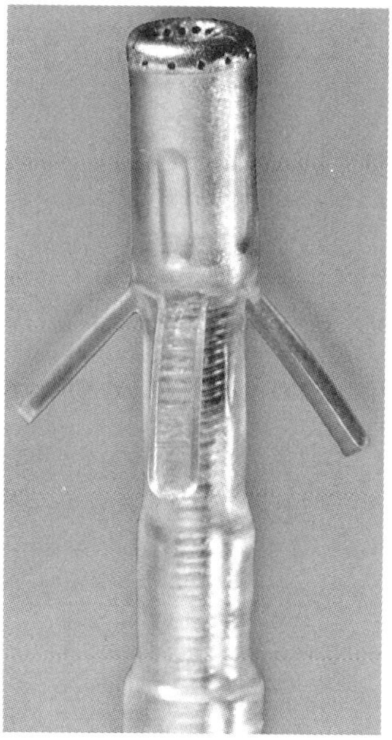

Figure 8-4 A passive fixation (tined) ventricular lead is demonstrated. The distal end of the lead is shown with an electrode; pores have been bored into the electrode to allow ingrowth of tissue. The lead is stabilized in the right ventricle by tines that wedge within the trabeculae. Reprinted with permission from Telectronics Pacing Systems, Inc.

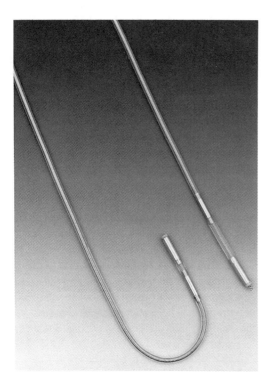

Figure 8-6 Active fixation leads with a J shape and a straight shape are shown. The helix is extended on the right. The J-shaped lead on the left demonstrates a helix that has not been extended from the electrode. These active fixation leads can be used in either the atrium or the ventricle. Reprinted with permission from Telectronics Pacing Systems, Inc.

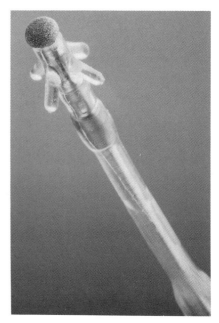

Figure 8-7 A ventricular permanent pacing lead with a porous electrode is demonstrated. This electrode overlies a reservoir of dexamethasone sodium phosphate that gradually elutes through the porous electrode to prevent inflammation at the myocardial-electrode interface. These electrodes have been shown to decrease the permanent pacing threshold over an extended period of time. Reprinted with permission from Medtronic, Inc. © Medtronic, Inc. 1990.

tensile strength to withstand the stress of flexing with millions of heartbeats. There are relative advantages and disadvantages to each type of insulating material, with no clear consensus regarding which insulator provides the best long-term durability (Figure 8-7).

Permanent pacemaker implantation is usually performed under local anesthesia, either in the operating room, a cardiac catheterization laboratory, or a specialized electrophysiology suite. The complication rate has been shown to be similar in each of these settings. Complications of permanent pacemaker implantation include cardiac perforation with pericardial tamponade, induction of ventricular and atrial arrhythmias, pneumothorax, hemothorax, pocket hematoma, infection, air embolization, and venous thrombosis. The risk of infection is less than 0.5% and may be associated with severe or indolent sepsis. The most frequent complications of permanent

pacemaker implantation involve dislodgement of pacing leads, poor positioning of leads, and long-term failure of the pacing system to sense intrinsic cardiac electrical signals. The experience of the operator is the one factor that most closely relates to the complication rate that can be expected with permanent pacemaker implantation.

In order to standardize pacemaker terminology and simplify understanding of pacing modes, the Pacemaker Study Group of the Inter-Society Commission on Heart Disease Resources (ICHD) introduced a three-letter code for pacemaker modes. This code was later revised to include five positions. The first letter in the code represents the cardiac chamber or chambers that are paced, the second letter indicates the cardiac chamber or chambers that are sensed, and the third letter denotes the mode of response to sensed events. Thus a ventricular demand pacemaker that paces the ventricle (V), senses ventricular activity (V), and is inhibited (I) from pacing by sensed R waves would be designated as a VVI pacemaker. Similarly, an atrial demand pacemaker that paces the atrium (A), senses atrial activity (A), and is inhibited by sensed P waves is coded as an AAI pacemaker. A pacemaker that paces the ventricle (V), senses only in the atrium (A), and is triggered (T) to pace the ventricle by atrially sensed events is a VAT pacing system. This pacing mode is now obsolete and has been replaced by pacemakers that pace both the atrium and the ventricle (D, or dual chamber), sense in both chambers (D), and are both inhibited by ventricular events and triggered by atrial events (D, or dual response mode)—DDD pacemakers. The fourth position in the code refers to the programmable functions available in the pacemaker, and the fifth position describes antitachycardia pacemaker function. The letter *R* in the fourth position of the code is used to describe the feature of rate-adaptation based on an artificial sensor. A DDDR pacemaker paces both chambers, senses both chambers, is both inhibited and triggered, and has the ability to change the pacing rate in response to the output of an artificial sensor or the rate of the sinus node.

Several important terms and concepts relating to cardiac pacing should be emphasized. First, the strength of the stimulation pulse is usually measured in volts. In addition, the stimulating pulse must be applied to the heart for a sufficient amount of time to excite the myocardium and generate a propagated complex. The minimum combination of stimulus amplitude and pulse duration that result in stimulation of the heart is referred to as the capture or stimulation threshold. In order for a pacemaker to provide reliable stimulation of the heart, the stimulus must exceed the stimulation threshold. This concept is of vital importance, as the proper stimulus strength should be at least twice threshold. In addition, the pacemaker should be able to respond to the heart's intrinsic electrical signals. This is ensured by recording electrical signals that are of sufficient amplitude to be sensed by the sensing amplifier of the pulse generator. The electrical signal is measured at the time of lead implantation to maximize the amplitude of the electrogram so that long-term sensing will be maintained. The sensitivity setting of a pulse generator should be programmed to allow consistent sensing. The stimulation threshold and sensing parameters are set by a complex interaction of the underlying myocardium and the pacing electrode. Successful permanent pacing requires meticulous attention to these concepts of stimulation and sensing.

Several other pacing concepts should be emphasized. The term "AV synchrony" refers to the normal sequence of atrial contraction that precedes ventricular contraction. There are several symptoms and signs that may develop in patients without AV synchrony. If the ventricles are paced without regard to the underlying atrial rhythm, the cardiac output may decline. This is especially true in patients with noncompliant ventricles who require the atrial contraction to completely fill the ventricles prior to ventricular systole. A properly timed atrial contraction may add as much as 50% to the cardiac output of patients with left ventricular hypertrophy. In patients with elevated atrial filling pressures and dilated, compliant ventricles, such as occurs in dilated cardiomyopathy, the atrial contraction is much less important. The importance of AV synchrony is also dependent on whether patients manifest retrograde conduction from the ventricles to the atria during ventricular pacing. If the AV conduction system is capable of retrograde conduction, ventricular pacing will be associated with a consistent contraction of the atria at a time when the ventricles are completing systole. In this instance, the atria contract against closed tricuspid and mitral valves, leading to elevations in right and left atrial pressures. This may produce severe symptoms in some patients, such as palpitations, shortness of breath, fatigue, lightheadedness, hypotension, and, rarely, syncope or even shock. The occurrence of this syndrome with ventricular pacing, is referred to as "pacemaker syndrome."

Another concept that should be appreciated regards the normal increase in heart rate that occurs in response to exercise, emotion, or other causes of increased metabolic demand. The normal cardiac output may increase up to 4- to 5-fold from rest to maximum exercise. Cardiac contractility and increased stroke volume may increase cardiac output 1.5-fold. The increased heart rate that occurs with exercise is responsible for up to a 3-fold increase in cardiac output. Patients with fixed heart rates that do not increase with exertion often complain of fatigue and poor exercise tolerance. Pacemakers that increase the heart rate in response to artificial sensors that indicate the level of exertion have been shown to markedly improve quality of life and exercise capacity as compared to fixed-rate devices. This property of appropriate regulation of heart rate is referred to as rate-adaptation or rate-responsiveness. If the sinus node is normal, pacemakers that sense and track atrial activity are capable of normal rate adaptation. In these individuals, the normal sinus node provides appropriate regulation of the cardiac rate (Figure 8-8).

In the absence of normal sinus function, pacemakers that rely on artificial sensor input can also provide appropriate regulation of the heart rate (Figure 8-9). The artificial sensors that have been developed include pacemakers that sense body vibration (activity sensors), respiration (minute ventilation or respiratory rate), cen-

tral venous blood temperature, right ventricular stroke volume or pressure, the QT interval, and mixed venous oxygen saturation.

In general, the optimal physiologic pacing mode is the one that most closely mimics the function of the normal AV conduction system. An ideal pacemaker would therefore provide for normal AV synchrony with a normal PR interval and would provide a physiologic range of heart rates based on the patient's metabolic needs. However, devices that offer the most sophisticated features often cost the most and may be more difficult to implant or require more intense follow-up. For example, dual-chamber devices require that both atrial and ventricular leads be implanted. The added cost and increased rate of complications associated with two leads require consideration of the clinical necessity for dual-chamber pacing.

Various clinical factors should be weighed when selecting the appropriate pacing mode for an individual patient. First, the indication for pacing is a crucial consideration. For example, if the indication is the occurrence of intermittent

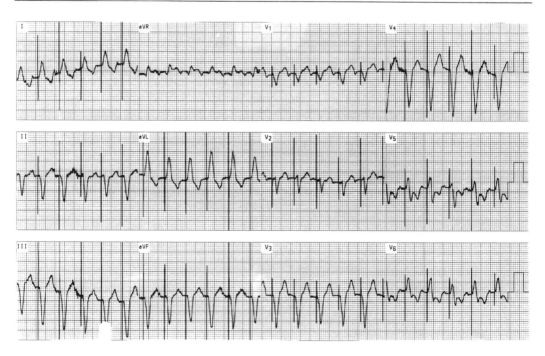

Figure 8-8 Normal DDD pacing in a patient with intact sinus node function at peak exercise. Notice that in lead V_1 P waves are seen prior to each ventricular pacing stimulus as the ventricle is paced synchronously with the atrium. Thus DDD pacing provides AV synchrony and rate response in patients with an intact sinus node.

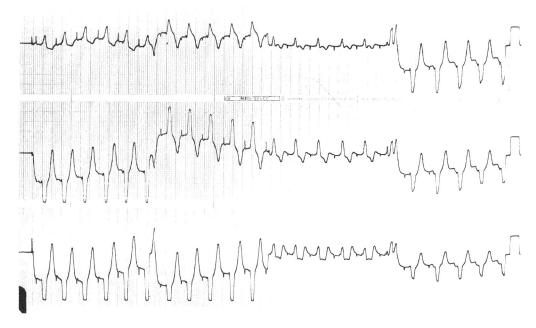

Figure 8-9 A 12-lead ECG demonstrating normal DDDR pacing during exercise is demonstrated. Notice that both the atrium and ventricles are paced with small bipolar pacing stimuli. The DDDR pacing system paces both the atrium and ventricle, senses in both chambers, and tracks atrial activity as well as the activity of an artificial sensor. Thus a DDDR pacing system provides both AV synchrony and rate adaptation to demand in patients with impaired sinus node function.

pauses that occur very rarely, the goal of pacing is to simply provide a rate floor. In these individuals a relatively simple device may be all that is needed. In other patients, pacing will be required at all times.

In these individuals the goals of AV synchrony and rate adaptation should be achieved. Next, the status of the atria is extremely important. For example, if there is chronic atrial fibrillation or flutter, atrial pacing will not be possible (Figure 8-10). In these patients it is of no value to implant an atrial lead. The competence of the sinus node to increase the heart rate appropriately with increased metabolic demand is another important consideration. If the sinus node is severely diseased, it will not be a reliable guide to the appropriate pacing rate (Figure 8-11). Thus dual-chamber devices that use the sinus node as the guide to heart rate will provide AV synchrony but not rate adaptation.

The status of AV conduction should be a prime consideration. If the sinus node is diseased, the atrial pacing mode would be appropri-
ate only if the AV conduction system is normal. However, if AV conduction is also impaired, the ventricle should be paced as well. The functional status of the patient also factors importantly into the choice of pacing mode. If the patient is severely demented or markedly limited in physical activity, a simple device may be important. Although implantation of the most sophisticated pacemaker in all patients would offer the widest range of programming possibilities, the constraints of cost and complexity warrant a more selective approach.

PACING FOR SINUS NODE DYSFUNCTION

Abnormal sinus node function is the most common indication for permanent pacemaker implantation in the United States. Dysfunction of the sinus node is highly correlated with age, with a progressive increase in the signs and

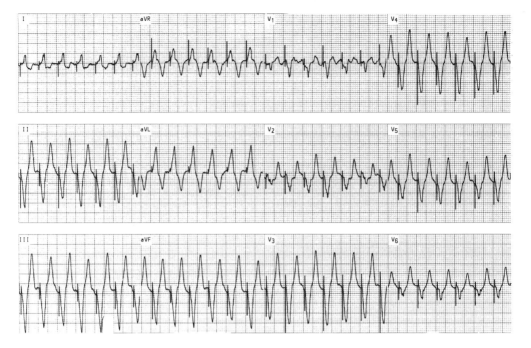

Figure 8-10 VVIR pacing at peak exercise. The tracing demonstrates a ventricularly paced rhythm at a rate of 150 beats per minute at peak exercise in a patient with a minute-ventilation pacemaker. This pacing mode provides rate response but not AV synchrony. Notice that in lead V_1 there is dissociation between the atrial and ventricular complexes.

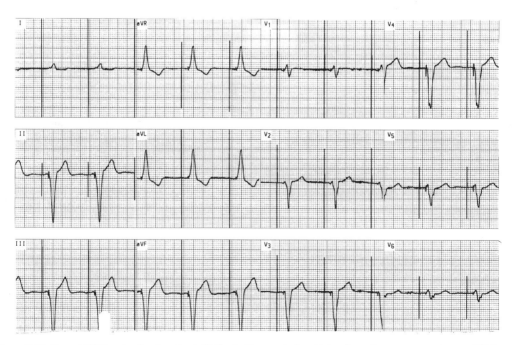

Figure 8-11 Normal DDD pacing function at rest. Notice that large unipolar atrial pacing spikes are present at a rate of 60 beats per minute with normal capture of the atrium. A bipolar pacing spike captures the ventricle. Notice that the bipolar pacing spike is much smaller than the unipolar spike, a feature that is characteristic of each of these pacing configurations. At rest the atrium and ventricle are paced in this patient with intrinsic sinus node dysfunction.

symptoms in older populations. Sinus node dysfunction may be manifest as an extreme sinus bradycardia, intermittent sinus pauses, or failure to resume normal pacemaker activity following spontaneous termination of atrial tachyarrhythmias or after cardioversion. The abnormalities in sinus node function may be present at rest or during exercise. In addition, patients may manifest any combination of these abnormalities. These clinical manifestations of abnormal sinus node function have been referred to as the sick sinus syndrome. The frequent association of abnormal sinus node function with atrial tachyarrhythmias, especially atrial fibrillation and flutter, is commonly described as the tachycardia-bradycardia syndrome.

Abnormal sinus node function may occur in association with virtually all forms of structural heart disease. Since sinus node dysfunction is generally a disorder of older individuals, many patients have concomitant coronary artery disease or hypertension. Despite the frequent occurrence of these structural cardiac abnormalities in the elderly, the most common cause of sinus node dysfunction is idiopathic degenerative fibrosis of the conduction system. Autopsy specimens in individuals without clinically evident sinus node dysfunction demonstrate a progressive degree of fibrous tissue infiltration of the sinus node with age. It is likely that an exaggeration of this process leads to impaired sinus node function in symptomatic patients. Since fibrosis of the conduction system is widespread throughout the heart, sinus node dysfunction is commonly associated with other conduction system abnormalities, especially AV block. Diffuse fibrosis of the atrium is the likely cause of the intermittent atrial fibrillation and flutter commonly observed in patients with sinus bradycardia and sinus pauses. Other structural heart disorders associated with sinus node dysfunction include cardiomyopathies, valvular heart disease, amyloidosis, and pericardial diseases. Sinus node dysfunction is relatively common in children with transposition of the great vessels and following repair of atrial septal defect, tetralogy of Fallot, tricuspid atresia, and Ebstein's anomaly of the tricuspid valve.

In addition to these chronic disorders, there are multiple causes of acute, reversible dysfunc-tion of the sinus node. The most common reversible cause of sinus bradycardia and sinus pauses is the use of drugs, including β-blockers, calcium channel blockers, digoxin, and antihypertensive agents. The antihypertensive medications causing sinus node dysfunction include clonidine, α-methyldopa, reserpine, and guanethidine. Class I antiarrhythmic drugs may also suppress the sinus node, especially procainamide, quinidine, propafenone, encainide, and flecainide. The worst of the antiarrhythmic drug offenders are amiodarone and sotalol. Use of these class III drugs requires permanent pacemaker implantation in up to 10% of patients. Other reversible causes of sinus node dysfunction include hypothyroidism, hypoxemia (especially sleep apnea), obstructive jaundice, and enhanced vagal tone. Each of these factors should be eliminated if clinically feasible. However, the frequent association of ischemic heart disease, hypertension, and atrial arrhythmias often requires that medications be given. In these cases, a permanent pacemaker may be required to allow drugs to be given for other clinical indications.

The clinical symptoms associated with extreme sinus bradycardia are most often fatigue, lightheadedness, and effort intolerance. Patients with marked sinus bradycardia may also experience a worsening of their angina or congestive heart failure symptoms. Elderly patients often experience a decrease in their level of alertness and other personality changes, including exacerbation of dementia. Sinus bradycardia, by itself, is an uncommon cause of true syncope. Sinus pauses are usually manifest by sudden lightheaded spells or episodes of syncope. Patients often complain of tachypalpitations followed by a feeling of profound lightheadedness. Patients commonly report a peculiar sense that blood is "draining from my head" or "rising up" during prolonged sinus pauses. Although the mortality rate of patients with sick sinus syndrome is on the order of 35% over 5 years of follow-up, the risk is approximately the same as in age- and disease-matched controls. In addition, while it is clear that sinus pauses rarely, if ever, produce sudden cardiac death, elderly patients may be exposed to the hazards of falling, including risk of hip fracture.

The diagnosis of sinus node dysfunction is usually made by correlation of symptoms with electrocardiographic recordings. If patients experience their typical symptom during documented sinus pauses, the diagnosis is clearly established, and further testing is not necessary. However, most patients with intermittent spells of lightheadedness, fatigue, or syncope present in an ambulatory setting to be evaluated when they are not having symptoms. If patients have been experiencing severe symptoms (frequent presyncope or syncope), hospitalization for telemetry is usually warranted. Most patients will have less severe symptoms and can be evaluated on an outpatient basis. The most valuable test for assessment of sinus node dysfunction is Holter monitoring. The demonstration of symptoms during sinus bradycardia (rate less than than 40 beats per minute) or sinus pauses (more than 3 seconds) clearly defines the diagnosis. Patients may also experience sinus pauses related to sinus exit block or sinoatrial Wenckebach block. Despite the diagnostic utility of Holter monitoring, patients with very intermittent symptoms may not demonstrate the cause of their symptoms on a 24-hour recording. In these patients, repeated Holter monitoring may improve the diagnostic yield. Transtelephonic monitoring is extremely helpful, especially the use of looping memory recorders, which are well suited to record episodes of short duration.

Noninvasive methods of evaluating the sinus node are the mainstay of diagnosis. However, occasional patients will not be diagnosed with these techniques. In addition, the findings on Holter monitoring may be equivocal and difficult to interpret. In these patients, exercise testing may prove of some value to assess the response of the sinus node to exercise. Patients who fail to increase their heart rate appropriately with exercise may be diagnosed as having chronotropic incompetence of the sinus node (Figure 8-12). Patients with chronotropic incompetence may develop symptoms of fatigue or exertional lightheadedness during treadmill exercise testing.

Sinus node recovery time and sinoatrial conduction are the two invasive indices used to evaluate sinus node function. (For further discussion, see Chapter 4). The sinus node recovery time should be less than 1500 milliseconds,

and, when corrected for the underlying heart rate, the duration of the postpacing pause can be calculated by subtracting the sinus cycle length prior to pacing from the duration of the postpacing pause. The sinoatrial conduction time should be approximately 250 milliseconds. Another measure of sinus node function has been termed the intrinsic sinus rate. The intrinsic sinus rate is the rate of sinus rhythm after blockade of autonomic influences on the node by intravenous atropine (0.04 mg/kg) and propranolol (0.2 mg/kg). The sinus rate following pharmacologic blockade usually increases in healthy subjects as a result of vagal withdrawal. The intrinsic heart rate decreases with age, with an expected heart rate equal to $118.1 - (0.57 \times age)$. The intrinsic heart rate is considered to be abnormal if it is less than 95% of expected.

Permanent pacemakers are indicated for patients with clinically important symptoms related to sinus bradycardia or sinus pauses that occur in the absence of reversible causes. It should be re-emphasized that the prognosis of patients with the sick sinus syndrome is the same as age-matched controls. There is no evidence that pacing prolongs longevity or that sudden death occurs with sinus node dysfunction. Because of these facts, the only reason to implant a permanent pacemaker for the treatment of sinus node dysfunction is to relieve symptoms. If the patient is asymptomatic, there is rarely a reason to implant a permanent pacemaker.

There has been some controversy as to whether atrial or ventricular pacing should be used for sinus node dysfunction. However, it has become clear that the risk of developing atrial fibrillation is less with atrial pacing than with ventricular pacing (3.9% versus 22.3%). Furthermore, atrial pacing has been shown to be associated with a lower risk of systemic emboli than ventricular pacing (1.6% versus 13%). In addition, pacemaker syndrome with retrograde ventriculoatrial conduction may occur in approximately 5% of patients with ventricular pacing but is not found with atrial pacing. It is our practice to pace the atrium and preserve atrial synchrony whenever possible.

The optimum choice of pacing mode for patients with sinus node dysfunction depends on several factors. If the patient has rare sinus

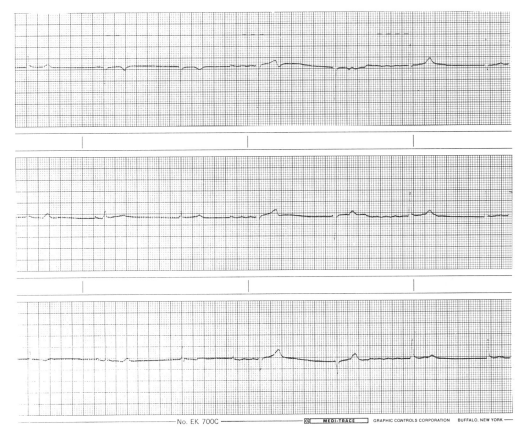

Figure 8-12 Complete AV block with a narrow QRS escape rhythm is demonstrated with concomitant sinus node dysfunction. This patient demonstrates dysfunction of both the sinus and AV nodes and would be an ideal candidate for a DDDR rate-adaptive pacing system.

pauses, normal AV conduction, and no history of atrial fibrillation or flutter, atrial demand (AAI) pacing is the preferred mode. However, many patients have both sinus pauses and periods of severe sinus bradycardia with failure to increase their sinus rate with exercise. In these individuals, the rate-adaptive AAIR pacing mode provides the most physiologic rhythm. If there is concomitant disease in the AV conduction system, a dual-chamber, rate-adaptive pacing mode (DDDR) is preferred. If the patient has very frequent episodes of atrial arrhythmias that cannot be controlled with antiarrhythmic drug therapy, the VVIR or DDIR pacing modes may provide optimal therapy. A more controversial situation involves patients with infrequent atrial tachyarrhythmias. In this group, atrial pacing itself may decrease the frequency of atrial fibrillation or flutter. We usually combine a DDDR pacemaker with antiarrhythmic drug

therapy in this clinical setting. If the only sinus pauses observed occur following termination of atrial fibrillation, AAI or VVI pacing to provide a rate floor may suffice. It has been demonstrated that AV block occurs at a rate of approximately 4% per year in patients with sick sinus syndrome. Thus if there is no bundle branch block, a normal PR interval, and AV Wenckebach block occurs at an atrial pacing rate of 120 beats per minute or more, atrial pacing is the preferred mode. If concern exists that atrial fibrillation or impaired AV conduction will develop, a dual-chamber pacing system capable of AAIR, VVIR, and DDDR modes is usually implanted.

PACING FOR ATRIOVENTRICULAR BLOCK

Impairment of AV conduction has been classified as first-, second-, or third-degree block based on the characteristics of the 12-lead ECG. The term "first-degree AV block" is a misnomer as there is conduction delay rather than conduction block. Second-degree block is characterized by intermittent loss of AV conduction, while third-degree block implies complete interruption of AV conduction. Second-degree block is further subdivided into Mobitz type I (Wenckebach) and Mobitz type II block. These terms are useful because they have important implications regarding the site of abnormal AV conduction. In this section, emphasis will be placed on discriminating block that is localized to the AV node from block in the His bundle and bundle branches.

The distinction between block in the AV node from block in the His bundle and bundle branches has important clinical implications. In general, spontaneous block in the AV node is associated with a relatively benign clinical course, whereas block in the His bundle or bundle branches is associated with a poor prognosis. The AV node is characterized by very slow conduction of electrical impulses, marked responsiveness to autonomic influences, and progressive slowing of conduction in response to rapid atrial pacing. The refractory period of the AV node lengthens in response to rapid atrial pacing. The AV node can conduct atrial

impulses with a wide range of conduction (AH) intervals. The AH interval gradually lengthens in response to rapid atrial pacing until AV block occurs. In contrast to this behavior, the His bundle and bundle branches are characterized by relatively rapid conduction, relative insensitivity to autonomic influences, and all-or-none conduction properties. Thus the conduction interval from activation of the His bundle to activation of the ventricles (HV interval) generally remains constant at rapid pacing rates until the refractory period is encountered and 2:1 block occurs. In addition, the refractory period of the His bundle and bundle branches shortens in response to rapid pacing.

Second-degree block occurring in the AV node is typified by the Wenckebach phenomenon, progressive PR prolongation prior to block (Figure 8-13). Following AV block, the first conducted beat is usually conducted with a much shorter PR interval. In addition, patients with intermittent Wenckebach block often demonstrate a prolonged PR interval during periods of 1:1 conduction. In keeping with the all-or-none conduction properties of the His bundle and bundle branches, second-degree block localized to these structures is usually associated with a constant PR interval before and after the blocked beat. It there is a fixed 2:1 AV ratio, the site of

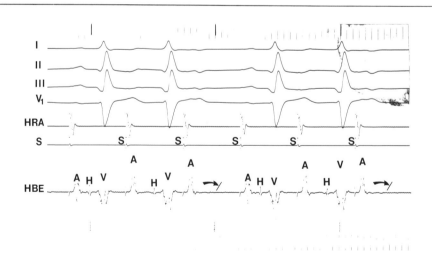

Figure 8-13 AV Wenckebach block. Surface electrocardiographic leads I, II, III, and V_1 are shown simultaneously with a bipolar electrogram from the high right atrium (HRA) and the His bundle electrogram (HBE). Pacing from the high right atrium (S) results in progressive prolongation of the AH interval. The third atrial deflection from the left demonstrates block between the atrial and His deflections, indicating block in the AV node. This is typical of AV Wenckebach block.

second-degree block is more difficult to localize. Clues that the block is confined to the AV node include a relatively narrow QRS morphology, improvement in conduction with exercise or atropine, and worsening of conduction with carotid sinus massage. In contrast, AV block within the His bundle or bundle branches is usually associated with a wide QRS, no change or worsening of conduction with atropine and exercise, and improvement in conduction with carotid sinus massage. Furthermore, if the PR interval exceeds 300 milliseconds, disease in the AV node is suspected.

Complete AV block localized to the AV node is generally associated with a narrow QRS complex and relatively rapid escape rate in the range of 45 to 60 beats per minute (Figure 8-14). Block occurs proximal to the His bundle in this instance and is known as suprahisian block.

Complete block in the His bundle (intrahisian) or more distally (infrahisian) is characterized by a wide QRS escape at a slower rate, usually 30 to 45 beats per minute. In rare clinical situations it may be necessary to record a His bundle electrogram to localize the site of AV block because of uncertainty with interpretation of the ECG. AV block confined to the AV node is diagnosed when the atrial deflection in the His bundle electrogram is not followed by His bundle deflections. In this way, the block is localized to the structure that joins the atrium and the His bundle, the AV node. In addition, when AV conduction is present, the conducted beats are usually remarkable for a long AH interval. AV block that occurs within the His bundle is often associated with a fractionated, split His deflection (Figure 8-15). In this situation, block occurs between the fractionated, split components of the His electrogram (Figure 8-16).

Infrahisian block is diagnosed when the blocked beats are associated with a His deflection but no ventricular deflection in the His bundle electrogram (block within the HV interval) (Figure 8-17).

Documentation of spontaneous AV block in the His bundle or bundle branches is an indication for permanent pacemaker implantation. In asymptomatic patients with bundle branch block but no documented AV block, His bundle recordings may provide prognostic information regarding the risk of progression. However, prophylactic pacemaker implantation has not been shown to influence subsequent mortality in these patients. An exception to this statement may

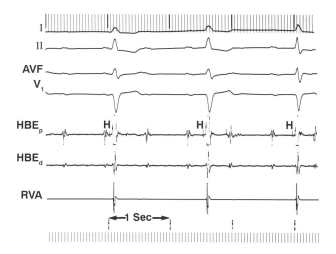

Figure 8-14 Suprahisian block is demonstrated. Surface leads I, II, and aVF are demonstrated simultaneously with bipolar intracardiac eletrograms from the His bundle electrogram proximal (HBEp) and distal (HBEd) electrode pairs and from the right ventricular apex (RVA). Note that there is dissociation between the atrial and ventricular deflections on both the intracardiac electrograms and the surface electrocardiographic tracings. A narrow QRS complex escape rhythm associated with a clearly defined His bundle deflection (H) prior to each QRS is demonstrated. This is typical of a His bundle escape rhythm and demonstrates that block occurred in the AV node.

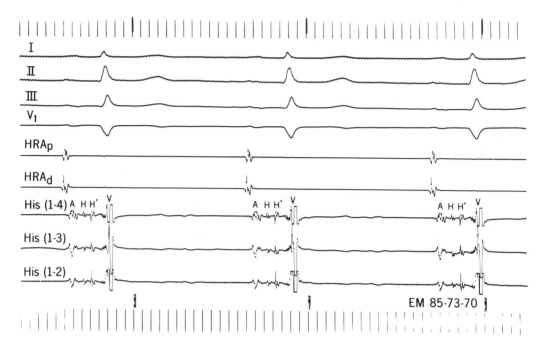

Figure 8-15 A split His potential is demonstrated. Surface leads I, II, III, and V₁ are recorded simultaneously with bipolar electrograms from the high right atrium proximal (HRAp) and distal (HRAd) electrode pairs, and from three electrode pairs from the His bundle catheter. Note that there is a fragmented split His deflection with an H and an H′ deflection. This demonstrates conduction delay within the His bundle. Notice that the QRS morphology is narrow, demonstrating that the bundle branches are intact.

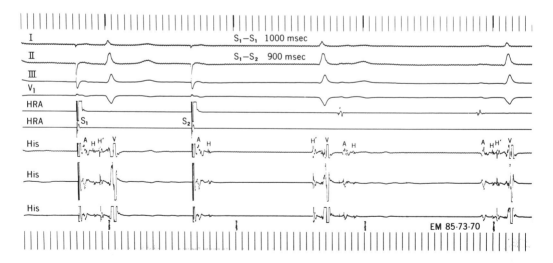

Figure 8-16 Intrahisian block is demonstrated in the same patient as in Figure 8-15. Note that with an S1-S2 coupling interval of 900 milliseconds there is block within the His bundle between the H and the H′ deflections. This patient subsequently was treated with a permanent cardiac pacemaker.

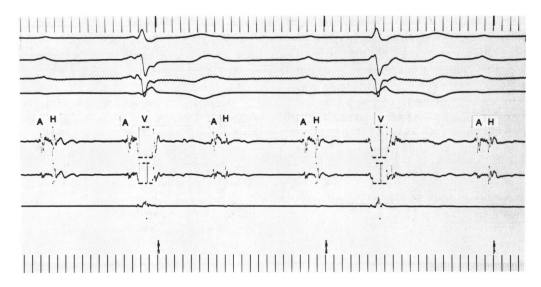

Figure 8-17 Complete infrahisian AV block is demonstrated. Surface leads I, II, aVF, and V₁ are shown with simultaneous His bundle electrograms, proximal and distal electrode pairs, and right ventricular apex. The His bundle electrogram demonstrates complete heart block occurring below the level of the His bundle. Note that each atrial deflection is followed by a His deflection. But there is no conduction from the His bundle to the ventricles.

involve the use of antiarrhythmic drugs. Since antiarrhythmic drugs usually slow conduction in the His bundle and bundle branches, His bundle recordings should be considered a routine part of any baseline electrophysiologic study. If the HV interval exceeds 80 milliseconds in the baseline state, the risk of developing infrahisian block is increased with the addition of an antiarrhythmic drug. If the HV interval exceeds 100 milliseconds, many laboratories proceed with prophylactic pacemaker implantation prior to initiation of long-term antiarrhythmic drug therapy.

The causes of acute AV nodal dysfunction include inferior myocardial infarction, increased vagal tone, drugs, idiopathic fibrosis, cardiac surgery, infiltrating diseases such as amyloidosis or sarcoidosis, and inflammatory processes such as rheumatoid arthritis or acute rheumatic fever. Acute inferior myocardial infarction is commonly associated with impairment of AV nodal conduction. Patients with acute inferior myocardial infarction often develop a prolonged PR interval that rapidly progresses to AV Wenckebach block and then to complete AV block. The escape rhythm is usually adequate, with a narrow QRS at a rate ranging from 40 to 60 beats per minute. The conduction abnormalities may improve with atropine. If there has been no damage to the His bundle and bundle branches, complete AV block associated with inferior myocardial infarction completely resolves in the vast majority of patients within 2 weeks. Pathologic specimens typically show acute edema but no infarction in the region of the AV node. Permanent pacing is rarely required, though a temporary pacemaker may be needed during the first 1 to 2 weeks postinfarction.

Enhanced vagal tone is a very common cause of AV nodal block. This may occur with simple vasovagal episodes, as a reflex during sleep or rest (especially in young patients), following vomiting or bowel movements, or as a reflex related to carotid sinus massage, carotid sinus hypersensitivity, or glossopharyngeal neuralgia. Enhanced vagal tone should be suspected as the cause of AV block when there is simultaneous slowing of the sinus rate and AV block. If the cause of AV nodal block is augmented vagal tone, atropine will reverse the impaired conduction. The drugs associated with AV nodal block include the β-blockers, calcium blockers, digoxin, clonidine, α-methyldopa, and guanethidine. As mentioned previously, block occurring in the AV node is usually associated with a good long-term prognosis.

The causes of chronic AV nodal block include congenital complete heart block, congenital heart diseases (transposition of the great vessels, ventricular septal defect), coronary artery disease, valvular heart disease, hypertension, cardiomyopathies, and systemic rheumatologic diseases. The most common cause of chronic block in the AV node is idiopathic fibrosis of the conduction system. There is often widespread fibrosis of the conduction system in this disorder.

Permanent pacemaker implantation is not required for chronic block in the AV node if the patient is asymptomatic. However, many patients complain of fatigue, effort intolerance, palpitations, lightheadedness, or syncope. Other patients may complain of exacerbation of congestive heart failure symptoms or angina. Since the escape rhythm is usually located within the His bundle when block is in the AV node, the rate is usually 45 to 60 beats per minute. If symptoms are present and there is no reversible cause of AV node dysfunction, a permanent pacemaker should be considered. As with sinus node dysfunction, there is no definitive evidence that pacemakers improve prognosis with block confined to the AV node. The goal of pacemaker therapy should be to alleviate symptoms.

Acute conduction block in the His bundle or bundle branches may occur as a consequence of anterior myocardial infarction, antiarrhythmic drugs, hyperkalemia, endocarditis, or surgical trauma. The clinical manifestations of acute block in the distal AV conduction system are often dramatic, with syncope, seizures, ventricular tachycardia (torsades de pointes), or sudden death possible. Development of Mobitz II or complete AV block in this site is often associated with a slow, wide QRS escape rhythm that is not reliable. If this form of AV block develops, a temporary pacemaker is almost always indicated, regardless of symptoms (Figures 8-18 and 8-19). In most patients who develop acute,

Figure 8-18 A single-chamber external temporary pulse generator is demonstrated. The pulse generator has controls for adjusting stimulus output (mA), pacing rate, and sensitivity. Reprinted with permission from Medtronic, Inc. © Medtronic, Inc. 1990.

Figure 8-19 A dual-chamber, (DDD) temporary external pacemaker is demonstrated. Programmed parameters are continuously displayed. It may also be programmed to deliver bursts of atrial pacing at up to 800 beats per minute. Reprinted with permission from Medtronic, Inc. © Medtronic, Inc. 1991.

transient AV block in the His bundle or bundle branches, permanent pacemaker implantation should be strongly considered.

Chronic AV block localized to the His bundle and bundle branches may occur as a consequence of coronary heart disease, hypertension, cardiomyopathies, calcific valvular disease, following surgery for congenital heart disease, or as an idiopathic fibrosis of the conduction system. Most patients manifest bundle branch block or hemiblocks prior to the development of Mobitz II or complete AV block. Patients often present to medical attention because of syncope, marked presyncope, fatigue, congestive heart failure, or chest pain. The patient may describe episodic symptoms over a long period of time. In other patients the first manifestation may be sudden death. The prognosis for patients with Mobitz II or complete heart block with a wide QRS escape is very poor without permanent pacing. Indeed, the mortality rate prior to the advent of permanent pacemakers was on the order of 50% by 1 year. Permanent pacing has dramatically improved the outlook for patients with symptomatic AV block.

The optimal pacing mode for the treatment of AV block depends on the status of the sinus node, the frequency of AV block, the underlying structural heart disease, the presence of atrial arrhythmias, and the functional status of the patient. The ideal pacemaker would restore the normal AV synchrony of the heart. In addition, the ventricular rate should increase in response to increasing demands for cardiac output. For patients with very rare episodes of AV block, a simple demand VVI pacemaker may suffice to prevent symptoms by providing a rate floor while allowing the patient's own conduction system to function the majority of the time. If the AV block is relatively frequent and the sinus node function is well preserved, a DDD or VDD pacemaker would provide both rate adaptation and AV synchrony. However, if the sinus node is unreliable or does not respond to exercise, the ideal pacing mode would include an artificial sensor, allowing function in the DDDR pacing mode. Patients with chronic atrial fibrillation or flutter cannot benefit from AV synchrony and are best treated with a rate-adaptive VVIR pacing system. There are several special considerations

regarding clinical indications for pacing that influence the selection of pacing mode. Patients with ventricular hypertrophy such as those with hypertension, aortic valve disease, or hypertrophic cardiomyopathy are dependent on the atrial transport function to achieve adequate ventricular filling and cardiac output. These patients should be implanted with a dual-chamber system whenever possible. An exception would be those individuals with chronic atrial fibrillation. Patients with carotid sinus hypersensitivity are also dependent on optimal ventricular filling during reflex vagal vasodilatation. These patients should also receive dual-chamber pacing systems. In addition, patients demonstrating ventricular to atrial conduction during ventricular pacing are at high risk for developing pacemaker syndrome and should also receive dual-chamber pacing systems.

BIBLIOGRAPHY

Alpert MA, Curtis JJ, Sanfelippo JF, et al. Comparative survival following permanent ventricular and dual-chamber pacing for patients with chronic symptomatic sinus node dysfunction with and without congestive heart failure. *Am Heart J.* 1987;113:958–965.

Alpert MA, Flaker G. Arrhythmias associated with sinus node dysfunction. *JAMA.* 1983;250:2160–2166.

Alt E, Volker R, Wirtzfeld A, et al. Survival and follow-up after pacemaker implantation: a comparison of patients with sick sinus syndrome, complete heart block, and atrial fibrillation. *PACE.* 1985;8:849–855.

Arguss NS, Rosin EY, Adolph RJ, et al. Significance of chronic sinus bradycardia in elderly people. *Circulation.* 1972;46:924–930.

Ausubel K, Furman S. The pacemaker syndrome. *Ann Intern Med.* 1985;103:420–429.

Belic N, Talano JV. Current concepts in sick sinus syndrome: anatomy, physiology, and pharmacologic causes. *Arch Intern Med.* 1985;145:521.

Belic N, Talano JV. Current concepts in sick sinus syndrome—ECG manifestations and diagnostic and therapeutic approaches. *Arch Intern Med.* 1985;145:722.

Bellinder G, Nordlander R, Pehrsson SK, et al. Atrial pacing in the management of sick sinus syndrome: long-term observation for conduction disturbances and supraventricular tachyarrhythmias. *Eur Heart J.* 1986;7:105–109.

Benditt DG, Gornick CC, Dunbar D, et al. Indications for electrophysiologic testing in the diagnosis and assessment of sinus node dysfunction. *Circulation.* 1987;75:93–99.

Bernstein AD, Camm AJ, Fletcher RD, et al. The NASPE/ BPEG Generic Pacemaker Code for antibradyarrhythmia and adaptive-rate pacing and antitachyarrhythmia devices. *PACE*. 1987;10:794–799.

Bhandari AK, Rahimtoola SH. Indications for intracardiac electrophysiologic studies in patients with atrioventricular and intraventricular blocks not associated with acute myocardial infarction. *Circulation*. 1987;75:107–109.

Brodsky M, Wu D, Denes P, et al. Arrhythmias documented by 24 hour continuous electrocardiographic monitoring in 50 male medical students without apparent heart disease. *Am J Cardiol*. 1977;39:390–395.

Carisma MBO, Manalo JM, Chua WT. Atrioventricular conduction in sick sinus syndrome. *PACE*. 1988;11:1636–1640.

Coplan NL, Schweitzer P. Carotid sinus hypersensitivity: case report and review of the literature. *Am J Med*. 1984;77:561–565.

Cortadellas J, Cinca J, Moya A, et al. Clinical and electrophysiologic findings in acute ischemic intrahisian bundle-branch block. *Am Heart J*. 1990;119:23–29.

Denes P. Atrioventricular and intraventricular block. *Circulation*. 1987;75:19–25.

DePasquale NP, Bruno MS. Natural history of combined right bundle branch block and left anterior hemiblock (bilateral bundle branch block). *Am J Med*. 1973;54:297–303.

Dhingra RC, Denes P, Wu D, et al. Prospective observations in patients with chronic bundle branch block and marked H-V prolongation. *Circulation*. 1976;53:600–604.

Dhingra RC, Denes P, Wu D, et al. Syncope in patients with chronic bifascicular block: significance, causative mechanisms, and clinical implications. *Ann Intern Med*. 1974;81:302–306.

DiCarlo LA, Morady F, Krol RB, et al. The hemodynamic effects of ventricular pacing with and without atrioventricular synchrony in patients with normal and diminished left ventricular function. *Am Heart J*. 1987;114:746–752.

Draper AJ. The cardioinhibitory carotid sinus syndrome. *Ann Intern Med*. 1950;32:700–716.

El-Sherif N, Scherlag BJ, Lazzara R. Pathophysiology of second degree atrioventricular block: a unified hypothesis. *Am J Cardiol*. 1975;35:421–434.

Ferrer MI. The etiology and natural history of sinus node disorders. *Arch Intern Med*. 1982;142:371–372.

Ferrer MI. The sick sinus syndrome. *Circulation*. 1973;47:635–641.

Feuer JM, Shandling AH, Messenger JC. Influence of cardiac pacing mode on the long-term development of atrial fibrillation. *Am J Cardiol*. 1989;64:1376–1379.

Frue RL, Collins JJ, DeSanctis RW, et al. Guidelines for permanent cardiac pacemaker implantation, May 1984. *Circulation*. 1984;70:331A–339A.

Garber GR, Popp H, Levine PA. Decision analysis for choosing the hemodynamically optimum pacemaker. *J Electrophysiol*. 1989;3:217–220.

Gilmore JP, Sarnoff SJ, Mitchell JH, et al. Synchronicity of ventricular contraction: observations comparing hemodynamic effects of atrial and ventricular pacing. *Br Heart J*. 1983;25:299–307.

Greenberg B, Chatterjee K, Parmley WW, et al. The influence of left ventricular filling pressure on atrial contribution to cardiac output. *Am Heart J*. 1979;98:742–751.

Gupta PK, Lichstein E, Chadda KD. Electrophysiological features of complete AV block within the His bundle. *Br Heart J*. 1973;35:610–615.

Gupta PK, Lichstein E, Chadda KD. Electrophysiological features of Mobitz type II AV block occurring within the His bundle. *Br Heart J*. 1972;34:1232–1237.

Hayes DL. Indications for permanent pacing. In: Furman S, Hayes DL, Holmes DR, eds. *A Practice of Cardiac Pacing*. 2nd rev. and enl. ed. Mt Kisco, NY: Futura Publishing Co; 1989;3–22.

Hayes DL, Furman S. Stability of AV conduction in sick sinus node syndrome patients with implanted atrial pacemakers. *Am Heart J*. 1984;107:644–647.

Hilgard J, Ezri MD, Denes T. Significance of the ventricular pauses of three seconds or more detected on 24-hour Holter recordings. *Am J Cardiol*. 1985;55:1005–1008.

Hoffmann A, Jost M, Pfifterer M, et al. Persisting symptoms despite permanent pacing: incidence, causes and follow-up. *Chest*. 1984;85:207-210.

Jutzy RV, Isaeff DM, Bansal RC, et al. Comparison of VVIR, DDD, and DDDR pacing. *J Electrophysiol*. 1989;3:194–201.

Kammerling JM. Sinus node dysfunction. In: Zipes DP, Rowlands DJ, eds. *Progress in Cardiology*. Philadelphia, Pa: Lea & Febiger; 1988;1–1:205–230.

Kaplan BM, Langendorf R, Lev M, et al. Tachycardia-bradycardia syndrome (so-called "sick sinus syndrome"): pathology, mechanisms, treatment. *Am J Cardiol*. 1973;31:497–508.

Kay GN, Anderson K, Epstein AE, et al. Active fixation atrial leads: randomized comparison of two lead designs. *PACE*. 1989;12:1355–1361.

Kay GN, Bubien R. Effect of His bundle ablation and rate responsive pacing on exercise capacity and quality of life in patients with atrial fibrillation. *PACE*. 1988;11:505.

Kay GN, Bubien RS, Epstein AE, et al. Effect of catheter ablation of the atrioventricular junction on quality of life and exercise tolerance in patients with paroxysmal atrial fibrillation. *Am J Cardiol*. 1988;62:741–744.

Kay GN, Bubien RS, Epstein AE, et al. Rate-modulated cardiac pacing based on transthoracic impedance measurement of minute ventilation: correlation with exercise gas exchange. *J Am Coll Cardiol*. 1989;14:1283–1289.

Kay GN, Epstein AE, Plumb VJ. Comparison of unipolar and bipolar active fixation atrial pacing leads. *PACE*. 1988;11:544–549.

Kay R, Estioko M, Wiener I. Primary sick sinus syndrome as an indication for chronic pacemaker therapy in young adults: incidence, clinical features, and long-term evaluation. *Am Heart J.* 1982;103:338–342.

Kerr CR, Grant AO, Wenger TL, et al. Sinus node dysfunction. *Cardiol Clin.* 1983;1:187–207.

Kriwisky M, Goldstein J, Gotsman MS. Accessory atrioventricular pathway, supra- and infrahisian conduction impaired due to mitral annulus calcification. *Clin Cardiol.* 1987;10:818–820.

Langendorf R, Pick A. Atrioventricular block, type II (Mobitz)—its nature and clinical significance. *Circulation.* 1968;38:819–821.

Langenfeld H, Grimm W, Maisch B, et al. Atrial fibrillation and embolic complications in paced patients. *PACE.* 1988;11:1667–1672.

Lehman MH, Steinman RT. Atrioventricular and intraventricular block. In: Zipes DP, Rowlands DJ, eds. *Progress in Cardiology.* Philadelphia, Pa: Lea & Febiger; 1988;1–1:281–312.

Lerman BB, Marchlinski FE, Kempf FC, et al. Prognosis in patients with intrahisian conduction disturbances. *Int J Cardiol.* 1984;5:449–457.

Lesaka Y, Rozanski JJ, Pinakatt T, et al. Intrahisian functional bundle branch block. *PACE.* 1982;5:667–674.

Levine Paul A. Physiologic pacing 1988: a comparison of single- and dual-chamber pacing systems with rate adaptive single- and dual-chamber pacing systems. *J Electrophysiol.* 1989;3:167–169.

Levine Paul A. Physiological pacing '88: summary and commentary. *J Electrophysiol.* 1989;3:221–222.

Madigan NP, Flaker GC, Curtis JJ, et al. Carotid sinus hypersensitivity: beneficial effects of dual-chamber pacing. *Am J Cardiol.* 1984;53:1034–1040.

Markewitz A, Schad N, Hemmer W, et al. What is the most appropriate stimulation mode in patients with sinus node dysfunction? *PACE.* 1986;9:1115–1120.

Mazuz M, Friedman HS. Significance of prolonged electrocardiographic pauses in sinoatrial disease: sick sinus syndrome. *Am J Cardiol.* 1983;52:485–489.

McAnulty JH, Murphy E, Rahimtoola SH. A prospective evaluation of intrahisian conduction delay. *Circulation.* 1979;59:1035–1039.

Morgan JM, Joseph SP, Bahri AK, et al. Choosing the pacemaker; a rational approach to the use of modern pacemaker technology. *Eur Heart J.* 1990;11:753–764.

Nishimura RA, Gersh BJ, Vlietstra RE, et al. Hemodynamic and symptomatic consequences of ventricular pacing. *PACE.* 1982;5:903.

Reddy CP, Damato AN, Akhtar M. Time dependent changes in the functional properties of the atrioventricular conduction system in man. *Circulation.* 1975;52:1012–1022.

Ogawa S, Dreifus LS, Shenoy PN, et al. Hemodynamic consequences of atrioventricular and ventriculoatrial pacing. *PACE.* 1978;1:8.

Parsonnet V, Bernstein AD. Pacing in perspective: concepts and controversies. *Circulation.* 1986;73:1087.

Rasmussen K. Chronic sinus node disease: natural course and indications for pacing. *Eur Heart J.* 1981;2:455–459.

Rosenqvist M, Arent C, Kristensson BE, et al. Atrial rate-responsive pacing in sinus node disease. *Eur Heart J.* 1990;11:537–542.

Rosenqvist M, Brandt J, Schuller H. Long-term pacing in sinus node disease: effects of stimulation mode on cardiovascular morbidity and mortality. *Am Heart J.* 1988;116:16–22.

Rosenqvist M, Obel IWP. Atrial pacing and the risk for AV block: is there time of change in attitude? *PACE.* 1989;12:97–101.

Samet P, Bernstein W, Levine S. Significance of the atrial contribution to ventricular filling. *Am J Cardiol.* 1985;55:195–202.

Scherlis L. Atrioventricular block and implantation of a permanent cardiac pacemaker. In: Fortuin MJ, ed. *Current Therapy in Cardiovascular Disease-2.* Philadelphia, Pa: Marcel Dekker, Inc; 1988:219–222.

Shaw DB, Hockness JM. Natural history of sinoatrial disorders. *Clin Prog Pacing Electrophysiol.* 1983;1:335–348.

Strasberg B, Amat-Y-Leon F, Dhingra RC, et al. Natural history of chronic second-degree atrioventricular nodal block. *Circulation.* 1981;63:1043–1049.

Sun RL, Wang FZ, Hu SJ. Intra-hisian block associated with unusual etiologies. *PACE.* 1987;10:1117–1124.

Sutton R, Kenny RA. The natural history of sick sinus syndrome. *PACE.* 1986;9:1110–1114.

Walter PF, Crawley IS, Dorney ER. Carotid sinus hypersensitivity and syncope. *Am J Cardiol.* 1978;42:396–403.

Wish M, Fletcher RD, Cohen A. Hemodynamics of AV synchrony and rate. *J Electrophysiol.* 1989;3:170–175.

Yee R, Strauss HC. Electrophysiologic mechanisms sinus node dysfunction. *Circulation.* 1987;75:12–18.

Chapter 9

Catheter Ablation of Physiologic Substrates of Cardiac Arrhythmias

INTRODUCTION

With the advent of antitachycardia pacing and catheter ablation, electrophysiologic testing has evolved from a purely diagnostic technique to a procedure with direct therapeutic application. Catheter ablation techniques include any approach to permanent modification of an arrhythmogenic focus or conduction pathway that is performed with intravascular catheterization. The delivery of high-energy shocks, radio-frequency energy, or thermal energy (either heating or cooling); lasers; and the intracoronary infusion of ethanol have all been successfully used to treat atrial and ventricular arrhythmias that are refractory to medical management. Ablative procedures involve selective interruption or modification of the AV conduction system, accessory AV connections, and regions of the atrial or ventricular myocardium that are sites of origin for clinical arrhythmias. Each of these techniques will be reviewed in this chapter, with an emphasis on the clinical indications, results, and complications of each approach.

ABLATION OF THE ATRIOVENTRICULAR CONDUCTION SYSTEM

Interruption of the AV conduction system may be indicated for selected patients with recurrent atrial or junctional arrhythmias that cannot be adequately managed by less invasive means.

The most common indications for this procedure are atrial fibrillation or flutter with rapid ventricular response. Patients who are considered for this procedure have typically failed medical trials of digoxin, calcium blockers, and β-blockers that are designed to slow the ventricular response. Patients who are candidates for the procedure should have also been given trials of class I drugs and cardioversion in an attempt to maintain sinus rhythm. In addition to the requirement that standard medical therapy has been tried and shown to be ineffective, patients must have sufficient symptoms to justify the risks and long-term imponderables of the procedure. Other arrhythmias that have been successfully treated with catheter ablation of the AV junction include ectopic atrial tachycardia, AV nodal reentrant tachycardia, orthodromic reciprocating tachycardia utilizing a concealed accessory pathway, incessant junctional tachycardia, and reentrant tachycardias utilizing a nodofascicular Mahaim fiber. It is vitally important that patients be told that the procedure is irreversible and that they will be totally pacemaker dependent. The long-term unknowns need to be emphasized, especially to young patients.

Direct Current Shock

Interruption of AV conduction by direct current discharge was first reported by Vedel in

1979. AV block was accidentally induced by external cardioversion with energy that was carried to the heart by an electrode catheter placed across the tricuspid valve to record His bundle activation. Subsequently, Scheinman reported that this technique could be reliably used to produce complete heart block in dogs by delivery of the defibrillating waveform from an electrode catheter recording from the His bundle region. Soon thereafter, Scheinman and Gallagher independently reported the successful application of this technique for the treatment of medically refractory atrial arrhythmias in humans. The technique gained widespread acceptance, and a national registry of patients treated with direct current shocks for the purpose of ablating the AV conduction system was established.

Direct current shocks are usually delivered with a standard clinical defibrillator using a backplate that is positioned behind the left scapula as the anode and the distal pole of a standard tripolar or quadripolar catheter as the cathode. The patient is sedated with intravenous thiopental, methohexital, or etomidate prior to the ablative discharge. The energy delivered to the catheter has ranged from 150 to 500 J in different studies. Our standard technique has involved use of a specially designed 8F bipolar catheter to deliver 300 J from the distal electrode. The catheter is positioned at a site recording the largest bipolar His deflection possible. Other authors have suggested using unipolar recordings and have delivered the shock more proximally, at a site recording a large atrial deflection in addition to a generous His potential. In our experience, the only factor predicting successful ablation of AV conduction has been a minimum amplitude of the His deflection of 160 μV.

The physical effects of direct current shocks have been extensively studied. In saline tank tests, the first effect during a direct current discharge of 400 J is a flash of light around the tip of the catheter that is rapidly followed by an audible explosion and vaporization of water. An initial wave of positive pressure is generated at the catheter tip that is followed in a few milliseconds by a negative pressure wave. This fireball generates at least 3 atm of pressure at the catheter tip. The temperature at the point of discharge has been measured to exceed 1700°C. Lowering the energy of discharge results in a decrease in the pressure wave and maximum temperature generated by the flash. The biologic effects of direct current shocks include hemolysis of red blood cells and creation of gas bubbles composed predominantly of hydrogen and nitrogen, with smaller amounts of carbon dioxide and oxygen. Microscopic examination of the canine heart following direct current shocks delivered to the region of the His bundle has demonstrated coagulation necrosis and extensive surrounding myocardial edema. Chronically, these lesions are replaced by dense connective tissue with fibrosis, fatty infiltration, and giant cell inflammation. It is likely that much of the necrosis is related to the very high electrical current passing through the tissue. The myocardial edema likely reflects the effects of barotrauma from the shock wave. The high-pressure shock wave that is generated by direct current shocks may temporarily interrupt AV conduction, with return of conduction following resolution of these transient effects.

The overall success rate of direct current ablation for producing complete AV block in the national registry has approximated 80%, with an additional 10% having modification of AV conduction and 10% experiencing failure of the procedure. The complications observed with direct current shocks have included cardiac tamponade, creation of intracardiac shunts, precipitation of ventricular fibrillation, transient hypotension, venous thrombosis, and a few instances of sudden death in late follow-up. Following catheter ablation, a permanent rate-adaptive pacemaker is implanted. The effect of catheter ablation of the AV conduction system and rate-adaptive pacemaker implantation on quality of life and exercise capacity was prospectively studied in 12 patients with medically refractory atrial fibrillation or flutter. All patients had failed multiple antiarrhythmic drug regimens prior to ablation. The results of this study demonstrated a significant improvement in the level of physical functioning, sense of overall well-being, and exercise tolerance following the procedures. Thus these techniques may offer medically refractory patients an improved quality of life and relief of disabling symptoms.

Radiofrequency Energy

Radiofrequency energy may also be used to create AV block for the treatment of atrial arrhythmias. Radiofrequency energy was introduced in 1987 as a clinical technique in humans to induce AV block in patients with medically refractory atrial arrhythmias. This technique has been associated with a high rate of success in inducing complete AV block comparable to that observed with high-energy direct current shocks. The development of specialized catheters with a larger surface area has further improved the efficiency of the technique. This technique has recently received widespread acceptance as an alternative to direct current shocks because of several advantages. First, since radiofrequency energy applied to the endocardium produces minimal discomfort in most individuals, ablative procedures using this energy form do not require general anesthesia or intravenous sedation. Because of this, radiofrequency energy may be applied to patients who are poor risks for sedation, especially those with chronic obstructive pulmonary disease. Second, radiofrequency energy does not generate a shock wave, so that this technique is not associated with barotrauma. This allows its use in the coronary sinus without the risk of perforation associated with direct current shock. Third, the use of radiofrequency energy produces small lesions and minimal elevation of serum isoenzyme creatine kinase–MB, as compared to direct current shock. Fourth, the minimal tissue damage caused by radiofrequency energy and the lack of requirement for anesthesia allows multiple lesions to be placed during a single session. Fifth, radiofrequency energy is easier to control than direct current shocks, allowing modification of AV conduction rather than producing complete AV block.

Radiofrequency ablation involves delivery of electromagnetic energy with frequencies ranging from approximately 150,000 to 1 million Hz.

This frequency range is capable of cutting and coagulating tissue and has been used in surgical operations for years. Electrosurgical devices used for a variety of surgical procedures generally deliver frequencies in the range of 500 to 750 kHz between an active electrode and a dispersive pad placed over the skin. The electrical energy actually passes through the tissue starting at the point of contact of the active electrode. Since the resistance to current flow offered by living tissues is far greater than the resistance of metal conducting wires, the electrical energy is converted to heat at the tip of the active electrode. Electrosurgical units may be used to cut or cauterize tissue. The sparking of high-power sine waves between the electrode and the tissue results in tissue dissection, whereas coagulation involves use of lower power, with intermittent pulses of energy. The efficiency of electrosurgical devices declines precipitously following accumulation of charred, desiccated tissue on the catheter. This charred debris results in a marked rise in impedance and requires that the catheter be withdrawn from the body and cleaned. The application of radiofrequency energy to myocardial tissue ablation involves lower-power continuous sine wave energy in the range of 300 to 750 kHz. Frequencies below 100 kHz may stimulate contraction in cardiac muscle and are not used.

Catheter ablation with radiofrequency energy is produced by delivery of the electrical energy to the heart using a specially designed electrode catheter and a dispersive pad placed on the skin. The voltage used is usually in the range of 25 to 50 V, with constant-voltage radiofrequency generators. This results in a current of 150 to 500 mA and a delivered power of 5 to 25 W. The current actually delivered to the tissue is determined by the voltage setting selected and the impedance to electron flow. If the impedance of the system is high, the current delivered is low. Higher voltages result in rapid charring of the tissue in contact with the electrode, which is associated with an abrupt increase in impedance (and an abrupt decrease in current flow). Thus care is taken to deliver lower-voltage currents to avoid this phenomenon. The energy is usually applied for 30 to 60 seconds with the catheter in firm contact with the precise site to be ablated. The current delivered is continuously monitored, and the power is turned off at the first sign of a decrease. If charring does occur, the catheter must be withdrawn and any charred debris removed. The technique of radiofrequency ablation has been improved by the development of catheters with large surface area electrodes and by the recognition that the catheter must be firmly in contact with the endocardial surface.

Catheter positioning involves recording of the His bundle electrogram, with delivery of energy from the distal electrode at a site recording a large atrial deflection in addition to the His deflection. The time required for successful ablation of AV conduction tissue is usually longer with radiofrequency energy than with direct current shock, though further experience with this technique may significantly shorten the duration of the procedure.

Radiofrequency energy may also be used to modify AV conduction without producing complete AV block, and the smaller lesions created by this energy form are likely to allow a greater degree of precision than direct current shocks. The radiofrequency technique is devoid of barotrauma, which may temporarily stun but not destroy AV conduction with direct current shocks. Because of this, more accurate assessment of the long-term effects on AV conduction may be possible with radiofrequency ablation. Radiofrequency ablation of the AV conduction system has proven painless and hemodynamically well-tolerated. Permanent pacemaker implantation is required after creation of complete AV block with radiofrequency energy. It is uncertain whether radiofrequency ablation of the AV conduction system will be associated with the rare episodes of late sudden death that have been observed with direct current shocks.

Intracoronary Ethanol Infusion

Direct injections of phenol or 96% ethanol into cardiac tissue have been used to induce AV block in experimental animals. The intraoperative injection of phenol into the AV groove has also been successfully used to treat Wolff-Parkinson-White syndrome for several years in China. Brugada introduced the technique of ethanol infusion into selective branches of the coronary arteries to ablate incessant ventricular tachycardia in humans. We have successfully applied the intracoronary ethanol ablation technique to patients suffering from medically refractory ventricular tachycardia and to patients with intractable atrial arrhythmias. In order to create AV block, ethanol must be delivered directly into the AV node artery, which is a branch of the right coronary artery in over 90% of individuals. Standard coronary arteriography is first performed to determine the location of the AV node artery. A standard guiding catheter is then advanced to the ostium of the right coronary artery, and guiding angiographic views are recorded with injections of an iodinated contrast medium into the right coronary artery. A high-torque guide wire (0.014 to 0.018 inch) is then advanced via the guiding catheter under fluoroscopic guidance into the AV nodal artery. A polyethylene catheter with an external diameter of 2.7F is then advanced over the guide wire into the AV nodal artery, and the guide wire is removed. Injections of cold saline and iodinated contrast medium into the AV node artery are then made, with careful recording of the AH, HV, and PR intervals. If the AH interval prolongs with selective injections into the AV nodal artery, 2 mL of 96% ethanol is then infused into this artery. Patients typically describe a sense of chest discomfort that lasts less than 30 seconds, as the ethanol is delivered into the coronary artery. The ethanol is infused over 2 to 3 minutes in order to minimize backleak into the distal right coronary artery.

Intracoronary ethanol ablation of the AV node has been highly successful for creating complete AV block (80%) or for markedly modifying AV conduction (10%) in patients with intractable atrial arrhythmias. The technique does not require intravenous sedation and can be accomplished quickly. The escape rhythm is a narrow QRS complex at a rate of 40 to 60 beats per minute. His bundle recordings have demonstrated that the His bundle is probably the site of the escape pacemaker. Although an adequate escape rhythm has been reliably present following intracoronary ethanol ablation, a permanent pacemaker is still implanted to provide a more normal chronotropic response.

Despite these initial encouraging results with ethanol ablation of the AV node, the potential for damage to the right coronary artery by indiscriminate use of ethanol should be carefully considered before using this technique. Although we have used intracoronary ethanol ablation of the AV node very successfully and without significant complications, this procedure is likely to gain slow acceptance because of these concerns.

Lasers

Laser energy has been used for intraoperative interruption of the AV conduction system as well as intraoperative ablation of ventricular tachycardia. Canine studies have demonstrated that it may be feasible to interrupt the AV conduction system with a transcatheter approach. Although these initial results are encouraging, the clinical application of laser energy for direct transcatheter ablation of arrhythmias has yet to be studied in humans.

ABLATION OF ACCESSORY PATHWAYS

Direct Current Shock

High-energy direct current shocks have been used successfully to ablate accessory pathways located in the posterior septum. This technique involves delivery of shocks via a catheter positioned at the ostium of the coronary sinus. The approach to accessory pathways in the posteroseptal location has involved using two linked poles on an electrode catheter in the mouth of the coronary sinus as the cathode and a backplate as the anode. The results of catheter ablation for the treatment of posteroseptal accessory pathways have demonstrated complete elimination of preexcitation in approximately 70% of patients. Effective ablation has required direct current shock energies in the range of 200 to 300 J. The complication rate has been very low, though a number of centers have experienced rupture of

the coronary sinus and pericardial tamponade with this procedure. This technique has also proven extremely effective for the treatment of the permanent form of junctional reciprocating tachycardia, an unusual incessant supraventricular tachycardia utilizing the AV node as the antegrade limb of the circuit and a very slowly conducting accessory pathway located in the posteroseptum as the retrograde limb. Although direct current shock has been used by many laboratories for ablation of posteroseptal pathways, a significant minority of patients will develop return of accessory pathway conduction over a period of minutes to days following the procedure. This observation suggests that barotrauma may produce temporary dysfunction in the pathway without permanent destruction.

Catheter ablation using direct current shocks has also been used to treat left free wall accessory pathways using a catheter in the coronary sinus. This technique has been associated with rupture of the coronary sinus and pericardial tamponade. Thus the use of standard high-energy shocks in the coronary sinus has been abandoned. Newer technologies involving modification of the waveform of the defibrillator to deliver direct current shocks without producing a fireball and shock wave have been reported. These modifications may allow catheter ablation with direct current shock to be used for accessory pathways in locations other than the posteroseptal region. Recent experience with direct current shock ablation for accessory pathways has demonstrated a very high success rate for pathways in virtually all locations. Whether the complication rate will be as low as with radiofrequency is uncertain.

Radiofrequency Energy

Radiofrequency energy currently holds the greatest promise for catheter ablation of accessory pathways. We and others have used radiofrequency energy to ablate accessory pathways in virtually any location in the heart, including septal, left free wall, and right free wall pathways. The technique involves precise recording of the atrial and ventricular insertion sites of the pathway during atrial and ventricular pacing as well as during reciprocating tachycardia.

Our standard approach to radiofrequency ablation for Wolff-Parkinson-White syndrome utilizes an ablation catheter with 4 mm^2 electrode surface area that is positioned at the ventricular insertion site of the accessory pathway. The catheter is placed along the ventricular side of the AV ring directly opposite an atrial or coronary sinus catheter positioned to record the site of earliest atrial activation during orthodromic reciprocating tachycardia. The ventricular ablation catheter is looped in the ventricle so that the tip is firmly wedged underneath the mitral or tricuspid valve in direct apposition to the valve ring. Ablation of the atrial insertion site of accessory pathways is also an effective method that is used by several centers. Radiofrequency energy is then applied, using 5 to 40 W for 30 to 60 seconds. The typical response is an abrupt loss of preexcitation and accessory pathway conduction after approximately 1 to 40 seconds. Precise positioning of the catheter is required for success with this procedure.

The approach to posteroseptal accessory pathways has also involved the use of a catheter positioned above the tricuspid valve ring within Koch's triangle just cephalad to the ostium of the coronary sinus, along the tricuspid valve anterior or caudal to the coronary ostium or within the ostium of the coronary sinus. Successful ablation of left free wall accessory pathways is highly likely with radiofrequency energy (greater than 95%). Posteroseptal or right free wall accessory pathways have proven more difficult to ablate with this technique, with a success rate of approximately 90%.

Radiofrequency ablation is likely to replace long-term antiarrhythmic drug therapy or surgery as the primary treatment of Wolff-Parkinson-White syndrome. However, it is likely that a small number of patients cannot be managed with this procedure. The complication rate with this method of ablation has been very low, and the success rate very high. At present, radiofrequency ablation is combined as part of our standard diagnostic electrophysiologic study for Wolff-Parkinson-White syndrome. Thus in a single study patients can be both diagnosed and effectively treated for their arrhythmias.

CATHETER ABLATION OF ARRHYTHMOGENIC SUBSTRATES OF VENTRICULAR TACHYCARDIA

Direct Current Shock

Catheter ablation of the arrhythmogenic substrates of ventricular tachycardia with high-energy direct current shocks has been used for several years with variable results. The initial success rate of this technique, using standard catheter mapping to localize the site of earliest ventricular activation during ventricular tachycardia, is in the range of 30%. More recently, the electrophysiologic concepts of resetting and transient entrainment have been demonstrated to localize the region of slow conduction within the reentrant circuit of ventricular tachycardia. By using these concepts in catheter mapping, more precise delivery of direct current shocks has been possible.

The results of catheter ablation have generally improved with the use of ventricular mapping to localize the region of slow conduction prior to delivery of standard high-energy direct current shocks. It should be emphasized that some authors have reported mortality rates as high as 10% with direct current ablation. Our experience with this technique has demonstrated that it may be a valuable clinical tool to decrease the frequency of incessant ventricular tachycardia and that it may allow successful control of arrhythmias that had been previously refractory to antiarrhythmic drugs. Only a minority of patients (30%) have had no inducible ventricular arrhythmias at predischarge electrophysiologic testing. As reported by other groups, the success rate of high-energy direct current shocks in ablating foci of ventricular tachycardia arising in the right ventricle has been considerably higher (approximately 70%). In patients with ventricular tachycardia arising from the right ventricular outflow tract or with right ventricular dysplasia, catheter ablation has been extremely successful.

A distinct variety of ventricular tachycardia with a reentrant circuit confined to the bundle branches may be especially well suited to catheter ablation. In this form of ventricular tachycardia, known as bundle branch reentry, there is unidirectional block in one bundle branch and slow conduction. The reentrant circuit consists of antegrade conduction over one bundle branch and retrograde conduction over the other bundle branch. Because of the requirement for unidirectional block, most patients manifest a typical bundle branch block during sinus rhythm. The QRS morphology during bundle branch reentry is often very similar to the QRS morphology during sinus rhythm. Bundle branch reentry may be effectively treated by delivery of high-energy shocks to the region of the retrogradely conducting bundle branch. This structure can be localized as a distinct, sharp deflection along the right or left side of the interventricular septum. Patients who would be considered excellent candidates for high-energy direct current shock ablation have hemodynamically stable ventricular tachycardia with a single QRS morphology. Patients with ventricular tachycardia arising in the right ventricle are likely to have a higher chance of success.

Radiofrequency Energy

Since the lesions produced by radiofrequency ablation are small, relatively shallow, and not associated with surrounding edema, this technique has not shown great promise to date for the treatment of ventricular tachycardia arising in the relatively thick-walled left ventricle. However, it seems likely that improvement in endocardial mapping strategies will increase the clinical utility of this technique. Radiofrequency energy can be used to ablate ventricular tachycardia, especially when the site of origin is in the right ventricle. The syndrome of right ventricular outflow tract tachycardia is especially well suited to treatment with radiofrequency ablation.

Intracoronary Ethanol Infusion

Intracoronary ethanol infusion has been used successfully to ablate sources of incessant ventricular tachycardia. We have extended this technique to ventricular tachycardia that is inducible in the electrophysiology laboratory. It has been observed for several years that ventricular tachycardia may be terminated by the intracoronary injection of an iodinated radiocontrast medium during this arrhythmia. Our standard technique for intracoronary ethanol ablation involves inducing ventricular tachycardia with programmed electrical stimulation, recording the sequence of intracardiac ventricular activation, and injecting a radiographic contrast medium into coronary arteries supplying the ventricular myocardium involved. If the ventricular tachycardia is thereby interrupted, a high-torque guide wire is passed via an angioplasty guiding catheter into very small branches of the coronary arteries. An infusion catheter with an outside diameter of 2.7F is then advanced over the guide wire into the branch of the coronary arteries suspected of supplying the abnormal myocardium involved in the reentrant circuit. Injections of cold saline or contrast medium into the cannulated artery during ventricular tachycardia will interrupt the arrhythmia if the correct artery has been selected. If reliable termination of ventricular tachycardia is demonstrated by selective intracoronary injections of cold saline or contrast medium, 2 mL of 96% ethanol is then infused slowly into the vessel. Patients develop transient chest discomfort with this infusion, which rapidly resolves. Initial experience with this technique demonstrates that intracoronary ethanol ablation is highly effective in abolishing ventricular tachycardia, provided that the correct feeding vessel can be identified. There appears to be a relatively high risk of complete AV block (approximately 20%) because of coronary vessels that provide collateral blood supply to the AV conduction system. Complications of intracoronary ethanol ablation include occlusion of branches of the coronary arteries, complete AV block, and pericarditis resulting from epicardial inflammation. Although this technique appears to be promising, it remains highly investigational. Widespread use of this procedure depends on further experience with this technique in treating ventricular tachycardia.

ABLATION OF ATRIAL FOCI

Catheter ablation has been used to ablate the abnormal focus of an ectopic atrial tachycardia in a small number of cases. Although the experience is limited, direct current shocks have been demonstrated to effectively treat ectopic atrial tachycardia arising in the right atrium. We have had excellent long-term results in a small number of patients. We have also experienced pericardial tamponade related to rupture of the high right atrium in one individual who received shocks of 200 J delivered to the high anterior right atrium. Radiofrequency energy has also been used for ablation of foci of atrial tachycardias. To date, the overall experience with catheter ablation of the sources of this arrhythmia is quite limited, and widespread application of this therapy awaits further clarification of the risks and success rate that can be anticipated.

MODIFICATION OF THE ATRIOVENTRICULAR CONDUCTION SYSTEM

Catheter ablation with high-energy direct current shocks has been demonstrated to result in permanent cure of AV nodal reentrant tachycardia in selected patients. Standard direct current shocks have been delivered to the region of the AV node. The postablation electrophysiologic studies performed after attempts at modification have demonstrated ablation of the slow antegrade pathway in some individuals and ablation of the fast retrograde pathway in others. This procedure has been associated with a relatively low risk of complete AV block. More recently, radiofrequency energy has been applied to the region of the AV node to permanently cure AV nodal reentrant tachycardia. Radiofrequency lesions placed near the apex of Koch's triangle at sites recording a large atrial deflection and a small His deflection have resulted in ablation of the fast pathway in approximately 75% of patients. The risk of complete AV block has been relatively low, in the range of 10%. An alternative technique using radiofrequency ablation for modification of the AV nodal reentrant tachycardia circuit has involved attempts to selectively ablate the slow pathway. The radiofrequency lesions are placed caudal to the AV node, more posteriorly in Koch's triangle. Similar long-term cure rates for AV nodal reentrant tachycardia have been demonstrated with either approach. In our experience, the selective ablation of the slow pathway has not produced AV block but has produced a high rate of success. These catheter ablation techniques have great promise as a permanent solution for recurrent AV nodal reentrant tachycardia.

BIBLIOGRAPHY

Bardy GH, Coltorti F, Ivey TD, et al. Some factors affecting bubble formation during catheter mediated electrical pulse. *Circulation.* 1986;73:525–538.

Brugada P, de Swart H, Smeets J, et al. Transcoronary chemical ablation of atrioventricular conduction. *Circulation.* 1990;81:757–761.

Brugada P, de Swart H, Smeets J, et al. Transcoronary chemical ablation of ventricular tachycardia. *Circulation.* 1989;79:475–482.

Budde T, Borgreff M, Martinez-Rubio A, et al. Acute and long-term results of radiofrequency ablation of the AV conduction system. *Circulation.* 1989;80(suppl 2):II-44. Abstract.

Calkins H, Sousa J, El-Atassi R, et al. Diagnosis and cure of Wolff-Parkinson-White syndrome or paroxysmal supraventricular tachycardias during a single electrophysiologic test. *N Engl J Med.* 1991;324:1612–1618.

Cunningham D, Rowland E, Rickards AF. A new low energy power source for catheter ablation. *PACE.* 1986;9:1384–1390.

Davis J, Scheinman MM, Ruder MA, et al. Ablation of cardiac tissues by an electrode catheter technique for treatment of ectopic supraventricular tachycardia in adults. *Circulation.* 1986;74:40.

Davis J, Scheinman MM, Ruder MA, et al. Ablation for treatment of ectopic supraventricular tachycardia in adults. *Circulation.* 1986;74:1044–1053.

Ellman BA, Parkhill BJ, Marcus PB, et al. Renal ablation with absolute alcohol: mechanism of action. *Invest Radiol.* 1984;19:416–423.

Epstein LM, Scheinman MM, Langberg JJ, et al. Percutaneous catheter modification of the atrioventricular node. *Circulation.* 1989;80:757–768.

Evans GT, Scheinman MM, Zipes DP, et al. The percutaneous cardiac mapping and ablation registry: final summary of results. *PACE.* 1988;11:1621–1626.

Fitzgerald DM, Friday KJ, Yeung Lai Wah JA. Electrogram patterns predicting successful catheter ablation of ventricular tachycardia. *Circulation.* 1988;77:806–814.

Friedman PL, Sosa-Suarez G, Wang PJ. Selective AV nodal artery catheterization in humans. *Circulation.* 1989; 80(suppl 2):40. Abstract.

Gallagher JJ, Svenson RH, Kasell JH. Catheter techniques for closed-chest ablation of the atrioventricular conducting system. *N Engl J Med*. 1982;306:194–200.

Gillette PC, Wampler DG, Garson A, et al. Treatment of atrial automatic tachycardias by ablation procedures. *J Am Coll Cardiol*. 1985;6:405–409.

Grogan EW, Nellis SH. Catheter ablation using radiofrequency energy: control of lesion volume and shape by varying power and duration of ablation. *J Am Coll Cardiol*. 1987;9:128A.

Huang SK, Bharati S, Graham AR, et al. Closed chest catheter desiccation of the atrioventricular junction using radiofrequency energy—a new method of catheter ablation. *J Am Coll Cardiol*. 1987;9:349–358.

Huang SK, Jordan N, Graham A, et al. Closed-chest catheter desiccation of atrioventricular junction using radiofrequency energy—a new method of catheter ablation. *Circulation*. 1985;72:III-389. Abstract.

Jackman WM, Wang X, Friday KJ, et al. Catheter ablation of accessory atrioventricular pathways (Wolff-Parkinson-White Syndrome) by radiofrequency current. *New Engl J Med*. 1991;324:1605–1611.

Kay GN, Bubien RS, Dailey SM, et al. A prospective evaluation of intracoronary ethanol ablation of the atrioventricular conduction system. *J Am Coll Cardiol*. 1991;17:1634–1640.

Kay GN, Bubien RS, Epstein AE, et al. Effect of catheter ablation of the atrioventricular junction on quality of life and exercise tolerance paroxysmal atrial fibrillation. *Am J Cardiol*. 1988;62:741–744.

Kay GN, Crossley GH, Epstein AE, et al. Facilitation of fast pathway conduction by selective radiofrequency ablation of the slow pathway in AV nodal reentry. *PACE*. 1991;14:659. Abstract.

Kay GN, Epstein AE, Bubien RS, et al. Intracoronary ethanol ablation for the treatment of recurrent sustained ventricular tachycardia. *J Am Coll Cardiol*. In press.

Langberg JJ, Chin MC, Herre JM, et al. Catheter ablation of the atrioventricular junction using radiofrequency energy. *J Am Coll Cardiol*. 1989;169A. Abstract.

Lee MA, Morady F, Kadish A, et al. Catheter modification of the atrioventricular junction with radiofrequency energy for control of atrioventricular nodal reentrant tachycardia. *Circulation*. 1991;83:827–835.

Little RE, Kay GN, Plumb VJ, et al. His-bundle ablation: determinants for return of atrioventricular conduction and final clinical outcome. *PACE*. 1988;11:161.

Morady F, Frank R, Kou WH, et al. Identification and catheter ablation of a zone of slow conduction in the reentrant circuit of ventricular tachycardia in humans. *J Am Coll Cardiol*. 1988;11:775–782.

Morady F, Scheinman MM, DiCarlo L, et al. Catheter ablation of ventricular tachycardia with intracardiac shocks: results in 33 patients. *Circulation*. 1987;75:1037–1049.

Morady F, Scheinman MM, Winston SA, et al. Efficacy and safety of transcatheter ablation of posteroseptal accessory pathways. *Circulation*. 1985;72:170–177.

Plumb VJ, Epstein AE, Kay GN. The ablation of recurrent sustained ventricular tachycardia by intracoronary ethanol infusion. *J Am Coll Cardiol*. 1990;15:133A. Abstract.

Scheinman M. Catheter ablation for patients with cardiac arrhythmias. *PACE*. 1986;9:551–564.

Scheinman MM, Davis JC. Catheter ablation for treatment of tachyarrhythmias: present role and potential promise. *Circulation*. 1986;73:10–13.

Scheinman MM, Laks MM, DiMarco J, Plumb VJ. Current role of catheter ablative procedures in patients with cardiac arrhythmias. *Circulation*. 1991;83:2146–2153.

Tullo NG, An H, Saksena S. Ablation using radiofrequency current and low energy direct current shocks. In: Saksena S, Goldschlager N, eds. *Electrical Therapy for Cardiac Arrhythmias*. Philadelphia, Pa: WB Saunders Co; 1990.

Zipes DP. Targeted drug therapy. *Circulation*. 1990; 81:1139–1141.

Chapter 10

Antitachycardia Pacing

INTRODUCTION

Pacing techniques are an effective method of terminating many varieties of clinical tachycardias. Pacing can also be used to prevent the occurrence of tachyarrhythmias. The effective use of antitachycardia pacing for the management of clinical arrhythmias requires an understanding of the underlying mechanism of the tachycardia. The arrhythmias that can be reliably interrupted by pacing are usually based on a mechanism of reentry with a gap of excitability in the circuit (also discussed in Chapter 2). The fact that many clinical arrhythmias can be treated with antitachycardia pacing reflects the frequency of reentry as the mechanism of clinical tachycardias. In this chapter, the underlying mechanism of arrhythmias that can be interrupted by pacing will be discussed, as well as the specifics of antitachycardia pacing strategies.

THE MECHANISM OF REENTRY WITH AN EXCITABLE GAP

In order for reentry to occur, two conditions must be satisfied: (1) unidirectional block and (2) slow conduction. These concepts are best explained by considering arrhythmias associated with Wolff-Parkinson-White syndrome. The prototypical clinical arrhythmia based on reentry

is orthodromic reciprocating tachycardia utilizing an accessory AV connection. In patients with Wolff-Parkinson-White syndrome, there are two connections between the atria and the ventricles, the AV node-His bundle and the accessory pathway. In many patients with Wolff-Parkinson-White syndrome, the pathway is capable of conducting from the atrium to the ventricles (antegrade) as well as from the ventricles to the atria (retrograde). During sinus rhythm there is fusion of ventricular activation as the atrial impulse travels in the antegrade direction over both the normal AV conduction system and the accessory pathway. If both pathways conduct simultaneously, no arrhythmias result. However, a reentrant tachycardia may be initiated when there is unidirectional block in one of these two connections between the atria and ventricles (Figure 10-1).

For example, if an atrial premature depolarization travels to the ventricles over the AV node but fails to propagate antegradely over the accessory pathway, the impulse may reach the ventricle and continue to travel back to the atrium by traversing the accessory pathway in the retrograde direction. The site of unidirectional block in this case is the accessory pathway. In order for the reentry circuit to be completed, the accessory pathway must recover its excitability, permitting it to conduct the impulse in the retrograde direction. This requires

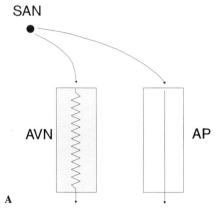

A

B

Figure 10-1 Initiation of orthodromic reciprocating tachycardia by an atrial premature depolarization (APD). In panel A, sinus rhythm is illustrated, with antegrade conduction over the AV node (AVN, shaded rectangle) and over the accessory pathway (AP, open rectangle). Since there is not a unidirectional block in either pathway, no arrhythmias occur. In panel B, an APD occurs, which conducts to both the AV node and the accessory pathway. There is an antegrade block in the accessory pathway when the APD encounters the refractory period of the accessory pathway. This beat is able to conduct antegradely over the AV node from the atrium to the ventricle, however. In Panel C, sustained reentry is then induced by the wavefront emerging from the AV node to reenter the distal portion of the accessory pathway and travel retrogradely to the atrium. SAN indicates sinoatrial node.

C

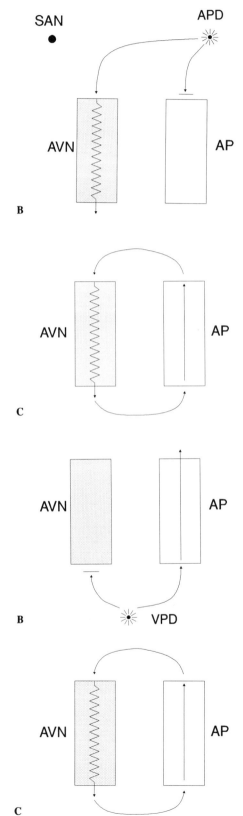

B

C

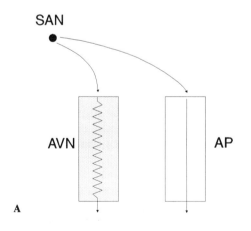

A

Figure 10-2 Initiation of orthodromic reciprocating tachycardia by a VPD. In panel A, a normal sinus beat occurs, with antegrade conduction from the atrium to the ventricle over the both the AV node (AVN, shaded rectangle) and over the accessory pathway (AP, open rectangle). In panel B, a VPD occurs, which blocks the AV node retrogradely. The VPD is able to conduct retrogradely through the accessory pathway to the atrium. In panel C, sustained reentry occurs as the atrial impulse reenters the proximal portion of the AV node to complete the circuit.

that there be a delay in antegrade conduction sufficient to allow the impulse to travel from the atrium to the ventricle over the AV node. Thus in this example of a prototype reentrant arrhythmia (orthodromic reciprocating tachycardia), unidirectional block occurs in the accessory pathway, and slow conduction is present in the AV node.

In addition to this mechanism of initiation, orthodromic reentrant tachycardia may be initiated by a VPD that blocks retrogradely in the AV node (the site of unidirectional block) but conducts over the accessory pathway to the atrium (Figure 10-2). The impulse may then reenter the AV node and conduct antegradely to begin the tachycardia. The site of slow conduction is also the AV node in this mechanism of initiation.

Antitachycardia pacing may be used to terminate a reentrant rhythm by converting unidirectional block in one limb of the circuit to unidirectional block in both limbs (Figure 10-3). For example, in the patient with orthodromic reciprocating tachycardia, rapid atrial pacing at a rate faster than the tachycardia may produce

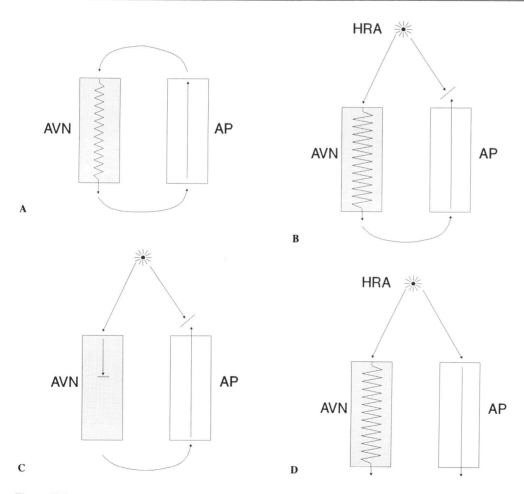

Figure 10-3 Interruption of orthodromic reciprocating tachycardia by atrial pacing. In panel A, sustained orthodromic reciprocating tachycardia is demonstrated, with antegrade conduction over the AV node (AVN, shaded rectangle) and retrograde conduction over an accessory pathway (AP, open rectangle). In panel B, rapid pacing from the high right atrium (HRA) results in collision between the paced wavefront and the retrograde wavefront emerging from the accessory pathway. The pacing impulse is able to traverse the AV node and simply resets the tachycardia. In panel C, the tachycardia is interrupted by bidirectional block. This occurs as a consequence of antegrade blocking in the AV node and block of the impulse emerging from the accessory pathway. In the subsequent beat (panel D) the paced impulse traverses both the AV node and the accessory pathway in the antegrade direction, and the tachycardia has been interrupted.

antegrade Wenckebach block in the AV node. The paced impulse travels to the atrial insertion site of the accessory pathway and collides with the preceding wavefront, spreading retrogradely over the pathway. The paced wave also travels to the AV node. If atrial pacing is stopped following a beat that blocks in the AV node, the tachycardia will be interrupted since an antegrade block will exist in both the AV node and the accessory pathway.

Rapid ventricular pacing may interrupt the same tachycardia by encountering the refractory period of the accessory pathway in the retrograde direction (Figure 10-4). The ventricular paced wavefront will travel to the AV node and collide with the beat that is conducting antegrade from the atria to the ventricles over the AV node. In this case, retrograde block in both the accessory pathway and the AV node will exist, and the tachycardia will have been interrupted.

The mechanism by which antitachycardia pacing interrupts reentrant tachycardias relates

to stimulating the atria or ventricles at rates that fail to propagate through the reentrant circuit. The conduction block that is produced by rapid pacing is a result of the pacing wavefront encountering the refractory period of cardiac tissue comprising a critical link in the reentrant circuit. If a paced wavefront is to be successful in terminating a reentrant tachycardia, there are several conditions that must exist. First, the pacing wavefront must be able to conduct to the reentrant circuit. Because of this requirement, the site of stimulation may be important for the success of antitachycardia pacing. Delivering a greater number of paced beats may increase the chances of interrupting the tachycardia circuit, as there may be progressively more atrial or ventricular tissue that is depolarized by the paced wavefront with each paced beat. This progressive activation of a greater amount of the heart by each successive beat in the pacing train has been referred to as "peeling back refractoriness" (Figure 10-5). Thus although single-

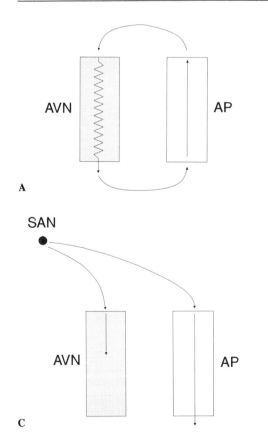

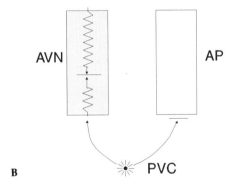

Figure 10-4 Interruption of orthodromic reciprocating tachycardia by ventricular pacing. In panel A, sustained orthodromic reciprocating tachycardia is illustrated with antegrade conduction over the AV node (AVN; shaded rectangle) and retrograde conduction over the accessory pathway (AP; open rectangle). In panel B, ventricular pacing results in collision of the wavefront traversing the AV node, producing retrograde block in the AV node. If the pacing stimulus also finds the accessory pathway refractory to conduction in the retrograde direction, bidirectional block occurs, and the tachycardia will have been interrupted. In panel C, sinus rhythm resumes with antegrade conduction over both the AV node and the accessory pathway.

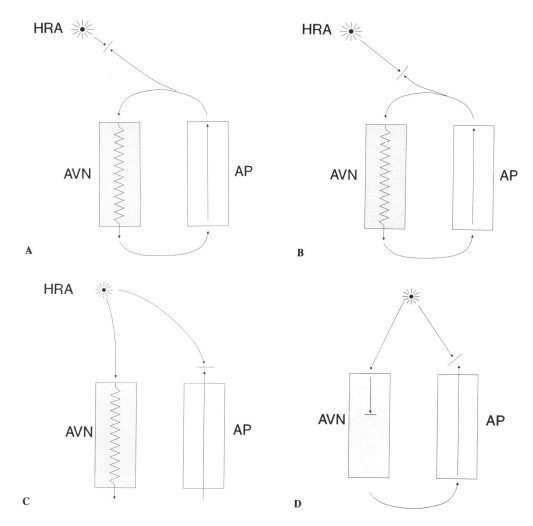

Figure 10-5 "Peeling back" of refractoriness. In panel A, orthodromic reciprocating tachycardia with antegrade conduction over the AV node (AVN; shaded rectangle) and retrograde conduction over the accessory pathway (AP; open rectangle) are shown. Pacing from the high right atrium (HRA) results in a wavefront of depolarization that collides with a wavefront that emerges from the reentry circuit. This paced beat does not affect the reentry circuit. In panel B, the next paced beat is able to advance further toward the reentry circuit before colliding with a wavefront that emerges from the reentrant circuit. Although this pacing beat does not affect reentry, the pacing wavefront has progressed further toward the circuit. In panel C, the paced wavefront is able to advance to the reentrant circuit and collide with the wavefront of activation spreading retrogradely over the accessory pathway. However, the pacing wavefront is able to traverse the AV node in the antegrade direction. In panel D bidirectional block occurs as a premature pacing beat encounters refractoriness in both the AV node and accessory pathway and results in termination of the tachycardia.

or double-paced beats may be effective in interrupting a tachycardia if delivered in close proximity to the reentrant focus, a train of several pacing stimuli often produces a greater chance of success by allowing the circuit to be depolarized.

A second requirement for interruption of a reentrant tachycardia by pacing is the presence of a gap of excitability within the reentrant circuit. A gap of excitability is a period of time during rotation of the reentrant wave when a portion of the circuit can be stimulated by the pacing wavefront. In other words, if the pacing wave can penetrate the reentrant circuit and activate a portion of it earlier than expected, there may be a chance that the paced wavefront will encounter refractoriness and produce conduction block. This excitable gap is a "window of opportunity" for antitachycardia pacing to interrupt the reentrant arrhythmia. The greater the gap of excitability, the greater the chance that pacing will succeed. The gap is usually widest during slower tachycardias (for example, those at a rate of 150 beats per minute) and much narrower during faster tachycardias. Thus a more aggressive approach (i.e., longer bursts of pacing) may be required to terminate faster tachycardias, as it may be more difficult for a pacing train to enter a narrow excitable gap. Tachycardias that do not have a gap of excitability cannot be interrupted by pacing. Examples of reentry without an excitable gap include micro–reentrant rhythms such as atrial fibrillation or rapid, type II atrial flutter. These arrhythmias cannot be interrupted since the paced wavefront cannot enter the reentrant circuit.

PACING ALGORITHMS FOR INTERRUPTION OF REENTRANT TACHYCARDIAS

There are several methods of delivering pacing stimuli to interrupt tachycardias. Despite these differences, the mechanism by which the tachycardia is interrupted is the same—a conduction block is created within the reentrant circuit.

Underdrive pacing involves delivering pacing stimuli at a rate slower than the tachycardia (Figure 10-6). An example of underdrive pacing is the application of a magnet to a VVI pacemaker during ventricular tachycardia. Application of the magnet converts the pacemaker to an asynchronous, fixed-rate, VOO pacemaker mode that competes in a random way with the tachycardia. The pacing stimuli will be delivered at random during the tachycardia cycle and may interrupt the arrhythmia if a single stimulus captures the ventricle and produces conduction block within the circuit. This technique requires that a single extrastimulus be capable of terminating the tachycardia and usually is effective for slow, well-tolerated arrhythmias.

Single, timed extrastimuli may be delivered in a synchronous manner during a reentrant tachycardia. The tachycardia cycle is scanned in a precise, orderly manner by progressive decrements in the coupling interval between the sensed tachycardia beat and the paced extrastimulus. In order for single extrastimuli to be effective, the tachycardia must be relatively slow, and the paced wavefront must be able to conduct into the tachycardia circuit. In general, there must be a relatively wide gap of excitability. Multiple timed extrastimuli can be delivered at a rate faster than the rate of a reentrant tachycardia (burst pacing) if the arrhythmia cannot be terminated by single pulses (Figure 10-7). This may be effective for tachycardias that are faster, when the gap of excitability is shorter, or

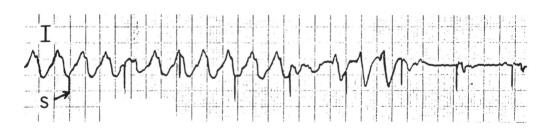

Figure 10-6 Underdrive pacing for termination of ventricular tachycardia. A surface electrocardiographic lead I tracing of sustained ventricular tachycardia at a rate of approximately 170 beats per minute is illustrated. Pacing stimuli (S) are produced by placing a magnet over a VVI pacemaker. This results in asynchronous pacing at a rate of 80 beats per minute. Because the pacing stimuli are delivered in a random fashion, a single pacing stimulus is able to capture the ventricle at a critical point during the reentry circuit and interrupt the tachycardia.

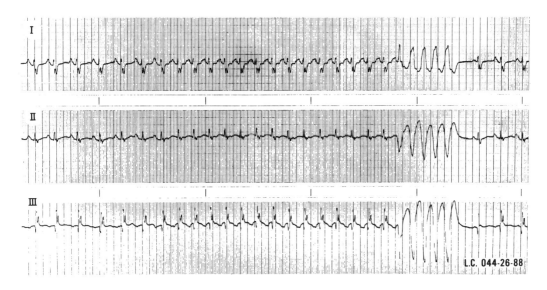

Figure 10-7 Antitachycardia pacing for termination of orthodromic AV reentrant tachycardia in a patient who has Ebstein's anomaly and a right-sided accessory pathway is illustrated. An Intertach antitachycardia pacemaker delivers a five-beat burst at the right ventricular apex.

when the tachycardia circuit is distant from the pacing site. In general, the more extrastimuli that are delivered, the greater the chance of success. Using trains (multiple beats) of extrastimuli may allow interruption of a tachycardia by pacing at a slower rate than is required with trains of fewer beats.

Several other variations on the same antitachycardia pacing theme have been used. For example, the rate of a pacing train may be gradually increased or decreased with each successive pacing stimulus. In addition, the pacing trains may be timed to begin at different coupling intervals from the last sensed tachycardia beat. In some cases the pacing train may be programmed to accelerate and then decelerate. Newer antitachycardia pacing devices have the capability to combine the features of each of these algorithms.

For example, timed extrastimuli may be programmed to occur at the end of a rapid train of stimuli. In addition, the antitachycardia device may automatically scan the tachycardia by delivering more rapid trains with each successive attempt. Scanning is the term used to describe an automatic change in the cycle length of the extrastimulus with successive attempts to terminate a tachycardia. Antitachycardia pacemakers may

be programmed to deliver extrastimuli at a fixed pacing cycle length or as a percentage of the spontaneous tachycardia cycle length (adaptive pacing). The algorithm used depends on whether the tachycardia always occurs at the same rate or at variable rates. If there is considerable variation in tachycardia rate, scanning antitachycardia burst pacing may be preferable to a fixed pacing cycle length. In addition, antiarrhythmic drug therapy may slow the rate of a tachycardia, allowing pacing at slower rates. If there is variability in serum drug levels (which may cause variability in the tachycardia cycle length), scanning pacing trains may be preferred. It should be emphasized that empiric trials of each algorithm should be tried in each patient to arrive at the program that is most likely to interrupt the tachycardia but minimize the risk of acceleration (Figure 10-8).

ACCELERATION OF TACHYCARDIAS BY PACING

In addition to the possibility for interrupting a reentrant tachycardia, antitachycardia pacing has the possibility for accelerating the tachycar-

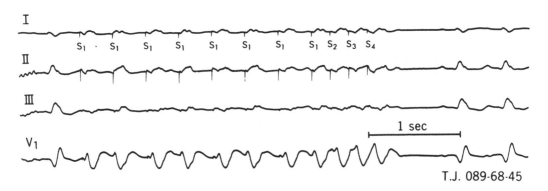

Figure 10-8 These tracings were recorded from a patient with ischemic heart disease and recurrent ventricular tachycardia treated with a combined implantable cardioverter defibrillator (ICD) and Intertach antitachycardia pacemaker system. Surface ECG leads I, II, III, and V_1 are shown. The figure demonstrates the antitachycardia pacemaker functioning to provide programmed stimulation in the noninvasive programmed stimulation (NIPS) mode during postimplant electrophysiology testing. S1, S2, S3, and S4 refer to the extrastimuli introduced in an attempt to induce the ventricular tachycardia to determine the effectiveness of the pacing algorithm.

dia to a more rapid or hemodynamically unstable rhythm (Figure 10-9). Pacing may convert a hemodynamically stable, well-tolerated arrhythmia into an unstable, life-threatening rhythm. Because of this fact, patients should always be carefully studied in the electrophysiology laboratory prior to implantation of an antitachycardia device.

In addition, the nature of a reentrant tachycardia may change over time as drugs are added or taken away or as the underlying structural cardiac condition changes. Thus what is an effective antitachycardia pacing strategy at one point in time may become ineffective or even dangerous at another point. Since tachycardia acceleration is always possible with pacing, it is useful to consider the worst-case scenario with antitachycardia pacing in all patients prior to device implantation. If the arrhythmia to be terminated is ventricular tachycardia, the worst-case scenario would be acceleration of the arrhythmia to ventricular fibrillation. Prior to the advent of combined pacemaker cardioverter defibrillators, our approach was to always implant an automatic defibrillator in patients in whom long-term antitachycardia pacing was planned as primary therapy for ventricular tachycardia. Although not all authors agreed with this approach, this strategy protected the

patient from more malignant arrhythmias. With the development of devices that incorporate antitachycardia pacing into standard implantable cardioverter defibrillators, this concern has been eliminated. Ventricular antitachycardia pacemaker trials were discontinued in 1990 when the combined pacemaker-cardioverter-defibrillator trials were initiated in the United States.

If the arrhythmia is an atrial tachycardia or AV nodal re-entrant tachycardia, the worst-case scenario may be that these arrhythmias will be converted to atrial fibrillation. Since atrial fibrillation is rarely life threatening, antitachycardia pacing may be used by itself without excessive concern about arrhythmia acceleration. We often deliberately induce atrial fibrillation in candidates for atrial antitachycardia pacemakers to determine how the arrhythmia is tolerated and whether the atrial fibrillation will spontaneously convert to sinus rhythm. One clinical situation in which atrial antitachycardia pacing is inadvisable is when the patient has Wolff-Parkinson-White syndrome with an accessory pathway capable of rapid antegrade conduction. If atrial fibrillation is induced by atrial pacing, the ventricular rate may be dangerously rapid if there is brisk antegrade conduction. In these individuals, antitachycardia pacing should not be used.

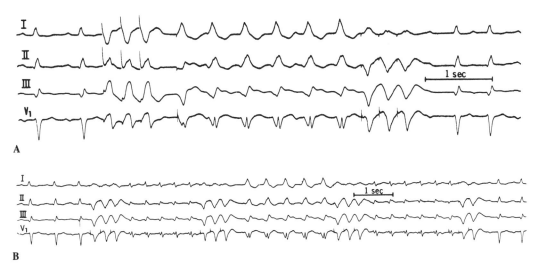

Figure 10-9 A PASAR antitachycardia pacemaker was implanted in the ventricle in this patient with recurrent ventricular tachycardia. An implantable cardioverter defibrillator was also implanted to provide defibrillation in the event of tachycardia acceleration. The two panels show the antitachycardia pacemaker being used both to provide programmed stimulation and to terminate ventricular tachycardia therapy during postoperative electrophysiologic study. In panel A, ventricular tachycardia is induced and terminated with a three-beat ventricular burst by the antitachycardia pacemaker. In panel B, programmed stimulation induces sustained ventricular tachycardia. The first antitachycardia pacing burst changes the morphology of the tachycardia. A second burst reverts the tachycardia to the first configuration and a third burst restores sinus rhythm.

DETECTION ALGORITHMS FOR ANTITACHYCARDIA PACEMAKERS

Antitachycardia pacemakers require predefined criteria to determine whether a tachycardia is a pathologic arrhythmia that should be interrupted. Several criteria may be used to initiate antitachycardia pacing. The most common criterion is the rate of a tachycardia. If the sole criterion for tachycardia detection is heart rate, antitachycardia pacing will be initiated whenever a selected rate is exceeded. This criterion is usually all that is needed for very rapid arrhythmias. However, if the rate of an arrhythmia such as ventricular tachycardia is relatively slow, there may be a range of ventricular tachycardia rates that overlap with the rate of sinus tachycardia. In such a situation, antitachycardia pacing could be triggered by sinus tachycardia. The antitachycardia pacing itself could induce ventricular tachycardia in this patient. Thus if there is a range of heart rates that overlap with sinus tachycardia, other criteria that are more specific for a pathologic tachycardia need to be specified.

Other criteria that may distinguish sinus tachycardia from abnormal tachycardias include the mode of onset of the arrhythmia, the range of heart rates that is sensed during the tachycardia, and the duration of the heart rate in excess of the rate criterion. For example, sinus tachycardia should have a gradual onset and gradually speed up and slow down. Pathologic tachycardias are usually abrupt in onset and demonstrate a fairly uniform rate. By specifying the change in heart rate at the onset of a tachycardia as a detection criterion, sinus rhythm may be distinguished from abnormal arrhythmias. In addition, by specifying the maximum allowable change in rate during an arrhythmia, the variability in the rate of sinus tachycardia can be used to distinguish this rhythm from pathologic arrhythmias. In addition to these detection criteria, the minimum number of tachycardia beats that will trigger antitachycardia pacing can be specified. Multiple combinations of these criteria can be used to define a tachycardia that should be interrupted (Figure 10-10). It should be emphasized that a trade-off between sensitivity and

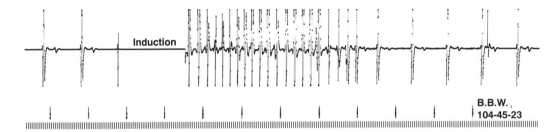

Figure 10-10 Stored electrograms from a Ventritex Cadence Model V-100 implantable tiered therapy defibrillator are shown. These electrograms were recorded during an electrophysiologic study. The two beats at the left of the screen are during sinus rhythm. Thereafter, programmed stimulation induces nonsustained ventricular tachycardia. The tachycardia was sensed by the device, but no shock or antitachycardia pacing therapy was delivered since the preselected criteria for pacing termination or defibrillator therapy was not met when the patient returned to sinus rhythm. A marker indicating return to sinus rhythm is the sharp spike after the second to the last beat, at the right side of the figure.

specificity must be made when selecting a complex set of detection criteria. If the criteria are too specific, there is a risk that a pathologic tachycardia will not be diagnosed appropriately. On the other hand, if only the rate of the tachycardia is used as the detection criterion, there will be high sensitivity but low specificity.

EVALUATION AND SELECTION OF ANTITACHYCARDIA PACING ALGORITHMS

Patients who are considered for antitachycardia pacing must have an invasive electrophysiologic study to define the mechanism of their arrhythmia and to uncover any other rhythm abnormalities that may not have been manifested clinically. Additional information that must be collected during the invasive study includes (1) the response to antitachycardia pacing and the risk of tachycardia acceleration, (2) the best antitachycardia pacing algorithm, and (3) the optimal detection criteria. Patients are studied in the baseline state, in the absence of antiarrhythmic drugs. The clinical arrhythmia is induced by programmed electrical stimulation and the mechanism of the tachycardia clearly defined. Attempts to interrupt the tachycardia are then made, beginning with the introduction of single extrastimuli into the tachycardia. The diastolic interval is scanned by introducing extrastimuli at progressively shorter intervals

until the tachycardia is interrupted or the stimulus encounters the refractory period of the myocardium. If the tachycardia cannot be reliably interrupted by single extrastimuli, the response to multiple extrastimuli is assessed in the same manner. Overdrive pacing is then used at progressively faster pacing rates to interrupt the tachycardia. By this empiric method, the optimal pacing algorithm can be determined. If antiarrhythmic drugs will be required, the pacing protocol described above is repeated on a steady-state level of the medications to be used.

If the arrhythmia to be treated is ventricular tachycardia, this arrhythmia is induced and terminated multiple times to determine the effectiveness of antitachycardia pacing, the ranges of tachycardia rates and QRS morphologies, and the risk of acceleration. If acceleration occurs, the use of this technique must be reconsidered.

The new generation of implantable defibrillators incorporates capabilities for antitachycardia pacing, bradycardia pacing, cardioversion, and defibrillation in a single device (Figures 10-11 and 10-12).

Antitachycardia pacing for atrial arrhythmias is often simpler than pacing for ventricular arrhythmias because the consequences of tachycardia acceleration are usually less severe. However, there are several exceptions to this statement. First, patients with the Wolff-Parkinson-White syndrome with rapid antegrade conduction over the accessory pathway should be

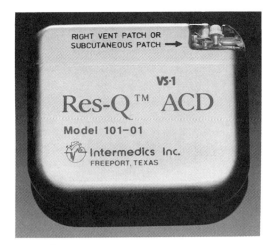

Figure 10-11 An automatic implantable antitachycardia pacemaker cardioverter defibrillator is shown. This device is designed for use with contoured patches, which are placed over the epicardial surface of the heart. Typical of newer generation antitachycardia devices, the Res-Q ACD provides tiered therapy with antitachycardia pacing, low-energy cardioverting shocks, and high-energy defibrillating discharges. *Source:* Courtesy of Intermedics, Inc., Angleton, TX.

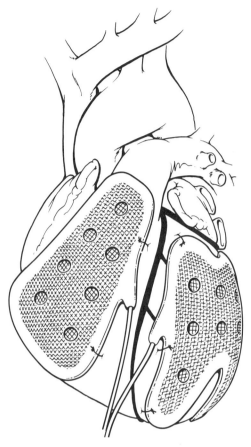

Figure 10-12 Placement of contoured defibrillating patches on the epicardium. Note that the patches are contoured, with different shapes for the right ventricular surface and the left ventricular free wall. A cardioverting defibrillating shock is delivered between the patches to depolarize the left and right ventricles. *Source:* Courtesy of Intermedics, Inc., Angleton, TX.

excluded, since rapidly conducted atrial fibrillation may be induced with pacing. Patients who develop atrial fibrillation with atrial pacing are also poor candidates for this therapy. We always assess the effects of isoproterenol on supraventricular tachycardias and the influence of a faster tachycardia rate on the response to antitachycardia pacing. This allows the pacing algorithm to be modified so that it may be effective for tachycardias that occur with different levels of autonomic tone. Supraventricular tachycardias are usually induced and terminated at least 50 times prior to reaching a decision to implant an antitachycardia pacing system. At the time of permanent antitachycardia pacemaker implantation, the clinical arrhythmia is induced, and electrograms are recorded at the site of permanent lead placement both during sinus rhythm and during the tachycardia. This is performed to ensure that adequate cardiac signals for proper sensing will be present during the arrhythmia. Following device implantation, the arrhythmia is reinduced several more times to be certain that the implanted system functions as intended. It should be stressed that the newer generation of implantable cardioverter defibrillators that

incorporate antitachycardia pacing will simplify the clinical evaluation of these patients.

The follow-up of patients with antitachycardia pacemakers is critically important to the success of this therapy. Patients may demonstrate a wider range of tachycardia rates during their usual daily activities than during invasive electrophysiologic testing. It is not uncommon for these devices to require adjustments in detection criteria settings or in the antitachycardia pacing algorithm following the patient's discharge from the hospital (Figure 10-13). The diagnostic data regarding tachycardia rates and the success of an algorithm for tachycardia termination made

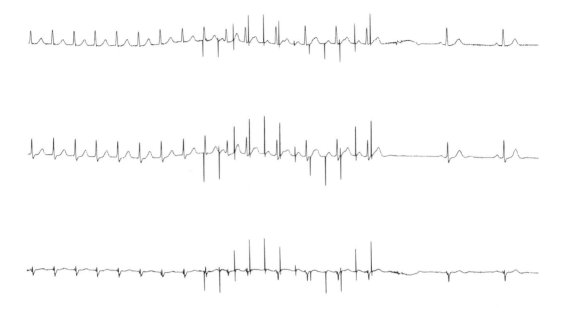

Figure 10-13 Antitachycardia pacing for termination of AV nodal reentrant tachycardia (AVNRT) is demonstrated. During an outpatient clinic visit the effectiveness of the programmed pacing algorithm to terminate AVNRT was assessed. Using noninvasive programmed electrical stimulation (NIPS), the AVNRT was initiated. On the left side of the figure, sustained AVNRT at a rate of 150 beats per minute is demonstrated. Twelve atrial pacing stimuli are delivered, followed by termination of the tachycardia and resumption of sinus rhythm. Antitachycardia pacemakers provide effective control of AVNRT by producing antegrade block in the slow pathway in most instances. Notice that during the burst of atrial pacing there is AV Wenckebach block, resulting in interruption of the tachycardia.

available by the memory storage capacity of these devices is especially important to tele-meter.

INDICATIONS AND CONTRAINDICATIONS TO ANTITACHYCARDIA PACING

Patients who are ideal candidates for anti-tachycardia pacing include those with hemo-dynamically well-tolerated AV nodal reentrant tachycardia or orthodromic reciprocating tachycardia utilizing a concealed retrograde con-duction accessory pathway, and sometimes those with atrial flutter, intra atrial reentry, or sustained ventricular tachycardia. Most patients will have failed multiple antiarrhythmic drug regimens before antitachycardia pacing will

have been considered for them. Patients who develop syncope or marked presyncope at the start of their tachycardia are poor candidates for antitachycardia pacing. As previously men-tioned, patients with Wolff-Parkinson-White syndrome who have rapid antegrade conduction over their accessory pathway are also poor can-didates for this therapy. If the rate of the tachycardia is very slow and overlaps with sinus rhythm, antitachycardia pacing may be more difficult to regulate. Patients who develop accel-eration of their tachycardia with pacing are less likely to have a good outcome with this therapy.

It should be emphasized that the success of radiofrequency ablation techniques for the treat-ment of AV nodal reentrant tachycardias and atrioventricular reentrant tachycardias has effec-tively replaced antitachycardia pacing as a wide-spread treatment modality.

CLINICAL RESULTS WITH ANTITACHYCARDIA PACING

Antitachycardia pacing has been an extremely effective treatment for supraventricular tachycardias, provided that the patients are carefully evaluated before, during, and after pacemaker implantation. Approximately a fourth of patients will require concomitant antiarrhythmic drug therapy to diminish the frequency of their arrhythmia. The satisfaction rate with this treatment has been approximately 90% in most studies. It should be emphasized to patients that antitachycardia pacing does not prevent tachycardia. Rather, pacing will usually interrupt the rhythm quickly. If patients know to expect a brief period of palpitations, their acceptance of this therapy is greatly enhanced. Most patients report a period of brief palpitations followed by resumption of normal sinus rhythm. This is a very reassuring feeling for patients who had previously required emergency room visits or hospital admissions to terminate their arrhythmias.

Antitachycardia pacing has been used successfully for a number of years to terminate ventricular tachycardia. It was our practice to implant an automatic defibrillator as a backup in case of tachycardia acceleration. The vast majority of patients receiving these devices have had excellent control of their arrhythmias, though approximately 40% have used their defibrillator. It has been our experience that many patients require antiarrhythmic drug therapy to slow the rate of ventricular tachycardia enough to minimize symptoms and allow successful antitachycardia pacing. As with most therapies for patients with sustained ventricular tachycardia, the long-term mortality rate is high, a fact that usually reflects poor left ventricular function and coronary artery disease.

The new generation of implantable defibrillators incorporates sophisticated antitachycardia pacing algorithms and bradycardia pacing support. These devices allow different antitachycardia strategies for ventricular arrhythmias at different rates, with antitachycardia pacing for relatively slow episodes of ventricular tachycardia, synchronized cardioversion for faster episodes, and high-energy defibrillation for more malignant arrhythmias. Use of these devices to effectively manage arrhythmias with varying characteristics has replaced the combined use of an antitachycardia pacemaker and a standard implantable defibrillator.

BIBLIOGRAPHY

Brugada P, Wellens HJJ. Entrainment as an electrophysiologic phenomenon. *J Am Coll Cardiol.* 1984;3:451–454.

Camm AJ, Davies DW, Ward DE. Tachycardia recognition by implantable electronic devices. *PACE.* 1987;10:1175–1190.

Charos GS, Haffajee CI, Gold RL, et al. A theoretically and practically more effective method for interruption of ventricular tachycardia: self-adapting autodecremental overdrive pacing. *Circulation.* 1986;73:309–315.

Cooper TB, Maclean WAH, Waldo A. Overdrive pacing for supraventricular tachycardias: a review of theoretical implications and therapeutic techniques. *PACE.* 1978;1:196.

Crick JCP, Way B, Sowton E. Successful treatment of ventricular tachycardia by physiological pacing. *PACE.* 1984;7:949.

Epstein AE, Kay GN, Plumb VJ, et al. Combined automatic implantable cardioverter, defibrillator and pacemaker systems: implantation technique and follow-up. *J Am Coll Cardiol.* 1989;13:121.

Falkoff MD. Long-term management of ventricular tachycardia by implantable automatic burst tachycardia-terminating pacemakers. *PACE.* 1986;9:885–895.

Fisher JD. Electrical devices for the treatment of tachyarrhythmias. *Cardiology Clinics.* 1986;4(3):527–542.

Fisher JD, Johnston D, Furman S, et al. Long-term efficacy of antitachycardia pacing for supraventricular and ventricular tachycardias. *Am J Cardiol.* 1987;60:1311–1316.

Fisher JD, Kim SG, Furman S, et al. Role of implantable pacemakers in control of recurrent ventricular tachycardia. *Am J Cardiol.* 1982;49:194–206.

Fisher JD, Matos JA, Kim SG. Antitachycardia pacing and stimulation—with particular reference to ventricular arrhythmias. In: Josephson ME, Wellens HJJ, eds. *Tachycardias: Mechanisms, Diagnosis, Treatment.* Philadelphia, Pa: Lea & Febiger; 1984:413–425.

Kay GN, Epstein AE, Plumb VJ. The incidence of reentry with an excitable gap in ventricular tachycardia: a prospective evaluation utilizing transient entrainment. *J Am Coll Cardiol.* 1988;11:530–538.

Manz M, Gerckens U, Funke HD, et al. Combination of antitachycardia pacemaker and automatic implantable cardioverter-defibrillator for ventricular tachycardia. *PACE.* 1986;9:676–684.

Nacarelli GV, Zipes DP, Rahilly TG. Influence of tachycardia cycle length and antiarrhythmic drugs on pacing terminations and accelerations of ventricular tachycardia. *Am Heart J*. 1983;105:1–5.

Newman DM, Lee MA, Herre JM, et al. Permanent antitachycardia pacemaker therapy for ventricular tachycardia. *PACE*. 1989;12:1387–1395.

Parsonnet V. Antitachyarrhythmia devices. *PACE*. 1988; 11:5–6.

Saksena S, Heselmeyer T, Batsford W, et al. Long-term clinical experience with a versatile antitachycardia pacemaker for tachycardia termination, induction and

monitoring: a multicenter study. *PACE*. 1988;11:493. Abstract.

Saksena S, Pantopoulos D, Parsonnet V, et al. Usefulness of an implantable antitachycardia pacemaker system for supraventricular or ventricular tachycardia. *Am J Cardiol*. 1986;58:70–74.

Vassalle M. The relationship among cardiac pacemakers: overdrive suppression. *Circ Res*. 1977;41:269–277.

Winkle RA. Nonpharmacologic therapy of tachycardias: the role of implanted devices. *PACE*. 1988;11:109–113.

Chapter 11

Surgery for Arrhythmias

INTRODUCTION

The introduction of electrophysiologic testing and catheter mapping techniques has allowed accurate localization of arrhythmogenic foci and reentrant conduction pathways. The ability to identify the anatomic origin of arrhythmias quickly led to surgical techniques to definitively treat these clinical problems. Surgery has become standard treatment for many patients with Wolff-Parkinson-White syndrome, ectopic atrial tachycardia, and ventricular tachycardia. The results of surgery have been gratifying for patients with these arrhythmias that cannot be controlled by antiarrhythmic medications. In this chapter, the indications, contraindications, and technique of intraoperative cardiac mapping and surgery will be discussed in relation to the growing capabilities of less invasive catheter techniques.

SURGERY FOR SUPRAVENTRICULAR ARRHYTHMIAS

The first successful report of surgery for Wolff-Parkinson-White syndrome occurred in 1968 at Duke University. During the surgery, the epicardial surface of the heart was mapped, which demonstrated that the earliest site of ven-tricular activation during preexcitation occurred at the AV groove along the free wall of the right ventricle. The surgical approach involved dissection of the AV groove in the area of the earliest ventricular activation. The postoperative course of the patient was marked by conversion of the ECG to a normal pattern and elimination of recurrent supraventricular tachycardia. Thus for the first time the anatomic and functional properties of Wolff-Parkinson-White syndrome were defined and eliminated by a combination of intraoperative mapping and surgery. Subsequently, thousands of patients with Wolff-Parkinson-White syndrome have been cured of supraventricular arrhythmias by surgery.

The indications for surgery in patients with Wolff-Parkinson-White syndrome include refractoriness to medical management, intolerance or adverse reactions to antiarrhythmic drugs, and a desire to avoid possible teratogenic effects of drugs in young women seeking to become pregnant. Patients who develop atrial fibrillation with very rapid ventricular response (shortest preexcited RR interval less than 240 milliseconds) or who have been resuscitated from ventricular fibrillation are best treated by nonpharmacologic procedures. In addition to these indications, young patients facing years of antiarrhythmic drug treatment may elect to have a definitive cure of their arrhythmias with surgery. With the emerging prominence of radiofrequency ablation for the treatment of accessory pathways, the role of surgery is likely to diminish and be reserved mainly for patients who fail catheter ablation techniques. Surgery will continue to be the therapy of choice for patients requiring additional operative procedures such as valvular replacement or repair and coronary bypass grafting.

In Wolff-Parkinson-White syndrome, accessory pathways may be located at any point around the tricuspid valve ring or interatrial septum and around the posterior and lateral portions of the mitral valve ring as far distally as the left atrial appendage (Figure 11-1). These accessory pathways cannot be identified visually. Therefore, intraoperative mapping is critical to the success of surgery for Wolff-Parkinson-White syndrome. Mapping is usually performed on the epicardial surface of the heart, with the heart exposed, warm, and beating. Atrial pacing at a rate from 100 to 180 beats per minute is used to accentuate the degree of preexcitation. With a preexcited QRS complex, the epicardial activation pattern is mapped with a roving electrode probe that is moved systematically along the ventricular edge of the AV groove. The location of the accessory pathway is identified by the site of earliest ventricular activation. Ventricular pacing is then performed in the same manner and the site of earliest atrial activation is identified. Attempts are made to induce orthodromic reciprocating tachycardia, and the sequence of retrograde atrial activation is again mapped along the atrial surface of the AV groove. If the pathway is mapped to the interatrial septum, the right atrium is opened and the right atrial surface of the interatrial septum is mapped just above the tricuspid valve. Although the technique of using a roving probe has been used with excellent success, it can be time consuming. Because of this limitation, some centers have developed computerized mapping systems that record from multiple sites around both AV rings simultaneously. These systems offer the advantage of

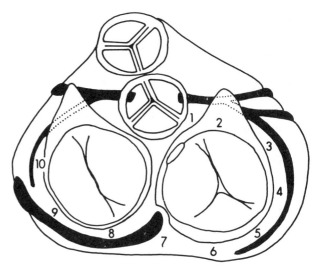

1 = RIGHT ANTEROSEPTAL
2 = RIGHT ANTERIOR
3 = RIGHT ANTEROLATERAL
4 = RIGHT LATERAL
5 = RIGHT POSTEROLATERAL
6 = RIGHT POSTERIOR
7 = POSTEROSEPTAL
8 = LEFT POSTERIOR
9 = LEFT POSTEROLATERAL
10 = LEFT LATERAL /
       ANTERIOR

Figure 11-1 Schematic representation of the epicardial location of accessory pathways. The atrium has been removed from the AV rings, showing the tricuspid and mitral valves. The coronary sinus circles the mitral valve ring posteriorly and laterally. The right coronary artery circles the tricuspid valve ring. Epicardial mapping is performed prior to opening of the heart, to localize the site of earliest antegrade and retrograde conduction over an accessory pathway prior to surgical division.

being able to record activation at each point for the same beat. Cardiopulmonary bypass is usually not required to obtain a complete map of the AV rings with computerized multichannel mapping systems. Despite its advantages, the cost of computerized mapping systems may be prohibitive for many medical centers.

The surgical technique for treatment of Wolff-Parkinson-White syndrome has involved two major approaches. The endocardial technique for the division of left or right free wall accessory pathways involves opening the left or right atrium following cold cardioplegia. An incision is made just above the mitral or tricuspid valve ring and the AV groove is dissected from the endocardium to the epicardial reflection of the visceral pericardium. The AV groove contains fat that surrounds the coronary arteries and coronary veins. The second technique for division of accessory pathways has been termed the epicardial approach. The epicardial approach can usually be performed without cardioplegia, while the heart is warm and beating. The epicardial surface of the AV groove is incised, and the coronary artery and vein are mobilized to prevent damage to these vessels. Following epicardial dissection of the AV groove, a cryoprobe is placed at the junction of the atria and ventricular myocardium to the valve annulus. This area is frozen to a temperature of $-60°C$ for 2 to 3 minutes to destroy any possible pathways that cross this region. The results of surgery with either the endocardial or epicardial approaches have been excellent, with most centers reporting over 95% success in dividing the accessory pathway and a surgical mortality less than 1%. The mortality rate has been somewhat higher when concomitant surgery for congenital cardiac anomalies has been required. Although surgery for accessory pathways located in the septal region has been associated with damage to the AV node or His bundle with permanent AV block in some patients, this complication has become rare as experience with the technique has grown. The long-term results of surgery have been excellent, with most patients enjoying a normal life, free of arrhythmias.

Ectopic atrial tachycardias are very often incessant and resistant to medical management. Because patients have had a chronic tachycardia over a period of years, a tachycardia-induced cardiomyopathy may have developed. This progressive dilatation of the heart may lead to fatal congestive heart failure. However, control of the arrhythmia results in complete reversal of the cardiomyopathy in most patients. Because of its incessant nature and resistance to treatment, surgery has become the therapy of choice for young patients with medically refractory ectopic atrial tachycardia. Since the site of origin of the ectopic focus may be located anywhere in either atrium or in the interatrial septum, mapping is crucial to the success of surgery. An unfortunate observation with this arrhythmia has been disappearance of the tachycardia following induction of general anesthesia. When this occurs, intraoperative mapping is not possible. Preoperative mapping in the electrophysiology laboratory is therefore vital to localize the ectopic focus.

The intraoperative approach to ectopic atrial tachycardia involves mapping of the epicardial surface of the atria to determine the earliest site of atrial activation. If the focus appears to arise in the interatrial septum, the right atrium is opened and the septal surface mapped with the heart warm and beating. When a recording electrode is placed directly over the abnormal focus, the tachycardia will often terminate. Cooling of the focus to 0°C will also result in termination of the tachycardia. If the site of origin of the tachycardia is located and confirmed in this manner, the site is then frozen to $-60°C$. We have usually excised the abnormal focus and placed cryolesions around the edges of the dissection. An alternative approach to left atrial tachycardias that has been reported involves electrically isolating the left atrium from the right atrium by an encircling incision. This left atrial isolation procedure allows the ectopic atrial rhythm to persist in the left atrium without conducting to the right atrium or AV node region. The sinus node then resumes regulation of the cardiac rhythm. The results of surgery have been excellent, provided that careful mapping is performed preoperatively and intraoperatively. In our experience, nearly all patients have maintained normal sinus rhythm in long-term follow-up and have returned to a normal life-style.

Surgery has also been introduced as a treatment for medically refractory AV nodal reentrant tachycardia in selected patients. Surgery for this arrhythmia involves placing multiple 3-mm cryolesions around the AV node from the right atrial surface in the triangle of Koch. An alternative technique has used sharp dissection at the site of earliest retrograde atrial activation during the tachycardia. Both techniques have produced excellent clinical results. These surgeries have resulted in ablation of the fast AV nodal pathway in some patients, the slow pathway in some patients, and modification of both pathways in others. However, the long-term results have shown that AV nodal reentrant tachycardia is not inducible in the vast majority.

SURGERY FOR VENTRICULAR ARRHYTHMIAS

Surgery for ventricular arrhythmias was first performed in 1959 when a blind left ventricular aneurysmectomy was performed to ablate ventricular tachycardia in a patient following myocardial infarction. The combination of aneurysmectomy and coronary artery bypass grafting has been used extensively to treat patients with ventricular tachycardia and coronary artery disease. The results of these procedures without the use of electrophysiologic mapping have been relatively poor, with most centers reporting that ventricular tachycardia recurs in approximately 50% of patients postoperatively. It is likely that the failure of blind aneursymectomy to eliminate ventricular tachycardia is due to this arrhythmia arising not within the aneurysm itself but at the border between scarred and more healthy myocardium. Modern surgical treatment of ventricular tachycardia involves the use of preoperative and intraoperative ventricular mapping to localize the site of the reentrant ventricular tachycardia circuit. Once localized, the focus is ablated by dissection, cryosurgery, or the use of laser energy. In addition to its role in the treatment of ventricular tachycardia related to coronary artery disease, surgery has been successfully used to treat this arrhythmia arising in a wide variety of structural heart disorders, such as right ventricular dysplasia.

Preoperative ventricular mapping is usually required to localize the origin of ventricular tachycardia. In the presence of coronary artery disease, programmed electrical stimulation can be used to induce ventricular tachycardia in over 90% of patients, which permits the sequence of ventricular activation recorded in both the right and left ventricles to be mapped. The use of preoperative mapping allows surgery to be performed in patients who do not have inducible ventricular tachycardia while under general anesthesia in the operating room. Intraoperative mapping is performed with the heart warm and beating. Most centers induce ventricular tachycardia and map the activation sequence over the epicardial surface of the heart. However, it has been demonstrated that ventricular tachycardia related to coronary artery disease usually arises in the subendocardial layer. The activation sequence of the tachycardia is not a straight pathway from the subendocardial surface to the epicardial surface. Thus the site of exit of the tachycardia on the epicardial surface may vary greatly from its subendocardial location. Therefore, the epicardial activation map may be considerably different from the map obtained directly from the endocardial surface of the ventricle. Following the epicardial map, the ventricle is opened with an incision in the region of a left ventricular aneurysm or in an akinetic region. Ventricular tachycardia is then reinduced by programmed electrical stimulation, and the endocardial surface of the ventricle is mapped using a roving electrode probe. Approximately 50 sites are usually mapped in a radial fashion around the incision in the ventricle. The location of the ventricular tachycardia circuit is generally in the proximity of earliest endocardial activation. This region is usually activated prior to onset of the QRS complex in the surface ECG.

There are several limitations to mapping with a roving probe, including the requirement that ventricular tachycardia persist for a sufficient period for a complete map to be obtained. In addition, the ventriculotomy itself may terminate ventricular tachycardia and render it noninducible. Because of these limitations, multiple electrode recording systems that can record activation over a wide area of the ventricles have been developed. An epicardial shock with up to

256 electrodes sewn into an expandable mesh can be placed over the heart to record complete epicardial activation in only a few beats. An even more valuable tool is a latex balloon covered with multiple electrodes that can be placed into the left ventricle through an incision in the mitral valve. The balloon is inflated to allow the electrodes to contact the endocardium. This recording system allows the endocardial surface of the left ventricle to be mapped without opening the ventricle. A major advantage of the multiple electrode recording systems is that the entire cardiac cycle can be analyzed. Since ventricular tachycardia is most often related to reentry, simply recording the site of earliest activation may not identify the critical point in the circuit, the region of slow conduction. Endocardial mapping systems offer the possibility of recording from these critical portions of the reentrant circuit. It is hoped that these multichannel endocardial mapping systems will allow mapping with a greater degree of precision for localizing critical components of the tachycardia circuit and improve the results of surgery.

Several surgical techniques have been used to ablate ventricular tachycardia. Subendocardial resection involves removal of scarred regions in the subendocardium that are associated with areas of early ventricular activation. Cryosurgery can also be used to destroy the subendocardial region. Cooling of the cryoprobe to 0°C can be used to map the ventricles in a functional way. If ventricular tachycardia is interrupted or becomes noninducible with reversible cooling of an area, permanent destruction can be achieved by freezing to $-60°C$. Laser energy has also been used to destroy the subendocardial region involved in ventricular tachycardia. An incision in the ventricle may be made around the region of earliest activation to isolate the site of ventricular tachycardia origin. This has been termed encircling endocardial ventriculotomy. Each of these strategies has been used successfully for the treatment of recurrent ventricular tachycardia. Mapped guided operations have been shown to be associated with a higher chance of success for eliminating ventricular tachycardia than operations without intraoperative mapping. However, the operative mortality has been the same with or without mapping.

The encircling endocardial ventriculotomy operation involves making an incision around the site of arrhythmia origin that extends from the endocardium to the subepicardial region. This procedure is associated with a high operative mortality and an increased likelihood of postoperative low cardiac output. The subendocardial resection operation involves peeling the scarred subendocardial layer in the region of infarction from the underlying, more healthy myocardium. This procedure is often combined with cryoablative lesions that are applied to the region surrounding the base of the papillary muscles. The papillary muscles are left intact to avoid creating mitral regurgitation. Cryolesions can be given to areas lying deeper within the ventricular wall that are not removed by peeling the subendocardial scar. The Nd:YAG laser has also been used to destroy the subendocardial region by photoablation. Each of these procedures can be performed with the heart warm and beating, or during cold cardioplegia. Although there is no clear consensus regarding the best technique, some groups have suggested that keeping the heart warm and beating allows the results of resection to be continually re-evaluated with programmed electrical stimulation. Most groups perform coronary revascularization following completion of the antiarrhythmic portion of the operation.

The indications for ventricular tachycardia surgery have gradually evolved with the introduction of competing technologies such as the automatic implantable cardioverter defibrillator and antitachycardia pacing. The decision to proceed with surgery for ventricular tachycardia is based on several clinical considerations, including the need for coronary revascularization, the presence or absence of a left ventricular aneurysm, the overall hemodynamic state of the left ventricle, the frequency of ventricular tachycardia, the presence of other medical diseases, and the response to antiarrhythmic drug therapy. Other factors that relate to the decision to approach ventricular tachycardia surgically relate to whether sustained ventricular tachycardia is monomorphic or polymorphic, and the inducibility of ventricular arrhythmias with programmed electrical stimulation. If the patient has class III or IV congestive heart failure, opening the ventricle with resection of a portion of the heart will likely worsen ventricular function and congestive heart failure. If ventricular tachycardia is very frequent and poorly tolerated despite medical therapy, surgery may be preferable. If there is no clear left ventricular aneurysm, the results of surgery are less favorable. In addition, optimal results depend on the inducibility of a monomorphic ventricular tachycardia with programmed stimulation. If the primary rhythm problem is ventricular fibrillation, the automatic defibrillator is a better therapy. Patients who have received long-term amiodarone treatment are more likely to have postoperative hemodynamic and pulmonary complications.

The results of surgery for ventricular tachycardia are likely to change with increasing experience and evolving techniques. However, reports published to date suggest that the operative mortality exceeds 10%. The success rate for rendering ventricular tachycardia noninducible averages approximately 80%. The only factors predicting risk of operative mortality are the presence of preoperative left ventricular congestive heart failure, lack of a discrete aneurysm, amiodarone therapy, and requirement for emergency operation. Patients with multiple morphologies of ventricular tachycardia and posterior-inferior locations of ventricular tachycardia are more likely to have persistently inducible ventricular tachycardia postoperatively.

Surgery for ventricular tachycardia should be placed in perspective in relation to the competing therapies of amiodarone, the implantable cardioverter defibrillator, new generation combined pacemaker-cardioverter defibrillators, antitachycardia pacing, catheter ablation, and cardiac transplantation. If the patient has severe congestive heart failure, consideration should be given to cardiac transplantation. If the patient is not a candidate for transplantation, amiodarone may be the preferred treatment. If there is polymorphic ventricular tachycardia, or ventricular fibrillation, the implantable cardioverter defibrillator is likely to provide the best treatment. If the patient has no congestive heart failure, a single morphology of ventricular tachycardia and a left ventricular aneurysm, surgery should be entertained. Several centers routinely implant defibrillating patches on the heart following ventricular tachycardia surgery. However, this may increase the chances of postoperative infection. If ventricular tachycardia remains inducible postoperatively, the defibrillating pulse generator is then implanted.

BIBLIOGRAPHY

Cobb FR, Blumenschein SD, Sealy WC, et al. Successful surgical interruption of the bundle of Kent in a patient with Wolff-Parkinson-White syndrome. *Circulation.* 1968;38:1018.

Cox JL. Anatomic-electrophysiologic basis for the surgical treatment of refractory ischemic ventricular tachycardia. *Ann Surg.* 1983;198:119–129.

Cox JL. The status of surgery for cardiac arrhythmias. *Circulation.* 1985;71:413–417.

Cox JL, Gallagher JJ, Ungerleider RM. Encircling endocardial ventriculotomy for refractory ischemic ventricular tachycardia, IV: Clinical indications, surgical technique, mechanism of action, and results. *J Thorac Cardiovasc Surg.* 1982;83:865–872.

Cox JL, Holman WL, Cain ME. Cryosurgical treatment of atrioventricular node reentrant tachycardia. *Circulation.* 1987;76:1329–1336.

Dailey SM, Kay GN, Epstein AE, et al. The comparison of endocardial and epicardial programmed stimulation for the induction of ventricular tachycardia. *J Am Coll Cardiol.* 1989;13:1608–1612.

Gallagher JJ, Gilbert M, Svenson RH, et al. Wolff-Parkinson-White syndrome—the problem, evaluation, and surgical correction. *Circulation.* 1975;51:767–785.

Gallagher JJ, Kasell JH, Cox JL, et al. Techniques of intraoperative electrophysiologic mapping. *Am J Cardiol.* 1982;49:221–240.

Gallagher JJ, Sealey JL, German LD, et al. Results of surgery for preexcitation caused by accessory atrioventricular pathways in 267 consecutive cases. In: Josephson ME, Wellens HJJ, eds. *Tachycardias: Mechanism, Diagnosis, Treatment.* Philadelphia, Pa: Lea & Febiger; 1984.

Guiraudon GM, Klein GJ, Gulamhusein S, et al. Surgical repair of Wolff-Parkinson-White syndrome: a new closed-heart technique. *Ann Thorac Surg.* 1984;37:67–71.

Harken AH, Josephson ME. Surgical Management of ventricular tachycardia. In: Josephson ME, Wellens HJJ, eds. *Tachycardias: Mechanism, Diagnosis, Treatment.* Philadelphia, Pa: Lea & Febiger; 1984:475–487.

Holman WL, Ikeshita M, Lease JG, et al. Alteration of antegrade atrioventricular conduction by cryoablation of periatrioventricular nodal tissue. *J Thorac Cardiovasc Surg.* 1984;88:67–75.

Josephson ME, Horowitz LN, Harken AH. Endocardial excision: a new surgical technique for the treatment of ventricular tachycardia. *Circulation*. 1979;60:1430–1439.

Josephson ME, Horowitz LN, Spielman SR, et al. The role of catheter mapping in the preoperative evaluation of ventricular tachycardia. *Am J Cardiol*. 1982;49:207–220.

Kirklin JW, Barratt-Boyes BG. *Cardiac Surgery*. New York, NY: John Wiley & Sons; 1986.

Kirklin JW, McGiffin DC, Plumb VJ, et al. Intermediate-term results of the endocardial surgical approach for anomalous atrioventricular bypass tracts. *Am Heart J*. 1988;115:444–447.

Klein GJ, Guiraudon GM, Perkins DG, et al. Surgical correction of the Wolff-Parkinson-White syndrome in the closed heart using cryosurgery: a simplified approach. *J Am Coll Cardiol*. 1984;3:405–409.

Krafchek J, Lawrie GM, Roberts R, et al. Surgical ablation of ventricular tachycardia: improved results with a map-directed regional approach. *Circulation*. 1986;73:1239–1247.

Leitch JW, Guiraudon GM, Klein GJ, et al. The corridor operation for atrial fibrillation: Initial results and long term follow up. *Circulation*. 1990;Supp. III 82:472. Abstract.

Lowe JE. Surgical treatment of the Wolff-Parkinson-White syndrome and other supraventricular tachyarrhythmias. *J Cardiac Surg*. 1986;1:117.

Mason JW, Stinson EB, Winkle RA, et al. Relative efficacy of blind left ventricular aneurysm resection for the treatment of recurrent ventricular tachycardia. *Am J Cardiol*. 1982;49:241–248.

McGiffin DC, Kirklin JK, Plumb VJ, et al. Relief of life-threatening ventricular tachycardia and survival after direct operations. *Circulation*. 1987;76:93–103.

Miller JM, Kienzle MG, Harken AH, et al. Subendocardial resection for ventricular tachycardia: predictors of surgical success. *Circulation*. 1984;70:624–631.

Sosa E, Marcial MB, Scanavacca MI, et al. Surgical treatment of atrioventricular nodal re-entrant tachycardia. *J Electrophysiol*. 1988;2:497–503.

Swerdlow CD, Mason JW, Stinson EB, et al. Results of operations for ventricular tachycardia in 105 patients. *J Thorac Cardiovasc Surg*. 1986;92:105–113.

Chapter 12

The Implantable Cardioverter Defibrillator

INTRODUCTION

Although automatic internal defibrillation was initially rejected as an unfeasible concept, the implantable cardioverter defibrillator (ICD) has gained acceptance as an effective therapy for the prevention of sudden cardiac death. The current enthusiasm for this device is due to several factors, including the ever-increasing numbers of patients who are successfully resuscitated from ventricular tachycardia and fibrillation and from broader recognition of the limitations of antiarrhythmic drug therapy. In this chapter the function of the ICD and its effect on mortality for patients with life-threatening ventricular arrhythmias will be reviewed. The indications and contraindications for implantation of the ICD, the preoperative evaluation, and follow-up care will be discussed.

RATIONALE: DEVELOPMENT OF THE IMPLANTABLE CARDIOVERTER DEFIBRILLATOR

Early reports of the long-term follow-up of patients resuscitated from ventricular fibrillation indicated that the subsequent mortality rate was at least 30% within the first year, with most deaths being sudden despite empiric therapy with antiarrhythmic medications. The initial enthusiasm for suppression of spontaneous ventricular premature depolarizations with antiarrhythmic drug therapy in patients with life-threatening arrhythmias has been replaced by recognition of a sudden death rate of 12% the first year in patients treated using this approach. Furthermore, although invasive electrophysiologic testing has several advantages over the noninvasive approach to the management of life-threatening ventricular arrhythmias, the 1-year incidence of sudden death after initiating therapy for malignant ventricular arrhythmias directed by electrophysiologic studies is also significant, underscoring the limitations of medical therapy. Persistence of inducible ventricular tachycardia or fibrillation on antiarrhythmic drug therapy is a predictor of poor prognosis on medical therapy. Although suppression of inducibility portends a more benign clinical outcome, electrophysiologically guided drug therapy fails to protect an important number of patients from arrhythmia recurrence and subsequent death.

The dominant factors influencing the prognosis of patients with life-threatening ventricular arrhythmias are the underlying etiology of their cardiac disease and the degree of left ventricular dysfunction. Mortality rates of 16% have been reported in patients with prior myocardial infarction and sustained ventricular tachycardia, compared to a 34% mortality in patients with ventricular fibrillation. Among patients without coronary disease, however, the mortality rate has been less than 5%. Long-term mortality and the probability of finding an effective antiarrhythmic agent are directly related to the left ventricular ejection fraction.

EFFECTIVENESS OF THE IMPLANTABLE CARDIOVERTER DEFIBRILLATOR

The ability of the ICD to reliably terminate sustained ventricular tachycardia and fibrillation is clear. The risk of sudden cardiac death following ICD implantation has consistently been shown to be less than 2% per year. This level of efficacy exceeds that of all competing therapies. Although it is evident that the ICD effectively terminates ventricular tachycardia and fibrillation, the overall mortality rate of patients receiving this device remains important. Since many patients with ventricular tachycardia or ventricular fibrillation have left ventricular failure, it is not surprising that this group also demonstrates significant mortality related to progressive underlying structural heart disease. Although ventricular arrhythmias may be controlled by the ICD, patients remain at risk for congestive heart failure and recurrent myocardial infarction. Thus effective therapies designed to prevent sudden cardiac death maintain patients on survival curves that are determined by the extent of their underlying cardiac diseases. Reports of mortality in patients implanted with an ICD have indicated 98%-99% freedom from sudden death at 1 year, with an overall survival of more than 90%. In our experience, the risk of sudden death has been very low in patients with an   ICD. Despite this, worsening congestive heart failure has been the major cause of death in our patients. Indeed, no trial has ever demonstrated that ICD therapy extends life. Such trials are currently underway in selected subsets of patients.

INDICATIONS FOR THE IMPLANTABLE CARDIOVERTER DEFIBRILLATOR

The automatic implantable defibrillator was initially indicated for patients suffering at least two cardiac arrests, with documented failure of antiarrhythmic medications. With accumulated experience regarding the overall safety and efficacy of the device, the indications have been broadened (Table 12-1).

The ICD is now approved for patients who have survived a cardiac arrest caused by hemodynamically unstable ventricular tachycardia or ventricular fibrillation that is not associated with acute myocardial infarction. Because of the unacceptably high risk for recurrence of sudden death with antiarrhythmic drug therapy, our current practice is to consider the ICD as a therapy of choice for these patients. The ICD is also indicated for patients with a history of cardiac arrest who have no inducible ventricular arrhythmias with programmed electrical stimulation. Patients with a history of cardiac arrest who have no reversible precipitating factors and no inducible ventricular arrhythmias have a high risk of recurrence of sudden death. This group of patients is also probably best treated with an ICD.

The device is indicated for patients with recurrent ventricular tachycardia in the absence of cardiac arrest who have inducible ventricular tachycardia or fibrillation despite conventional drug therapy. Even if inducible ventricular

---

Table 12-1 Indications for ICD Implantation

- clinical occurrence of hemodynamically unstable ventricular tachycardia or ventricular fibrillation not associated with acute myocardial infarction
- cardiac arrest or unstable ventricular tachycardia not associated with myocardial infarction
- inducible ventricular tachycardia not suppressed at electrophysiologic study
- cardiac arrest without inducible ventricular tachycardia or ventricular fibrillation
- recurrence on drugs despite electrophysiologic study findings
- an alternative to pharmacologic management with amiodarone in selected instances

arrhythmias are suppressed by an antiarrhythmic drug regimen, the ICD offers a proven survival advantage with respect to the risk of sudden death in patients who have hemodynamically unstable ventricular arrhythmias. Furthermore, antiarrhythmic drugs suppress the inducibility of ventricular tachycardia or fibrillation in only a minority of patients, making the ICD a more likely option for many patients. Long-term therapy with amiodarone is associated with a wide variety of adverse effects, and many patients receiving this drug will eventually require its discontinuation and be considered for ICD therapy.

The ICD may also be used as a "bridge to transplantation" for patients with poor ventricular function and ventricular arrhythmias without sufficient congestive heart failure to warrant immediate cardiac transplantation. These patients may be protected from sudden death while the course of their underlying structural heart disease is carefully monitored for signs of worsening. Thus the ICD may prevent premature cardiac transplantation and serve to extend the limited supply of donor organs.

Since high energy shocks delivered from an ICD are uncomfortable, hemodynamically stable sustained ventricular tachycardia has not been considered an ideal clinical indication for this device. However, the ICD may be combined with an antitachycardia pacemaker and low energy cardioversion, both well tolerated. Until recently, the use of antitachycardia pacing in combination with an ICD required implantation of two devices. This combination presented the potential for adverse device-device interactions, including double counting by the ICD (counting both pacemaker stimulus artifacts and QRS signals and interpreting the rate as indicating a ventricular arrhythmia), inhibition of the ICD from detecting ventricular arrhythmias, and damage to the antitachycardia pacemaker. Despite these technical limitations, the combination of an antitachycardia pacemaker for the interruption of ventricular tachycardia with an ICD for backup in case of acceleration of the arrhythmia or the occurrence of ventricular fibrillation has proven to be a highly satisfactory therapy. At present, several implantable

Figure 12-1 A newer generation of implantable pacemaker-cardioverter defibrillator, the Ventritex Cadence Model V-100. The pulse generator is attached to electrode patches that are placed over the surface of the heart. A separate sensing lead allows tachycardia detection. This device offers tiered therapy of ventricular arrhythmias with antitachycardia pacing capability, low-energy cardioverting shocks, and high-energy defibrillating shocks and bradycardia pacing support. *Source:* Courtesy of Ventritex, Sunnyvale, CA.

defibrillators that combine the features of antitachycardia pacing with cardioversion and defibrillation are being tested in clinical trials (Figure 12-1). These devices are devoid of these adverse interactions.

CONTRAINDICATIONS FOR THE IMPLANTABLE CARDIOVERTER DEFIBRILLATOR

The major contraindication to use of the ICD is ventricular tachycardia or fibrillation occurring during transient, reversible conditions that are unlikely to recur (Table 12-2).

Ventricular arrhythmias that occur only during the first 48 hours of transmural myocardial infarction are associated with a low risk of recurrence. Patients with clear reversible precipitating factors such as idiosyncratic reactions to antiarrhythmic drugs, severe electrolyte abnormalities, rapid ventricular response to atrial fibrillation, or myocardial ischemia also have a

Table 12-2 Contraindications to ICD Implantation

1. ventricular arrhythmias associated with acute myocardial infarction
2. reversible precipitating factors
   - idiosyncratic drug reactions
   - electrolyte imbalance
   - rapid ventricular response to supraventricular arrhythmias
   - acute myocardial ischemia
   - frequent or incessant ventricular tachyarrhythmias
   - aortic stenosis
3. intractable congestive heart failure
4. severe refractory ischemia

low risk of arrhythmia recurrence and should not have an ICD implanted. Patients with very frequent or incessant episodes of sustained ventricular tachycardia or fibrillation that cannot be controlled with antiarrhythmic medications are poor candidates for the device. However, antiarrhythmic drug therapy may decrease the frequency of either atrial or ventricular arrhythmias enough to allow ICD implantation. Patients with intractable congestive heart failure or angina pectoris are unlikely to receive long-term benefit from an ICD. In these patients in whom survival is likely to be compromised because of poor ventricular function, cardiac transplantation may be the better treatment. Although transvenous defibrillator lead systems are now available, they are still being studied in clinical trials, so patients unable to tolerate a thoracotomy cannot be implanted with a standard ICD.

The effective use of the ICD requires meticulous follow-up care that may be quite demanding for the patient. Patients with an ICD may develop significant psychologic complications. Thus the emotional and psychologic stability of the patient must be carefully considered before implantation of an ICD. If patients are not psychologically stable, the ICD should not be implanted. Since the cost of implantable antitachycardia devices is very high, these devices will have a very limited role to play in societies with limited medical resources. Initial reports have suggested that the decrease in hospitalization following implantation of an ICD may make this device cost-effective. Ultimately, the uti-

lization of this expensive therapy will have to be carefully studied in relation to competing therapies.

IMPLANTABLE CARDIOVERTER DEFIBRILLATOR SYSTEM DESCRIPTION

Currently, the implantable cardioverter defibrillator system that is approved for routine use in the United States is marketed as the AICD™ (Cardiac Pacemakers [CPI], Inc., St. Paul, Minnesota). Many centers are investigating other antitachycardia systems from several other manufacturers. The ICD system consists of a pulse generator and leads. The leads are used for monitoring ventricular electrograms and for the delivery of the cardioverting or defibrillating shock. The standard AICDs™ have several programmable features (Model 1550, 1555, 1600, CPI). The physical dimensions of the pulse generator are $10.1 \times 7.6 \times 2.0$ cm. The volume of the pulse generator is 145 mL and the weight 235 g. Two lithium-silver vanadium pentoxide batteries are used to power the circuitry and charge the defibrillating capacitors. The pulse generator delivers shocks of 26 or 30 J that are synchronized to the QRS complex. The battery capacity provides for approximately 200 shocks at the beginning of battery life.

To enable prompt recognition of a ventricular arrhythmia that should be shocked, the ICD continuously monitors the intracardiac electrogram. A sensing amplifier monitors the rate of the ventricular electrogram from a bipolar transvenous lead that is positioned in the right ventricle. Alternatively, two unipolar sensing leads may be placed directly on the pericardium or screwed into the myocardium. The rate of the ventricular electrogram is used as a detection criterion. When the detection criterion is exceeded, charging of the capacitors is initiated. The sensing electrograms are also used to synchronize the delivery of cardioverting shocks to the intrinsic R wave. The defibrillating pulse is delivered from one of two different lead configurations. The implantable defibrillator may use a coiled titanium spring electrode positioned transvenously in the superior vena cava as the anode and an epicardial patch lead positioned on the left ventricle as the cathode, for direct current defibrillation. Another approach is to use two silicone-insulated epicardial patch leads that are positioned directly on the right and left ventricles to deliver defibrillating shocks. The two-patch configuration has been shown to provide lower defibrillation thresholds in most patients (see Figure 10-9); "defibrillation threshold" refers to the minimum energy required to successfully defibrillate the heart. The presently approved patch electrodes are available in two sizes, large (28 cm^2) and small (14 cm^2). The choice of patch size depends on the size of the heart and the exposure that can be achieved during implantation. Investigational ICD systems will allow the use of patches contoured to the shape of the heart.

INTRAOPERATIVE TECHNIQUES AND CONSIDERATIONS

The ICD presently requires intrathoracic placement of at least one defibrillating lead. In order to place the defibrillating patch electrodes on the heart, several surgical approaches may be employed, including a left lateral thoracotomy, median sternotomy, and subxiphoid or subcostal incisions. A left lateral thoracotomy is most commonly used unless other cardiac surgical procedures such as coronary bypass grafting or ventricular tachycardia surgery are planned. If other procedures are planned, a median sternotomy approach is used. The subxiphoid and subcostal approaches provide only limited access to the heart and limit optimal positioning of the patch electrodes.

Although the defibrillation threshold is often lower with a two-patch system compared to the spring electrode and one epicardial patch system, positioning two patches on the surface of the heart may be technically difficult. If there are coronary artery bypass grafts, the implantation of two patches may be especially difficult. Because of these surgical limitations, a totally extrapericardial approach has been developed that avoids opening the pericardium. The placement of patches on the parietal pericardium also minimizes postoperative adhesions, damage to

bypass grafts, and postoperative morbidity. Epicardial patch electrodes generate a marked fibrotic reaction that may preclude future coronary bypass grafting; placing patches on the parietal pericardium minimizes fibrosis and preserves access to the native coronary arteries.

Following initial placement of the defibrillating and sensing electrodes, ventricular tachycardia and ventricular fibrillation are induced with programmed electrical stimulation or alternating current to assess the sensing signals and the amount of energy required to cardiovert and defibrillate the heart. In order for the ICD to function reliably, it must be able to deliver more energy than the defibrillation threshold. An external device with sensing characteristics and defibrillating waveforms similar to those of the implantable device is used to terminate the induced arrhythmias and determine the defibrillation threshold. If the defibrillation threshold is unacceptably high, the patches are repositioned and testing is repeated until optimal defibrillating lead positions are located. This may involve testing multiple patch configurations. After satisfactory defibrillation thresholds are achieved, the sensing and defibrillating leads are tunneled subcutaneously to a pocket in the left upper quadrant of the abdomen for connection to the pulse generator. The pulse generator is then positioned in the subcutaneous abdominal pocket. The final step in implantation is to reinduce ventricular fibrillation with the device implanted, to be certain that the entire system functions as anticipated. When replacement of the pulse generator is required due to battery depletion, the procedure is relatively simple and a thoracotomy is not required. The old generator is explanted, and a new generator is installed using the preexisting lead system.

FUNCTION OF THE IMPLANTED CARDIOVERTER DEFIBRILLATOR

As noted above, the ICD detects ventricular arrhythmias by continuously analyzing the ventricular rate recorded from the bipolar sensing leads. When the rate of the tachycardia exceeds the programmed tachycardia detection rate, charging of the capacitors is initiated. The arrhythmia detection rate criterion ranges from 125 to 200 beats per minute typically in 5 beat per minute increments and is noninvasively programmable with currently available ICD models. Early generation ICDs had a fixed detection rate that could not be changed. Besides rate, the electrogram morphology can also be used as a tachycardia detection criterion. The electrogram morphology is analyzed from the signal recorded across the defibrillating leads. By analysis of the proportion of the cardiac cycle that the electrogram occupies the isoelectric line (termed the probability density function [PDF]™), certain ICD models may discriminate wide QRS complex tachycardias from narrow QRS complex tachycardias. In this manner, wide QRS ventricular arrhythmias that have only a small portion of the cardiac cycle at the isoelectric line may be distinguished from narrow QRS complex supraventricular tachycardias such as sinus tachycardia that occupy the isoelectric line for a greater proportion of the cardiac cycle. There are, however, several disadvantages to using the electrogram morphology. It may inappropriately prevent the detection of ventricular tachycardia that is recorded as a relatively narrow QRS in the defibrillating patches and it increases the time required for arrhythmia detection. Also, the electrogram morphology may be satisfied in patients who have an intraventricular conduction delay or bundle branch block. Patients with underlying conduction system disease may meet electrogram morphology if they develop a rate-dependent bundle branch block with sinus tachycardia. Whereas the PDF sensing function was either present or absent in older AICDs,™ the current generation of ICDs allow electrogram morphology to be programmed on or off. In many instances using the rate as the only criterion for arrhythmia detection is preferable.

Once the tachycardia detection criteria of the ICD have been satisfied, the capacitors are charged using the power supplied by the batteries, and the cardioverting or defibrillating shock is delivered to the heart. The time required for detection of a ventricular arrhythmia is usually only 2 to 5 seconds. After the ventricular tachyarrhythmia has been recognized, new generation ICDs reconfirm detection to ensure that the arrhythmia is sustained. The time required to charge the capacitors is variable and depends on several factors, including the battery capacity, the interval from the last capacitor charge, and the programmed shock energy. Thus the total duration of an arrhythmia prior to delivery of a shock ranges from about 5 to 25 seconds. If the arrhythmia is not interrupted by the initial therapy, a redetection will ensue and further shock therapies delivered. Multiple shocks can be delivered for a single arrhythmia.

The newer implantable defibrillators incorporate antitachycardia and antibradycardia pacing. As described in Chapter 10, single or multiple extrastimuli may be delivered to interrupt the tachycardia. Rapid overdrive pacing with scanning capabilities is also a possibility. These devices have the capacity to deliver different antitachycardia pacing therapies depending on the rate of the tachycardia. For example, ventricular tachycardia at a relatively slow rate may be treated by single extrastimuli. If the rate of ventricular tachycardia is faster, rapid overdrive pacing may be used (Figure 12-2). For other tachycardias, low-energy cardioverting shocks may be delivered (Figure 12-3), and for very rapid ventricular tachycardia or ventricular fibrillation, a high-energy shock may be used. The sequence of therapies to be used, the energy to be delivered, and the number of times a therapy should be tried can all be programmed.

In addition to these antitachycardia capabilities, the newer generation of defibrillators offers real-time and storage of electrograms to determine the nature of any arrhythmias detected and the response to the therapy given by the device (Figure 12-4). Investigators continue to explore ways to decrease the defibrillation threshold and prolong device longevity. Biphasic pulse waves are one promising technique that has been successfully incorporated into some of the new combined devices. A biphasic pulse is delivered with an abrupt reversal of polarity during the shock. The positive pole for the initial portion of the shock becomes the negative pole for the terminal portion of the shock. Biphasic waveforms have been demonstrated to decrease the energy required for defibrillation by as much as 50% (Figure 12-5). Another innovation that may decrease the

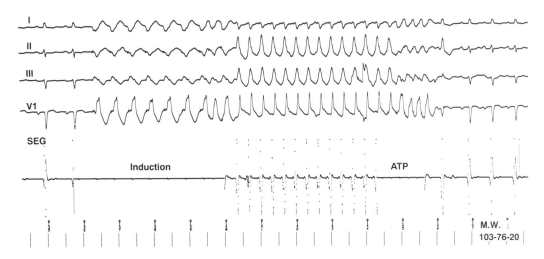

Figure 12-2 The patient has coronary artery disease and repetitive monomorphic ventricular tachycardia. He has a Ventritex Cadence Model V-100 antitachycardia pacing system implanted. These tracings were recorded at postoperative electrophysiologic study. Surface electrocardiographic leads I, II, III, and V$_1$ are displayed in the first four channels. The Ventritex Cadence has the capability of storing electrograms of sensed arrhythmia events. The stored electrograms (SEG) corresponding to the real-time ECGs are displayed in the fifth channel. The first two beats are sinus rhythm. Thereafter, programmed stimulation using the Ventritex Cadence induces monomorphic ventricular tachycardia. The tachycardia is recognized, and antitachycardia pacing (ATP) successfully terminates the arrhythmia and restores sinus rhythm. The pacing stimulus artifacts are easily visible in lead V$_1$.

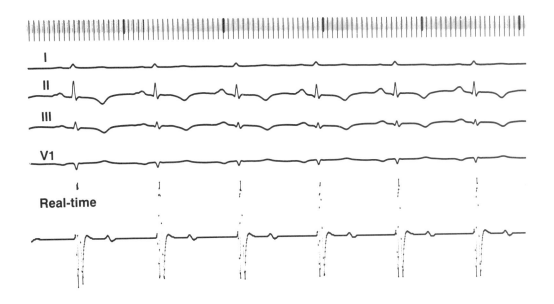

Figure 12-3 These tracings are from the same patient described in Figure 12-2. The five recorded channels are as in Figure 12-2. Programmed stimulation induces monomorphic ventricular tachycardia, and a 50-V synchronized shock (0.1 J) successfully restores sinus rhythm. The patient was hardly aware that the shock was given in this instance since the delivered energy was so low.

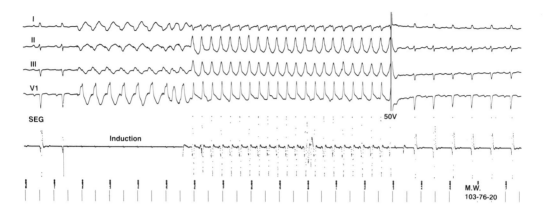

Figure 12-4 Surface electrocardiographic leads I, II, III, and V_1 are recorded with simultaneous real-time electrograms from a Ventritex Cadence Model V-100 implantable defibrillator.

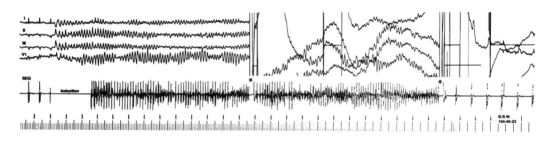

Figure 12-5 The patient has coronary artery disease and was resuscitated from a cardiac arrest. He had inducible ventricular fibrillation that was treated with a Ventritex Cadence model V-100 implantable pacemaker-cardioverter defibrillator. These tracings were recorded at postoperative electrophysiologic study. Channels 1 to 4 record ECG leads I, II, III, and V_1. The fifth channel records a stored electrogram from the implanted device, which is superimposed on the real-time electrocardiogram. After two sinus beats, programmed stimulation (rapid ventricular pacing from the implanted defibrillator) induces ventricular fibrillation. At the first asterisk, a 550 V shock fails to restore sinus rhythm. At the second asterisk, a 750 V shock restores sinus rhythm. The Ventritex Cadence may be programmed to deliver biphasic shocks.

defibrillation threshold is the delivery of the shock between more than two poles. This system, known as bidirectional shocks, delivers the defibrillating discharge over two distinct axes and may further decrease defibrillation energy requirements.

PREOPERATIVE ASSESSMENT

Patient selection is critical for successful use of the ICD, and several factors must be considered prior to device implantation (Table 12-3). First, reversible factors that are arrhythmogenic,

such as coronary ischemia, the presence of proarrhythmic drugs, or electrolyte abnormalities, must be corrected. If there is congestive heart failure that cannot be controlled with medications, cardiac transplantation may be indicated instead of an ICD. Definition of coronary artery anatomy, left and right ventricular function, valvular abnormalities, and functional status of the patient is usually required prior to device implantation. Thus it is our standard practice to perform coronary arteriography and left ventriculography in all patients prior to ICD implantation. The findings at cardiac catheterization may require surgical correction before ICD

Table 12-3 ICD Preoperative Evaluation

- reversible causes of arrhythmias
- functional classification congestive heart failure and angina pectoris
- psychologic status
- social support
- bradycardia and/or antitachycardia pacing
- exercise stress testing to determine maximum sinus rate, rate-dependent bundle branch block, exercise-induced arrhythmias, ischemia
- coronary arteriography and left ventriculography to determine coronary artery disease or spasm, coronary artery anomalies, left ventricular status, valvular function
- electrophysiologic testing to determine rates and mechanisms of induced arrhythmias, response to drug therapy and antitachycardia pacing, and conduction in the His-Purkinje system
- Holter monitoring to determine frequency of nonsustained arrhythmias, supraventricular arrhythmias

implantation. Exercise stress testing is performed to determine if ischemia can be provoked and the maximum exercise heart rate that may be expected for the patient. Invasive electrophysiologic testing is required for all patients to determine the rate and mechanism of all inducible ventricular arrhythmias and response to drugs. If concomitant antiarrhythmic drug therapy will be required to reduce the frequency of spontaneous ventricular or supraventricular arrhythmias, the effects of these agents on tachycardia rate must be known. In addition, antitachycardia pacing algorithms that are effective or result in acceleration need to be defined. For patients who do not have inducible ventricular arrhythmias, the rate of the detection criteria is determined by the rate of the spontaneous arrhythmia event.

Adverse interactions between pacemakers and the ICD must be considered prior to ICD implantation (Figure 12-6). These device-device interactions can be minimized by positioning the rate-sensing electrodes on the surface of the left ventricle at a site that records a small amplitude of the pacing stimulus. Since unipolar pacemakers produce large pacing stimulus artifacts, a unipolar permanent pacemaker should be changed to a bipolar system prior to ICD implantation.

In selected patients requiring cardiac surgery, it may be appropriate to implant sensing and defibrillating electrodes on the heart without implanting the ICD pulse generator. This is most commonly done with surgical procedures designed as primary therapy for ventricular arrhythmias, such as endocardial resection, aneurysmectomy, or cryoablation. If ventricular tachycardia or fibrillation remain inducible at electrophysiologic testing following surgery, the ICD pulse generator can be implanted without the need for another thoracotomy. Routine placement of ICD leads for patients undergoing

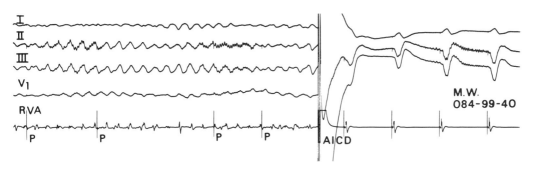

Figure 12-6 Postoperative electrophysiologic testing to assess potential adverse device-device interaction. The patient had an ICD implanted as therapy for ventricular fibrillation and a VVIR pacemaker implanted for the bradyarrhythmia. At postoperative electrophysiologic study, the ICD was tested to ensure that there was no adverse device-device interaction with the pacemaker inhibiting ventricular fibrillation detection. Shown are ECG leads I, II, III, and V₁, with an intracardiac recording from the right ventricular apex (RVA) during induced ventricular fibrillation. The pacing stimulus artifact is seen on the ventricular electrogram (P). A single ICD shock successfully terminates the ventricular fibrillation without detection inhibition. Note that the patient is pacemaker dependent after the shock.

coronary artery surgery is neither warranted nor wise because of the risk of infection. It should be appreciated that the presence of epicardial patch electrodes generates a marked fibrotic reaction that may preclude future coronary bypass grafting. Patch placement on the parietal pericardium may avoid this problem.

POSTOPERATIVE CARE

The postoperative care of patients who have had an ICD implanted is similar to that of other patients having cardiac surgical procedures. Although the policy varies among institutions, it is common practice for the defibrillator to remain deactivated during the initial postoperative period. It is of paramount importance that the nurse know whether the device is active or inactive. If the device is in the inactive mode, external defibrillation must be immediately available, and any arrhythmias that develop should be managed in the standard manner. The length of hospitalization following implantation varies considerably and is dependent on such factors as the underlying condition of the patient and other surgical procedures performed. Patients who are having pulse generator replacements may be discharged within two days.

Patients are provided with information through audiovisual aids and patient education booklets that discuss commonly asked questions about device function and life-style changes. In addition, many centers have clinical nurse specialists and both in-hospital and extended outpatient support groups to assist patients with adjustment to the device, their altered self-image, and life-style changes. The emotional support of patients with an ICD is an important part of successful therapy with this device. Patients require support and encouragement from their family and health professionals preoperatively through extended outpatient follow-up. Reports in the literature have focused on the psychologic ramifications of the ICD on patients and their spouses, particularly fear of painful countershocks, anxiety regarding whether the device will function appropriately, depression regarding the seriousness of the condition, and loss of independence. Patients may

become overly dependent on their physician and nurses. Psychiatric counseling by individuals experienced in the care of emotional problems associated with the ICD should be readily available. Patient support groups may play an important role in aiding patients to cope with this long-term therapy. Careful preoperative screening of patients at particular risk for psychologic problems is especially important.

Perhaps the most dramatic change that patients must cope with is relinquishing driving their automotive vehicle, a privilege that is closely linked with a sense of freedom and independence. Since the ICD does not prevent arrhythmia occurrence and presyncope or syncope may result prior to termination by the device, driving is prohibited. While it is recommended that patients with defibrillators not drive, some centers are relaxing this restriction if the patient has not experienced a shock for at least 1 year. Patients are cautioned to use common sense in making life-style changes and are urged to seek positive alternatives.

FOLLOW-UP CARE OF PATIENTS WITH IMPLANTABLE CARDIOVERTER DEFIBRILLATORS

The AIDCHECK™ (CPI) was used to perform battery tests on all AICD™ models prior to the current 1550 and 1600 series. The present programmable AICD™ has a programmer and software module that allows determination of the battery status and retrieval of diagnostic data such as the number of shocks delivered to the patient, the number of test shocks, the last charging time, the programmed parameters, and the lead impedance of the last shock delivered (Figure 12-7). The programmable AICD™ programmer is also capable of monitoring detection, delay, and charging intervals during electrophysiologic testing. Interrogation of the 1600 series also indicates the programmed delay to the first shock and the number of joules to be delivered with each shock. Whereas models prior to the 1550 series dumped their charge internally, resulting in decreased longevity, the 1550 and later models are designed to allow gradual dissipation of the capacitor charge. This process markedly reduces battery depletion, resulting in

Figure 12-7 CPI Model 1550 AICD™ and Model 2035 programmer. The current generation of AICDs has programmable features for tachycardia detection and the level of cardioverting defibrillating shock energy. *Source:* Courtesy of Cardiac Pacemakers, Inc., St. Paul, MN.

a projected 5-year longevity rather than the 2-year longevity of earlier models. Other ICD systems by a variety of manufacturers require comparable follow-up and elicit similar information. The Cadence, however, is capable of providing stored and real-time electrograms and automatically reforming capacitors. During each follow-up visit the battery charge time is assessed to determine if the device is at the elective replacement indicator.

Inappropriate magnet applications can result in inactivation of an ICD, false activation of an ICD, and energy depletion secondary to inadvertent capacitor charging. Patients must be educated to avoid strong magnetic fields to prevent inactivation of an ICD. Patients are cautioned to contact their physician if they suspect they inadvertently entered a magnetic field or if a beeping tone is emanating from their defibrillator. As with pacemakers, patients are instructed that magnetic resonance imaging is contraindicated, that prophylactic antibiotics are required for dental work, and that all health professionals caring for them must be informed that they have an ICD. It should be emphasized that use of a magnet by health professionals must also be avoided unless they are thoroughly familiar with the function of the device.

Evaluation of shocks received by the patient can present a vexing problem since the present 1500 and 1600 models of the AICD™ do not have the capability to store information about the appropriateness of the shock (stored electrograms). If the discharge was preceded by syncope or presyncope, an appropriate response to a ventricular arrhythmia can be inferred. However, shocks that are not associated with symptoms may have been either an appropriate response to ventricular tachycardia or an inappropriate response indicating another arrhythmia or malfunction of the device. Verification of the active status of the device is done by the physician. Holter monitoring is a useful method for evaluating the patient who has received an unexplained shock. Transtelephonic monitoring has also been demonstrated to be useful. Appropriate treatment can be given if ventricular or supraventricular arrhythmias are documented. If no arrhythmias are detected by these methods, the integrity of the sensing circuitry of the device should be assessed by radiographs of the leads and noninvasive recording of the audible tone produced synchronously with the sensed intracardiac electrogram. Manipulation of the pulse generator and movement of the arms may allow recognition of spurious signals that may indicate fracture of the sensing leads.

Patients are instructed to notify their physician when they receive a shock and to record the date, activity, and symptomatology associated with the shock. Patients are queried at each follow-up visit as to whether they have experienced a shock. Typically, one or two shocks associated with appropriate symptoms do not require further intervention. After a brief rest period, the patient may resume his or her daily activities. Hospitalization is indicated for patients experiencing multiple discharges of the ICD over a brief period of time. Frequent episodes of sustained or nonsustained ventricular tachycardia may require suppression with antiarrhythmic drugs. Multiple countershocks related to supraventricular arrhythmias are best managed by temporary inactivation of the ICD until the arrhythmias can be controlled pharmacologically. The defibrillator patches may act as an insulation barrier to external defibrillation, resulting in higher external defibrillation energy requirements. It should be recognized that antiarrhythmic drugs may raise the defibrillation threshold or slow the rate of ventricular tachycardia below the rate detection criterion of the ICD. Because of these concerns, repeat electrophysiologic testing is usually necessary to ensure proper function of the device following changes in an antiarrhythmic drug regimen. Similarly, if a permanent pacemaker becomes necessary in a patient with an ICD, careful electrophysiologic evaluation for adverse device-device interactions is required.

FUTURE DEVELOPMENTS IN IMPLANTABLE CARDIOVERTER DEFIBRILLATOR TECHNOLOGY

Newer ICDs offer the capability for increased programmability, storage of data regarding electrograms associated with shocks, and both antitachycardia pacing and bradycardia support.

Bradycardia support is particularly useful because following termination of a tachyarrhythmia, bradycardias are not uncommon. Sensor technology such as implantable pressure sensors may allow future devices to determine the hemodynamic stability of the patient and to tailor therapy appropriately. The shape of the defibrillating waveform is programmable with the newer devices, and biphasic and triphasic shocks can be delivered. In addition, bidirectional countershocks will be used with several newer devices. These newer shock delivery methods will decrease the energy required for arrhythmia conversion and provide greater patient comfort, device efficacy, and pulse generator longevity.

Although still in clinical trials, totally transvenous defibrillating systems that use a subcutaneous electrode and right ventricular leads offer the potential to eliminate the need for a thoracotomy (Figures 12-8 and 12-9). If cardioverter defibrillators can be reduced in size,

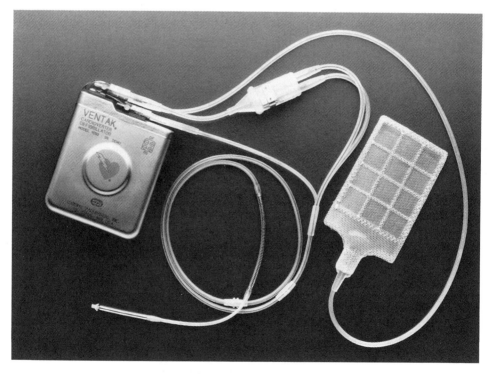

Figure 12-8 The CPI Model 1550 AICD™ is shown in combination with an Endotak-C catheter, which is placed transvenously into the right ventricular apex (RVA). Spring electrodes for defibrillation are located in the RVA and in the superior vena cava. A subcutaneous patch electrode is placed over the left chest. This device allows effective defibrillation without the need for thoracotomy. *Source:* Courtesy of Cardiac Pacemakers, Inc., St. Paul, MN.

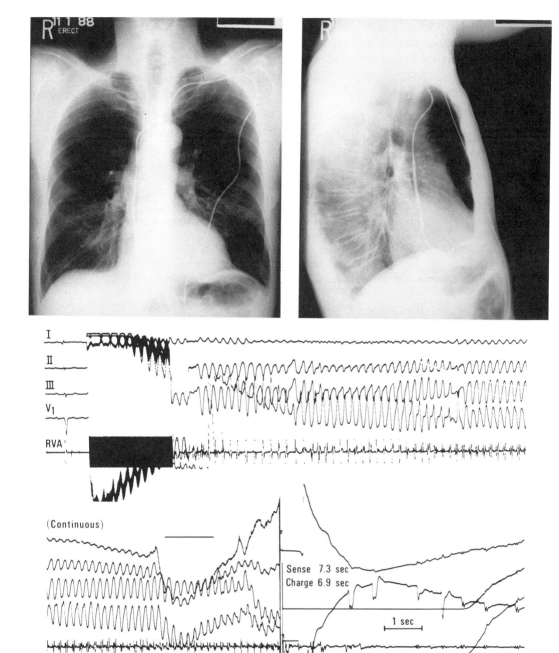

C

Figure 12-9 The patient has ischemic heart disease and was resuscitated from a cardiac arrest. He is treated with an Endotak nonthoracotomy implantable defibrillator system. Various lead configurations were tested employing the Endotak-C transvenous lead with a subcutaneous patch, the Endotak-SQ, and it was determined that the lowest defibrillation threshold was used when delivering a shock between the distal and proximal catheter electrodes without the use of a subcutaneous patch. The chest x-ray (panels A and B) shows the implanted transvenous lead in the final configuration used in this patient. In panel C, a postoperative electrophysiologic study is shown in this patient. Surface ECG leads I, II, III, and V_1 are shown in the first four channels, and a recording from a temporary transvenous lead in the right ventricular apex (RVA) is shown in the last channel. After a single sinus beat, alternating current is introduced and ventricular fibrillation precipitated. After a sensing time of 7.3 seconds and capacity charging time of 6.9 seconds, a single ICD shock terminates the ventricular arrhythmia.

with the possibility for implantation under local anesthesia using a technique similar to that used for permanent pacemakers, the use of these devices will become more widespread. Indeed, if the implantation technique can be made similar to that used for permanent pacemakers, implantable defibrillators are likely to become the treatment choice for the majority of patients with ventricular arrhythmias.

BIBLIOGRAPHY

Babbs CF, Yim GKW, Whistler SJ, et al. Elevation of ventricular fibrillation threshold in dogs by antiarrhythmic drugs. *Am Heart J*. 1979;98:345–350.

Badger JM, Morris PL. Observations of a support group for automatic implantable cardioverter-defibrillator recipients and their spouses. *J Cardiovasc Nurs*. 1990;4:20–32.

Baum RS, Alvarez H, Cobb LA. Survival after resuscitation from out-of-hospital ventricular fibrillation. *Circulation*. 1974;50:1231–1235.

Brodman R, Fisher JD, Furman S, et al. Implantation of automatic cardioverter-defibrillators via median sternotomy. *PACE*. 1984;7:1363–1369.

The Cardiac Arrhythmia Suppression Trial Investigators. Preliminary report: effect of encainide and flecainide on mortality in randomized trial of arrhythmia suppression after myocardial infarction. *N Engl J Med*. 1989; 321:406–412.

Chapman PD: Patient selection and preoperative evaluation for the implanted defibrillator. *Clin Prog Electrophysiol Pacing*. 1986;4:255–259.

Chapman PD, Troup P. The automatic implantable cardioverter-defibrillator: evaluating suspected inappropriate shocks. *J Am Coll Cardiol*. 1986;7:1075–1078.

Ciccone JM, Saksena S, Shah Y, et al. A prospective randomized study of the clinical efficacy and safety of transvenous cardioversion for termination of ventricular tachycardia. *Circulation*. 1985;71:571–578.

Cobb LA, Werner JA, Troughbaugh GB. Sudden cardiac death, I: A decade's experience with out-of-hospital resuscitation. *Mod Concepts Cardiovasc Dis*. 1980;49: 31–36.

Cooper DK, Luceri RM, Thurer RJ, et al. The impact of the automatic implantable cardioverter-defibrillator on quality of life. *Clin Prog Electrophysiol Pacing*. 1986;4: 306–309.

DeBelder MA, Camm AJ. Implantable cardioverter-defibrillators (ICDs) 1989: how close are we to the ideal device? *Clin Cardiol*. 1989;12:339–345.

Dixon EG, Tang AS, Wolf PD, et al. Improved defibrillation thresholds with large contoured epicardial electrodes and biphasic waveforms. *Circulation*. 1987;76:1176–1184.

Echt DS, Armstrong K, Schmidt P, et al. Clinical experience, complications, and survival in 70 patients with the automatic cardioverter-defibrillator. *Circulation*. 1985;71:289–296.

Echt DS, Winkle RA. Management of patients with the automatic implantable cardioverter-defibrillator. *Clin Prog Electrophysiol Pacing*. 1985;3:4–16.

Epstein AE, Kay GN, Plumb VJ, et al. Combined automatic implantable cardioverter-defibrillator and pacemaker systems: implantation techniques and follow-up. *J Am Coll Cardiol*. 1989;13:121–131.

Epstein AE, Shepard RB, Kirklin JK, et al. Failure of elective replacement indicator to predict end-of-life of the automatic implantable cardioverter-defibrillator. *PACE*. 1988;11:569–574.

Fisher JD, Kim SG, Mercando AD. Electrical devices for treatment of arrhythmias. *Am J Coll Cardiol*. 1988; 61:45A–57A.

Fogoros RN, Fiedler SB, Elson JJ. The automatic implantable cardioverter-defibrillator in drug-refractory ventricular tachyarrhythmias. *Ann Intern Med*. 1987;107: 635–641.

Freedman RA, Swerdlow CD, Soderholm-Difatte V, et al. Prognostic significance of arrhythmia inducibility or noninducibility at initial electrophysiologic study in survivors of cardiac arrest. *Am J Cardiol*. 1988;61:578–582.

Grayboys TB, Lown B, Podrid PJ, et al. Long-term survival of patients with malignant ventricular arrhythmias treated with antiarrhythmic drugs. *Am J Cardiol*. 1982; 50:437–443.

Guarnieri T, Levine JH, Griffith LSC, et al. When "sudden cardiac death" is not so sudden: lessons learned from the automatic implantable defibrillator. *Am Heart J*. 1988; 115:205–207.

Haluska EA, Whistler SJ, Calfee RJ. A hierarchical approach to the treatment of ventricular tachycardias. *PACE*. 1986;9:1320–1324.

Hamer A, Vohra J, Hunt D, et al. Prediction of sudden death by electrophysiologic studies in high risk patients surviving acute myocardial infarction. *Am J Cardiol*. 1982; 50:223–229.

Herre JM, Sauve MJ, Malone P, et al. Long-term results of amiodarone therapy in patients with recurrent sustained ventricular tachycardia or ventricular fibrillation. *J Am Coll Cardiol*. 1989;13:442–449.

Jones DL, Klein GJ, Guiraudon GM, et al. Internal cardiac defibrillation in man: pronounced improvement with sequential pulse delivery to two different lead orientations. *Circulation*. 1986;73:484–491.

Jones DL, Klein GJ, Guiraudon GM, et al. Prediction of defibrillation success from a single defibrillation threshold measurement with sequential pulses and two current pathways in humans. *Circulation*. 1988;78:1144–1149.

Kastor JA. Michel Mirowski and the automatic implantable defibrillator. *Am J Cardiol*. 1989;63:977–982, 1121–1126.

Kay GN, Plumb VJ, Dailey SM, et al. Current role of the automatic implantable cardioverter-defibrillator in the treatment of life-threatening ventricular arrhythmias. *Am J Med.* 1990;88:25N–34N.

Kim SG, Furman S, Waspe LE, et al. Unipolar pacer artifacts induced failure of an automatic implantable defibrillator to detect ventricular fibrillation. *Am J Cardiol.* 1986;57:880–881.

Klein LS, Fineberg N, Heger JJ, et al. Prospective evaluation of a discriminant function for prediction of recurrent symptomatic ventricular tachycardia or ventricular fibrillation in coronary artery disease patients receiving amiodarone and having inducible ventricular tachycardia at electrophysiologic study. *Am J Cardiol.* 1988;61: 1024–1030.

Kuchar DL, Thornburn CW, Sammel NL. Prediction of serious arrhythmic events after myocardial infarction: signal-averaged electrocardiogram, Holter monitoring and radionuclide ventriculography. *J Am Coll Cardiol.* 1987;9:531–538.

Kuppermann M, Luce B, McGovern B, et al. An analysis of the cost effectiveness of the implantable defibrillator. *Circulation.* 1990;81:91–100.

Langer A, Heilman MS, Mower MM, et al. Considerations in the development of the automatic implantable defibrillator. *Med Instrum.* 1976;10:163–167.

Lampert S, Lown B, Grayboys TB, et al. Determinants of survival in patients with malignant ventricular arrhythmias associated with coronary artery disease. *Am J Cardiol.* 1988;61:791–797.

Lehmann MH, Steinman RT, Schuger CD, et al. The automatic implantable cardioverter-defibrillator as antiarrhythmic treatment modality of choice for survivors of cardiac arrest unrelated to acute myocardial infarction. *Am J Cardiol.* 1988;62:803–805.

Luceri RM, Habal SM, Castellanos A, et al. Mechanism of death in patients with the automatic implantable cardioverter-defibrillator. *PACE.* 1988;11:2015–2022.

Manolis A, Rastegar H, Estes NAM. Prophylactic automatic implantable cardioverter-defibrillator patches in patients at high risk for postoperative ventricular tachyarrhythmias. *J Am Coll Cardiol.* 1989;13:1367–1373.

McGovern B, Garan H, Malacoff RF, et al. Long-term clinical outcome of ventricular tachycardia or fibrillation treated with amiodarone. *Am J Cardiol.* 1984;53: 1558–1563.

Mirowski M. The automatic implantable cardioverter-defibrillator: an overview. *J Am Coll Cardiol.* 1985;6: 461–466.

Mirowski M, Mower MM, Langer A, et al. A chronically implanted system for automatic defibrillation in active conscious dogs. Experimental model for treatment of sudden death from ventricular fibrillation. *Circulation.* 1978;58:90–94.

Mirowski M, Reid PR, Mower MM, et al. Clinical performance of the implantable cardioverter-defibrillator. *PACE.* 1984;7:1345–1350.

Mirowski M, Reid PR, Mower MM, et al. Termination of malignant ventricular arrhythmias with an implanted auto-

matic defibrillator in human beings. *N Engl J Med.* 1980;303:322–324.

Mirowski M, Reid PR, Watkins L, et al. Clinical treatment of life-threatening ventricular tachyarrhythmias with the automatic implantable defibrillator. *Am Heart J.* 1981; 102:265–270.

Mirowski M, Reid PR, Winkle RA, et al. Mortality in patients with implanted automatic defibrillators. *Ann Intern Med.* 1983;98:585–588.

Morady F, DiCarlo L, Winston S, Davis et al. Clinical features and prognosis of patients with out-of-hospital cardiac arrest and a normal electrophysiologic study. *J Am Coll Cardiol.* 1984;4:39–44.

Myerburg RJ, Kessler KM, Estes D, et al. Long-term survival after prehospital cardiac arrest: analysis of outcome during an 8 year study. *Circulation.* 1984;70:538–546.

Myerburg RJ, Luceri RM, Thurer R, et al. Time to first shock and clinical outcome in patients receiving an automatic implantable cardioverter-defibrillator. *J Am Coll Cardiol.* 1989;14:508–514.

Olinger GN, Chapman PD, Troup PJ, et al. Stratified application of the automatic implantable cardioverter-defibrillator. *J Thorac Cardiovasc Surg.* 1988;96: 141–149.

Reid PR, Griffith LSC, Mower MM, et al. Implantable cardioverter-defibrillator: patient selection and implantation protocol. *PACE.* 1984;7:1338–1344.

Roy D, Waxman HL, Kienzle MG, et al. Clinical characteristics and long-term follow-up in 119 survivors of cardiac arrest: relation to inducibility at electrophysiologic testing. *Am J Cardiol.* 1983;52:969–974.

Ruskin JN, DiMarco JP, Garan H. Out-of-hospital cardiac arrest. Electrophysiologic observations and selection of long-term antiarrhythmic therapy. *N Engl J Med.* 1980;303:607–613.

Saksena S, Calvo R. Transvenous cardioversion and defibrillation of ventricular tachyarrhythmias: current status and future directions. *PACE.* 1985;8:715–731.

Saksena S, Parsonnet V. Implantation of cardioverter defibrillator without thoracotomy using a triple electrode system. *JAMA.* 1988;259:69–72.

Schaffer WA, Cobb LA. Recurrent ventricular fibrillation and modes of death in survivors of out-of-hospital ventricular fibrillation. *N Engl J Med.* 1975;293:259–262.

Shepard R, Kirklin JK, Kay GN, et al. Use of pericardial surface, rate-sensing electrodes for defibrillator implantation. *PACE.* 1989;12:663. Abstract.

Smith WM, Lubbe WF, Whitlock RM, et al. Long-term tolerance of amiodarone treatment for cardiac arrhythmias. *Am J Cardiol.* 1986;57:1288–1293.

Stevenson LW, Fowler MB, Schoreder JS, et al. Poor survival of patients with idiopathic cardiomyopathy considered too well for transplantation. *Am J Med.* 1987; 83:871–876.

Swerdlow CD, Winkle RA, Mason JW. Determinants of survival in patients with ventricular tachyarrhythmias. *N Engl J Med.* 1983;308:1436–1442.

Tang AS, Seitaro Y, Wharton JM, et al. Ventricular defibrillation using biphasic waveforms: the importance of phasic duration. *J Am Coll Cardiol*. 1989;13:207–214.

Teplitz L, Egenes KJ, Brask L. Life after sudden death: the development of a support group for automatic implantable cardioverter defibrillator patients. *J Cardiovasc Nurs*. 1990;4:20–32.

Troup PJ, Chapman PD, Olinger GN, et al. The implanted defibrillator: relation of defibrillating lead configuration and clinical variables to defibrillation threshold. *J Am Coll Cardiol*. 1985;6:1315–1321.

Vlay SC. The automatic internal cardioverter defibrillator: comprehensive clinical follow-up.—the Stony Brook experience. *Am Heart J*. 1986;112:189–194.

Vlay SC, Olson LC, Fricchione GL, et al. Anxiety and anger in patients with ventricular tachyarrhythmias. Responses after automatic implantable cardioverter defibrillator implantation. *PACE*. 1989;12:366–373.

Watkins L, Mirowski M, Mower M, et al. Implantation of the automatic defibrillator: the subxiphoid approach. *Ann Thorac Surg*. 1982:515–520.

Wilber DJ, Garan H, Finkelstein D, et al. Out-of-hospital cardiac arrest. Use of electrophysiologic testing in the prediction of long-term outcome. *N Engl J Med*. 1988;318:19–24.

Winkle RA, Bach SM, Echt DS, et al. The automatic implantable defibrillator: local ventricular bipolar sensing to detect ventricular tachycardia and fibrillation. *Am J Cardiol*. 1983;52:265–270.

Winkle RA, Mead RH, Ruder MA, et al. Long-term outcome with the automatic implantable cardioverter defibrillator. *J Am Coll Cardiol*. 1989;13:1353–1361.

Winkle RA, Stinson EB, Bach SM, et al. Measurement of cardioversion/defibrillation thresholds in many by a truncated exponential waveform and apical patch-superior vena caval spring electrode configuration. *Circulation*. 1984;69:766–771.

Zheutlin TA, Steinman RT, Mattioni TA, et al. Long-term arrhythmic outcome in survivors of ventricular fibrillation with absence of inducible ventricular tachycardia. *Am J Cardiol*. 1988;662:1213–1217.

Index